Anne Morrow Lindbergh

Also by Dorothy Herrmann

S. J. Perelman: A Life

With Malice Toward All: The Quips, Lives,
and Loves of Some Celebrated 20th-Century American Wits

ANNE MORROW LINDBERGH

A Gift for Life

Dorothy Herrmann

Ticknor & Fields NEW YORK 1992

For information about permission to reproduce selections
from this book, write to Permissions, Ticknor & Fields,
Houghton Mifflin Company, 215 Park Avenue South,
New York, New York 10003

Library of Congress Cataloging-in-Publication Data
Herrmann, Dorothy.
  Anne Morrow Lindbergh : a gift for life / Dorothy Herrmann.
    p.   cm.
  Includes bibliographical references and index.
  ISBN 0-395-56114-0
  1. Lindbergh, Anne Morrow, 1906–   — Bibliography. 2. Authors,
American — 20th century — Biography.   I. Title.
PS3523.I516Z68   1993
818'.5209 — dc20   92-30280
[B]   CIP

Printed in the United States of America

HAD 10 9 8 7 6 5 4 3 2 1

Grateful acknowledgment is made to the following for permission to reprint copyrighted
material: Excerpts from *Bring Me a Unicorn: Diaries and Letters of Anne Morrow Lindbergh,
1922–1928,* copyright © 1972, 1971 by Anne Morrow Lindbergh; *Hour of Gold, Hour of Lead:
Diaries and Letters of Anne Morrow Lindbergh, 1919–1932,* copyright © 1973 by Anne Morrow
Lindbergh; *Locked Rooms and Open Doors: Diaries and Letters of Anne Morrow Lindbergh,
1933–1935,* copyright © 1974 by Anne Morrow Lindbergh; *The Flower and the Nettle: Diaries
and Letters of Anne Morrow Lindbergh, 1936–1939,* copyright © 1976 by Anne Morrow Lindbergh; *War Within and Without: Diaries and Letters of Anne Morrow Lindbergh, 1939–1944,*
copyright © 1980 by Anne Morrow Lindbergh. Reprinted by permission of Harcourt Brace
Jovanovich, Inc. Excerpts from *The Wartime Journals of Charles A. Lindbergh,* copyright
© 1970 by Charles A. Lindbergh; *Charles A. Lindbergh: Autobiography of Values,* edited by
William Jovanovich, copyright © 1978, 1977, 1976 by Harcourt Brace Jovanovich, Inc. and
Anne Morrow Lindbergh. Reprinted by permission of the publisher. Excerpts from *Harold
Nicolson: Diaries and Letters, 1930–1939,* edited by Nigel Nicolson. Copyright © 1966 by William Collins Sons & Co., Ltd. Reprinted with the permission of Atheneum Publishers, New
York, and HarperCollins Publishers, Ltd., London. Quotations from the unpublished letters
of Harold Nicolson and Vita Sackville-West. Reprinted by permission of Nigel Nicolson and
the Lilly Library, Indiana University, Bloomington, Indiana. Excerpts from the unpublished
journals of Selden Rodman. Reprinted with the permission of Selden Rodman. Quotation
from the unpublished reminiscences of Senator William Benton. Reprinted by permission of
the Columbia University Oral History Research Office, Columbia University, New York. Excerpts from *The Honeycomb,* by Adela Rogers St. Johns. Copyright © 1969 by Adela Rogers
St. Johns. Reprinted by permission of Doubleday and Co., Inc.

For Lucille Fletcher Wallop

. . . For whither thou goest, I will go;
and where thou lodgest, I will
lodge: thy people shall be my
people, and thy God my God:
  Where thou diest, will I die,
and there will I be buried:
the Lord do so to me, and more also,
if aught but death part thee and me.
                    — Ruth 1:16–17

Women have served all these
centuries as looking-glasses
possessing the magic and delicious
power of reflecting the figure of
man at twice its natural size.
                    — Virginia Woolf,
                      A Room of One's Own

Contents

Preface

O N A LATE spring afternoon in 1929, a handful of guests threaded their way past a group of reporters staked out at the gate of a Georgian mansion on the outskirts of Englewood, New Jersey. As they entered the palatial home, which was owned by Dwight Morrow, the U.S. ambassador to Mexico, and his wife, Elizabeth, many of the guests were still under the impression that they had been invited to a diplomatic reception. But entering the living room they realized to their surprise that they had been summoned for an entirely different reason. The Morrows' pastor, Dr. William Adams Brown, of the Union Theological Seminary, was present. Next to him stood a tall, boyishly handsome blond young man named Charles Lindbergh who two years earlier had astounded the entire world by flying alone nonstop from New York to Paris.

As soon as everyone was assembled, the Morrows' daughter Anne entered the room on her father's arm. She was wearing a white chiffon wedding dress. On her dark hair was a cap of Brussels lace with a small transparent veil that partially concealed her eyes. She carried a bouquet of columbine and larkspur that her older sister had picked that morning from the family garden. In contrast to her bridegroom, who resembled a prince out of a Nordic fairy tale, she was petite and dark haired, with a shy, uncertain, almost childlike manner. Had it not been for her eyes, she might have been considered plain. A luminous violet-blue, they seemed to be drinking in everything around her. As she came toward her famous bridegroom and stood beside him to repeat the wedding vows, they brimmed with tears.

The wedding reception was brief, as if the participants could hardly wait for it to end. Although the Morrows were very wealthy, it was far from a lavish occasion. There was no music, no dancing, no elaborate wedding feast with multiple courses and bottles of French champagne. Instead, guests were offered a slice of wedding cake and a glass of ginger ale or water to toast the bride and groom.

After a few minutes of chatting with their guests, the newlyweds excused themselves, went upstairs to change their clothes, and then departed in a motorcar. To escape attention from the waiting press, Anne lay down in the bottom of the automobile. As it turned out, when the gate opened and the Lindbergh automobile drove past, many of the reporters didn't even bother to look up.

Only hours later, when Arthur Springer, Dwight Morrow's private secretary, went down to the gate to read them an announcement, did the newspapermen realize the trick that had been played upon them.

"Mr. and Mrs. Dwight W. Morrow announce the marriage of their daughter Anne to Charles A. Lindbergh at Englewood, New Jersey, May 27, 1929," Springer read. Then he turned on his heel and walked back to the house without answering any questions.

The reporters groaned.

"My God, we're all going to get the ax," someone said. " 'Lucky Lindy' just took himself a bride, and we didn't even know it!"

On May 21, 1927, Charles Augustus Lindbergh completed his spectacular transatlantic solo flight from New York to Paris in the *Spirit of St. Louis* and became a hero overnight. Everywhere he went, he was feted, cheered, photographed, given honors and surrounded by hordes of awestruck admirers, including many worshipful flappers who yearned to marry him. Women were so crazy to meet "Lucky Lindy" that some checked into hotel rooms he had just vacated so that they could bathe in his bathtub and sleep in his bed.

When, two years after his flight, word leaked out that Lindbergh was engaged to be married, the world again went wild. Who was the lucky woman who had snared this most eligible of bachelors? Was she a Clara Bow type, with bee-stung red lips and short, thigh-baring skirts? Or a dedicated colleague, some woman flier like Amelia Earhart who was beginning to garner headlines for her aviation feats? As it turned out, Lindbergh's choice of a wife was a surprise to everyone. She was Anne Morrow Lindbergh, the second daughter of Dwight Whitney Morrow, the recently appointed ambassador to Mexico and a multimillionaire.

Shy yet sensitive and well educated, Anne was awed when she met Lindbergh at a gala reception her father held in his honor at the U.S. embassy in Mexico City. She could barely say a word to him, which, as it turned out, attracted his notice. As he confessed to a friend many years later, the main reason he had been drawn to this small, bookish young woman was that, unlike the countless other women vying for his attention, she didn't "flirt" or try to engage him in silly chatter about airplanes.

They were an odd couple. An aviation and technical genius, Lindbergh craved constant adventure and new challenges, while Anne was an intellectual who felt most at home in the world of books and ideas. He was a realist who tended to conceal his intimate emotions, while she lived an inner life of subtle thoughts and observations she expressed in poems, diaries, and letters to her family and friends. Yet these two dissimilar personalities shared many of the same contradictions. Although they were regarded by the public as a golden couple in a fairy tale romance, both were shy, reclusive, and extremely private individuals who yearned for what they called a "simple life" in which they could live like ordinary people. And although both maintained that they hated publicity, they were nevertheless intensely conscious of their own public images. From the 1920s to the 1940s, they commanded the headlines and were cultivated by many important people, some of whom would later become as controversial as themselves. The Duke and Duchess of Windsor were their friends; so were J. Pierpont Morgan, Henry Ford, Lady Nancy Astor, Harold Nicolson and his novelist wife, Vita Sackville-West, Alexis Carrel, Robert Goddard, as well as presidents Kennedy and Johnson. Although some of these people were obviously drawn to them because of Lindbergh's fame, others were genuine admirers of Anne, whose beautifully written books about the flying adventures she shared with her husband were attracting a wide audience and critical acclaim.

When tragedy struck on March 1, 1932, and their twenty-month-old son, Charles, Jr., was kidnapped, the public mourned as though one of their own family had lost a child. Later, when many Americans turned against the Lindberghs for their isolationist views before the Second World War, people were inclined to be harder on Charles than they were on Anne. Although he was suspected of being a Nazi sympathizer and an anti-Semite, she was regarded as merely misguided and too devoted a wife. Her major fault — and what woman could not identify with it — was that she was guilty of being so blindly in love she could not bring herself to express any disapproval of her husband.

Thanks in part to Anne Morrow Lindbergh's extraordinary literary gifts, the enduring Lindbergh marriage has become a part of the American myth. Few other writers have lived so documented a life. In her diaries and innumerable letters, her fiction and essays, Anne drew almost entirely on her own experiences, all of which paint a poetic and idealistic picture of her life with Charles. Her spiritual yearnings and love of nature are also described in prose that often reads like poetry. For many women, her famous best seller, *Gift from the Sea,* published in 1955, sounded a note of quiet rebellion heralding the new feminist movement of the 1960s.

Between them, the Lindberghs published thousands of pages about their lives and opinions. At the same time, they rarely granted interviews and refused to cooperate with biographers and scholars or with journalists exploring the still unanswered questions about their careers. Not only did they seal their private papers at the Sterling Library at Yale University, but whenever a rumor arose that someone was planning a biography of Charles Lindbergh, their friends were instructed not to talk to the biographer if they wished to stay in the couple's good graces. Obviously, they wanted only their own points of view to be official; by writing so exhaustively about themselves, they tried to ensure that posterity's view of their lives would be sympathetic.

Since Anne Morrow Lindbergh has minutely chronicled her life from an early age, the question may legitimately be raised whether she needs a biography. Why not let her own thoughts and observations speak for themselves? Yet, even as honest and forthright as Anne appears to be in her writing, there are aspects of her life that still remain obscure. For example, how did being the wife of Charles Lindbergh help or hinder her own development as a woman and as a writer? Did she often lay aside her own work to write portions of her husband's books and speeches, as some of his detractors have suggested? As for her private life, was her affection for Lindbergh equal throughout their marriage? Or did she grow gradually disillusioned as his political views and growing unpopularity condemned her and their children to a wandering life and to increasing isolation?

How did the kidnapping and murder of her son affect the rest of her life — her attitude toward her subsequent children, her faith in her country, and her feelings about the American public and its press? And how has she coped with the public's continuing morbid curiosity about the crime? Even though the execution of Bruno Hauptmann took place more than a half century ago, a number of crime scholars think that he had nothing to do with the kidnapping and murder of the Lindbergh baby, while others are of the opinion that he was in fact guilty and committed the crime alone, while still others believe that he was merely a minor player in an elaborate scheme engineered by an unknown person or persons who also enlisted the help of a member of either the Lindbergh or the Morrow household staff.

A candid biography of Anne Morrow Lindbergh still needs to be written, for, aside from the public interest in her as the wife of Charles Lindbergh and the mother of a famous crime victim, she is an important figure in her own right. Few critical evaluations of her literary work exist, even though many of her books were best sellers in their day and her writing was highly praised by many distinguished literary critics. This critical neglect of her work seems a vast oversight, for Anne, aside from detailing her life as Mrs. Charles Lindbergh, wrote beautifully about a variety of fascinating subjects, including the early days of aviation and the world of her youth. Her exquisite descriptions of what it was like to be in the air in a small plane have seldom been matched, even by her spiritual and literary mentor, Antoine de Saint-Exupéry, or by the Kenyan aviator Beryl Markham. After the publication of her first book, *North to the Orient,* which described a 1931 survey flight she and Lindbergh made to China, one critic observed, "She has the quiet courage of an explorer, an artist's sensitiveness to beauty, and a poet's gift of phrase. Very few books of travel contain more intrinsically interesting material, and fewer still are written with such grace and charm." One might add that in the early days of aviation, when many were afraid to fly, Anne's evocative descriptions of her journeys in a small plane over long distances helped people overcome their fear of this new form of travel.

An intensely private woman despite her copious autobiographical writings, Anne Morrow Lindbergh has stated that she wishes no biography of herself to be published during her lifetime. Why she does not want one is cause for conjecture. Is it because she believes that since she has been her own and her husband's best biographer, no one else should presume to chronicle their lives? Or does she fear that another author might dig deeper than she has, and perhaps undercut the glamorous Lindbergh legend she has spent her life attempting to create?

Whatever the motives behind her views, an honest portrayal of her life should be written, for in her day she was considered one of this country's most gifted writers. Beyond her literary achievements, her marriage to Charles Lindbergh was a love story that outlasted not only the loss of their son, but also the loss of his prestige when he opposed the United States' entry into World War II, as well as the constant restlessness and turmoil of their lives. Despite these stresses, Anne's devotion to her husband has never seemed to falter — and one may well ask why. Was it his fame and charisma that held her spellbound? Or her own lack of self-esteem? Was she the epitome of the "perfect wife"? Or a woman who sacrificed her own identity and remarkable talent for her husband's image?

Today, when feminine and masculine roles are being re-evaluated, the story of Anne Morrow Lindbergh may offer new insight into the nature of love and marriage, and will perhaps prompt men and women to examine the truths about their own relationships.

Anne Morrow Lindbergh

CHAPTER 1

"The Sleeping Princess"

I T WAS BOTH Anne Morrow's fortune and her misfortune that her father, Dwight Whitney Morrow, was one of the most famous men of his time. In the course of his long and extraordinary career, he was a Morgan partner, the U.S. ambassador to Mexico, and a senator from New Jersey. Besides these achievements, Dwight Morrow was very well-to-do. In fact, he was so wealthy that his death during the Depression saved New Jersey from bankruptcy — his estate taxes of well over $1 million put the state into the black by some $400,000.

Like the offspring of most celebrities, Anne was ambivalent about her famous father. On the one hand, she loved him and was proud of his accomplishments. On the other, she knew that she was far from the most important person in his life. In fact, he barely noticed her, and breakfast was the only time of the day when she ever saw him.

It was a meal she dreaded.

As she was eating her breakfast, she would hear the sounds of his small, brisk steps descending the stairs as he whistled a patriotic tune. The moment he entered the breakfast room, she knew that it was her task to jump up from the table and kiss him. It was always a mad scramble, for her brother and sisters knew that they were also expected to kiss their father good morning. Then, after kissing him, she would sit back down at the table and resume eating, only to be interrupted by her father, who, unsure which of his children had embraced him, insisted that she get up from the table and kiss him again.

Although Anne longed to have her father notice her, she was embarrassed by his kisses. They always left a large wet spot on her cheek, which she tried to dry off as soon as she thought he wasn't looking.

Then came the part of breakfast that she loathed most. As soon as he had polished off the last morsel of his runny eggs, he would put his children to a test. There were four of them, and Anne was the second oldest.

Dwight Morrow would turn to his eldest daughter, Elisabeth, a blond Botticelli-type beauty, and ask, "Who do you like best, your mother or your father?"

Anne was already squirming in her chair with dread. She knew that her father was going to question her next, and the thought terrified her.

"I like Mother best — and *next* to Mother I like you," Elisabeth answered candidly, looking her father straight in the eye.

He laughed loudly, as if he thought her response were the funniest joke in the world. To Anne, tensely awaiting her turn, it was obvious that he admired her sister's blunt honesty and didn't seem hurt at all. Yet Anne was timid and retiring by nature, a person who liked to remain in the background, placate people, and keep the atmosphere pleasant, while Elisabeth was her opposite — practical, independent, and fearless.

Her father's piercing blue eyes were focused next on her.

"Now, Anne, it's your turn. Who do you like best, your mother or me?"

"I like you both the same," Anne said quickly.

"Now, Anne, tell me the truth. Who do you love best?" He persisted, smiling.

"But I like you . . . *differently!*"

"Now . . . Anne."

Still chuckling, he asked her the question several more times, until finally, with a mock sigh, he gave up and told her to give him another kiss.

Pecking her father's cheek for the third time that morning, Anne was relieved that she had been able to avoid telling him the truth, that she, like Elisabeth, loved her mother most. If she confided her real feelings, he might stop teasing her and demanding kisses, which, as much as she hated it, meant that at least he was aware of her existence.

It was not that Dwight Morrow didn't love his children. But like many busy, ambitious men, he was simply too engrossed in his many intellectual, business, and political interests to make them a priority. Whatever time he had to spare was spent with his wife, Elizabeth, with whom he was passionately in love, and who returned his ardor, even though Dwight Morrow could hardly be called a physically attractive man. In fact, he might have been described as ugly, and one of his contemporaries, Judge Learned Hand, went so far as to say that he was "physically rather revolting." Short in stature, with an incongruously large head and an arm that had been improperly set after being fractured in childhood, he was misshapen, almost dwarflike. Elegant, well-tailored suits might have helped camouflage his physical deficiencies, but his clothes were always rumpled. Yet despite his odd appearance and his casualness as a father, Dwight Morrow was known as a brilliant and charming man who was not only a mesmerizing conversationalist but also a superb diplomat who lived and breathed his profession.

His absent-mindedness, caused by his obsession with work, was legendary. It was rumored that once, when he was taking a bath, he called his valet to ask him why the soap was not lathering properly; his servant pointed out that he was still wearing his pajamas.

Yet, in the words of his close friend political columnist Walter Lippmann, Dwight Morrow was a "public figure of the first magnitude." In fact, for many Americans of his generation, Dwight Morrow commanded even more respect than the president of the United States, an office to which they had no doubt he would one day be elected.

A visitor to Next Day Hill, Morrow's fifty-six-acre estate in Englewood, New Jersey, with its well-kept grounds, elegant furnishings, and army of servants, might have assumed that this vague little man had inherited his wealth, but this was not the case. Morrow's fortune was of his own making.

Dwight Morrow was born at Marshall College in Huntington, West Virginia, on January 11, 1873, where, two years earlier, his father, James Elmore Morrow, had accepted the post of president. Despite the imposing title the presidential salary was meager, but James had taken the job for one reason: he and his wife, Clara, and their growing family (they would have a total of eight children) could stay in free lodgings on campus.

When Morrow was two years old, his father accepted a post as a teacher of mathematics at the Oakdale Academy on the Ohio River, in Allegeny, which later became part of the city of Pittsburgh. Scarcely a beautiful or inspiring place, Allegheny was an industrial town, with factories on every side and the nearby Ohio blackened with coal dust.

It was from his father that Morrow inherited his superb mathematical mind, as well as his passion for collecting books. To Clara's dismay,

James, who was also well versed in Hebrew and Latin, spent what little extra money the couple had on rare volumes.

Precocious and brilliant, Morrow graduated from high school when he was fourteen. From the start he appears to have been a complex character, a bright, friendly boy whose indefatigability — he was known to his classmates as "Bulldog Morrow" — and optimism masked violent inner tensions. According to his biographer, Harold Nicolson, he suffered from headaches all his life, even in infancy.

After a rejection from West Point and a brief, unhappy semester at Washington and Jefferson College, Morrow entered Amherst College in 1891. He became class orator, and in perhaps the first manifestation of his penchant for making friends and influencing people, he struck up a close acquaintance with Calvin Coolidge. The silent and aloof Coolidge was notoriously hard to know.

Another friend was Elizabeth Reeve Cutter, whom Morrow met in the spring of 1893 at a dance given at a girls' school in Amherst. At the time Elizabeth was attending Smith College in nearby Northampton. Elizabeth, who was from Cleveland, was a petite, sensitive young woman with heavy eyebrows and a small, tight mouth, which gave people the impression that she was a disagreeable person. On the contrary, she was a warm, outgoing woman who was cultured and educated. Like Morrow, she possessed a superabundance of energy. Her one peculiarity was that she couldn't bear to be alone and constantly needed people around her.

Morrow was greatly attracted to the gregarious, high-minded young woman. Soon he began visiting her in Northampton.

Although she was drawn to Morrow, Elizabeth evidently had doubts about his suitability as a husband. Before convincing her to marry him, "Bulldog Morrow" was forced to court Betty (or, as he called her, Betsey) for ten years. It seems that Betty felt he lacked her appreciation of literature and art, was not cultured enough, and had little perception of other people's needs and wishes.

For a time Elizabeth was more attracted to his older brother Jay, although Morrow was blissfully unaware of this infatuation.

After graduating from Smith with honors, Elizabeth taught at a private school in Cleveland. Her father was in poor health, and in the hope of regaining his strength, he took his family on an extended trip to Europe. The Cutters stayed in Paris for a year, and Elizabeth studied at the Sorbonne and later in Florence. While she was away, Morrow kept peppering her with letters, which evidently were so brilliantly written that soon Elizabeth began "comparing the quality of his mind and character with those of her superficially more cultured friends."

In 1901, on her return to the United States, Morrow and Elizabeth became engaged. They had known each other for eight years. But even then she had second thoughts about her fiancé. In any event, she insisted on an extended engagement, but finally capitulated and married him on June 16, 1903.

After the wedding, the couple lived in Englewood, New Jersey, a small city in Bergen County, across the Hudson River from New York City, where Morrow worked as a corporation lawyer for Reed, Simpson, Thacher and Bartlett, a utility firm. Their first house was on Spring Lane, which they rented from a doctor who had just built it. They were then so poor that they made their furniture out of the packing cases in which their wedding presents had arrived. Their first child, Elisabeth Reeve, was born on March 17, 1904. Two years later, Anne Spencer was born on June 22, 1906. Their son, Dwight Whitney, Jr., followed Anne by two years, on November 28, 1908. Constance Cutter, the youngest, was born on June 27, 1913.

With motherhood, whatever doubts Elizabeth had felt about her husband vanished. She wrote in her diary a few months after Elisabeth was born, "Another happy evening together alone. Dwight and I. We are just as happy together as two people could be, I believe."

In the spring of 1909, when Anne was three years old, the Morrows moved to a new house higher up the hill on Palisade Avenue. The new house, which was large, with gingerbread trimming, stood on an acre of ground with lovely old shade trees. By then the Morrows had become prominent in the Englewood community. Although most of their friends were middle-class married couples like themselves, they had also become intimate with some wealthy people, including Thomas W. Lamont, a partner in the prestigious banking firm of J. P. Morgan and Company.

In 1912, when Anne was six years old, her father began to tire of his career as a corporate lawyer. While he was casting about for some other profession, members of J. P. Morgan and Company were considering adding a new senior member to the staff. Lamont suggested Morrow's name to Henry P. Davison, another partner in the firm, but Davison, who knew Morrow only casually, did not think he would be suitable for the job.

A year later the civic-minded Dwight Morrow gave a speech, urging his fellow Englewood citizens to donate $1 million to help rebuild the local hospital. Henry P. Davison happened to be present at the meeting, and he was deeply impressed by Morrow's intelligence as well as his ability to persuade his fellow citizens to part with a contribution. Some weeks later, during a violent rainstorm, Davison was venturing along an Englewood street when he collided with a very small man whose umbrella became interlocked with his own. The owner of the other umbrella turned out to be Dwight Morrow. Remembering the eloquence of Morrow's speech about the hospital, Davison, after extricating his umbrella, went to the office and told Lamont that he had changed his mind about not asking Morrow. Together, they approached J. P. Morgan about the possibility of hiring Morrow, and a few days later an offer was made. Would Mr. Dwight Morrow consider joining J. P. Morgan and Company, with a view to eventually becoming a partner?

Although other men would have jumped at the opportunity, Morgan's offer sent Morrow into a tizzy. For days he agonized over whether to accept the position. "It arose from an endeavor to assure himself that this new career, however promising, would not conflict with those values which he had elaborated as essential to the good life," Nicolson reported. Once, when he and Betty were still living in their modest house on Spring Lane, he woke up in the middle of the night to report to his wife, "I have had the most horrible nightmare. It was truly horrible. It was all so vivid, it was all so ghastly. It seemed real, Betsey, it seemed so *real* . . . I dreamt, Betsey, that we had become rich. But *enormously* rich." This conflict between materialism and spiritual values in a devout Scottish Presbyterian like Morrow became so acute that he tottered on the edge of a nervous breakdown. He had to go to Bermuda for three weeks to recover "his intellectual balance," although in the very act of taking a luxurious island vacation Morrow had perhaps already come to terms with his real values. In any event, he decided to accept J. P. Morgan's offer.

Morrow joined the firm of J. P. Morgan and Company on April 15, 1914. Several months later he became a partner. According to his biographer, he was not "elated" by his new job and was plagued by feelings of homesickness for his old one, which had paid him a mere $35,000 a year, a marked contrast to the $5 million a year he would eventually make as a Morgan partner.

Although he gradually adjusted to his new job and the prospect of enormous wealth, Morrow tried to remain true to what he felt were his real values. He was fond of telling his children, "The world is divided into people who do things and people who get the credit. Try if you can to belong to the first class; there is far less competition."

Although the Morrows were never overly extravagant in their tastes, as were their friends J. P. Morgan and Pierre du Pont, they nevertheless soon succumbed to the lifestyle of the very rich. Their new home, Next Day Hill, on fifty-six wooded acres in Englewood, New Jersey, which was built by their friend the architect Chester Aldrich, was showy but dignified. It boasted wood-paneled rooms, deep pile carpets, original paintings by the famous Scottish artist Sir Henry Raeburn, and a vast cathedral-like library with thousands of books. A stream cut through the property, plunging at intervals into small waterfalls, and the immense grounds were always immaculately groomed. There were chauffeurs, valets, and private secretaries.

Every winter, Morrow took the family to Nassau in the Bahamas. When they grew older and he had become a Morgan partner, he often took them abroad when he traveled on business. These excursions to Europe were no mere pleasure trips but were designed to educate his children about history and foreign civilizations. He frequently instructed his children to behave not like tourists but like "leisurely observers."

Education and reading were his passions. After his death, his daughter Elisabeth remembered him reading in the old Morris chair in the living room, surrounded by his "fantastic curlicues of paper." Morrow had the eccentric habit of making paper spills to save on the cost of matches. He would tear off the corner of a sheet of paper, twist it, screw it into his ear, throw it on the floor, and then begin a new spill by tearing off a section of a fresh sheet of paper.

Since Dwight and Elizabeth both valued education, they urged their children to perform on the highest moral and intellectual levels. Every evening, at home, there were prayers, as well as readings from the classics or ancient myths. Both parents regularly attended the local Presbyterian church, and in addition to Sunday school, the children began their Sunday mornings with prayers next to their mother and father's bed.

When Dwight Morrow wasn't teasing his children at breakfast, he quizzed them on their mathematical ability. As Anne later pointed out, "To this day, if someone asks me suddenly: 'How much is 7 times 8?' my mind blanks to the child's frozen landscape of panic."

In her diaries and letters, Anne always portrayed her family in idealized terms, as if she were modeling them after a loving, closely knit colorful clan in a Dickens novel. To some extent this description was true, but there was also a darker side to her family that she never mentioned in her published writing.

Her shy younger brother, Dwight, Jr., was the victim of a severe mental illness that began to manifest itself at an early age. According to several friends and classmates, he suffered a number of episodes of what appears to have been a manic-depressive illness when he was a student at Groton.

Whether the cause of his illness was biochemical or psychological — the result of an only son's having to live in his brilliant father's shadow — is unknown. In his early youth, Dwight, Jr., tended to hear voices and had to be hospitalized several times.

Understandably, his chronic illness put a severe strain on the family. Although the Morrows did everything they could to help him, as time went on Mrs. Morrow seemed to blame her son for his condition. "She was not too nice to him," Mina Curtiss, a close family friend, reported to Harold Nicolson some years later. (Although Nicolson, after meeting Dwight, described him as being "a dumpy little youth in pince-nez" with a bad stammer, he rapidly modified his assessment and found him to be intelligent.) In contrast to her mother, Anne continued to love her brother without reservation. "She really loved him and was always supportive and understanding," a friend reported, "and Anne was Dwight's idea of the most wonderful person in the world."

Elisabeth's illness was another source of worry for the family. As a young girl she contracted rheumatic fever, a disease characterized by fever, pain in the joints, and inflammation of the pericardium and heart valves. Although the Morrows were not immediately aware of it, the disease severely damaged one of her heart valves and left her particularly susceptible to serious infections. As a result, she was often sickly and confined to her bed for days. By nature emotional and high-strung, she became even more nervous and excitable when ill.

With two sickly children, a workaholic father who was eaten up by nervous energy, and a highly energetic mother who escaped from her woes by incessant activity and socializing, the Morrow family was hardly the happy, easy-going group that Anne portrayed in her early diaries. On the contrary, according to a friend, "they were more like a bunch of high-strung thoroughbreds." Unlike her mother, Anne appears to have coped with the family's complex problems by withdrawing into herself. She was by nature a shy child who found it difficult to talk to people outside the family.

At Miss Chapin's School, a private girls' finishing and college preparatory school in New York City, she had trouble engaging the other students in conversation. At home, she took refuge in a world of her own imagination, writing fairy tale plays, in which Elisabeth, Constance, and Dwight would act.

Like many young girls, Anne was emotionally closer to her mother and two sisters than she was to her busy father and unpredictable brother. Of her two sisters, she was especially close to Elisabeth, who could be very witty, daring, and outgoing when she wasn't ailing. The bond between the sisters was so intense that when their mother read them the leper colony scenes in the novel *Ben-Hur,* they both began worrying about contracting leprosy themselves. "Anne made a solemn compact that if she caught it she would immediately touch Elisabeth, and Elisabeth promised to do the same for Anne, so that if they had to be sent away, at least they could go together," Elisabeth later recalled.

As is often the case with sisters, there was strong, unspoken sibling rivalry between the two oldest girls. Anne did not consider Constance, who was seven years younger than herself, much of a threat, but she was painfully aware of the differences between Elisabeth and herself. Not only was Elisabeth smart, sophisticated, and witty, but she was a strikingly attractive blonde with an appealing ethereal quality that was in part due to her delicate health. She was somewhat taller than Anne, who had inherited her mother's plain looks and her father's tiny stature. As they grew older and began to date, Anne felt sure that men would prefer Elisabeth.

Despite all her education, travel, and wealth, Anne felt hopelessly immature. In comparison with the wild flappers of her era, who wore rolled stockings and short skirts and were sexually sophisticated, she and even the older Elisabeth seemed to live a cloistered existence. They were "sleeping princesses." "Only in college did I begin to realize how much I resembled the 'sheltered Emelye' of Chaucer's *Knight's Tale,* enclosed in a walled garden," she later wrote. Although she was loath to admit it, she longed for someone to scale the wall and let her out. She also dimly sensed that he — the "Prince Charming" whom the other girls at school were always prattling about — couldn't be just any ordinary male. On the contrary, he had to be someone famous and powerful, just like her awe-inspiring father.

CHAPTER 2

"A Modern Galahad"

THE TIMID, DREAMY YOUNG WOMAN who watched the autumn leaves drift into Paradise Pond at Smith College in Northampton, Massachusetts, longed to be a freshman on some other college campus. She wanted to be able to enter a classroom or dormitory without everyone knowing who she was. She also yearned to be independent. In fact, some months before, she had worked up the courage to tell her mother that she did not want to attend Smith, Mrs. Morrow's alma mater. When her mother asked her why, she replied that she did not want to be endlessly compared with her mother and Elisabeth, who was already enrolled at Smith and on the dean's list.

"I want to go to Vassar!" she told a shocked Mrs. Morrow.

Her wish was instantly squelched. Mrs. Morrow, who was a trustee of the college and the first woman chairman of the board, could not countenance a daughter of hers entering another college, especially a Seven Sister rival like Vassar. Anne, despite her own wishes, was marched off to Smith in the fall of 1924.

Although outwardly obedient and conscientious, she seems to have retaliated subconsciously by suffering from a devastating case of stage fright at exams. Even though she had studied diligently, her brain froze at the sight of a test, as she took pains to point out to her mother in several letters.

Gradually, however, she began to like college life, although the academic pressures continued to exhaust her.

At the time Anne attended college, education for women was undergoing something of a revolution. As Smith's president, William Allan

Neilson, observed, the route to higher learning blazed by the nine-teenth-century feminists had "become a highway," although it was still traveled by a privileged group. By 1920, 431,000 women were enrolled in colleges and universities — almost 45 percent of the total college population. The generation of women who had fought for higher education was succeeded by a generation that more or less took it for granted. The debate of the 1920s centered not on whether women should attend college, but on the type of education that would best pre-pare them for the future. For many women, this consisted of both mar-riage and a career, although in the case of a Seven Sisters school like Smith, academics were stressed to the point where women were said to receive on graduation a "spinster of the arts" degree.

Although Anne was dubious about her ability to attain a husband or a career, she was more confident about her literary ability. She had be-come interested in writing in her second semester when she took a course from Mina Kirstein, a well-known writer of the time who published her books under her married name, Mina Curtiss. Mrs. Curtiss, who later became a loyal friend, encouraged her in her literary efforts.

Anne continued to work hard at her college courses, but the "stage fright" that overwhelmed her whenever she took a test continued to plague her, and her marks were merely average. Her failure to achieve scholas-tic glory undermined the feeble self-confidence she had been able to mus-ter. Again and again she compared herself with her brilliant parents and to beautiful, bright Elisabeth and longed to do something special that would prove to them — and to herself — that she was as clever and re-markable as they.

Her one consolation was that Mrs. Curtiss thought she had ability as a writer. The older woman kept praising her work, even telling her that some of it was good enough to publish. But despite this encour-agement, Anne was riddled with self-doubt, confiding in her diary in 1927, "I want to write — I want to write — I want to write and I never never will. I know it and I am so unhappy and it seems as though nothing else mattered. Whatever I'm doing, it's always there, an ulti-mate longing there, saying, 'Write this — write that — write — ' and I *can't.* Lack ability, time, strength, and duration of vision. I wish someone would tell me brutally, 'You can *never* write *anything.* Take up home gardening!' "

Despite this lack of faith in her own talent, Anne kept on writing es-says, stories, and poems. Eventually a number of her literary efforts were published in the *Smith College Monthly* magazine. The first, "A Six

O'clock Story for Constance," appeared in the April 1927 issue, along with "Grand Opera," a review of Edna St. Vincent Millay's text for music that had been composed by Deems Taylor. These contributions were followed by two more prose works, one a prize-winning essay, "Madame d'Houdetot," which was published in the October issue, the other a prize-winning story, "Lida was Beautiful," published in June 1928, her senior year. In addition, she had eight poems published in the college magazine between October 1926 and June 1928. These included "Caprice," "Unicorn," "Letter with a Foreign Stamp," and "Remembrance," which would be reprinted in the *Literary Digest* after her engagement to Charles Lindbergh was announced.

Not surprisingly, some of her poems revealed her awakening sexuality. In one verse, she wrote about a modest "brown-haired Quaker maiden" who yearned to be "a scarlet, Spanish dancer." In other poems, she revealed her secret desire to escape from her loving but overwhelming family and, simultaneously, to do something extraordinary that would make them admire her. She not only imagined "silver birds" and "a sudden fluttering of wings in silver flight," but also fancied herself astride a unicorn with "polished bright" hoofs, soaring over the rooftops in the moonlight. The unicorn was to become a recurring image in her work, and it was evident that for her, even as a young woman, it held a special meaning. According to legend, this beautiful, fierce white creature, which resembled a horse or a kid, was notoriously difficult to capture and could be caught only if a virgin was thrown before it. After the unicorn leaped into her lap, she suckled it and then led it into a king's palace.

While she was away at college, Anne wrote many letters home. Her favorite correspondent was her mother, about whom she had mixed emotions. On the one hand, she adored Mrs. Morrow and wanted to emulate both her lifestyle and her accomplishments. On the other, she resented her, feeling that she could never match her mother's prodigious energy and intellect, as well as her charming social manner.

Her other main correspondents were her two sisters, especially in 1926, when Elisabeth went to France for a semester to study languages at the University of Grenoble. Although Elisabeth by her absence was no longer much of a threat, Anne missed her sister intensely and expressed her love in a series of long, affectionate letters. At the same time she also began writing regularly in her diary, which she had started before entering Smith.

In later years, Anne remarked on the difference between these two forms of personal writing. "There is, naturally, a distinction between diaries and letters," she observed.

> Letters are usually written not only to communicate with the recipient, but also to amuse and please him. So that the truth here is sometimes veiled or colored. Diaries are written for oneself and reveal the writer as he is when alone. My diaries were written primarily, I think, not to preserve the experience but to savor it, to make it even more real, more visible and palpable, than in actual life. For in our family an experience was not finished, not truly experienced, unless written down or shared with another.

Shy, contemplative, and more preoccupied with writing about an experience than actually living it, Anne was then a slender, serious young woman who wore her dark, unruly hair in a long ponytail. Her clothes were expensive but not particularly stylish; she favored simple dresses and blouses with starched white collars. She appeared to prefer the world of her thoughts and the safety of her family to the dances, parties, and other social events favored by her classmates. People meeting her for the first time were often struck by her air of restraint and desire for privacy. Despite her inner longing to be popular, she did not warm up to other people easily, becoming friendly only when she was sure of their feelings toward her. Even so, several of her fellow students were able to penetrate her reserve, and she did make some close friends, including an insecure and troubled freshman named Frances Smith who clung to her in her senior year and often sought her advice.

Women were not Anne's only friends at Smith. Like many shy young girls, she dated a few of the sons of family friends or an occasional male friend of her brother, Dwight. None of these young men interested her romantically, and she secretly pronounced them as "middling" boys who lacked dash, intelligence, and character. It was not surprising that these men failed to stir her. Overly protected and sexually naive, she found the prospect of an intimate relationship with a man frightening. Even if she did meet one who was physically attractive, what chance did he have of competing with her father? Because Dwight Morrow was such a powerful and distinguished man, she feared that it would be harder for her than it was for other women to fall in love and marry. Once, after visiting the happily married wife of an English teacher on campus, she confided to Elisabeth, "Don't you often wish this marrying business were all over? I would be willing to sacrifice 'falling in love,' and all that — honeymoon, etc. — if I could just jump into an everyday life like hers. A home, a nice husband (if necessary), and a baby — everything settled and everyday, no romance but a kind of humdrum divinity."

Ironically, she would soon be propelled into a romantic relationship that was entirely the opposite of such girlish visions.

Anne spent a good part of May 20 and May 21, 1927, holed up in the Smith College library, writing a paper on Erasmus. While she was deep in her thoughts, everyone else in the United States was focusing their attention on quite a different type of man.

On Friday morning, May 20, 1927, a twenty-five-year-old airmail pilot named Charles Augustus Lindbergh, Jr., was taking off from a muddy runway on Roosevelt Field on Long Island. He was headed for Paris in his single-engine plane, the *Spirit of St. Louis,* and what thrilled the public was the fact that he hoped to make the perilous 3,500-mile trip nonstop and that he was alone.

As soon as his overloaded plane cleared the telephone lines near Roosevelt Field by barely twenty feet, people all over the country crowded around their small crystal sets to hear the news of his progress across the Atlantic. Those living near his flight path rushed out of their houses, scrambled up trees, or even climbed on rooftops to see if they could glimpse his small silvery plane as it passed overhead. Could he make it? Would he survive the cold and darkness, the fog, rain, and wind, and land before his fuel and strength gave out? In America, England, Paris, and all over the world, people waited for word that his plane had been sighted. That night, forty thousand boxing fans attending the Maloney-Sharkey heavyweight fight at Yankee Stadium in New York stood and bowed their heads when the announcer asked them to pray for "Lindy." The humorist Will Rogers, himself a flier, spoke for millions of Americans when he wrote in his nationally syndicated news column, "No attempt at jokes today. A slim, tall, bashful, smiling American boy is somewhere over the middle of the Atlantic Ocean, where no lone human being has ever ventured before."

When Lindbergh and the *Spirit of St. Louis* landed thirty-three and a half hours after takeoff at Le Bourget airport just north of Paris, people went crazy with admiration and joy. The mayor of Paris was so thrilled by the aviator's heroic feat that he immediately offered him the keys to the city's bordellos, an offer which Lindbergh graciously declined. In the streets and cafés of Paris, people sang all night, "*Le jeune Américain, il la fait, nom d'un chien."* ("My God, he did it!") It was, as one observer pointed out, "as if Icarus had at last succeeded, a daring man alone had attained the unattainable." Americans, of course, went wild with pride and amazement. Not only had one of their countrymen achieved the impossible, but he was accepting his triumph with a charming modesty and decorum.

In little more than a day, Charles Lindbergh, a former Minnesota farm boy, was transformed from an unknown pilot into a historical figure. Tall and handsome, with a shy smile and a wayward lock of blond hair over his forehead, he captured the imagination of millions.

There were other reasons for his enshrinement as a hero. In the cynical twenties, people desperately wanted someone to worship. Weary and disillusioned after World War I, Americans longed for a hero who could make them feel good about life and their country again. Lindbergh, with his clean-cut good looks, quiet dignity, and modesty, seemed made to order. This daring young American of twenty-five, this "unheralded boy," as people often called him, had done what seemed to be the impossible. Furthermore, he had done it *alone,* in the best American tradition.

"A disillusioned nation fed on cheap heroics and scandal and crime was revolting against the low estimate of human nature which it had allowed itself to entertain," observed Frederick Lewis Allen in *Only Yesterday: An Informal History of the Nineteen Twenties.*

> For years the American people had been spiritually starved . . . Romance, chivalry, and self-dedication had been debunked; the heroes of history had been shown to have feet of clay . . . Something that people needed . . . was missing from their lives. And all at once Lindbergh provided it. Romance, chivalry, self-dedication — here they were, embodied in a modern Galahad for a generation which had foresworn Galahads.

For days the world's newspapers were largely devoted to Lindbergh and his achievement. When he returned home to the United States, he was greeted in New York by 200 boats and 75 planes, then showered with 1,800 tons of paper in a spectacular ticker-tape parade up Broadway. According to one historian, "So avid was the interest in him that the nation's newspapers used up some 25,000 tons of newsprint beyond the normal amount . . . Millions of Americans in thousands of churches all across the land, that Sunday morning, bowed their heads in prayers of thanksgiving for him, and few were the sermons that did not mention him. Of many, he was the only subject . . ." Four thousand poets composed verse in his honor. A new dance was named for him (the Lindy Hop), and hastily composed songs bearing such titles as "Oh, Charlie Is My Darling" and "Lucky Lindy" proclaimed his new status as the world's idol. He was deluged with mail congratulating him, including 3¹/₂ million letters and 100,000 telegrams and cables. A Texas town, streets, schools, and restaurants were named after him. His photograph was displayed in classrooms and thousands of homes. In St. Louis, women fought over a corn cob from which he had just eaten.

The newspaper tycoon William Randolph Hearst offered Lindbergh a half-million-dollar movie contract to star in a film about aviation, and he was presented with an airplane, dogs, monkeys, a horned toad, diamond stickpins, and crocheted doilies, as well as proposals of marriage. He turned them down, including the lucrative film offer. Far from being incensed, a reverential Hearst presented the aviator with two antique celestial and terrestrial globes that he had casually admired in Hearst's apartment. They were worth almost fifty thousand dollars, but Lindbergh sent them, along with the truckloads of gifts, trophies, and medals he had received, to the Missouri Historical Society for permanent display.

After he became famous, Lindbergh soon learned to stop sending his shirts to the laundry. They were never sent back. Nor were his checks, which were never cashed. People kept them as souvenirs, reminders that life could be something more than the crime, graft, cheap theatrics, and meaningless sexual encounters of the jaded Jazz Age.

Because he was so modest and unassuming, the public's image of a pilot changed overnight. No longer was an aviator considered a crazy daredevil who told tall tales about his flying exploits in World War I. Lindbergh was the exemplar of the new pilot — a peacetime aviator who proved a spectacular boon to American business when his epic flight gave a boost to the fledgling commercial airline industry. Within weeks of his historic flight, aircraft and engine factories were under construction throughout the United States, and flying schools and air taxi services could not keep up with the demand for their services. People flocked to buy aeronautical stocks. As one airline company official described it at the time, "From a picturesque aeronautical movement of uncertain financial status, aviation has changed into an established business enterprise."

"No living American — no dead American, one might almost say, save perhaps Abraham Lincoln — commanded such unswerving fealty,"

Frederick Lewis Allen noted. "If you decried anything that Lindbergh did, you knew that you had wounded your auditors. For Lindbergh was a god."

But the young man who was the object of all this attention was ill-suited for fame and celebrity. Although undeniably the epitome of what author Tom Wolfe was later to describe as "the right stuff," that quality beyond bravery and courage, Charles Augustus Lindbergh, Jr., was no simple American boy who reveled in his supercelebrity image. As he later said, all "this hero guff" was beginning to make him so fed up that he felt like "shouting murder." In actuality, he was a very complicated and contradictory young man who until the end of his days would remain an enigma to almost everyone who knew him. As the historian Max Lerner said many years later, "He was someone who had recesses within recesses, and I doubt whether anyone knew him with the possible exception of his wife. I'm not sure that he ever knew himself."

Charles Augustus Lindbergh, Jr., was born in Detroit, Michigan, on February 4, 1902, the only child of Charles Augustus Lindbergh, a taciturn and unapproachable, though prosperous, lawyer from Little Falls, Minnesota, and Evangeline Lodge Land, an attractive, intelligent, but reserved young woman who had briefly taught chemistry at the Little Falls High School. Evangeline was twenty-five at the time of their marriage; her husband, forty-two. Evangeline was the elder Lindbergh's second wife. His first wife, Mary LaFond, had died following surgery to remove an abdominal tumor at the age of thirty-one, having borne him three daughters: Lillian, Edith, who died at ten months of age, and Eva.

Charles's ancestors on his father's side were Swedes, who had changed their name from Månsson to Lindbergh when they emigrated from Sweden to Minnesota in 1859. His grandfather, Ola Månsson, who adopted the name August Lindbergh when he left the country, had been a prominent figure in Sweden — he was one of the leaders of the Riksdag, the Swedish parliament, and a close friend of the king. On his mother's side, the family was of English, Scottish, and Irish descent.

Charles Lindbergh's childhood was lonely and unhappy. Soon after their marriage, his parents discovered they were incompatible. According to his half-sister Eva, her father and stepmother "were attuned mentally, but not emotionally." Evangeline was a high-strung, moody, and private woman, while, in the words of his biographer, Bruce L. Larson, the elder "Lindbergh was the sort of man who did not show emotion at all." He did not appear to crave human society and spent a great deal of his spare time reading, especially books written by Charles Darwin and Herbert Spencer, the philosopher who first proposed the theory of social Darwinism, namely the belief that Darwin's theory of evolution can be applied to society.

When Charles was five, his parents separated. By this time, however, the elder Lindbergh, a Republican, had been elected to the U.S. House of Representatives where he served from 1907 to 1917, and consequently the Lindberghs did not divorce. For appearance's sake, they would meet occasionally in Washington or Little Falls, sleeping in separate rooms in the same house. Both parents tried earnestly to impress on young Charles the fact that their separation did not alter their feelings for him and that they continued to hold each other in high regard. Inevitably, however, their bizarre style of life affected him deeply, although he never discussed their separation publicly, merely stating some years later that their relationship was "a tragic situation" and that perhaps his mother's education and closeness to her family were "not good background for a Minnesota one-generation-beyond-the-frontier life."

Perhaps Charles's observation also had something to do with the fact that his mother's sense of intellectual superiority prevented him from enjoying a normal upbringing. Whatever she felt about her husband privately, Evangeline was highly conscious of her position as a congressman's wife. A coldly polite woman who took great pride in her advanced degrees in science, she shunned the residents of Little Falls as her social and mental inferiors and invited few neighbors to visit her. Charles was discouraged from mingling with other boys his age.

The only trait Charles's parents appear to have had in common was a fanatical stoicism, which they communicated to their son. The elder Lindbergh once insisted on enduring a hernia operation without any anesthetic. Determined that his son would be equally self-sufficient, he refused to rescue the boy when he fell into the Mississippi River near the family farm, counting on young Charles to be able to swim. Fortunately, he could. Although a doting and overprotective mother, Evangeline was peculiarly distant and undemonstrative. To the end of her life, she shook hands with her son when they said good-night rather than kissing him. An unhappy woman, she undoubtedly compensated for her failed marriage by making her only child the center of her life.

The tradition of stoicism and self-reliance ran as strong in Evangeline's family as it did in her husband. Evangeline's father, Dr. Charles Henry Land, was a well-known Detroit dentist and inventor who was widely recognized as a pioneer in porcelain dentistry. A short, balding man with a white mustache, he was an iconoclast who, like Lindbergh, Sr., believed in Darwin's theories and mocked many aspects of organized religion.

As a child Charles loved to work in his grandfather Land's laboratories on the ground floor of his small, gray-painted house in Detroit. There he could bake clay, make electric batteries, and melt lead, carrying out some of the more dangerous experiments with the help of his grandfather and his uncle, a mining engineer. The two men liked to engage in long discussions about science, and Charles loved to listen to them talk about Edison's and Marconi's inventions, Darwin's theories, and Wilbur and Orville Wright's wonderful flying experiments. Like Charles's father, Dr. Land would remain a major influence on Charles, who, to the end of his life, would continue to espouse many of his father's and grandfather's beliefs, including social Darwinism, a reverence for science and technology, and a distaste for the movies, which Dr. Land felt created a false and unwholesome view of the world.

Although they were both fiercely independent thinkers and "loners," Charles's father and grandfather Land did not see eye-to-eye on many issues, especially politics. The Lands were conservative Republicans who believed in the value of private property, while the elder Lindbergh was an insurgent and progressive Republican who as he grew older became increasingly anticapitalistic and fervidly opposed the big money trusts.

During his five terms in Congress, Representative Lindbergh believed that national prosperity was founded on the work of the farmer, and he steadfastly protected the interests of Midwestern farmers. He also called for sweeping reforms in the financial policies of government, banks, and businesses, including government ownership of transport and public utilities.

In 1913 he published a book, *Banking and Currency and the Money Trust,* in which he attacked the "unfair practices" of such private banking organizations as those of the Rockefellers and J. P. Morgan. He feared they were devising a new banking scheme, the Aldrich plan, that they would then control and that they would also propel the United States into a war to protect their financial interests abroad.

As a congressman, Lindbergh made the serious political error of questioning the role of the Roman Catholic Church in the United States. Concerned about reports from the Free Press Defense League which accused the Church of attempting to destroy such free institutions as public schools, the press, and separation of church and state, he requested on the House floor a "true and impartial investigation" of the matter. According to Bruce Larson, "Lindbergh's character would substantiate the sincerity of his motives, but in a sense it seemed politically naive to introduce such a controversial resolution. Though an investigation was never conducted, reaction against Lindbergh could be expected . . . In the opinion of his friends and biographers . . . , 'There is nothing that more surely brought about his political defeat.' "

In 1917 Lindbergh gave up his seat in the Congress and ran for governor in the 1918 Republican primary in Minnesota. It turned out to be one of the most bitter campaigns in American history. For opposing the United States' entry into World War I and refusing to take an anti-German stance, Charles Lindbergh, Sr., was pelted with rotten eggs when he spoke at meetings, hanged and burned in effigy, shot at, and run out of town. He was called "an anarchist and Bolshevik," "anti-religious," "a traitor," "an ass," and worse. The book he wrote and published at his own expense, entitled *Why Is Your Country at War?*, was confiscated, and he was arrested on the grounds of "sedition," although formal charges were never brought against him.

When he lost the primary by only fifty thousand votes to the incumbent, Republican governor Joseph A. Burnquist, few people were upset. Although he had behaved courageously during the vituperative campaign, writing to his daughter Eva that she "must prepare to see me in prison and possibly shot for I will not be a rubber stamp to deceive people," his personality was so distant and eccentric that he failed to elicit sympathy and compassion.

The teenaged Charles, Jr., was his father's chauffeur during much of his campaign. It was later reported that the sixteen-year-old boy "appeared to take little interest in the speeches, the hooting, cheering and jeering, or the riots." He would "stay by the car during the meetings, tinkering with its machinery." Both the elder Lindbergh and his son stoically endured the humiliation, although by this time young Charles was discovering how to deal with stress and uncertainty by retreating into the clear and precise world of science and technology, which he had now come to believe was far easier to understand and control than unpredictable human emotions.

Although Charles Lindbergh spent the first four years of his life in Little Falls, Minnesota, he seldom spent more than a few months in the same place after his father was elected to Congress. He spent the winters in Washington, which he disliked because it was a city and he "could not go hunting with a gun," and the summers in Minnesota. His education was erratic, due to his father's unsettled lifestyle. As a child and young man, he attended twelve schools, both public and private, from Washington to California. An indifferent student, he did poorly at all.

Of the many places where Lindbergh lived during his youth, Little Falls was unquestionably his favorite. In the center of a farming and timbering community, it was surrounded by woods and streams where he developed a deep feeling for nature and wildlife. His love of the outdoors was partially an escape, for he had little personal contact with his classmates and teachers, joined no extracurricular groups, and attended no parties given by his peers. Perhaps one of the reasons, aside from his antisocial nature, was that he hated to dress up. As he later remembered, the first time he was taken to church in Little Falls, he created such an uproar when his mother made him "wear scratchy new clothes" that he was never again taken to a service. "The incident left me skeptic toward religion, questioning the beneficence of God," he wrote.

His classmates at the Little Falls High School also later confirmed the fact that they never saw him in a white shirt or in anything but the most casual clothes. Even his relatives had to concede that he was "shy and a little odd," a young man who was always by himself, had no friends, neither smoked nor drank, was obsessed by physical fitness, and was uninterested in girls. "His mother is his only 'girl,' " his aunt insisted to a reporter in 1927, shortly after her nephew's famous flight.

In 1920, after graduating from the Little Falls High School, he decided to study mechanical engineering at the University of Wisconsin. This step proved to be a mistake since, as he himself later admitted, he chose the school "probably more because of its nearby lakes than because of its high engineering standards." Always a poor student, he earned dismal grades in every subject except shop, and, in the middle of his sophomore year, he decided to drop out before he was expelled.

A motorcycle buff who had traumatized the residents of Little Falls by racing through town at a breakneck speed, he climbed on board his twin-cylindered Excelsior and rode to the Nebraska Aircraft Corporation in Lincoln. He had decided what he wanted to do with his life. As a boy lying in the tall grass of his father's Minnesota farm, he would watch the white clouds drift overhead. "How wonderful it would be, I'd thought, if I had an airplane — wings with which I could fly up to the clouds and explore their caves and canyons — wings like that hawk circling above me. Then, I would ride on the wind and be part of the sky . . . "

When, some time later, he saw his first airplane, he at first thought it sounded like an automobile that had been going by the house all summer. Then he realized that no automobile engine could make that strange sound. "I ran to the window and climbed out onto the tarry roof. It was an airplane! . . . Flying upriver below higher branches of trees, a biplane was less than two hundred yards away — a frail, complicated structure, with the pilot sitting out in front between struts and wires. I watched it fly quickly out of sight, and then rushed downstairs to tell my mother."

A short time later his mother took him to an air meet in Fort Myer, Virginia. The experience was so enthralling that he wanted to fly himself.

To promote the Lincoln Standard planes the firm manufactured, company pilots were giving flying lessons, and Lindbergh immediately signed up. On April 9, 1922, he had his first flight as a passenger in a Lincoln Standard. A few days later he received his first instruction in the same plane from an I. O. Biffle, a tough and demanding ex–military pilot.

"My early flying seemed an experience beyond mortality," he later recalled. "There was the earth spreading out below me, a planet where I had lived but from which I had astonishingly risen. It had been the home of my body. I felt strangely apart from my body in the plane. I was never more aware of all existence, never less aware of myself."

"The life of an aviator seemed to me ideal," he added. "It involved skill. It commanded adventure. It made use of the latest developments of science . . . I could spiral the desolation of a mountain peak, explore caverns of a cloud, or land on a city flying field and there convince others of aviation's future. There were times in an airplane when it seemed I had partially escaped mortality, to look down on earth like a god."

And although he was loath to admit it, he seemed to be venerated like one, for by the end of World War I, aviation was only fifteen years old and pilot-worship was at its most heady. Or as one aviation historian put it, "The only modern counterparts to aviators during this first postwar decade were the first few groups of astronauts, particularly the original seven. During the decade after World War I, any flight was considered newsworthy, with a record flight or racing triumph the clear equivalent of the world series or a championship boxing match. The war had created a need for heroes; aviation could provide them. . . . The aviator heroes of the Twenties could literally do no wrong."

For young men and women in the twenties, flight was equated with freedom and romance, as well as with extreme danger. The statistics proved it. A pilot's life was likely to be a short one — about eight hundred flying hours.

In the twenties, the vast majority of people in the United States had not yet experienced the exhilaration of flight. In 1914 only wealthy and euphoria-seeking sportsmen, often attired in bizarre flying outfits, and carnival-style aerial performers flew a few hundred aircraft. By 1919, even though thousands of planes were available as war surplus, few people purchased them. They were more expensive than yachts to operate and maintain, and far more dangerous. "Man was never made to fly" was the opinion of most Americans, who felt that any person who dared set foot in a plane was openly suicidal. And although commercial aviation did exist in the United States prior to 1927, the public was largely unaware of it.

Lindbergh became one of those select few to master the sky. Well aware that flying was a very dangerous pursuit, he gradually learned to conquer his fear of heights by climbing a high water tower near his home. After ascending a few rungs, he would stop and look down, trying "to rationalize away the strangeness that grew in me with each foot of height." This desensitization technique was successful, and he rapidly became not only an expert pilot but also a stunt flier, learning wing walking and parachuting. His stunts were so breathtaking that soon he was billed as "Daredevil Lindbergh," although to his fellow barnstormers he was known as "Slim," because of his lean and tall physique (he stood six feet three inches tall). His specialties were the double parachute jump and a spectacular stunt in which he would climb thousands of feet into the air and then dive straight down, only pulling out at the last minute, so near the ground that his wheels sometimes touched tall grasses.

Although he was as nervous at first about performing these death-defying stunts as he had been about flying, he convinced himself that he would not die like so many of his colleagues simply because he wouldn't make the same mistakes they had made. This is what psychologists would later call "magical thinking," and like many daredevils he perhaps only felt truly alive when he was attempting something dangerous. Whether this was due to an innate love of thrills, a death wish as a result of his unhappy family situation, or his physiology remains a matter of conjecture.

The dangerous profession Lindbergh took up, barnstorming, had become a popular occupation among many trained pilots who had returned from World War I with an appetite for flying and no means of earning a living. Unwilling to exchange their life of adventure and thrills for one of routine and safety, many bought flimsy surplus planes from the U.S. Army and traveled to county fairs or anywhere they could attract a crowd with their stunt flying. The real money, however, lay in giving rides, usually "ten dollars for ten minutes."

Lindbergh made his first solo flight in April 1923 when he purchased his first plane in Georgia. It was a salvaged World War I training plane, a Curtiss Jenny, and soon he began to earn his living as a flier from barnstorming expeditions in the Midwest. His fee for introducing people to the excitement of flight was lower than that of most barnstormers: he took up passengers at five dollars a ride. On one early flight, he almost killed his first passenger, barely clearing some trees and a hill on takeoff, but his expertise soon manifested itself on subsequent flights.

In 1924 he enlisted in the army, so that he could attend the army flying school at Brooks Field, San Antonio, Texas. Determined to make good this time, he decided to devote himself to his studies and graduated second in his class. He did even better at Kelly Field, where he went on for advanced training and graduated at the top of his class. He was commissioned a second lieutenant in the Army Air Service Reserve in March 1925.

By this time he was not only a top-notch pilot but also a confirmed practical joker whose fondness for crude pranks seemed to know no limits. Although practical jokes were the rage in the twenties, Lindbergh's seemed more cruel and hostile than humorous — undoubtedly an outlet for the anger and confusion about his traumatic family situation which he could never bring himself to express directly. His fellow cadets at Brooks and Kelly soon learned that having him as a barracks mate could be annoying. He squirted mounds of shaving cream into the open mouths of sleeping men and surreptitiously placed grasshoppers in the beds of those cadets he knew were deathly afraid of insects, and once the entire barracks had to sleep outdoors for several days after he stuffed a dead skunk into one cadet's pillowcase.

While he was at Brooks, Lindbergh was bombarded by letters from his mother. Undoubtedly she feared that at age twenty-two he was growing up fast and that she was losing him — in the early 1920s Evangeline had gone on a ten-day barnstorming tour through southern Minnesota with him and had adored every minute of it.

According to Brendan Gill, one of his biographers, as the letters kept coming, "his fellow cadets . . . assumed from the volume of mail he re-

ceived that an infatuated girl friend was in feverish pursuit of him."
Further,

> he begged his mother to spare him embarrassment by writing to him
> less often. She replied that she had·a solution to the problem: she would
> address envelopes to him in a number of different hands. There! she said, in
> effect — now they will envy you because they will think that you have a
> lot of girl friends, and it will really be only me. There was a coquetry in
> the suggestion, and there was sometimes a coquetry in the letters, espe-
> cially when she would hint at the approach and subsequent dismissal of
> unidentified admirers.
>
> . . . When reporters descended upon the town [of Little Falls] in the
> summer of 1927, seeking every scrap of information about Lindbergh's
> past, few of the townspeople could remember much of anything about
> him, except that he had a mechanical bent, liked to ride a motorcycle,
> and never dated. Little as she may have been aware of it, Evangeline's
> need to sequester and dominate her son was very strong. Charles was
> hers, and the evidence is that for twenty-seven years no other woman
> came within touching distance of him. Few mothers have held the abso-
> lute fealty of their sons for so long.

Outwardly Lindbergh may have seemed to worship his mother, but
some evidence exists that he also felt suffocated by her strange brand of
overpossessiveness. In a recent interview, his younger daughter, Reeve
Lindbergh, stated that perhaps the reason her father made his historic
flight across the Atlantic was to "get away" from his mother. Reeve pref-
aced her remark by saying that it was a "frivolous explanation," but
given Evangeline's single-track devotion and Lindbergh's lifelong restlessness, the comment may offer more of an insight into Lindbergh's enigmatic character than his daughter was willing to admit.

After Brooks, Lindbergh was hired by the Robertson Aircraft Company
in St. Louis as the chief pilot on the mail run to Chicago. He made the
inaugural run southward from Chicago on April 15, 1926.

American women in the 1920s thrilled whenever they glimpsed an
airmail pilot flying overhead. The rugged airmail men were considered
the bravest and most glamorous of men, undoubtedly because flying
the mail was a very dangerous occupation. As there were no radios aboard
and weather reports were unreliable, the pilots had no idea when they
descended in a fog or in poor atmospheric conditions whether they
would encounter clear air or a barn, high-tension wires or a mountain.

Sadly, they all too often hit obstacles, and thirty-one of the first forty airmail pilots were killed.

Charles Lindbergh was not among them. He managed to survive two forced landings during the day and two crashes at night when he parachuted at the last minute to safety. Despite his luck, he could not envision continuing as an airmail pilot. "There was nothing to match yourself against," he later said, obviously forgetting about death. That year, during one of his routine night flights to Chicago, he started considering the possibilities of long-distance flights and "startled" himself by thinking, "I could fly non-stop between New York and Paris."

He was not the first flier to whom the idea had occurred. For seven years American and French pilots had been attempting unsuccessfully to win the twenty-five-thousand-dollar Orteig Prize, the brainchild of Raymond Orteig, a rotund middle-aged Frenchman who operated the Brevoort and Lafayette hotels in New York City and who had a dream about linking France and the United States by air. He stated that the cash prize would be awarded "to the first aviator who shall cross the Atlantic in a land or water aircraft (heavier than air) from Paris or the shores of France to New York, or from New York to Paris or the shores of France, without stop."

Orteig had originally issued the challenge in 1919, with the provision that the flight be completed within the next five years. During that time no one had taken him up on his offer. The planes in the early twenties lacked engines powerful enough to sustain the long-distance trip, and even those pilots who dreamed of attempting it knew that to fail was to suffer certain death in the Atlantic Ocean. In fact, seven or eight years later, when pilots did start to compete for the prize, six men lost their lives in the attempt. They included two crew members of a four-man team headed by the tiny, debonair French ace, Captain René Fonck. The men burned to death when Fonck's enormous, elegantly appointed silver biplane, designed by the famous aeronautical engineer Igor Sikorsky, crashed on takeoff. (Undaunted, Fonck planned another attempt with another Sikorsky-designed plane in the spring.) Other victims included Lieutenant Commander Noel Davis and Lieutenant Stanton H. Wooster — their heavily overloaded plane, the *American Legion*, crashed on takeoff during a test run from Langley Field — and two French fliers, Captain Charles Nungesser and François Coli, both war heroes and skilled pilots. On May 8, a few weeks before Lindbergh made his historic flight, their French-built Levasseur, *L'Oiseau Blanc* (the White Bird), a biplane powered by one engine, took off from Le Bourget airport near Paris. It was later sighted on the coast of Ireland and then never seen again.

In 1927, another contender for the Orteig Prize was Commander Richard E. Byrd, who had astounded the world the previous year when he flew over the North Pole, a feat that was later questioned. His plane, the *America,* an enormous trimotored Fokker, crashed after its first test flight on April 16. Byrd's left wrist was broken, but the injuries of the other crew members, with the exception of famous test pilot Anthony J. Fokker, who escaped unharmed, were more serious, although they eventually recovered.

Studying the details of Fonck's crash, Lindbergh realized that the monster three-engine plane had been dangerously overloaded. There were two heavy radio sets on board, as well as a bed and a stove, so that the crew could cook a hot dinner for themselves en route. They also carried presents for their French friends, including a dozen croissants made in an American bakery which came on board at the last minute before the crash. In addition, the plane's cabin was decorated in red leather. Although these touches were undeniably handsome, Lindbergh felt that all that trimming added unnecessary weight.

In his opinion, a lone flier might succeed in making the trip in a much lighter plane. As he later explained, "A single-engine plane would have greater range, and it seemed to me it would offer its pilot greater safety." As he went back and forth along the mail run from St. Louis to Chicago, he became convinced that he could fly nonstop from New York to Paris and win the Orteig Prize. But two things were imperative for success: he needed the right sort of plane for such a long, extremely hazardous journey, and to obtain it, he would need backers.

A man who could suddenly be charming and outgoing if it helped him reach a goal, Lindbergh managed to convince some rich and civic-minded St. Louis businessmen to whom he was giving flying lessons to put up the money for a plane. What better way to promote your town than by helping me fly nonstop to Paris, he told them. After getting the runaround from several well-known aircraft companies, he was finally able to purchase a monoplane from the Ryan Aircraft Company, a small firm in San Diego that no one had ever heard of but which seemed eager for his business. It would cost only six thousand dollars, plus the price of the engine and instruments. As one writer inelegantly sized it up, the plane was "one giant gasoline tank with wings, a propeller and a bucket seat." This was an accurate description, but it neglected to mention that the plane boasted a powerful, new Wright J-5 whirlwind, 225 h.p. air-cooled engine, which Lindbergh had the foresight to recognize as the first truly reliable aircraft engine and without which his 1927 flight might well have ended in disaster.

The plane's top speed was 135 mph, and it had a range of nearly 4,000 miles, 500 more than the 3,500 miles between New York and Paris. Harold Bixby, a banker who was one of the backers, suggested that the plane be named the *Spirit of St. Louis* in honor of the city, its citizens, and the eight St. Louis businessmen who had made its manufacture possible.

Although he worked closely with Donald Hall, Ryan's young chief engineer and designer, Lindbergh made the final decision on the plane's design. Reasoning that its position would better help him survive a crash, he insisted that the major fuel tank be placed in front rather than behind the pilot's seat, even though this meant he could not see forward and would have to look out through a periscope while airborne.

Weight, he knew, remained a critical factor, the difference between death and life. Unlike his predecessors, who were doomed to failure because of a love for ostentation and paraphernalia, he decided to carry no sextant or radio, parachute, night flying equipment, or extra food — his only sustenance during the long flight would be five sandwiches and two canteens of water. No unnecessary items would be carried with him, not even a razor or a toothbrush. To save a few ounces, he even trimmed the margins of his maps. He would navigate the perilous sea by dead reckoning. The only clothing he wore was his flying suit, and he brought a watch that had belonged to his grandfather.

He was well aware that time was running out and that the pilots of two other planes were getting ready to take off for Paris. Byrd's trimotored Fokker was being repaired, and two ace pilots, Clarence D. Chamberlain and Bert Acosta, who had already beaten the world endurance record by nearly six hours in a Wright-Bellanca, were poised to set off for Paris at any moment.*

On May 11, 1927, Lindbergh took off from San Diego in the *Spirit of St. Louis,* arriving the next day at St. Louis's Lambert Field, where he convinced his backers that with his competitors about to take off at any moment, there was no time to spare for the scheduled christening cere-

---

*Chamberlain, with a passenger, would follow Lindbergh across the Atlantic two weeks later, breaking his record by some five hundred miles when he crash-landed in a marsh in Eisleben, Germany. Three weeks after Lindbergh's flight, Byrd, with three companions, would complete another transatlantic flight, barely escaping death when their plane crash-landed in bad weather in the ocean off a French coastal village.

monies. That same day he left for Long Island, landing at Curtiss Field on May 12, where hundreds of reporters and photographers were on hand to greet him. To his dismay, some crowded into the area where he wanted to land. Like other planes of the period, the *Spirit of St. Louis* had no brakes and was hard to maneuver on the ground, so Lindbergh shifted his approach and landed a safe distance away. But as he was taxiing to the hangar, reporters began to swarm around the plane and he was afraid that someone would be struck by a propeller.

Although Charles Lindbergh had lost all respect for reporters when they attacked his father for his antiwar stand, he was also well aware that they could be useful in helping him promote himself. "I wanted publicity for the St. Louis–New York–Paris flight," he candidly admitted some years later.

> It was part of my project. It would draw public attention to aviation. It would increase my personal influence and earning capacity. I found it exhilarating to see my name in print on the front pages of America's greatest newspapers, and I enjoyed reading the words of praise about my transcontinental flight. I did not begrudge the time I spent with the press — at first. I answered all the questions I could about my airplane and flight, and tried to laugh off questions that seemed too silly or too personal. But I was shocked by the inaccuracy and sensationalism of many of the articles resulting from my interviews. I had encountered nothing like it in San Diego or St. Louis. I found myself quoted as saying things I had neither said nor thought.

In the 1920s mass production had spread from the manufacture of automobiles to the production of news and ideas. There were fewer newspapers, which boasted larger circulations than the ones in the previous decade, and the majority of these newspapers had become standardized by their increasing use of press association material and syndicated features. Throughout the country newspapers were becoming part of chains under more or less centralized control. By 1927 the success of the Hearst and Scripps-Howard systems and the move toward cutting overhead costs had led to the formation of no fewer than fifty-five of these chains, which controlled 230 daily papers, with a combined circulation of over 13 million.

At the same time, there were many more national magazines with enormous circulations, and there was also the new phenomenon of radio broadcasting, so that when Lindbergh came home later in triumph to the United States, everyone heard his speech in their own living rooms. As Frederick Lewis Allen put it,

> The national mind had become as never before an instrument upon which a few men could play . . . They discovered — the successful tabloids were teaching them — that the public tended to become excited about one thing at a time. Newspaper owners and editors found that whenever a trial or a disaster took place, they sold more papers if they gave it all they had . . . They took full advantage of this discovery. Thus, Lindbergh's flight got a bigger play in the press than the Armistice and the overthrow of the German Empire . . . The result was that when something happened which promised to appeal to the popular mind, one had it hurled at one in huge headlines, waded through page after page of syndicated discussion of it . . . and (unless one was a perverse individualist) enjoyed the sensation of vibrating to the same chord which thrilled a vast populace.

The 1920s were also a decade in which the privacy of almost every prominent person was routinely invaded by the newspaper photographer with his handheld camera and magnesium flash lamp, an intrusive device in which a spark would ignite the magnesium, which would explode with a blinding flash, and then a dense, acrid, white smoke would fill the air.

During this era, the tabloids were crowded with many photographs, more than in today's newspapers. The photographer, eager to satisfy the public's insatiable curiosity about the lives of the rich and famous, thus made it his or her business to snap as many photos as possible of newsworthy people in unguarded moments. Other frequent subjects included accidents, disasters, and murder victims.

"Newspapering was entirely different," recalled Alex Handy, a *New York Daily News* photographer who covered Lindbergh's takeoff from Roosevelt Field. "The competition was fierce, and you had to know what you were about to take pictures quickly and effectively. We worked with plates, and we worked with flashpowder. We had to make our own flash equipment. The camera work was tough, a real challenge."

Although Charles Lindbergh may have wanted publicity for himself and his flight, he certainly had no desire to become "the news story of the week" or to have reporters and photographers constantly invade his privacy. Arriving at Curtiss Field, he had been dismayed when reporters bombarded him with questions that he considered either asinine or none of their business, such as whether he had a girlfriend or whether he planned to carry a rabbit's foot on the journey. His distaste escalated to outright hatred the following day when his mother, agitated by sensational newspaper reports that his chances of completing his flight were slim, arrived in New York to bid him farewell, perhaps for the last time. By this time she was his only living parent, his father having died of brain cancer in 1924, a death that Lindbergh had tried to accept stoically though it pained him to see his courageous, strong-willed father robbed of his intelligence.

Although mother and son obliged the press by posing for photographs, they refused to interact in a manner that Lindbergh felt might be construed as "maudlin" or "sentimental," and he was appalled to pick up the papers the following morning and discover that one tabloid had actually gone so far as to pose a middle-aged woman and a young man hugging each other and had superimposed photographs of his mother's and his face over the models'. "I thought it cheaply sentimental and thoroughly dishonest on the part of the papers," he later wrote. "At New York I began to realize how much irresponsibility and license can lurk behind the shining mask called 'freedom of the press.'"

When he took off on May 20, 1927, at 7:54 A.M., Eastern Standard Time, from Roosevelt Field, he had been awake for twenty-three hours, since newspapermen assigned to cover the takeoff had spent the night playing a noisy game of poker downstairs at his hotel and had prevented him from getting any sleep. On the second day of the thirty-three-and-a-half-hour flight, he was sometimes so exhausted that he had to hold his eyes open with his fingers in a desperate effort to stay awake. During that endless day he also sometimes drifted into a strange trancelike state, in which he was neither awake nor asleep and he saw translucent figures that seemed to appear "suddenly in the tail of the fuselage while I was flying through fog. I saw them clearly although my eyes were staring straight ahead. Transparent, mistlike, with semihuman form, they moved in and out through the fabric walls at will. One or two of them would come forward to converse with me and then rejoin the group behind." As he remembered later, "It was the only occasion in my life when I saw and conversed with ghosts."

Finally emerging from this fantastic world, he spotted some fishing trawlers below and buzzed the nearest one. He was filled with joy when he saw a man's face staring at him from one of the portholes. Flying close to the trawler, he leaned out of the cockpit and yelled, "Which way is Ireland?" But the man's face registered no reaction.

Disappointed, he turned his plane in the direction of what he hoped was Europe. He was right. An hour later he spotted what he realized from his chart was the southwest coast of Ireland. He felt uplifted as he passed overhead to see people dashing out of their houses to wave up at him and cheer him on.

On Saturday, May 21, 1927, the *Spirit of St. Louis* touched down in darkness at Le Bourget airport northeast of Paris. The time was 10:24 P.M. Thinking there was no one there to greet him, a pale and worn-out Lindbergh started to taxi the plane toward some hangars when an enormous wave of people — 100,000 French people — rushed to meet him. They were shouting, "Lindbergh! Lindbergh! Lindbergh!"

In that instant the life of Charles Augustus Lindbergh was changed forever. He had become the most famous man in the world. It was, however, as if he had struck a Faustian bargain. After he landed at Le Bourget, fame, adulation, and riches were soon heaped upon him, but he lost something precious in the bargain — his privacy. An avid public, convinced that he now belonged to them, clamored to know every detail of his personal life.

No longer could he lead a simple, knockabout life in which he could fly where he pleased and nobody would care. Suddenly he was forced to exchange the casual clothes he had always favored for formal dress and his sleeping bag for the grandest room at an American embassy or a deluxe hotel. Ordinary citizens were thrilled to shake his hand, but then so were presidents and kings. Although he was secretly flattered by some of the attention and took advantage of the connections that fame brought him, he also despised it. It spelled the end of his personal freedom and independence. Only in a plane, far above the world that hounded him incessantly, could he escape to a sense of his former self. "I began to realize that as one gains fame one loses life. Life meant more to me than fame," he wrote. Often, after returning to his luxurious hotel room after yet another evening of droning speeches in his honor, he would throw his pillow off the bed in disgust, grab his blanket, and sleep on the floor.

Had she been aware of some of the tremendous inner tensions of Charles Lindbergh, Anne Morrow might have found him more interesting. But unlike most of her classmates, who swooned at the mere mention of his name, she remained unimpressed by the clamor surrounding him. For one thing, she thought the nickname "Lucky Lindy" was silly. For another, she could tell just by looking at his pictures in the newspapers that he wasn't her type at all. The tall, stoop-shouldered bachelor, with his tousled blond hair and bashful, forced smile, didn't look "intellectual" at all, and she concluded in her diary that he was probably "the baseball-player type."

Meanwhile, the young flier had made a deep impression on another member of the Morrow family — Dwight Morrow, who had had the opportunity to observe Lindbergh firsthand.

In 1925 Calvin Coolidge, who had become president in 1923 after Harding's death, had asked his friend Morrow to be chairman of the president's Aircraft Board, later known more generally as the Morrow Board, which would study the relationship of airplanes to the national defense.

Under Morrow's leadership, the board had made recommendations for the use of airplanes in the army and in the navy. It also rejected the idea of an independent air arm, instead changing the name of the Army Air Service to the Army Air Corps to reflect its increased responsibilities. In that same year, Morrow's friends Daniel and Harry Guggenheim had set up the Guggenheim Foundation for the Promotion of Aeronautics. According to Ron Chernow, author of *The House of Morgan,* "Through Morrow, they got Coolidge to accept the [Guggenheim] money on behalf of the government to speed up airplane development."

After the historic flight, Coolidge sent the cruiser *Memphis,* flagship of the U.S. European fleet, to bring Lindbergh and the *Spirit of St. Louis* back to the United States, where he was awarded the Distinguished Flying Cross, the first in the nation's history, and made a full colonel in the United States Officers Reserve Corp.

During his elaborate reception in Washington, Lindbergh was invited by the president to stay at the temporary White House at 15 Dupont Circle. (The Coolidges were living there temporarily while the White House roof was being repaired.) Shrewdly, Coolidge sensed that Lindbergh's fame would be a major asset to the infant airline industry and that the young flier should meet his friend Dwight Morrow, who, as the head of the Aircraft Board, was creating the framework for the growth of aviation.

Although Charles Lindbergh, Sr., had spent a good part of his life opposing people like Dwight Morrow, the son evidently did not share the father's enmity toward the small group of men who controlled much of the United States' wealth and resources. He immediately liked Morrow, who was not only personally charming but wanted to help him publicize aviation and had many wealthy, important friends who would be willing to back him. For example, Morrow introduced the aviator to Harry Guggenheim, who would soon sponsor his three-month U.S.

tour in the *Spirit of St. Louis*. And Morrow himself became Lindbergh's personal financial adviser. One wonders what Lindbergh's father would have thought about such an arrangement.

During Lindbergh's visit, Coolidge approached Morrow about becoming ambassador to Mexico. In yet another of his restless professional moods, Morrow had become disillusioned with Wall Street, and rumors had evidently been circulating about his discontent. Morrow told Coolidge that he was excited by the prospect, and the offer was formally made a month later.

Anne was thrilled when she heard the news, although she was nervous at the thought of her mother and father going so far away. She also worried about her mother, who felt bitter that Coolidge, when he first became president, had not offered her husband a cabinet position.

Adding to Mrs. Morrow's distress was the fact that they would be living far away from their recently purchased New York apartment on East Sixty-sixth Street, an elegant pied-à-terre that she adored as much as Next Day Hill, still their primary residence. Hardly a cozy flat, the new acquisition boasted a marble hall, a sitting room, a library, and a ballroom, as well as fifteen bedrooms, with spectacular views of Central Park from every window.

As a dutiful wife, however, Mrs. Morrow did not put her own desires above her husband's needs. The couple, with Constance and their white West Highland terrier, Daffin, departed for Mexico City on October 19.

Mrs. Morrow was putting it mildly when she wrote that her husband's ambassadorship would be "a hard job." Relations between the United States and Mexico had never been worse. The president of Mexico, Plutarco Elías Calles, was regarded by Coolidge's secretary of state as a communist. Many Americans were horrified by the Mexican government's policy of nationalizing church property, closing parochial schools, and defaulting on its foreign debts.

To ease U.S.-Mexican tensions, Morrow knew that he would require something more than his own good brains and decent intentions. In short, he needed a miracle, and, fortunately for his career, he managed to produce one. Before leaving the United States, he acted on a tip from his good friend Walter Lippmann and invited Charles Lindbergh to visit him at his posh Manhattan apartment. During the meeting, he proposed that the aviator fly the *Spirit of St. Louis* from New York to Mexico City.

Lindbergh quickly agreed to help him out. After completing the Guggenheim-sponsored U.S. tour with the *Spirit of St. Louis,* he wanted to make one more long-distance nonstop flight with his beloved plane before retiring it to a museum. The flight to Mexico piqued his interest. Not only would it be the gesture of friendship toward Mexico that Morrow desired, but he would be able to "demonstrate still more clearly the capabilities of modern aircraft." Made in the winter, the trip would be under conditions entirely different from those of his spring New York to Paris flight, over terrain ranging from vertiginous mountains to a low coastline to high plains. "I wanted to experiment with these conditions," he later wrote, "and if possible to demonstrate that flying could be practical under them," adding that he "loved any opportunity to fly, particularly in the *Spirit of St. Louis.*"

Morrow was upset when he learned that the flight of slightly more than twenty-one hundred miles was going to be nonstop. He thought it *too* hazardous. He suggested that the aviator make the trip in easy stages as he had when touring the country after his historic flight, stopping in every state. But Lindbergh demurred. "I told him to leave flying problems to me and not to worry."

The airman took off from Washington's Bolling Field at 12:25 P.M. on December 13 for Mexico City. The flight went smoothly until the following day, when his plane crossed the mountains into the valley of Mexico, and suddenly he got lost. "The best maps of Mexico I had been able to obtain showed little detail," he later wrote. "Straightish black lines, representing railroads, crossed wavy blue lines, representing rivers. I could not make them fit the railroad and the dry river beds below me." Passing over a small dusty village, Lindbergh hoped that a sign on the local railroad station would give a clue to its identity. He glided the *Spirit* down with throttled engine to read it. "The name of the village was CABALLEROS. I unfolded my maps as I climbed. But I could find no Caballeros. Too small a place, I thought. I flew over cactus-bordered tracks to the next village. Its name was CABALLEROS, too! I tried a small town, with the same result. All the stations in Mexico appeared to be named alike. Slowly, after my sleepless night, I realized that 'Caballeros' marked a convenient place for men."

Later he flew over a city and after coming down to low altitude could read the words " 'hotel Toluca' on the side of a building." Consulting his map, he realized that Toluca was about thirty-five miles from Mexico City.

When Lindbergh did not arrive at Mexico City's Valbuena Airport at noon, as scheduled, Dwight Morrow became understandably upset. He and President Calles, whom Morrow had completely disarmed by greeting with a customary Latin hug and two kisses when they were introduced, had been waiting at the airfield since 8:30 in the morning. As the hours dragged by, premonitions of disaster swept the enormous crowd of 150,000 Mexicans who had gathered to see the famed aviator. Finally, Morrow could stand it no longer. Breaking off his polite chitchat with Calles, he descended from the grandstand set up for the dignitaries and nervously began to pace up and down the airfield to the alarm of the spectators. It was swelteringly hot, and perspiration poured off his small, earnest face. Undoubtedly, he was trying to compose a diplomatic speech to the Mexican multitudes explaining why a man who had had no trouble finding Paris had no idea of the location of Mexico City.

Suddenly, at 2:44 P.M., the agonizing wait was over. The tremendous crowd roared its approval as the lone engine of the *Spirit of St. Louis* was heard overheard. It had taken Lindbergh twenty-seven hours and fifteen minutes to make the first nonstop airplane trip from Washington, D.C., to Mexico City, a journey that ordinarily took more than a week by train. "It was perfectly thrilling when the plane came to earth," Betty Morrow recorded in her diary that evening. "Dwight brought him [Lindbergh] to the President who welcomed him and gave him the keys of the city. Lindbergh only said 'thank you' very simply. The throng on the field shouting and screaming with joy was indescribable. As we went to the car, our clothes were almost torn off . . . Flowers and confetti were flung every moment."

Lindbergh was staying at the embassy with the Morrows when Anne and Elisabeth took the train to Mexico City during their Christmas break. Anne had never been to Mexico before, and she was enchanted when the train crossed the border from Texas, with its monotonous sagebrush, cactus, and sand, into Mexico, with its brilliant flowers, brightly painted houses, and majestic landscape of mountains, cornfields, and sweeping valleys, which she described as a "miracle of warmth and sun and color."

The lush sensuality of the Mexican landscape stirred her senses, and she wrote evocative, almost sexual descriptions in her diary of the farmers with their straw hats and the peasant women in their colorful, sweeping skirts. "Suddenly, through the canyon and over the hills the mist melted. We were in bright sun . . . A woman held up a basket of oranges and limes, brilliant with the sun on it. It was warm — deliciously, unbelievably warm . . . You could take your coat off and the sun turned you inside out."

She and Elisabeth arrived in Mexico City in the evening and were met at the station by Constance and Dwight Morrow, radiant with having pulled off the diplomatic coup of the year. Before they even had a chance to catch their breath, they were hurried off to the embassy for a gala official reception to honor the aviator.

Meeting the man everyone in the world was talking about at the crowded reception, Anne realized she had misjudged him. "I saw standing against the great stone pillar — on *more* red plush — a tall, slim boy in evening dress — so much slimmer, so much taller, so much more poised than I expected. A very refined face, not at all like those grinning 'Lindy' pictures — a firm mouth, clear, straight blue eyes, fair hair, and nice color," she confided to her diary, in a passage so smooth and polished that it suggests having been reworked before its publication almost forty-five years later.

When Anne and the young flier were introduced, he did not smile but rigidly bowed and shook her hand. As he turned to the next person, she continued down the line, shaken by new, unfamiliar feelings. She had just touched the hard, masculine flesh of the incredibly brave — and handsome — aviator who had become the first person in history to fly nonstop from New York to Paris. And now, like millions of other silly, love-struck women, she found herself wondering what it would be like to have him hold her in his arms.

CHAPTER 3

"The Romance of the Century"

Anne still felt dazed later that evening, when she, Elisabeth, her father, and Charles Lindbergh gathered around the great stone fireplace at the embassy after the guests had departed. Although she longed to say something charming and brilliant that would attract the attention of this celebrated young man, she sat tongue-tied with embarrassment as she listened to her older sister converse easily with him. It didn't seem fair, she told herself, that handsome men always brought out the best in Elisabeth while they "terrified" her and made her feel more awkward and childish than ever.

Although Lindbergh was not aware of it, the silent, dark-haired young woman in the corner was sizing him up. Her conclusion, as she watched him stand stiffly by the desk, shifting from one foot to another, was that despite his enormous fame and virile good looks, he was almost as awkward and shy as herself. "He is very, very young and was terribly shy — looked straight ahead and talked in short direct sentences which came out abruptly and clipped," she later noted in her diary. "You could not meet his sentences: they were statements of fact, presented with such honest directness; not trying to please, just bare simple answers and statements, not trying to help a conversation along. It was amazing — breathtaking. I could not speak. What kind of boy was this?"

She was still intoxicated the following morning when she and her family went to the airfield to meet Lindbergh's mother, who was arriving in a large silver Ford trimotor plane from San Antonio, Texas, to take part in the festivities. Anne was curious to meet her. From newspaper reports, she had gathered that the one woman to whom the pilot was devoted was his mother. But what would she be like? Would she be tall and vivacious, a "manager" like Elisabeth or her mother? But when Evangeline Lindbergh stepped from the plane, Anne noted with some relief that she was a "small, sweet-faced, shy little woman." She might have been describing an older version of herself, for Mrs. Lindbergh was not only reticent but well educated, having graduated from the University of Michigan with a degree in chemistry at the turn of the century. Like Anne, she was literary and loved writing letters, especially to her mother.

Physically, the two women bore some resemblance. Although Evangeline was somewhat taller than Anne, both might be described as petite, and, as Kenneth S. Davis, one of Lindbergh's biographers has pointed out, their facial expressions were uncannily similar. "In her [Anne's] eyes was often a hurt, withdrawn look, not unlike that seen in many photographs of the hero's mother," he noted.

Anne had no trouble conversing with Mrs. Lindbergh, whom she found refreshingly modest and down-to-earth. Evidently considering the daughter of an ambassador to be her social and intellectual equal, Evangeline dropped her mask of haughty remoteness and was at her most relaxed and charming. She confided to Anne that she felt that the enormous publicity about her son's exploit was verging on the ridiculous. But Anne still felt ill at ease and embarrassed around Charles Lindbergh, who evidently shared her sentiments. "He avoids us — at least me — as much as I do him, for *I can't* treat him as an ordinary person (and *will* not treat him as an extraordinary one), so I just avoid him as much as possible."

A few days later Lindbergh offered to take the entire Morrow family flying in the Ford trimotor that had brought his mother from San Antonio. It is not known whether Anne had ever flown before, but the invitation from Lindbergh, the world's greatest flier, was an undeniable thrill, and as the plane soared, "like a bird, like one's dreams of flying," high above Mexico City, she found it "a complete and intense experience." Undoubtedly, like her pilot, she was immediately enthralled by the power and majesty of flight, as well as by the feeling of being far above the world of mortals, for in a plane even the awesome Aztec ruins were quickly reduced to matchstick size.

But there was something else about flying that she felt but never mentioned publicly, and that was its quasi-sexual quality. It had to do with the rush of speed and power that she experienced as the plane acceler-ated down the runway, followed by the terrifying moments as it lifted off the ground and began its steep ascent, and then finally with the sense of relief and bliss when the machine entered safely a new dimen-sion and she was no longer chained to the earth but floating through the clouds.

This ecstatic feeling was, of course, intensified by the fact that her pilot was the world's most famous aviator as well as an unusually hand-some man. Even though other members of her family were present during the flight, she felt as if the experience were a romantic prelude to some-thing intimate that might happen between them. When Lindbergh landed the plane back on the field, she knew that she would "not be happy" until she was in the air with him again.

But her next flight with Lindbergh would not take place until Octo-ber of the following year. Three days after Christmas, on December 28, 1927, the young aviator left for the remainder of his good-will mission to Central and South America, which would link together by air the continents of the Western Hemisphere. In the early morning darkness as she watched the wings of the *Spirit of St. Louis* dipping in salute to her family, which had gone to the airfield to see him off, Anne was cer-tain that she would never see Lindbergh again. And yet the mere thought that such a man existed and that she had had the privilege of knowing him made her feel both joyful and strange. For she knew that her world, as she had always experienced it, would never be the same. "The idea of this clear, direct, straight boy — how it has swept out of sight all other men I have ever known, all the pseudo-intellectuals, the sophisticates, the posers — all the 'arty' people. All my life, in fact, my world — my little embroidery beribboned world is smashed. . . . Clouds and stars and birds — I must have been walking with my head down looking at the puddles for twenty years."

She knew now that her feelings for Charles Lindbergh and flying were inextricably linked. From then on, she vowed to gaze only sky-ward, toward the exhilarating new world that was his domain, a realm that promised not only adventure and freedom, but sexual excitement.

Reality quickly descended again on her return to Smith in January for her final semester. Frances Smith, the young, insecure freshman whom she had befriended, disappeared. Aware that Frances was suffering from a severe depression, Anne feared that she might have committed suicide. She was plagued with guilt that although she had been a good friend to Frances and had talked to her at length about her problems, she hadn't done more to help her. Detectives and reporters came to the college to question the students. As the weeks passed and Frances still hadn't been found, Anne began to suffer from terrible attacks of insomnia, waking up at 4:30 every morning. The only way she could get through the night was to recite poetry and to mull over in her mind every detail of meeting Lindbergh in Mexico City.

Morbidly Anne began to identify with Frances and at times suffered from the delusion that people were watching her. Although she does not mention it in her diary, surely she must have feared that she might suffer a nervous breakdown like her brother.

"The frightful sense of tragedy — not tragedy but a dry, black, despairing horror all the time; not tears, just that dry, black horror everywhere, like a burned and blackened landscape . . .

"Is there *anything* beautiful, is there anything good, anything lovely in this world, if such things can happen? . . .

"A nightmare of reporters, papers, reports, clues, detectives, questioning . . . ," she wrote in her diary, at the time little realizing that the disappearance of Frances Smith at Smith College was only a prelude to a far greater horror she would have to face later in life.

Adding to her emotional distress was the fact that her brother Dwight had again become "very ill" while he was attending Amherst College, his father's alma mater. Although she did not specify the cause in her published diary, he had undoubtedly suffered another nervous breakdown.

Fortunately Dwight recovered his emotional equilibrium within a few months, but Anne's premonitions about her friend proved correct. Frances Smith's body was later found floating in the Connecticut River.

Anne had begun to feel in control of her life again only to learn that Charles Lindbergh was coming to visit the family at Deacon Brown's Point, their newly built summer home on the island of North Haven, Maine. Given her feelings, the chance to see the flier again should have made her deliriously happy, but instead it filled her with dread. He was not coming to see her, but Elisabeth, and Anne was convinced that he was in love with her beautiful, vivacious twenty-four-year-old sister. The thought of Elisabeth's becoming romantically involved with Lindbergh made her wildly jealous. Adding to her misery was the fact that she loved her sister, whom she had once compared to a "patch of sunlight." In an emotional passage, she confided to her diary,

> He will turn quite naturally to E., whom he likes and feels at ease with. I will back out more and more, feeling in the way, stupid, useless, and (in the bottom of my vain heart) hoping that perhaps there is a mistake and that I will be missed. But I am not missed. They never notice and become more and more interested in each other and you must be more and more careless and happy, although *you notice* every little thing, and you have long sessions with yourself stamping out the envy, persuading yourself it is only fair and right.

Although Anne was beginning to receive some recognition as a writer — her poem "Height" was being published in the March issue of *Scribner's Magazine* and at her graduation from Smith, she won not one but two coveted literary prizes — her literary accomplishments seemed to bring her little satisfaction. Nor did it matter that several young men were interested in her.

Her life seemed dull in comparison with the glamorous world that she believed Elisabeth and Charles Lindbergh inhabited. Timid and unadventurous, while they were vibrant and active, she couldn't possibly hope to live on the same exalted plane as they did.

When Anne wrote about sitting spellbound in a Northampton movie theater, as she watched a film about Lindbergh's exploits, both her fixation on the flier and her inferiority complex became painfully apparent:

> Overwhelming. I sat sick with amazement, realizing it and saying to myself. "Did I ever meet this boy? How could I possibly comprehend him or it? I am much too small."
>
> I must say over and over to myself. *Make your world count* — it is little, but you must find something there . . . The nearest I can get to it is that perhaps I could be useful and happy trying to help people to appreciate (by teaching or some other way — writing, *perhaps*) (and perhaps through a family and children) the things I care most about: the beauty and poise and completion of flowers, or birds, of music, of some writing, of some people — glimpses of perfection in all of these.

Although besotted with physical desire for the aviator and caught up in the glamour of his legend, Anne appears to have abandoned all hope of having him view her as anything more than Elisabeth's kid sister. She was convinced that the older woman had snared this spectacular prize, just as she had gotten everything else that Anne wanted.

In June 1928, after her graduation with special honors from Smith, Anne spent the summer with her parents at Deacon Brown's Point. Although she loved the large, elegantly furnished wood-shingled house, with its spectacular views of the sea and beautiful plantings of dahlias, she was again plunged into an agony of longing and jealousy as she waited for Lindbergh to visit Elisabeth.

It certainly didn't improve her mood to witness her older sister, in preparation for his call, playing the Southern belle, with a legion of male admirers, to whom she read poetry nightly, vying for her attention. Another source of tension was her mother, whose abundant energy and vitality always made her feel small and unworthy. Although Anne felt close to her mother when they corresponded, the intimacy they shared through letters seemed to evaporate once they were together. They became emotionally distant, and as usual Anne blamed herself: "Why do I meet people better in letters? Perhaps the dross of me is somewhat purged in letters."

Watching Elisabeth's beaus smile every time her sister opened her mouth, Anne reminded herself that she must smother all feelings of envy when Lindbergh visited the family.

In a sense, it came as a relief when a relative called to tell her that Lindbergh wasn't coming to North Haven after all. Elisabeth had gone to New York, and he was going to visit her there.

Anne tried to tell herself that it didn't matter, writing in her journal,

> It was like that sudden falling down you have in a dream — kaplunk — and I have woken up.
>
> But it is not so bad now. "When I was fearing it, it came." It was inevitable and now I feel almost reconciled. The tooth is pulled.
>
> That dream is peacefully dead — speedy burial advised.

Like many people who feel rejected, she took refuge in humor, staying up half the night laughing with her sister Constance as they imagined Elisabeth and Lindbergh's wedding to the last detail.

She confided to her diary, "I want to be married, but I never, never will."

The exact nature of Lindbergh's relationship with Elisabeth and the cause of their breakup remain unknown. What is known, however, is that shortly after Anne returned to Englewood three months later, in early October, from her summer vacation, the telephone rang and the housekeeper said a male caller wanted to speak to her. To her utter surprise and confusion, it was Lindbergh. He wanted her to go flying with him. And as soon as possible.

Anne put him off, not because she had fallen out of love with him, but because, as luck would have it, she would be going into Presbyterian Hospital for minor surgery.

A little more than a week later, when she was out of the hospital, Lindbergh arrived in a chauffeur-driven car to discuss plans to take her for a flight over New York. Although Anne had been ecstatic at the thought of seeing him again, her enthusiasm palled once she was actually in his presence and he asked her when Elisabeth would return from her trip abroad. She was suddenly convinced that he had come to see her only because Elisabeth was unavailable, and her old feelings of inferiority and jealousy resurfaced. In a rare instance of anger, she later described him in a letter to her sister Con as being "cold — the coolest man I've ever met."

Even though his aloofness and lack of empathy repelled her, she could not break his physical hold over her. A few days later, as planned, she met him at the New York apartment of a friend of her father, and they drove in Lindbergh's car, a new black Franklin sedan, to the Guggenheim estate on Long Island where he had been staying. The secrecy was necessary, Lindbergh had told her at their last meeting, because if they flew from any of the local airfields, they'd "be engaged the next day." To Anne, the implication was obvious.

Perhaps in the hope of giving the impression that she wasn't the slightest bit interested in him, she decked herself out in a bizarre flying outfit. It consisted of Constance's riding pants, her mother's wool shirt, her father's gray golf stockings, a red leather coat, her street hat, and high heels — she had debated wearing boots but decided they would be too clumsy.

When she told him about deciding not to wear boots, he grinned and said that "boots would have helped to weigh me down if I had to jump. 'But I hope we don't have to use it [a parachute]!' "

Her choice of attire proved even more ill-advised when they arrived at the grand Guggenheim estate, with its sweeping lawns, peacocks, baronial rooms, and religious statuary, and she was asked to stay for lunch. She had not expected to dine in such elegant surroundings and refused to take off her leather coat; she "boiled" in it. "Oh, it was priceless, I and the Madonnas!" she wrote to Constance.

During their hour-long ride to the Guggenheim estate, her attitude toward Lindbergh appears to have undergone a transformation. "I discovered that I could be *perfectly* natural with him, say anything to him, that I wasn't a *bit* afraid of him or even worshipful any more. That Norse god has just gone. I can't understand why I saw what I did before. He's just *terribly* kind and absolutely natural . . ."

After lunch, Lindbergh left Anne with the Guggenheims, who regaled her with stories of the practical jokes that "Slim," as they called him, had played on the family, while he drove to Roosevelt Field to fetch a plane. Soon a silver De Havilland Moth biplane descended into the field in back of the Guggenheims' house, and Lindbergh got out. After presenting Anne with a helmet, goggles, and a parachute — "Don't jump unless I tell you to," he grinningly admonished — he took her for a flight over Long Island.

Anne found this second flight with him even more of an aphrodisiac than the first. The De Havilland was an open plane, with dual controls, and Lindbergh, who had let her drive his car part of the distance to the Guggenheims', made it even more apparent that he had faith in her mechanical abilities by allowing her, after giving some basic instructions, to help fly the plane. At first she was frightened, but then, "finding that the things actually worked, I stopped being afraid," she wrote to Constance. "Only it was so funny — I couldn't keep in a straight line. There are tremendous forces in the air that one doesn't realize. It was like an unwieldy and stubborn elephant."

This flight would be one of many in the next few months, as she and Lindbergh continued to see each other. Their dating was, of course, a secret. After his Paris flight, when he had become one of the first "mega media celebrities," Lindbergh grew even more distrustful of the press, which he felt badgered him for interviews and continued to make up untrue stories about him in order to sell newspapers. He communicated his hatred of the press to Anne, and she too began to live in fear that she would become the target of publicity. She became so fearful of the news leaking out about their dates that she started referring to him in her letters by the code name of Boyd. And she even cautioned Constance, now her closest confidante, not to mention the fact that she was seeing Lindbergh to their mother. It was the first instance in which she would side with him over her own family, a schism that would grow wider as the years passed.

The myth of Charles Lindbergh, the handsome, daring young American who was the most admired man in the world, still dazzled her, and she couldn't quite believe that of all the women in the world, including her beautiful, socially adept older sister, he had picked her as his date. Yet, just as her mother had worried about Dwight Morrow's lack of culture, there were moments when Anne had terrible agonizing doubts about his suitability as a boyfriend. "He never opens a book, does he? How that separates him from our world!" she confided to Constance. "It is hideous to think about — a hideous chasm. Do you ever think we could bridge it and get to know him well? Oh I'm afraid — terribly afraid. I do not want to see him again. It is terribly upsetting, liking someone so utterly opposed to you."

In her darker moments, she thought that Lindbergh was a gauche young man who was ill-read and liked to play tasteless practical jokes. And like her own father, he had little appreciation for music or poetry. "Sometimes he will say something that wrenches terribly, that 'Yes, he liked poetry: when he was a boy he read Robert W. Service'! (that just hurt *terribly*) . . ."

But she was also aware that he was "appreciative of all the essentials in our world. He is amazingly understanding — sees far outside of his world, even into ours."

His real hold on her, however, she discreetly neglected to mention to Constance. His tall, lean, hard body, tousled blond hair, and china blue eyes made her weak with longing and at the same time fearful that he would suddenly no longer find her attractive. It was a powerful sexual attraction that she continued to feel for him, heightened, of course, by his immense fame and the fact that by now she realized she was the only woman, with the exception of his own mother, he had ever permitted to get close to him.

"I don't think my parents had any idea why they fell in love," their daughter Reeve said many years later. "In large part, it was a physical relationship, a passionate, and always described by each of them as an inexplicable connection."

But even though he was as good-looking as a movie star and projected an aura of intense sexuality, Charles Lindbergh was not a ladies' man. On the contrary, this romantic figure for millions of women had practically no experience with the opposite sex. In fact, it is entirely possible that he was a virgin when he met Anne at the age of twenty-five, although from his own account, it seems more likely that he had had prior sexual experience with prostitutes. "A barnstormer's relationships with women were facile," he remembered with evident distaste in his posthumously published memoirs, *Autobiography of Values*, also recalling that when he became a flying cadet, "frequently a soldier's relationships with women were paid for in cash." In his book, he was hazy on the subject of his own sexual involvements, giving the impression that while he wasn't exactly a virgin when he married, he had been too busy walking on airplane wings to have time to date women. But, as he was careful to point out, after his New York to Paris flight he suddenly found he had the time to meet "girls," even though he knew that any relationship he had with a woman would be "exaggerated and complicated by the attention of the press," which had already reported him engaged to at least a dozen women.

There was another reason why Charles Augustus Lindbergh was attracted to Anne Spencer Morrow, and it could hardly be considered romantic. A confirmed social Darwinist long after the theory had gone out of fashion in the early 1900s, he wrote in his old age about his decision to marry:

> A girl should come from a healthy family, of course. My experience in breeding animals on our farm had taught me the importance of good heredity. I knew that qualities of the father and the mother, and the ancestors before them, invariably came out in the offspring, mixed though they must be . . .
>
> You did not have to be a scientist to realize the overwhelming importance of genes and chromosomes. When you saw the mothers and fathers, you could tell a lot about their offspring, and I found it interesting to try guessing the other way around. Here the relationship between heredity and environment was subtle; training, after all, had its effect on character. But you could see features of the parents in a son's or daughter's face. A nervous daughter had at least one nervous parent, often two of them.
>
> . . . The physical characteristics I wanted in a woman were not difficult to describe — good health, good form, good sight and hearing. Such qualities could be outlined in sequence like the specifications for an airplane. I wanted to marry a girl who liked flying, because I would take her with me on the expeditions I expected to make in my plane.

After his flight, Lindbergh was introduced to many prominent political and business leaders who, like himself, were interested in developing aviation. As he later wrote in *Autobiography of Values*, it was obvious that they had more than a new industry in common:

> There is the saying that "like tends to like," and while I did not consider this at the time, it was obviously enough taking place. The men I associated with and I were spearheading scientific and technical and material

progress. Possibly, but not certainly, our genetic compositions embodied various combinations of physical and mental acuities that resulted in our being what we were and doing what we did. It was reasonable to assume that the daughter I married would have these characteristics, too, and that they would be combined and enhanced in our offspring.

Ironically, this ardent believer in eugenics and social Darwinism failed to notice the serious mental and physical illnesses that plagued the Morrow family. In fact, he appears to have had no inkling of their problems, and one wonders whether he would have had the same enthusiasm for mingling his gene pool with theirs had he known about their darker side.

As Anne had originally suspected, it was not she who initially impressed Charles Lindbergh but Elisabeth, the only Morrow daughter who was in extremely frail health. "The second daughter, Anne, was blue-eyed, dark-haired, extremely pretty, but she stood very much in the background, as though resting in a shadow thrown by the sparkling vivacity of her older sister, Elisabeth," Lindbergh later wrote in an unflattering comparison. "Anne was twenty-one and midway through her final year of college. I had noticed her casually. She looked so very young, more of high-school than of college age, and she had not made a deep impression on my conscious mind. Rationally, I was surprised when I found her becoming conspicuous in memory months after I had left the hospitality of her father's embassy in Mexico. But in the fall of 1928 I began laying plans to meet her again."

Himself well aware of the aphrodisiac effect of flight on women from the locker room talk of his fellow cadets and barnstormers, he decided that the fastest way to attain his goal was to invite Anne to go flying with him. "Dating a girl was seldom difficult for the pilot of an airplane if he used some discretion in his method of approach. I knew that from the experience of others," he admitted many years later. "He simply asked her to accompany him on a flight around the nearby country. Aviation was romantic, adventurous, spectacular, and, except for timid creatures, the invitation seldom had to be extended twice . . ."

For Anne too there was another reason for her attraction to Charles Lindbergh which had nothing to do with romance and sexual passion. Competitive with her mother and Elisabeth, she had managed to outshine them both by dating the world's hero. And what better way to get her oblivious father to notice her than by having a romance with a man who was far more famous and powerful than himself. For the first time in her life, she was the star of the family, the golden girl, the one with the glittering life.

In November 1928 Anne left for Mexico City to visit her parents. After a hunting trip in the state of Chihuahua, Lindbergh joined her in Mexico City, which understandably aroused much speculation on the part of the press. To the small army of reporters who crowded around his plane, peppering him with questions about why he had come back to Mexico, he simply said that he had liked the country so much the first time he had visited that he had wanted to return as soon as possible. He spent the next fifteen days with Anne and her parents, staying the weekend at the Morrows' newly purchased weekend home in Cuernavaca and even taking Mrs. Morrow for a ride in his Curtiss Falcon biplane.

Although there were items in the Mexican newspapers saying that Lindbergh was engaged to marry Anne, the American embassy kept issuing denials that the flier was engaged to a "member of the Morrow family." Lying, Anne herself told her relatives that there was no truth whatsoever to the rumors.

And what about the other "member of the Morrow family," Elisabeth? In October, during her trip abroad, she was stricken with a severe case of bronchial pneumonia and forced to enter a nursing home. Although Anne was genuinely distressed to learn about her sister's illness, she was also eager for her to stay in London, which was far away from Mexico and Lindbergh. She kept urging her sister not to come home before she had made a complete recovery.

But Elisabeth did come home in late November 1928. She continued her recuperation at the Long Island home of Russell Leffingwell, a Morgan partner. Evidently she had wanted to return to the family home in Englewood during the Christmas season, when the family returned from Mexico City, but again Anne tried to dissuade her sister from making the short trip from Long Island to New Jersey. "I think it's quite natural you should be weak and have no resistance. I don't see *how* you could take that trip so soon. It seems pretty suicidal to me," she cautioned her in a letter. "And if you are comfortable and quiet there at the Leffingwells', *of course,* stay. It will be hectic at Christmas and you *can't* be quiet when Mother feels energetic . . . I think it's much better for you to be out at the Leffingwells."

To her relief, Elisabeth decided to stay on Long Island.

*

In December, Anne's wildest fantasies were realized. Lindbergh proposed marriage. Although she should have been delirious with happiness, the reality of being married to a man so different from herself seems to have put her into a somber, reflective mood. "Apparently I am going to marry Charles Lindbergh," she wrote to Corliss Lamont, the son of Thomas Lamont, a Morgan partner. "It must seem hysterically funny to you as it did to me when I consider my opinions on marriage. . . . Don't wish me happiness — I don't expect to be happy . . . Wish me courage and strength and a sense of humor — I will need them all."

This was a strange thing for a bride-to-be to write about her forthcoming marriage. Like her mother, who had hesitated about marrying her father, Anne had grave doubts about Charles Lindbergh's suitability as a husband. As she was painfully aware, he was not of her class and education, and she knew that many of her friends could not understand what she saw in him and joked among themselves about "his lack of sense of humor, his practical jokes, his one-track mind." Still, the thought of not marrying him seemed unendurable, and two months later, on February 12, 1929, the news was made official. Dwight Morrow summoned the press to the American embassy in Mexico City and handed them the announcement: "Ambassador and Mrs. Morrow have announced the engagement of their daughter, Anne Spencer Morrow, to Col. Charles A. Lindbergh."

Although Morrow refused to say when or where the wedding would take place, the press immediately began to speculate that the ceremony would occur in Mexico City.

Some evidence exists that the Morrows were not as pleased with Anne's choice of Charles Lindbergh as a husband as they pretended to be. When Lindbergh first dined with them in Mexico City, the servants were wild with excitement. After the evening was over and he had departed for his room, Betty Morrow's maid brought her a spoon that the flier had used during dinner. The maid explained that she thought Mrs. Morrow might like to keep it as a memento. Betty Morrow merely smiled indulgently, however, and handed back the piece of silver to her maid in silence.

"My mother was surprised when I said that I was going to marry Charles Lindbergh," Anne admitted many years later, "but she rose to the occasion and said, 'Anne, you'll have the sky.' "

On familiar terms with presidents, kings, and all manner of distinguished people, Dwight and Betty Morrow could hardly have been expected to have the same kind of awestruck reaction to the young aviator as the average American. Worldly wise and highly educated, they possibly regarded him as naive and limited. "Although the Morrows were themselves of humble origin yet they were cultured and distinguished people," Mina Curtiss, Anne's friend and mentor from Smith, told Harold Nicolson shortly after the couple were married. "Thus Lindbergh, who came from a lower social stratum, they treated with aloof politeness. He was himself simple and not easy. His wife Anne had a difficult task." As for Mrs. Curtiss herself, she and Betty Morrow were among the few women who refused to succumb to "Lindbergh mania." In Mrs. Curtiss's harsh opinion, "Lindbergh was really no more than a mechanic and, had it not been for the lone eagle flight across the Atlantic in 1927, would then have been in charge of a gasoline station on the outskirts of St. Louis."

In the past, Dwight Morrow hadn't been impressed by the young men Anne and Elisabeth had dated. But he seemed to approve thoroughly of Charles Lindbergh as "a nice clean boy" who didn't drink, smoke, or chase girls. However, when Anne announced that she and the aviator wanted to get married, Morrow was flabbergasted, possibly because suddenly he felt threatened by his future son-in-law's enormous fame and glamour. Many years later Anne also recalled her father's less than enthusiastic reaction to her fiancé. "He's going to marry Anne? What do we know about this young man?" He insisted the couple be formally engaged first and get to know each other better.

When the story of her engagement to Charles Lindbergh broke in the press, Anne Morrow's life as a private person ended. Suddenly thrust into the public eye as the fiancée of the "catch of the century," this shy, introspective young woman became the object of relentless publicity and speculation. Everyone wanted to know more about the "poetic" Miss Morrow who had won the affections of the man who, along with the Prince of Wales, was considered one of the world's most eligible bachelors.

Anne's picture — with Anne looking dazed and wild-eyed as if somebody had strong-armed her into facing the camera — appeared in numerous magazines. Almost inevitably, it was captioned "The Lone Eagle's Future Mate" or something similar. Another favorite among magazine editors of the time was a photograph of Lindbergh with his future in-laws, Dwight and Betty Morrow and their youngest daughter,

Constance. Seated stiffly in chairs on the patio of the American embassy in Mexico City, the four are staring grimly in different directions.

For the frivolous, fun-loving flappers of the twenties, Anne Morrow's engagement to America's most desirable bachelor must have been a comeuppance. For the "Lone Eagle" had not picked a liberated, sexually sophisticated woman for "his mate," but a shy, retiring child-woman, who was steeped in traditional values. And wasn't that, as the moralists liked to point out to the flaming youth of America, an argument for the return of "old-fashioned femininity"?

The couple's three-month engagement period was one of excitement, secrecy, and getting to know one another. It appears that Dwight Morrow was right when he insisted that they not marry immediately.

Anne continued to find herself the center of world attention. Thousands of people wrote letters to her, expressing their congratulations and offering advice about married life. Everywhere she went, people rushed up to her and told her how lucky she was to be the future bride of America's hero.

Reporters dogged the celebrated pair wherever they went. Eventually, the most ruthless ones offered bribes to the Morrow servants, or climbed across the roofs of neighboring buildings in the hope of glimpsing the sweethearts in the garden of Anne's parents' home in Cuernavaca, or they printed anecdotes that had no basis in fact. Their actions, especially those of the tabloid press, infuriated Lindbergh. "I had found relationships with the press difficult before I had a fiancée," he later wrote. "I found them next to impossible thereafter."

While a more narcissistic woman might have been titillated by these carryings on, Anne found them an ordeal. "From the creative darkness of anonymity, a sheltered family life, and intimate communication," she wrote, "I was suddenly thrust into the blaze of a naked stage. Even in the first days of our courtship, the freedom of privacy was denied us. Because of the merciless exposure we lived in, it was hardly possible to get to know this stranger well enough to be sure I wanted to marry him. The abnormality of our life explains many of my doubts during the engagement period."

In order not to be harassed, the couple had to avoid doing ordinary things, like taking a walk or shopping or dining in a restaurant. If they did venture out in public, they often resorted to disguises in the hope of not being recognized.

The only place where they were safe from curiosity seekers was in an airplane, but, as Anne soon discovered, the sky, which had always seemed to her an exotic, thrilling place, was not without its dangers.

In late February, after a picnic lunch on a prairie near Mexico City, Lindbergh lost a wheel on takeoff from the borrowed plane that he was flying. Realizing that landing on only one wheel and an axle would make the plane dangerously unstable and that it would probably nose over on landing, he flew for several hours to get rid of the fuel so as to minimize the risk of fire upon impact. He also packed seat cushions around Anne and told her to hang on tightly to the seat bottom when the plane touched the ground. Although his landing on one wheel was skillful (he managed to keep the plane level for some thirty yards), the plane turned upside down shortly after the axle made contact with the ground.

Lindbergh dislocated his right shoulder in the crash, but Anne was uninjured. Nor had she been frightened during their ordeal, until just before they landed, when she had "one terrible moment of panic." Only the thought that she might appear a coward in her future husband's eyes enabled her to retain her composure. She kept saying to herself, "Now here is the test. Suppose you can't face it. You will just be ruined in his eyes. Suppose I can't. Suppose I *can't . . .*"

But even though their engagement was marred by crises, Anne was gradually learning to feel at ease with Charles, as she now called him. In private, they teased each other, and Anne was charmed by the natural and unrestrained way he treated her and by his sense of humor, which others often found gauche. Knowing that she was always watching her weight, he heaped cans of nuts beside her plate at dinner. And he did a very amusing imitation of her secretly "making eyes" at him the first time he had taken her and her family up in a plane in Mexico City.

But she was also discovering he could be serious, and they had many thoughtful discussions about religion and the people they knew. In contrast to her high-strung, frenetic family, he offered laconic remarks and practical reactions, which gave her a feeling of sanity and calm, as well as dependability.

By the middle of March, she was able to write to Constance, "I am sure *sure sure* that it is right now, and the pangs are not *doubt* any more."

Anne and Charles were married in front of the fireplace in the large parlor at Next Day Hill on May 27, 1929. Somehow managing to elude the press, they fled not to the air, as the reporters had expected, but to the sea and Maine, where they secretly boarded the *Mouette,* a rented thirty-six-foot-long motor yacht, for what they devoutly hoped would be a private honeymoon.

Gazing at her handsome husband as he steered the boat out of the harbor, Anne couldn't believe that she was now Mrs. Charles Lindbergh. From now on, she was going to discover what it was like to be in an intimate relationship with the most famous young man in the world.

CHAPTER 4

Soaring

ANNE AND CHARLES'S SECRET HONEYMOON abruptly came to an end two days later when reporters and photographers in a flying boat spotted the *Mouette* in York Harbor. When Anne spied them, she quickly retreated into the cabin, but Lindbergh was forced to remain on deck to steer the boat. As the yacht lay at anchor, newspapermen in a speedboat mercilessly buzzed them for over six hours. One reporter yelled that he would let the couple finish their honeymoon in private if they would just come out on deck to have their picture taken. A stone-faced Lindbergh did not reply. To escape the reporters, he headed the boat out of the harbor into the open ocean until the press boat finally turned around, without obtaining any photographs. He and Anne spent an uncomfortable night on a fishing bank. The sea was rough, and their sleep was interrupted by the sound of pounding waves and breaking china.

The Lindberghs' dislike of the press, which Anne likened to a "cops-and-robbers" chase that made her feel like an "escaped convict," was intensified when they made their first public appearance after their honeymoon. The occasion, which took place at Mitchel Field, Long Island, was on behalf of the Guggenheim Foundation, which was active in promoting commercial aviation and for which Lindbergh was now a $25,000-a-year consultant. As part of an effort to convince the public that aviation was a safe and convenient way to travel, Anne and Charles went on a short demonstration flight. As they got off the plane, the reporters clustered around Lindbergh, and one asked, "Is it true that Mrs. Lindbergh is pregnant?"

Charles Lindbergh flushed with anger and stalked away, refusing to confirm or deny the question.

Outraged by the press's incessant curiosity about his private life, he continued to avoid the reporters, even though, as several friends pointed out, he might not be the object of such intense speculation if he granted a few interviews. He cautioned Anne, "Never say anything you wouldn't want shouted from the housetops, and never write anything you would mind seeing on the front page of a newspaper."

For his wife, who was accustomed to revealing her innermost feelings in letters to her family and in her journal, it was a smothering restriction. "The lid of caution was clapped down on all spontaneous expression," she later wrote. "I was convinced I must protect him and myself from intrusion into our private life, but what a sacrifice to make never to speak or write deeply or honestly!"

Still, anxious to please her new husband and putting his wish for privacy above her own need for self-expression, Anne does not seem to have imagined going against his wishes. For three years she obediently laid her diary aside and didn't make as much as a single entry. Her letters to her mother and sisters, which had once been a source of consolation and great pleasure, became stilted and mundane, filled with trivial descriptions of the small events of her daily life.

The Lindberghs' marriage was destined to be a traditional one, with Charles as the dominant partner. Active, eternally restless, eager for new adventure, he was the one who set the pace, and Anne the one who had to follow. As she herself later admitted, she was used to being dominated by her brilliant and charismatic father, her strong-willed, energetic mother, and by her beautiful, highly efficient sister Elisabeth. Certainly it seems that in the early years of their life together she did not expect their marriage to be one of equals but rather saw her husband as "a knight in shining armor," with herself as "his devoted page." This meant, of course, accompanying him on all his flying trips, whether or not she was physically or emotionally fit for them.

After their honeymoon, on July 7, 1929, Anne and Charles, along with Amelia Earhart, the first woman to cross the Atlantic Ocean by plane in 1928, and Mary Pickford, the silent screen star, participated in the festivities publicizing the newly inaugurated Transcontinental Air Transport route between New York and Los Angeles. Dubbed the "Lindbergh Line" and a predecessor of TWA, Transcontinental Air Transport (or TAT, as it was called) was one of the first airlines to begin cross-continental air service, although passengers had to make part of the trip on the Pennsylvania and Santa Fe railroads.

The fact that Lindbergh himself piloted the first passenger plane flying east from Los Angeles to Winslow, Arizona, and then the first passenger plane going west back to Los Angeles, was supposed to demonstrate to a wary public that the fledgling passenger airline industry was a safe and time-saving mode of travel. Anne helped add to the impression of calm by sitting in the sleekly outfitted cabin of the huge Ford trimotor plane and explaining to the jittery passengers that the flight would be perfectly safe because the plane boasted three motors and there was no such thing as an "air pocket."

In August 1929 they visited the Cleveland Air Races, where Lindbergh flew as a member of the "High Hat" aerobatic team. Although she had looked forward to the event, Anne found the races "deadly" after the fourth day, and all the publicity and crowds that attended Lindbergh's aerial stunts began to get on her nerves.

Her spirits were further depressed by the news that the large TAT Ford trimotor planes weren't as safe as she had described them to her fellow passengers: one had disappeared en route from Albuquerque to Los Angeles. She and Charles had eagerly anticipated a visit to her parents at their summer home in North Haven, but now the trip was out of the question. They would have to postpone their family reunion to make an emergency flight to Albuquerque to search for survivors. By the time they arrived in New Mexico in a borrowed Lockheed Vega, the wreck had been discovered on Mount Williams. No one had survived the crash.

The doomed plane preyed on Anne's mind. "I have thought of that until it is an obsession," she wrote to her mother. "It seems so terrible and close to me. I can picture it all: the plane, the trip, the pilot, the families saying good-bye to all those passengers. . . . It seems to me the most terrible accident in all the history of aviation, because the best in every way that can be done is being done on that line."

The thought of giving up flying because it was too dangerous seems never to have entered her mind. Despite her timorous manner, she was a brave and feisty woman who loved being in the air almost as much as her husband did. Besides, she hated the thought of being separated from him for even a few hours. "Flying with my husband cast a kind of bright golden bloom over everything," she once said. "Maybe it's just the way we feel — Charles and I — when we get off together all alone. All gold."

In September she and Charles embarked on a flight to Central and South America at the request of Juan Trippe, president of the newly formed Pan American Airways, who wanted Lindbergh to inaugurate airmail service from Puerto Rico to Dutch Guiana — the first time the mail had ever been flown from the United States to the South American mainland.

In the late 1920s, Juan Terry Trippe was being touted in Washington as the most important young man in the field of commercial aviation. A daredevil as well as a dreamer, Juan was the son of a rich New York investment banker. Like Lindbergh, he had fallen in love with aviation as a young boy when he saw his first air race. He learned to fly at the age of seventeen, and, after serving as a navy pilot in World War I, he graduated from Yale in 1920. Six feet tall and weighing almost two hundred pounds, Trippe was a skilled athlete who excelled at rowing, golf, and football until he was kicked in the spine in a pileup. Severely injured, he underwent one of the first spinal fusion operations. It was a success, but his athletic days were over. Flying remained his only physical outlet. In 1925, with the backing of some wealthy friends, he formed Eastern Air Transport, two years later reaching the first step of his goal of operating an overseas airline by purchasing two companies that later became Pan American Airways. An affable, well-bred man who gave the impression of being professionally unassertive, Trippe was nonetheless determined to make aviation a multimillion-dollar business.

By the time of the September 1929 flight, Lindbergh had already opened Foreign Airmail Route No. 5 from Miami to Panama. He had also signed on as a technical adviser to Pan American at a salary of $10,000 a year, plus options to buy thousands of shares of Pan Am stock at reduced price. That opportunity, which he quickly took advantage of, as well as the one from TAT, which also paid him $10,000 a year as a technical adviser, in addition to stock options at below market value, would enable him to acquire close to his first million dollars by 1930.

From the moment they approached the plane, the Lindberghs and Trippes made it obvious to a mesmerized public that this was no ordinary air journey. For their well-publicized takeoff from Florida, the Lindberghs were smartly attired in civilian clothing. Charles, at the controls, wore a gray business suit; Anne, a becoming blue silk traveling outfit. Undoubtedly hoping to impress the wealthy Central Americans they would be meeting en route, Trippe himself wore a tropical white suit. Adding to the gala atmosphere were the bouquets of roses that lined the cabin of the plane, a twin-engine amphibious Sikorsky S-38.

Despite the glamour and the hype, the journey was often unpleasant. Since Lindbergh had to keep to a schedule of delivering the mail, they were aloft for hours at a stretch, and usually there was little food on board. At their frequent stops for refueling, people made endless speeches and pressed fresh flowers on them but offered them nothing to eat.

According to Robert Daley, Juan Trippe's biographer, when they neared Venezuela, Lindbergh, who had brought along an aerial camera, wanted to take some pictures.

> But this was difficult from the S-38 because of its rather odd construction. The fuselage of the plane was shaped like a shoe with the pilot at the top of the laces, and the passengers behind that. . . .
>
> Unable to get the camera angles he wanted from the pilot's cockpit, Lindbergh crawled forward through "the shoe," opened a hatch . . . and stood up in the slipstream with his clothes almost blowing off him. The plane was cruising at 1,500 feet at around 110 miles an hour. Apparently, this angle didn't suit Lindbergh either. To everyone's horror he stepped up out of the hatch and began to crawl forward over the toes of the "shoe" toward the forward compartment, where the anchor was stowed. He was not wearing a parachute. Balanced on hands and knees on top of the cowling in the wind, he at last stepped down in this compartment and shot his pictures. . . . His new bride watched him crawl back inside and slip behind the controls again, but she said nothing . . .

Many years later, when Daley asked Anne whether she had been frightened when her daredevil husband stood up to take pictures, leaving the plane in the hands of his copilot, Charles Lorber, she replied that she had not. "He was the hero. I really didn't believe anything could happen to him. I was very young, and I was in love."

Although Charles Lindbergh had flown in this part of the world in 1927, after he had made his good-will trip to Mexico City, it was Anne's first flight into the region, and the sight of its rugged mountainous terrain inspired some of her finest descriptive writing:

> We rose above the harbor to the left (turquoise reef-water formation), climbed up over some mountains on that jut of land . . . climbed and climbed, and suddenly abruptly over the edge and down at the feet of them curled the sea, a misty violet blue. It was breathtaking: the rugged green tropical mountains dropping into that deep blue violet; added to

this were big heaped-up golden clouds piled over the mountains, superbly beautiful and wild — untouched.

On her return to the United States in the middle of October, Anne began to suffer bouts of intense nausea. She consulted the family physician, who confirmed her suspicions that she was pregnant. The doctor wanted Anne to have the baby in a hospital in New York, but both she and Charles wanted it to be born in her parents' mansion in Englewood. Undoubtedly, they felt that the guarded estate offered them more protection from the press and curiosity seekers than a private room in a maternity ward.

Anne was amazed that her family and friends weren't surprised by the news of her pregnancy after five months of marriage. They seemed to accept it as "a matter of course," she wrote to her mother, adding, "I suppose most people think of it as following marriage and I . . . just don't feel married. We have no 'little room' to do over in sky blue or anything. I'm not sewing on 'tiny garments,' and it all seems quite marvelous, inconceivable, and ridiculous."

Ridiculous or not, Anne had no intention of letting her pregnancy put an end to her flying trips with Charles.

In November 1929, shortly after learning that Anne was expecting a baby, Lindbergh decided that he wanted not only to lay out the first commercial air route between California and New York, but also to break the transcontinental flight record. The plane he wanted to use was a Lockheed Sirius that had been built to his exact specifications in Burbank, California. The *Sirius,* which was named after the brightest star of the night, was a two-seater and boasted three times the horsepower of the *Spirit of St. Louis.* Although still intensely nauseated with morning sickness, Anne flew with him to pick it up.

In Hollywood, the Lindberghs spent several days at the home of Jack Maddux, head of the western end of Transcontinental Air Transport, who would become one of the founders of TWA. Another of Maddux's houseguests was Amelia Earhart. Tall and attractive, with boyish hair and a disarming grin, Earhart bore a striking resemblance to Charles Lindbergh, a fact that had encouraged some reporters to dub her "Lady Lindy." Although Earhart was embarrassed by the comparison — in her opinion, she bore no resemblance to Lindbergh — Anne was amazed at how much alike her husband and Earhart looked, as if they were brother and sister.

She and Lindbergh had first met Earhart six weeks after their marriage in Winslow, Arizona, at the inauguration of TAT. She liked Earhart and at the time described her to her parents as "*very* likeable and very intelligent and nice and amusing." During this visit to the Madduxes, she got to know Earhart better and wrote to Constance that the flier "is the most amazing person — just as tremendous as C., I think." In her mind, there were many similarities between the two celebrated aviators. "She has the clarity of mind, impersonal eye, coolness of temperament, and balance of a scientist. Aside from that, I like her."

Amelia Earhart was also favorably impressed with Anne, whom she later described as being "small of stature," with "a charming dignity when surrounded by people . . . Her dress is simple, like her direct manners . . . About her mouth a smile always seems to lurk." She also thought that "under her gentleness lies a fine courage to meet both physical and spiritual hazards with understanding."

According to one of Earhart's biographers, Doris Rich, "Amelia had unlimited admiration for [Charles Lindbergh's] aviation expertise, but may have liked him less as a person. In writing about her departure from New York with Norah [her secretary] and thirteen pieces of luggage that comprised their winter and summer wardrobes, plus what Amelia called her 'itinerant office,' she noted that Lindbergh watched with disapproval."

> During our explanation I sensed he was making a comparison with the impedimenta of a typical Lindbergh journey.
> He turned to his wife with a grin. "Don't get any foolish ideas from this," he admonished.

Rich also points out that, unlike Anne, Earhart would not have permitted her husband to dictate what luggage she could bring on a trip.

Earhart was not amused by Lindbergh's practical jokes, which she felt were not only tiresome but revealing of his hostility toward people, including those to whom he was closest. She wrote her husband-to-be, the publisher George Palmer Putnam, a blow-by-blow description of one of his peculiarly adolescent stunts, which in this case was directed against Anne. As the following account indicates, Earhart clearly reveled in the fact that his wife had been able to turn the joke on him.

> Anne, the Colonel and AE [Amelia Earhart] were fellow guests at the home of Jack Maddux in Hollywood. One night they were sitting close to the icebox. Anne and AE were drinking buttermilk. Lindbergh, standing

beside his wife munching a tomato sandwich, had the sudden impulse to let drops of water fall in a stream on his wife's shoulder from a glass in his hand.

Anne was wearing a sweet dress of pale blue silk. Water spots silk. AE observed a growing unhappiness on Anne's part — but no move toward rebellion, not even any murmur of complaint. AE often said that Anne Lindbergh is the best sport in the world.

Then Anne rose and stood by the door, with her back to the others, and her head resting on her arm. AE thought, with horror, that the impossible had come to pass, and that Anne was crying. But Anne was thinking out a solution to her problem, and the instant she thought it out, she acted upon it. At once — and with surprising thoroughness.

With one comprehensive movement she swung around and — quite simply — threw the contents of her glass of buttermilk straight over the Colonel's blue serge suit. It made a simply marvellous mess! Lindbergh's look of utter amazement changed into a tremendous grin, and he threw his head up and shouted with laughter. The joke, very practical, was on him!

AE always suspected that no more of Anne's wardrobe ever got spotted — at least in that way.

George Palmer Putnam, who had published *We*, Lindbergh's first account of his historic flight, also took a dim view of the man. After numerous tedious business lunches with him, in which Lindbergh talked only about his current aviation project, the urbane and well-educated Putnam came to the conclusion that the flier had little appreciation of literature, history, or music, or of other people's wit or sophisticated social discourse — his idea of humor was the crude kind involving horseplay and practical joking.

In Putnam's opinion, the outstanding characteristic of Lindbergh's puzzling personality was his "single-trackness," which enabled him to think solely of the matter at hand without digressions. "The core of the Lindbergh make-up is an utter absence of imagination, in that subjective sense that the quality is ordinarily meant," he observed. "It may be that he is thus fortunate. Certainly a freedom from that sensitivity — that quality which enables a person to picture in the mind what will or may happen next — is particularly helpful to a calm facing and clear-cut execution of such exploits as those which established Lindbergh's well-justified fame."

If Lindbergh lacked imagination, his wife made up for his deficiency. Sensitive and observant, she had an uncanny ability to sense the nuances of the world around her and record them. Before her marriage, her literary talents had been appreciated mostly by her family, her college teachers, and classmates, but now her husband would give her a new perspective on the world and its horizons which would affect her life and her writing.

Unlike many other male pilots, who flew alone or were accompanied by other men, Lindbergh insisted that his wife accompany him on most of his flying adventures. He wanted her to experience with him the adventuresome world of aviation, but he also wanted to have the pleasure of her company when they landed. Of course, taking a woman with him on his travels was hardly a new experience. In 1913 he and his mother had taken a trip to Panama together to see the construction of the canal. Three years later, in 1916, they spent a month driving together to California, which Evangeline decided would be a "wonderful educational experience" for her son, even though it meant he would have to complete his junior year in a high school in another state. Lindbergh later remembered the experience of driving his father's new Saxon-Six car out West as "the greatest adventure of my life up to that time."

When he became a pilot, Evangeline, who loved flying, often flew with him, and in the early 1920s she accompanied him on a barnstorming tour through the Midwest. A photograph of mother and son in flying gear beside their plane is uncannily similar to one taken of Anne and Charles some years later as they were about to depart on one of their survey flights. There is one important difference, however. In the picture with his mother, Lindbergh looks grim and unsmiling, while in the one with his wife he looks happy, obviously pleased that she was going along.

As soon as Lindbergh met Anne, she replaced his mother as his traveling companion. When he surveyed air routes for TAT, Pan American and Transcontinental and Western (TWA), she was his copilot and navigator. When he became fascinated by the possibilities of aerial photography, she steadied their open-cockpit Curtiss Falcon biplane as he took hundreds of photographs in his search for ancient cliff-dweller ruins in the American Southwest. When, during the course of his travels in the Yucatán, he had seen what appeared to be a Mayan city, she returned with him, a well-known archaeologist, and two other men to explore and photograph the ruin in the Central American wilderness. The expedition, funded by the Carnegie Institution of Washington, proved to be an arduous one, with many hours of low flying over wild and treacherous terrain. The only woman in the five-member party, Anne did more than her share of the work and roughed it along with everyone else. It was an exhilarating experience for her, made possible by her husband's faith in her abilities and courage. The ruin they filmed turned out to be a lost Mayan site, and Lindbergh was later praised as a "pioneer of aerial archaeology."

At her husband's insistence, Anne even made her first trip in a glider. Long intrigued by the possibilities of powerless flight, Lindbergh had a friend in Los Angeles, Hawley Bowlus, who had built what he called a "sail plane." With its long wings and tiny body, it reminded Anne of a large beautiful seagull. Lindbergh flew in it several times and was so enthusiastic about the experience that Anne was willing to try it even though she was several months pregnant. After she had made a few test flights in a training glider, which was towed behind a car racing across an airfield, Lindbergh picked out the highest hill in the area, Soledad Mountain, from which the sailplane, carrying his pregnant wife, would be launched. No one had ever taken off from Soledad Mountain, but a trusting Anne thought it would be "a perfect place." Years later she admitted that she was actually "frightened to death being pulled off the mountain alone in a glider, but I could not admit fear to my knight. Once in the air, however, it was an ecstatic experience I have never forgotten or regretted."

After one day's instruction, Anne was the first woman in the United States to be issued a first-class glider pilot's license.

Now seven months pregnant, Anne helped Lindbergh break the transcontinental speed record on Easter morning, 1930. In the Lockheed *Sirius,* they flew from Los Angeles to New York in fourteen and three-quarter hours, three hours ahead of the previous record. Even if Anne had not been pregnant, the flight would have been an ordeal, however. The weather was mostly stormy, and to get above it, Lindbergh had to fly at what was then considered a high altitude. This was not by chance, because, according to one of his biographers, Kenneth Davis, a main purpose of the flight was to prove that flying at altitudes above the weather "was safest and fastest." There was no oxygen aboard and gas fumes began to leak into the cockpit, and Anne felt sick to her stomach and in pain for the last hours of the trip. Although she was tempted to ask her husband to land, she restrained herself because she did not want to ruin the record flight. "I was about to have a baby and I was just terribly airsick, but I knew I couldn't complain because that would spoil the record and would also prove I was a weak woman which I didn't want either," she later recalled.

She also knew that if the press learned that she had been sick during the flight, this would be played up in all the papers and would adversely affect the public's attitude toward commercial aviation, a cause she was now espousing as enthusiastically as her husband.

When they landed in New York, they were immediately surrounded by reporters, and Anne asked Charles to make the press leave as soon as possible. She wanted no one to see her poor physical condition. Lindbergh agreed, and when the press tried to interview him about his record-breaking flight, he was curt, saying that it was merely "an experiment in high-level flying." By then many of them had left the field, but some stayed long enough to see Anne being lifted out of the *Sirius* and carried to a waiting automobile.

When various stories of Anne's difficulties during the flight appeared in the papers — a story in one paper stated that she had suffered a nervous breakdown — a spokesman for Lindbergh vehemently denied them all. As Leonard Mosley, one of Lindbergh's biographers, has pointed out, Anne only admitted that the rumors were true many years later, when she confessed that, with the hindsight of forty years, flying while she was in an advanced stage of pregnancy was possibly not the wisest thing to do. "No doubt since I had difficulty believing I was married, I could hardly imagine I was having a baby. All that flying around in open cockpits . . . making a transcontinental record flight . . . was, I now think, tempting providence. But I felt young and strong and invulnerable."

And, one might add, anxious to please her demanding husband, who also seemed to be unaware of the perils of pregnancy.

After that, Anne prudently decided that she would make no more flights with Charles until after their child was born. She took her doctor's advice and retired to Next Day Hill for the final two months of her pregnancy.

But the family home proved anything but a haven. No longer an ambassador, Dwight Morrow was in the midst of a hectic election campaign in the New Jersey primaries for the U.S. Senate. The rigors of the campaign left him harried and tense, and he spent much of his time closeted behind locked doors with his advisers.

Elisabeth was also at home, confined to her bed and deeply depressed. Some months before, she had opened a nursery school in Englewood with her friend Constance Chilton which was known as "The Little School." She had been happily immersed in running the school until she suffered another mild attack of heart failure. The doctor insisted that she be confined to bed rest at Next Day Hill for a prolonged period of time.

Perhaps the spectacle of her former suitor and her happy, pregnant younger sister was more than Elisabeth could bear, because she suddenly decided that she would be more comfortable recuperating at North Haven than in Englewood. Anne wrote to her often in Maine, upbeat, cheerful letters that tried to convince Elisabeth that one day she would permanently regain her health and that although it was true that Charles and the baby were "the most glorious thing there is," she knew that Elisabeth would soon find marital happiness too.

Adding to the household tensions was Anne's awareness that people were spying on her and Charles at her parents' mansion. This was not a new situation, for in the past reporters had offered bribes to the servants to get them to tell everything they knew about the young couple's private lives. At the time of their engagement, a newspaper chain had bribed a workman to steal a bundle of Anne's letters to her fiancé. And one of Mrs. Morrow's recently hired servants proved to be not a servant at all but a reporter.

Fed up with the newspapers' intrusion into her privacy, Anne wrote to her mother-in-law that since she didn't want the newspapers to know when the baby's birth occurred, Lindbergh would wire her a message in code. If the baby was a girl, the telegram would read, ADVISE ACCEPTING TERMS OF CONTRACT; if it were a boy, ADVISE PURCHASING PROPERTY. Both messages would be signed "Reuben Lloyd."

On June 22, 1930, her twenty-fourth birthday, Anne gave birth to a son. That the infant was a boy delighted the young couple, especially Lindbergh. They named him Charles Augustus, Jr.

Like his father after his historic flight, Charles Augustus Lindbergh, Jr., immediately became a "media celebrity," and perhaps it is no exaggeration to say that rarely has a child been the object of such widespread public interest. When the Lindberghs, in a change of heart, permitted the news of his birth to be announced to the press on June 22, reporters who had waited outside the gates of the Morrow estate for several days dashed to their cars to get to the nearest telephones and telegraph offices. Radio broadcasters stepped to their microphones and sent the message out over chains of stations. Soon a song based on the baby's arrival was sung on the air, and he was dubbed by the press the "Little Eaglet."

Within an hour of the baby's birth, thousands of messages began to pour in to Next Day Hill. Hundreds of strangers drove up to the gate of the Morrow estate to offer their congratulations. So many presents were sent to the child that Anne and Charles could not find enough space for them all.

Dignitaries from all over the world deluged the couple with telegrams. From Mexico City, where Anne and Charles had met, President Ortiz Rubio sent his congratulations, as well as the best wishes of the Mexican people. And in France, where Lindbergh's name was applauded every time it was mentioned, the nation "adopted" his newborn son as its own.

In Englewood, local children handed bouquets of wildflowers they had picked to the guards at the Morrow estate for "Lindy's baby." Since no strangers were admitted, not even the children, one ingenious person tried to gain entrance by pretending that he was delivering a baby carriage Anne and Charles had ordered. He and his baby carriage were denied entry.

But along with the congratulations came ugly rumors. One particularly cruel story claimed that little Charles Augustus was hideously deformed, a monster, which was why the Lindberghs had permitted no photographs to be taken of him. To put a stop to this tale, Lindbergh released pictures of the boy — blond and beguiling, obviously a perfectly normal child. Unfortunately, however, this only created an even greater demand for more photographs of him.

When Anne first saw her newborn son, she was dismayed because she thought that the baby looked just like her, with dark hair and "a nose all over its face." But then, as she wrote to her mother-in-law, she discovered to her delight that, on closer inspection, Charles, Jr., had inherited his father's mouth and cleft in the chin. His only imperfection — and it was a very minor one — was that two toes of his right foot overlapped slightly.

Although she and Lindbergh had relented about allowing the press to know about the birth, sixteen days would pass before Lindbergh released the child's name to reporters, with photographs of the baby he had snapped himself. At that time he also stated that he would no longer be cooperating with several New York tabloids that had repeatedly printed outrageous and hurtful stories about him and his wife.

To the couple's delight, the press left them alone for the most part for several months following the baby's birth. Although they still couldn't dine in restaurants without being swamped by well-wishers, by resorting to ingenious disguises, in which Anne smeared on lots of lipstick and Lindbergh wore a false mustache, they occasionally enjoyed an undisturbed evening at the theater.

As she rocked Charles, Jr., whom she had almost immediately nicknamed "the fat lamb," Anne tried to convince herself that she was like any other young woman with a husband and a baby.

CHAPTER 5

"But She's Crew"

Although Anne doted on her infant son, she had no intention of giving up her flying adventures with Charles to become a full-time mother. Even though they had been married for more than a year, being alone with her husband in a plane thrilled her as much as it had the first time she had flown with him. Flying together meant that nothing separated them, not even his work, and she knew that he was allowing her to share his world, as well as his vision of aviation's future. But there was another reason why Anne adored flying with her husband. When they were in a plane, where he was clearly the pilot and master, the vast differences in their personalities, class, and education seemed to vanish. He was no longer Charles Lindbergh, a college dropout who had no appreciation for the arts and played tasteless practical jokes, but an aviation pioneer who right before her eyes was breaking new records, making important archaeological discoveries, and conquering the secrets of the heavens.

After a month's recuperation from childbirth, which was complicated by a painful breast abscess while she was nursing, Anne resumed flying with her husband in late August. Or, as she explained in a letter to her mother-in-law, "I jumped from bed into a plane, almost."

Anne bathed, dressed, and fed the baby, but a full-time young Scottish nurse named Betty Gow was mainly responsible for his care. Like many new mothers, Anne was jittery at first with the infant. She leaned heavily not only on Betty but also on her mother for help in taking care of him. When the baby became sick with a minor ailment, she had no idea what to do, and it was Mrs. Morrow who had to take him to a pediatrician. Cuddling the baby seemed unnatural to her, as she wrote to Elisabeth: "I don't want to 'fondle' it at all, so perhaps there is something wrong about me. I do like to talk to him and get his attention."

Anne's reliance on a nurse and her somewhat distant attitude toward the baby were not unusual for her times and her class. In imitation of wealthy European women, many well-to-do American women in the 1930s hired nannies for their children. They also slavishly followed the advice of Dr. John B. Watson, a child psychologist who advocated in his 1928 study *Psychological Care of Infant and Child* that children be treated as adults. "Never hug and kiss them, never let them sit on your lap," Watson cautioned. "If you must, kiss them once on the forehead when you say good night. Shake hands with them in the morning. Give them a pat on the head if they have made an extraordinarily good job of a difficult task." In the psychologist's opinion, coddled children soon became mama's boys. "Let the child learn as quickly as possible to do everything for itself . . . Build a routine for him to prepare to go out into the world at two." A loving mother despite her initial awkwardness with the baby, Anne seemed amused by Watson's harsh advice, pointing out to Elisabeth in the same letter that the baby did not like to be "fondled" either, but "knocked his fists about, so perhaps there's something wrong with him! A new mother-child complex for Watson."

When they weren't traveling, the Lindberghs were still spending most of their time at Next Day Hill. Considering that Anne was now twenty-five and Charles twenty-nine, for them still to be living with her parents seemed a peculiarly adolescent lifestyle, one that was certainly inconsistent with Lindbergh's enormous fame and increasing wealth. Yet, like many grown children who refuse to leave the parental nest, the famous young couple undoubtedly chose to stay at the mansion because it was an easy, almost effortless sort of life.

At the fifty-six-acre estate, staffed by twenty-nine servants, Anne and Charles had everything done for them. Not only were their physical needs immediately taken care of, but they were also protected from both an avid press and a public they had come to detest. Furthermore, the socially adept Morrows also provided Anne and Charles with advice on how to handle the dignitaries and famous people they met during the course of their travels. And as a financial wizard, Dwight Morrow was of inestimable help to his son-in-law in managing his growing fortune.

Separating themselves from such luxury and protection could not have been an easy decision, but Anne and Charles, after the birth of

Charles, Jr., finally decided that the time had come for them to stop living full-time with the Morrows and have at least a country retreat. They began to look for property, first in the Palisades and then in other parts of New Jersey. Their search came to an end in September, when Anne and Charles flew over a large piece of land in the foothills of Sourland Mountain, near Hopewell and about ten miles north of Princeton. According to Lindbergh, they decided to buy the four-hundred-acre wooded property after they had landed and climbed a tree on the hillside and looked down "on the place where we finally built our house." The site was far off the regular highways and could be approached only by dirt and gravel roads, which wound through dense woods of old oak trees, brooks, and fields. Their new home, in which Lindbergh planned to include a basement biological laboratory where he could conduct the scientific experiments that had begun to absorb him, would not be finished until November, so while the house was being constructed, they rented a small farmhouse outside Princeton with a large field in front that could serve as an airstrip.

Anne was ecstatic at the thought of their finally having a permanent home. "Our own home — Imagine it!" she wrote to Evangeline.

Yet, as much as she adored Lindbergh and looked forward to building their dream house together, there were moments when she desperately longed to be alone, to experience life unencumbered by either husband or child. Finding it difficult, if not impossible, to express openly any dissatisfaction with her husband, her negative feelings, if she expressed them at all, came out obliquely. For example, in an emotional letter to Constance, she described the exquisite thrill of attending a César Franck concert by herself and the luxury she felt at not having to share her impressions with "anyone else," although she was quick to add that if she were to share the experience with someone, it would be Constance, who she now felt was the closest to her spiritually of any of her siblings.

The missing companion to whom she alludes in her letter was, of course, her husband. Undoubtedly, one of the reasons she relished going to the occasion alone was because, like George Palmer Putnam, she was well aware that Lindbergh was bored by classical music. Dreaming up practical jokes was more his idea of a good time. Lately, he had been dumping guests out of canoes at Deacon Brown's Point. And she herself remained one of his favorite targets. For some reason he thought it outrageously funny to snatch the hat off her head every time she entered the house, and he teased her unmercifully about wearing stockings. Although she always laughed off his pranks whenever she described them to anyone, by this time she must surely have come to realize that her husband, despite his technical genius, often acted like an adolescent.

While their house was being built, the Lindberghs alternated their time between the farmhouse in Princeton and Next Day Hill, where Elisabeth was now living, after having just returned from a trip to Nassau. Anne was happy to see her frail, often despondent sister suddenly in a good mood — an attentive new boyfriend had evidently lifted her spirits — but she also fretted that Elisabeth was becoming too vibrant and cheerful, and her overexcitement was affecting her physical health. "It is nice to see her like that again — if she doesn't get too tired," she confided to Constance. "But it has been a great strain, trying 1) not to get her too upset physically so as not to get her too upset emotionally and 2) not to get her too upset emotionally so as not to get her too upset physically. Get it?"

Their roles were now reversed, and this time it was the lovely, regal Elisabeth who felt inferior and jealous. Although Anne herself never stated the association, undoubtedly it was not the new beau but the sight of her younger sister with a handsome, world-famous husband and beautiful baby boy — the husband and baby that might have been hers — which precipitated Elisabeth's agitated, almost manic state.

While Elisabeth was housebound by her chronic heart condition and excitable moods, Anne was increasingly airborne. Her husband was teaching her to fly a plane. In his usual blunt and practical manner, he had informed her that if something were to happen to him during a flight, he would want her to know how to be able to take over. Other women might have been traumatized by the thought of learning how to fly a plane, especially since the ones the Lindberghs flew seemed, from a modern perspective, fragile and exposed, but Anne was thrilled. She had always adored flying, once confiding to Amelia Earhart that she had longed to learn to fly as a young girl, long before she met Lindbergh.

The plane Anne learned to fly was a Bird biplane, which, as she later recalled, her husband thought was the perfect plane for her to fly because it was so small that "it could land in a tree." She and Lindbergh spent many hours in it as he taught her all the things she must remember during the course of a flight. Predictably, he was a strict teacher, and Anne was often intimidated and infuriated by his exacting demands, although she did everything in her power to please him. "I wanted terribly to live up to my husband's expectations," she said later.

At the time, most novice female pilots were coddled by their flying instructors — a lesson lasting longer than an hour was considered too arduous for a woman — but Lindbergh's training sessions with his wife went on for hours. Finally, he pronounced her ready to fly solo around the field. She made one hopelessly bumpy landing after another. Although she was overjoyed simply to return to earth in one piece, he was a perfectionist and he insisted that she continue training until she could make a succession of perfect three-point landings.

Her first solo flight was from the Long Island Aviation Club to the Teterboro Airport. As she scrambled out of the cockpit in New Jersey, she felt "like a queen." She received her pilot's license in May 1931, but her days as an aviation student were far from over. She learned how to operate a high-frequency radio set, a course that took many weeks of study in radio theory; she also studied navigation with Harold Gatty, Wiley Post's navigator on his around-the-world flight, and learned how to transmit and receive Morse code.

All this instruction and practice was for a specific purpose. Interested in exploring new aerial survey routes, Lindbergh had proposed to Juan Trippe of Pan American Airways flying to China via Canada and Alaska to open a new path to the Orient for commercial air travel. Anne would be his copilot, and she would serve as radio operator and navigator during the trip of several months as they flew over many uncharted regions of the world. Trippe was highly enthusiastic about the project. If Lindbergh were successful, it would mean that commercial flights would be possible across far northern areas, the shortest intercontinental routes.

Although elated about the prospect of making such an important trip with her husband, Anne was worried about leaving one-year-old Charlie, as she called him, with Betty and her parents, who were spending the summer in North Haven. She had grown more confident as a mother, and even though she knew he would be in good hands, she gave Mrs. Morrow detailed instructions about taking the child's picture monthly and keeping a record of his activities for Anne to see on her return. She also was anxious that the Morrows and the servants constantly be on guard against the intrusion of reporters or curiosity seekers who might want to photograph the boy. She had ample reason to fear. In March, Daffin, the white West Highland terrier who had accompanied the Morrows to Mexico City and had been Anne's favorite pet, was killed by sightseers who careened into the front courtyard of Next Day Hill. The curiosity seekers never bothered to stop after hitting the animal. Their callousness had upset Anne terribly. Seldom roused to rage, she wrote to Constance that the dog's unnecessary death "makes me boil with anger."

Dwight Morrow was now a senator from New Jersey, having been elected the previous November in a landslide victory. Although he had been hugely successful as the U.S. ambassador to Mexico, his last months in that country had been fraught with tension as a result of disagreement with President Pascual Ortiz Rubio, Calles's successor, over a national debt settlement.

Exhausted from infighting, he had returned to the United States and begun his campaign for the Senate. The campaign itself only made him feel more weary and tense, for it centered on the thorny issue of Prohibition. Morrow was the first federal official to favor outright repeal of the Eighteenth Amendment, but his stance privately unnerved him.

It was perhaps no coincidence that Dwight Morrow was in favor of repealing Prohibition, for by this time he had himself developed a drinking problem. Its severity and cause are unknown, though in the late twenties drinking had become increasingly fashionable. By 1930 it was heavy and open, with people holding bathtub gin parties, and there was a great deal of public drunkenness. As the Depression deepened, growing numbers of Americans tried to drown their financial troubles in liquor, and, according to one source, alcoholism was so widespread that "there seemed to be a collapse of public morals."

As for evidence of alcoholism, at least one close friend confided after Morrow's death to his biographer Harold Nicolson that Morrow "drank rather," and Nicolson himself once described his subject as "a shrewd and selfish little *arriviste* who drank himself to death" — a nasty and questionable remark since Nicolson alluded to the problem neither in his biography nor in the letters he wrote to his wife, Vita Sackville-West, when he was researching his book at Next Day Hill.

Whether the Senate race caused or aggravated Dwight Morrow's drinking problem is a matter of conjecture. Clearly, however, it was a source of stress, and he again began to suffer from bouts of insomnia and excruciating headaches. His wife worried about him constantly. "Dwight is so tired; so discouraged; so *wild* that he has been trapped into this Senatorial campaign. He is exhausted, does not want it, would be glad to lose," she confided to her diary.

As Morrow feared, the pressures only increased when he became senator. Rattled, or perhaps hoping not to be re-elected, he dismayed his liberal followers by voting against food relief, the soldiers' bonus bill, and stricter utility regulation. A journalist was merely voicing popular sentiment when he wrote that Morrow had "spent a lifetime getting a reputation as a great liberal only to spend three months in the Senate blasting it." Morrow was deeply wounded by such criticism. He felt that he was doing a conscientious job and resented having to vote on an issue if he didn't know anything about it.

One issue on which he wanted to be knowledgeable was the unemployment problem. Many nights he stayed up until dawn reading voluminous documents and studies on the subject, which prompted the ever vigilant Betty to remind him that he was not getting enough sleep. "That's nonsense," he replied. "Most people have exaggerated ideas about sleep. If I can get two solid hours, I'm all right."

Despite such denials, he was aware that overwork was beginning to undermine his physical and mental health. In the midst of a happy July 4 family reunion in 1931, surrounded by his loving wife and children and precious little grandson, he turned suddenly to his son-in-law and said darkly, "Charles, never let yourself worry. It's bad for the mind."

On July 27, three weeks after the family reunion, the Lindberghs were finally ready to take off on their survey flight from College Point, Long Island. Anne's anxieties about Charlie and the situation at home were temporarily dispelled as she and Charles climbed into the twin cockpits of the *Sirius*, which had just been rolled down a pier into the waters of Long Island Sound. Since its last major flight, the *Sirius* had undergone a transformation. It was now outfitted with large pontoons for water landings, which made the plane itself seem "small and dainty" to Anne. The addition of pontoons was necessary because the largely uncharted areas over which they would fly included thousands of lakes and inlets, and, in some instances, expanses of ocean. The pontoons would also perform another function: they carried most of the fuel, enough to take them almost two thousand miles.

Amid yells, screams, and cheers from the vast crowd that had assembled to see them take off, the *Sirius* sped across Long Island Sound with the spray churning up from its pontoons, a cool, refreshing sight on the sweltering hot midsummer day. Soon, to the onlookers, the sleek black plane with its sporty orange wings was just a dot in the sky, and then it was out of sight.

Alone together once more, the couple headed toward Washington, D.C., to obtain the necessary clearances and passports, and then they flew to the family summer home in Maine to say goodbye to the Morrows and to Charlie. As they approached North Haven, they looked down from their cockpits and could see almost the entire population of the community watching their descent from boats in the harbor. For once, Anne, who hated crowds, did not mind, for this group of curiosity seekers consisted mostly of friends and neighbors she had known all her life.

They spent that night at Deacon Brown's Point. Before going to bed, they sat for a long time in front of the fire, answering the Morrows' questions about their imminent journey. Her parents, Anne later reported, were impressed by her knowledge of the short-wave radio. She was even more pleased to note that whenever a member of the family asked them about it, Lindbergh let her provide the answer, even though, as she told everyone later, she was positive she knew far less about the subject than he.

As they took off the following morning, Anne was able to see the landscape of her childhood from an airborne perspective. Later she was eloquently to describe the experience in her first book, *North to the Orient:*

> The island falling away under us as we rose in the air lay still and perfect, cut out in starched clarity against a dark sea. I had the keenest satisfaction in embracing it all with my eye. It was mine as though I held it, an apple in my hand. All the various parts of it were mine at the same moment; the crowd on the pier, the little rocking boat in the harbor where my family waved, the white farmhouse on the point where my baby was. What a joy to hold them all in my eyes at once, as one tries, saying goodby to a person, to possess all of them in one look.

Although she did not realize it at the time, the one person she would never hold in her eyes again was a harried little man madly cheering them on from a boat — her father, Dwight Morrow.

From North Haven, the Lindberghs flew to Ottawa, where they were to dine with several noted Canadian aviators, explorers, and meteorologists. As they landed, Anne felt especially pleased with herself. That day, she had felt more comfortable using the radio and was able to contact two stations regularly. Still unsure of her technical abilities, however, she worried that she was not operating the instrument more efficiently.

In actuality, her job was a very complicated one, since, as Robert Daley pointed out in his biography of Juan Trippe,

Pan Am radio gear in 1931 had to be virtually assembled and disassembled each time one wanted to send or receive a message. To change frequencies one inserted a different transmitting coil, and the *Sirius* would carry six. A second set of coils had to be worked into place in order to receive. She [Anne] learned to crank the trailing antenna in and out; it had a heavy ball weight on the end, and had to be cranked out precise distances for each frequency. For instance, 48 reel turns equaled 3,130 kilocycles. The radio operated on 400 volts, and she learned, each time she stuck her fingers in there, to be prepared to be jolted nearly out of her seat.

Later in the flight, Anne was overjoyed when a radio operator, impressed by her skill in taking and receiving messages, informed her over the radio, "No man could have done better." She felt it was the highest accolade anyone could give her.

In her eyes, the supreme compliment was the one bestowed on her by her husband. That night at the dinner in Ottawa, some of the veteran Canadian pilots tried to dissuade Lindbergh from the route he had originally mapped out, describing it as desolate and dangerous, as well as unscenic. But Lindbergh stubbornly stuck with his original plan to fly from Ottawa to Moose Factory and then onward to the Hudson Bay and from there to Baker Lake and north to the Arctic. When one of the pilots had the cheek to reply that he considered a part of the journey so hazardous that he wouldn't consider taking his wife along, Lindbergh smiled at Anne and said, "You must remember that *she* is *crew*."

When she heard Lindbergh's remark, Anne was overwhelmed with pride and joy. "Have I then reached a stage where I am considered on equal footing with men!" she tremulously asked herself.

Secure in the knowledge that her husband now regarded her as being on a par with any seasoned male pilot, Anne flew with him next morning to Baker Lake, a remote Canadian fur-trading post fifteen hundred miles northwest of Ottawa. Her welcoming committee consisted of a member of the Royal Canadian Mounted Police and a few Eskimos in parkas and pointed hoods to protect them against the clouds of mosquitoes. As she descended from the plane, the Eskimos stared at her curiously. She was the first white woman to arrive at the trading post.

Life in this remote place reminded Anne of a prison. That night, when she and Lindbergh checked on the *Sirius,* which had been pulled up on the beach, she had a sudden feeling of panic that she would be stranded forever at Baker Lake, like the men who always talked of leaving it but never would.

> How terrible to be left here, I thought, glancing at our orange-winged ship. It looked so tame and domesticated, tethered placidly to shore, like some barnyard animal. I could hardly believe that there was power and freedom in that smooth body, as life and death lie imprisoned in the shining shell of a bullet — that at a touch it would wake roaring and, once released, would rise easily as a bit of bark caught under a rock in a stream rises. But now, the engine asleep, the pontoons caught in the sand, the wings tied to shore, it looked as earth-bound as we. This was our one hope of escape. I turned to the *Sirius* and said with silent passion, "You *must* take us out."

On the evening of August 4, they departed, flying north from Baker Lake into a motionless world where the sun seemed never to set. Far beneath them, the landscape was monotonous, with endless stretches of bleak, treeless tundra punctuated with forbidding, frigid lakes. Nothing in the scenery ever seemed to change, and Anne felt that had it not been for the engine's vibration, which hummed through the soles of her feet, that they would seem motionless too, "caught, frozen into some timeless eternity there in the North."

They were to refuel at Point Barrow, Alaska, the northernmost point in their journey, but when they arrived they found that the yearly supply boat, with their fuel aboard, was locked in ice a hundred miles down the coast. Donning their electrically heated flying suits, they took off again for the small mining town of Nome, leaving the land of the midnight sun behind them.

Darkness began to fall when they were still an hour and a half from their destination. Obviously worried, Lindbergh sent a penciled message to Anne, who was sitting tired and cramped in the back cockpit. WHAT TIME DOES IT GET DARK AT NOME? it said.

Anne tried repeatedly to radio Nome, but no message was forthcoming. Lindbergh switched on the instrument lights. Their fuel supply was running low. And they could see mountain peaks ahead. Suddenly Anne felt terrified by the approaching blackness. Although they were finally able to contact Nome, they realized that it would be night when they finally got there. Already there were dense patches of fog on the mountains around them.

Suddenly Lindbergh pulled the *Sirius* up into a stall, throttled down on the engine, and shouted to Anne that they were going to land.

"Where are we?"

"I don't know — somewhere on the northeast coast of the Seward Peninsula" was his curt reply.

As he banked steeply toward unknown waters, Anne began frantically sending a message reporting their location. Then she began winding in the radio antenna. She reeled it in so quickly that her arms began to ache. Then she braced herself for the landing.

From the air Lindbergh had spotted the murky outlines of a lagoon, and it was on its dim waters that they finally landed. In the distance they could see the dark outline of a shore. When they were about half a mile from it, Lindbergh cut the plane's engine, climbed out on one of the pontoons, and threw out the anchor. Although it landed with a splash, the rope stayed on top of the water. Shocked, he and Anne realized that they had landed in about three feet of water. They spread out their parachutes, flying suits, and sleeping bag in the baggage compartment and slept.

After takeoff next day, they landed in Nome and spent the day exploring the former Alaskan gold-mining town. Its heyday had been in the 1890s when gold was discovered in nearby creeks and on the coast. After refueling, they flew across the Bering Sea to Karaginski Island, a fur station off the coast of Soviet Kamchatka, where she felt very much at home. The local people reminded her of the villagers and trappers she had met at Point Barrow. One of them, a trapper's wife, persuaded Anne to show some pictures of her son. Examining the photographs with the woman made Anne feel close again to Charlie, and later she wrote, "When I left, my boy seemed nearer to me because they had seen his picture and had talked of him."

CHAPTER 6

"A Very Great Man"

By SEPTEMBER they were in Tokyo. They stayed for two and a half weeks and visited the U.S. ambassador, the Japanese prime minister, and other dignitaries, taking time off from their official duties to witness a Japanese tea ceremony during a private visit to a tea garden. Anne was deeply moved by the tea ceremony, which "gave a new appreciation of art and of the beauty in everyday life," and she promised herself that when she returned home, she too would "withdraw occasionally from the bustle of daily routine" and "in a place of quiet and simplicity sit with a few friends, and, in the act of sharing tea, contemplate the surrounding beauty."

They had been gone for more than two months, and by this time Anne was anxious to return home to her son. "I'm afraid I'm rather wanting to be back with the baby now," she wrote to Evangeline Lindbergh. "I rather counted on being back in the fall. But I can't fuss too much before Charles — it is such poor sportsmanship — when this *is* a marvelous experience. But I *am* thinking a good deal about that baby now summer is over. They're calling for us any minute: more sightseeing. Much love and *please* see the baby."

Ever the "good sport," she refrained from mentioning to her husband that she missed the baby. One wonders whether Lindbergh ever talked with her about their son and the conflicts she felt about leaving him, or was he too busy with flight patterns, fuel problems, and landing sites? In any event, Anne was scheduled to fly with him to Nanking, where they would soon encounter many more dangers. The Yangtze River, thirty-four hundred miles long, was in flood, and a vast sea of yellow water and mud had engulfed the lower Yangtze Valley. The villagers were dying by the thousands of famine and epidemic; their crops were destroyed and their livestock drowned in the rising waters.

Horrified by the devastation, the Lindberghs offered to assist the Chinese and the National Flood Relief Commission by making several survey flights to map the damaged areas. Lindbergh also offered to transport doctors and medical supplies, a gesture that almost cost him his life. His plane, carrying medical supplies, a Chinese doctor, and an American doctor — Anne had given up her seat — had just landed on water near the flooded walled city of Hinghwa, when the starving Chinese mistook the medicine being transferred onto a sampan for food. Attracted by the strange-looking plane, hundreds of sampans — "like flies on a summer day" — suddenly appeared out of nowhere. As some of the starving people reached the *Sirius,* they climbed onto its pontoons. Their weight was about to sink the plane when Lindbergh whipped out a revolver and fired above their heads. The sound succeeded in scaring the frenzied villagers away long enough for him to scramble into the cockpit and take off.

Seven days later, both Anne and Charles narrowly escaped death while preparing for yet another medical relief flight from the British aircraft carrier *Hermes.* A crane lowering the *Sirius* into the Yangtze jammed, and the plane, with Anne and Charles in their cockpits, tipped and began to turn over.

Charles yelled to Anne to jump. Without hesitation, she did as she was told, jumping into the fetid, rushing waters. After making sure she was clear of the plane and in the water, Lindbergh also dove into the Yangtze, and when he surfaced he saw "Little Anne Pan, perfectly happy paddling along like a little mud turtle." The soaking wet couple swam quickly toward a tender and heaved themselves onto it. Once she was back aboard the *Hermes,* Anne rushed to her cabin to drink a cup of bouillon and hot brandy and to take a dose of castor oil to kill the germs from the river.

To her surprise, Anne had felt calm and detached during the incident, even though she knew she had almost been hit by the wing of the capsizing plane. "I felt quite exhilarated because I have been afraid of an accident, and of being dragged out of life terrified," she later wrote to Elisabeth. "I don't want to die that way — screaming. But I don't think you do — you are spared that. There is no time for fear or much consciousness in an accident. It is over in three seconds; even if you can realize the danger, as I did, it does not frighten you at all — you are outside of it. C. says, though, that even if I'd been hit I wouldn't have been badly hurt. It wasn't as dangerous as it seemed for a moment."

In the mishap, the *Sirius* had been badly damaged, and major repairs were needed before it could fly again. The delay frustrated Anne. Overcome once more with longing for her baby, she wrote in despair to her older sister, "How long will it take to repair, and *when* will we get home?"

Anne and Charles planned to have the plane repaired at Shanghai, but on October 5, while they were still aboard the *Hermes,* Anne received a cable from her mother saying that her father had died.

The details were incomplete, and only weeks later, when she finally returned to Englewood long after the funeral, did Anne get the full story. Evidently, on September 10, while Anne was busy sightseeing in Japan, Dwight Morrow had suffered a minor stroke while lunching with his wife and Roy Howard, the newspaper publisher, on a yacht in Maine. His right arm and leg were briefly paralyzed, but the doctors who saw him failed to realize the seriousness of his condition. They diagnosed it as a "vascular spasm."

The next day, feeling fully recovered, Morrow resumed his hectic lifestyle. Intensely concerned by the specter of growing unemployment and the world's economic problems, he again began to have trouble sleeping at night. On October 2, 1931, while Anne was describing to Elisabeth her brush with death on the Yangtze, Dwight Morrow, after spending a sleepless night on a Pullman from Washington to New York, explained the reason for his insomnia to a fellow passenger the following morning: "I kept waking up thinking what a hell of a mess the world is in." That afternoon, in Englewood, he hosted a large reception for his fellow senator from New Jersey. He shook hands with thousands of well-wishers until his hands became blistered. The following evening, he was the keynote speaker at a dinner supporting Jewish philanthropies at the Commodore Hotel in New York.

When he returned to Englewood late that night, the house was in darkness, and he went to bed, no doubt thinking about the next day's commitments.

On Monday morning, October 5, Dwight Morrow could not be roused by his wife or the servants. Sometime during the night he had suffered a cerebral hemorrhage. By that afternoon, he was dead.

His death at age fifty-eight came as a shock to the nation. It had been rumored that he would be the Republican presidential nominee in the

1932 election, and many people thought he would win. Radio programs throughout the United States were interrupted to announce his death, and the *New York Times* ran a front-page obituary.

When Morrow's friend Walter Lippmann heard the news, he wrote a few hours later, "It would require more composure than I can muster in the first shock of the news of Dwight Morrow's death to attempt an estimate of the man or a just tribute to his qualities. It is too sad a day for such things." Some years later Morrow's biographer, Harold Nicolson, provided an intriguing summary of the character of this complex, dynamic, yet always elusive man: "There was about him a touch of madness or epilepsy, or something inhuman and abnormal . . . He had the mind of a super-criminal and the character of a saint. There is no doubt at all that he was a very great man."

When Lindbergh learned of his father-in-law's death, he immediately canceled the rest of their survey flight. He arranged for the *Sirius* to be shipped back to the Lockheed Air Factory for repairs and booked passage on a ship sailing from Shanghai to Seattle. His wife, he realized, as well as the plane, was in no condition to complete the rest of the trip.

The sudden loss of her father deeply depressed Anne, but if she was tempted to give normal vent to her emotions, Lindbergh's matter-of-factness and cool reserve stopped her. "It has been so much easier for me, with Charles, and then strangers to steel me to a calm. I cannot conceive of what it must have been for you and everyone at home," she wrote to Constance after reaching the United States and preparing to fly back to Englewood. "But I won't go over it, though it does seem to me strange that Daddy, who would be the most magnificent about death, cannot be here to explain and show us its reality. He would look at it calmly and deeply and sanely. I can only try to look at it as some kind of great cycle turning in the earth — a broad, impersonal cycle of birth, life and death."

Counterbalancing her sadness was her happiness at being reunited with her child, whom she hadn't seen for nearly two and a half months. Although Charlie did not seem to recognize his parents, he wasn't afraid of them, and Anne was overjoyed to observe Lindbergh, who had formerly been a diffident father, suddenly paying a great deal of attention to his son. He fed the child pieces of toast smeared with jam from his own plate and liked to take him "ceiling flying," which the baby appeared to find as exhilarating as his father did the real thing.

Lindbergh conceded to Anne that the boy was "good-looking and pretty interesting." He nicknamed him "Buster" and soon, when Charlie began to talk, was greatly amused at being called "Hi."

Glad to be home again with her son, Anne spent that winter quietly, preoccupied with domestic pursuits and writing. She had begun working on an account of their trip, and when she wasn't writing, she was putting the final decorating touches on their new home north of Hopewell. They planned to move into it in February.

During that month Lindbergh was asked to give a speech over the Columbia and National Broadcasting networks on behalf of the China Flood Relief. He thought that Anne would be able to speak more eloquently about the horrendous conditions they had encountered, and he urged her to give the speech in his place. Although still plagued by shyness and stage fright, she felt so strongly about the need to make the public aware of the Chinese people's plight that she agreed to talk publicly about their experiences.

It was the first time she had spoken on the radio, but listeners detected no trace of nervousness when her pleasing, well-modulated voice, with its perfect enunciation, came over the air. In her speech, she described how the devastated region had looked from the air and how her husband had managed to escape the hungry mob that threatened the plane in which he was carrying vaccine. As she spoke, Lindbergh, sitting nearby, smiled approvingly to offer her encouragement.

To Anne's surprise, not only was her speech a success, but she was dubbed a "radio personality." "One of the very best radio voices I have ever heard is that of Mrs. Charles Lindbergh," pronounced John Carlile, a Columbia production director. "She has what we in radio call 'a universal voice' that is not tied down too evidently to any particular locality."

But not even this success could take Anne's mind off her father's death. She had her own feelings of loss to contend with, but furthermore she was aware of her mother's grief and her own responsibility to help her mother make a new life for herself. It was no easy task, for the Morrows had been such a devoted, perfectly matched couple, so passionately in love with each other that their all-absorbing happiness often had made their children feel excluded from their lives. Perhaps as a result of her family problems, Anne developed a stomach ailment, or, as she described it, "a kind of ptomaine poisoning," which confined her to her bed during the early part of December.

Around this time Anne learned that she was pregnant again, but the news that she was expecting a second child did not exhilarate her. What roused her from her feelings of dullness and apathy was Charlie, who was no longer a baby but "a boy, a strong independent boy swaggering around on his firm little legs." Just the sight of his golden curls filled her with joy. "I know you said he would just look like himself and that was all one wanted," she wrote to Evangeline Lindbergh, "but it does make me happy to have him look like Charles. His hair gets curlier and lighter. He has a real twinkle in his eye."

But unlike his seemingly invincible father, Charles Augustus Lindbergh, Jr., was both vulnerable and helpless, a toddler who sat down and cried when a bully hit him at Elisabeth's nursery school, where he was now enrolled. As Anne later reported to Constance, "He was utterly bewildered; that anyone should hurt him *purposely* — that hadn't entered his life before."

CHAPTER 7

"Anne, They Have Stolen Our Baby"

STILL RELUCTANT to live entirely on their own, Anne and Charles did not reside in their Hopewell residence full-time. It was their habit to stay at Next Day Hill during the week, drive down to their country house on Saturday afternoon, and return to Englewood on Monday morning. Seldom did they prolong their stay in the country until Tuesday, partly because Lindbergh, in addition to doing aviation consulting work, was now collaborating with famed French surgeon Alex Carrel at the Rockefeller Institute in New York on the development of a perfusion pump, a precursor of the mechanical heart.

Fascinated by biology since childhood, Lindbergh began to study the subject seriously after his long transcontinental survey flights in 1928. "Then my mind, often wandering without conscious direction, began reconsidering childhood questions about life and death . . ." he wrote many years later. "Aviation showed what miracles man could accomplish. If he could learn to fly on wings, which was once considered impossible, why could he not learn how to live forever? With science now at his disposal, nothing seemed beyond his grasp."

Perhaps not surprisingly, Lindbergh's experimental interests soon became focused on finding a way to cure Elisabeth's heart condition. Shortly after his marriage, doctors had discovered what was causing her chronic fatigue and weakness. They diagnosed a cardiac lesion, the result of childhood rheumatic fever, and to take the load off her severely damaged heart, they advised Elisabeth to spend a year in bed.

In his copious writings, Lindbergh never alluded to his personal feelings about Elisabeth, merely referring to her in his usual noncommittal fashion as "my wife's older sister," but it was clear from his actions that he was deeply distressed by her illness and wanted to help her. Whether his motives extended beyond the clinical and resulted from lingering romantic feelings remain a matter of conjecture. In any event, when he asked Elisabeth's physician why surgery could not be done to correct her condition, he was told that the heart could not be stopped long enough for an operation to be performed because blood had to be kept circulating through the body, an impossibility at that time.

Lindbergh soon learned that his interest in this complex medical problem was shared by Alexis Carrel, head of the Rockefeller Institute's Department of Surgery and a 1912 Nobel Prize winner for his contributions to the surgery of blood vessels, transfusion, and the transplantation of organs. Swiftly he arranged to meet with Carrel, and at lunch he was informed by the world-famous surgeon that solving the problem was far more difficult than it might first appear. For almost two decades, Carrel had been trying to construct an apparatus that would perfuse isolated organs without infection. To illustrate, after lunch he took the aviator on a tour of his laboratories and let him see for himself the instruments that Carrel had designed.

Although impressed by the doctor's biological techniques, Lindbergh was "astounded by the crudeness of the apparatuses" he was shown. He told Carrel that he would like to design a better perfusion pump and to his delight was offered the use of the laboratory facilities. "By contributing my understanding of mechanical design, I could work side-by-side with a man who was a philosopher, a mystic, and one of the greatest experimental surgeons in the world," he later recalled.

The other reason the couple always returned promptly to Englewood on Monday was that Anne wanted to spend time with her mother. The formerly vivacious Mrs. Morrow had become despondent after her husband's sudden death, and her depression often became particularly severe on Monday, the day on which he had died.

Anne looked forward intensely to the weekends in Hopewell. She now felt thoroughly secure as a mother and took care of the baby herself, while Betty, the nurse, remained behind in Englewood. Charlie, or "the fat lamb," as she still liked to call him, was beginning to talk, and Anne was ecstatic every time she heard him calling for "Mummy" instead of his young Scottish nursemaid. Another deeper pleasure was watching her husband play with the child. Although still a toddler, the boy was already displaying an independence of spirit like that which Lindbergh's father had instilled in him, and which he in turn wanted passed down to his son.

Motherhood had changed Anne's life and marriage in profound ways. No longer were her letters to her mother-in-law and sisters filled with glowing descriptions of Lindbergh's exploits and their flying adventures. Instead, her correspondence was almost exclusively devoted to Charlie, his first baby step, his first word, his relationship to her and to Charles.

Although Anne continued working on a manuscript about their aborted flying trip to the Orient and had contacted some publishers about it, she only mentioned the book in passing to her various correspondents. It was Charlie and her wonder at watching him grow that absorbed most of her attention.

These joys of motherhood came to a tragic end on the bleak, windy evening of March 1, 1932.

In late February, the Lindberghs decided to go to Hopewell for the weekend. They had not visited the house for two weeks and were anxious to spend some time there. On Saturday afternoon, February 27, Anne, Charlie, and Miss Root, a member of her mother's household staff, were driven from Englewood by Henry Ellerton, one of Mrs. Morrow's chauffeurs.

At about five-thirty in the afternoon, the automobile, carrying Anne, with her twenty-month-old son snuggled on the seat beside her, entered the half-mile winding driveway leading up to the house, which was surrounded by four hundred acres of dense woods and meadow.

Oliver Whateley, the Lindberghs' affable English butler, and his wife, Elsie, the housekeeper, were at the door to greet them. After exchanging pleasantries with the couple, Anne took the baby upstairs to his nursery. With the help of Miss Root and Elsie, she fed, washed, and undressed him. Later, she put Charlie to bed at seven o'clock, his usual time.

Vaguely resembling a French manor, the house was a rambling two-and-a-half-story structure built of native fieldstone and covered with a white cement wash. Although the house was quite large, the rooms, by today's standards, were relatively small and poky. The extensive use of dark woodwork, which Lindbergh personally selected, helped to create an atmosphere of gloom and darkness, which was intensified by the dense woods on every side.

The couple had planned the nursery carefully. Though fairly small, it was sunny, with three windows, one of which was a French window facing south. Charlie ate his meals at a small maple table in the middle of the nursery and slept in a crib, which was also made of maple. A pink and green screen with gaily painted pictures of barnyard animals was placed around the crib to protect him from drafts. There was a fireplace in the room, with blue and white Dutch tiles. On its mantel rested an ornamental clock, as well as a porcelain rooster surrounded by other birds. The child's toys were kept in a large box under the French window.

After Anne had put the baby to bed, she closed and bolted all the shutters on the windows, except for the ones on the corner window. They had become warped and would not close. Before leaving the room, she opened the French window slightly.

That weekend Charlie developed a slight cold, which Anne thought he had probably caught on the way down in the car. On Monday morning he was still ill. By lunchtime his condition remained unimproved, so Anne telephoned Betty Gow in Englewood and informed her that they would not be returning to Next Day Hill as planned. She explained that the child's cold might get worse if he were subjected to a trip in a drafty car. As she later told the police, she said nothing to the nursemaid about returning to Englewood on Tuesday or about the possibility of the young woman's coming to Hopewell to help her.[*]

When Anne woke the following morning, she felt tired, feverish, and achy, as if she too were coming down with a cold. As for Charlie, he seemed to be no worse, although the cold had gone into his chest, which worried her. Feeling too unwell to care for a sick toddler alone, she decided that the time had come to call Betty and ask her to come down to Hopewell. As she later stressed to the police, she said nothing to the nurse about when she might return to Englewood. Although Betty had planned to travel to Hopewell by train, she called Anne back and told her that Mrs. Morrow had insisted that Henry, the chauffeur, drive her to Hopewell. She and the chauffeur arrived at about 1:30 in the afternoon.

---

[*]Anne's testimony helped clear Betty, who immediately became the police's chief suspect after Charles Augustus, Jr., was kidnapped. Suspicions focused on her, as well as on the Whateleys and other members of the Lindbergh and Morrow staffs, because the child had never before stayed at the house on a Tuesday night, and the kidnappers knew not only precisely when to strike but the exact location of his room. After considerable interrogation, however, the police found Betty to be "a highly sensitive girl of good morals . . . above being in any way connected with the persons responsible for the kidnapping of the baby." She was cleared. As were the Whateleys.

Later that day, the child's health seemed to be improving, so Anne, who was beginning to feel a bit better herself, left him with his nurse and went for a walk alone down the long, winding driveway.

Returning from her walk, she gazed up at the nursery windows, hoping to see her little boy standing inside. But he wasn't at the window, so she stooped and picked up a few pebbles and tossed them up against the windowpane. Soon Betty came to the window, and when she saw Anne smiling up from below, she disappeared and came back with Charlie in her arms. Anne waved at him and smiled, and Betty raised his small, chubby hand in greeting.

Later, when Anne had afternoon tea in the living room, she brought the toddler downstairs to keep her company. He romped around the floor and then disappeared into the kitchen, where he greeted Mrs. Whateley with a cordial "Hello, Elsie." As Betty later recalled, Charlie circled the kitchen several times before she caught him by the hand and took him back upstairs to the nursery where she read to him for a while and then gave him his supper. As he was finishing it, Anne came upstairs to prepare him for bed. She and Betty put drops in his nose, rubbed his chest, and gave him a physic. To ensure that he would not be chilled during the night, they decided to make him a high-necked shirt of flannel. Anne played with her son while Betty cut and stitched the shirt, which was made out of one of Elsie's old nightgowns. After slipping it on, they placed him under the covers to sleep. It was 7:30 P.M., a little later than his usual bedtime. Finally, mother and nurse closed all the shutters, except the one they couldn't fasten because it was warped. Anne left the nursery before Betty, who had not yet opened a rear window or switched off the lights. Anne knew that her husband would be coming home in about an hour, and she wanted to work on her manuscript. Recently she hadn't been able to devote much time to it since she had been busy answering letters of sympathy for her father's death.

As she sat writing at her desk that early spring evening, she kept listening for the sound of her husband's car. It was a cold, damp night, and the wind was howling, making it difficult to distinguish one sound from another. Once she thought she heard the sound of tires on gravel but then realized she had to have been mistaken, for Lindbergh did not drive up and toot the horn until at least fifteen minutes later, at about 8:25 P.M.

Shortly after he arrived, they had dinner. Afterward, they sat for a short time by the fire in the living room and discussed the day's events. It was just after nine when Lindbergh suddenly broke off their conversation.

"What was that?" he asked.

"What do you mean, Charles?" Anne asked.

"I thought I heard a sound like breaking wood," he answered.

"I didn't hear anything," she replied.

Charles Lindbergh did not get up immediately to investigate the source of the sound. A few minutes later they went upstairs and continued the conversation in their bedroom for about fifteen minutes. Then he took a bath. After dressing again, he told Anne that he was going downstairs to read.

Anne then drew a bath for herself. The symptoms of her cold had reappeared, and she decided to go to bed, even though it was still early. Realizing that she had left her tooth powder in the baby's bathroom, she went down the hall and retrieved it without turning on any lights. After brushing her teeth, she rang for Elsie and asked her to fix some hot lemonade.

It was now ten o'clock, the hour when Betty always paid her last visit of the evening to check on the baby. That night, after washing the child's clothes in his bathroom, she had looked in on him at around eight o'clock. He was fast asleep, breathing easily, with no sign of a chest cold. She had fastened the covers to his mattress with two large safety pins and then put out the bathroom light.

Before Betty re-entered the nursery for her final check, she turned on the light in the bathroom so that she could see into the baby's room without awakening him. When she entered the nursery, she found the room chilly, so she first closed the open French window and plugged in the electric heater. After warming her hands over it for a couple of seconds, she turned to the crib. Suddenly, she realized that something was amiss. There were no sounds of the toddler's soft, even breathing. Her first thought was that his bedclothes had smothered him. But soon in the dim glow of the electric heater she became aware of something just as alarming. The child wasn't in the crib. She began feeling frantically all over the cot for his small form.

She kept telling herself not to be frightened. The Colonel was an inveterate practical joker, wasn't he? Perhaps he had crept up and "stolen" the baby when she and Mrs. Lindbergh weren't looking, just to be funny at everyone's expense.

Quickly she walked through the passage to the Lindberghs' bedroom. Anne was coming out of the bathroom.

"Do you have the baby, Mrs. Lindbergh?"

"No," Anne replied.

She was not immediately alarmed. Like Betty, she thought that Charles had undoubtedly taken the child as a joke.

"Perhaps Colonel Lindbergh has him," she said. "Where is Colonel Lindbergh?"

Betty dashed downstairs to find Lindbergh. He was seated at his desk, with the lamp on, reading some papers.

"Colonel Lindbergh, have you got the baby, please don't fool me," Betty gasped from the doorway.

"The baby? Isn't he in his crib?" Lindbergh's face was puzzled as he looked up from his work.

"No."

Lindbergh jumped up from his desk and raced up the stairs, where he met Anne, who was just coming out of the nursery.

"Charles, do you have the baby?" she asked, although one look at his grim face made clear the answer.

Not pausing to reply, Lindbergh dashed into the nursery. After seeing the empty crib, he ran back into his bedroom, flung open the door of his closet, and drew out a Springfield rifle.

He strode back into the nursery, with Anne and Betty following close behind.

Again he glanced at the empty crib.

"Anne, they have stolen our baby," he said.

"Oh, my God . . ." Anne whispered.

Not yet believing what her husband had just said, she began searching wildly through the baby's bedclothes, the closets filled with his tiny outfits, and the large box underneath the French window containing all his toys.

By this time, the Whateleys had learned from Betty that Charlie was missing. On hearing the news, Elsie rushed upstairs to the nursery, where she found Anne in her dressing gown wandering around in a daze.

"You must get dressed, Mrs. Lindbergh," Elsie said gently.

"Elsie, get my clothes and I will dress in here," Anne replied, obviously loath to leave the room where her son had last been seen. Then, realizing it was vital that she pull herself together and help in the search, she said, "I will dress in my own room, Elsie."

Anne returned to her bedroom, with Elsie trailing behind. Impulsively, she threw open one of the windows and leaned far out, peering into the bleak, impenetrable night beyond. Suddenly she thought she heard a cry outside her window. "That was a cat, Mrs. Lindbergh," Elsie said.

Sadly convinced that she had been mistaken — that the sound was either made by a cat or by the roaring wind — Anne got dressed. With Betty and Elsie's help, she began searching every closet, every bureau drawer, every nook and cranny of the newly built house for her twenty-month-old son.

Finding nothing, she and the servants returned to the living room. Anne sat quietly, frozen, lost in thought. It was obvious to Elsie and Betty that she was still in shock and that her only concern now was for her child and whether the person who had taken him would be good to him. They longed to say something to comfort her, but they knew it would be useless under the circumstances even to try.

After learning that his son was missing, Lindbergh quickly donned the black jacket he often wore during his flights. Carrying the rifle, he went out into the night. Under the nursery window, he saw a broken ladder; he immediately realized that it had collapsed as the kidnapper, carrying his boy, had made the perilous descent. Realizing that it was too dark and stormy to search the surrounding fields, he returned to the house and put in an emergency call to the state police.

When they arrived and searched the grounds with flashlights, the state police officers quickly discovered, as had Lindbergh, the sections of a homemade extension ladder about sixty feet from the nursery window. Crudely built, with rungs set much farther apart than usual, the ladder was of an ingenious design: the middle and top sections could be folded into the bottom section so that the ladder could be easily carried. The top rung and one of the rails of the bottom section, where it was joined to the middle section, were splintered, a possible explanation, Lindbergh had thought when he saw it, for the sound of breaking wood that he had heard while he and Anne were talking before the fire in the living room.

Earlier, in the nursery, Lindbergh had noticed an envelope lying on the radiator grating. He insisted that no one open it until a fingerprint expert arrived. One came soon after midnight and tested the envelope, with its enclosed note, for fingerprints. None were obtained. Then the note, written in pencil in a peculiar, obviously heavily disguised handwriting, was handed over to Lindbergh. It read:

Dear Sir
    Have 50000$ ready 25000$ in 20$ bills 15000$ in 10$ bills and 10000$ in 5$ bills After 2–4 days we will inform you were to deliver the mony

We warn you for making anyding public or for notify the police The child is in gut care

Indication for all letters are singnature and three holes

The signature struck Lindbergh and everyone who saw it as bizarre. It consisted of two interlocking circles outlined in blue. In the section where they overlapped was an oval, colored red. Piercing the weird arrangement were three square holes in a horizontal line.

CHAPTER 8

"He Was Such a Gay, Lordly, Assured Little Boy"

Aⁿᶠᵗᵉʳ FTER READING THE NOTE, with its clumsy spelling and construction, Anne and Charles knew beyond a shadow of a doubt what had happened to their son. He had been kidnapped, abducted, they guessed, by an underworld gang, for whom kidnapping had become a big business in the early thirties. Almost always, the victims were released unharmed, and so the Lindberghs tried to reassure themselves that if they paid the ransom that the kidnappers demanded, Charlie would be returned safely to them.

By then, the news of the kidnapping of Charles Augustus Lindbergh, Jr., had been made public. In churches across the nation and over the radio, formal prayers were offered for the abducted child. New York's Bishop William T. Manning sent his clergy a special prayer to be used immediately. "In a case like this, we cannot wait until Sunday," he cautioned. In Madison Square Garden, a game was halted and people were asked to stand in silence for three minutes and pray for the child's well-being and safe return.

On vacation aboard the presidential yacht *Sequoia,* Herbert Hoover found it impossible to enjoy his time off under the circumstances and sent one of his Secret Service agents ashore at Glen Cove Springs, Florida, to obtain the latest information.

He was certainly not the only one who wanted to be kept up to date. The *New York Times* reported that in a single day 3,331 people called the newspaper, asking for information. In New York City, schoolchildren joined in a prayer for the child's safe return, while at least six hundred mothers pressured the police to have plainclothesmen guard their children at play in Central Park. Outside of Hopewell, five hundred children, wards of the St. Michael's Orphanage, prayed daily that the missing Lindbergh child would be left like any foundling, on the door of their orphanage. At Columbia University, football players volunteered to form a "kidnap patrol" that would guard children who might be likely kidnap victims. Meanwhile, dozens of Princeton undergraduates organized searches for the missing child near Hopewell and Princeton. Detective agencies such as Pinkerton and Benjamin Kerin could not keep up with the demand for their services and had to quadruple their staffs. In several states, legislators began preparing antikidnapping bills.

All over the United States people were on the lookout for Charles Augustus Lindbergh, Jr. Wild rumors abounded. Children resembling the Lindbergh toddler were spotted in cars all over the country. And the proprietor of a Jersey City cigar store told the police he was positive that a man he had overheard talking in a phone booth in his store was the kidnapper — since his conversation was so garbled, he had to be relaying a secret message to his fellow conspirators. Everywhere men and women were scanning buses, trolleys, subway cars, and lonely neighborhoods for a golden-haired, blue-eyed child who answered the following description, published all over the United States: "At the time of his abduction, the child was dressed in a white sleeping suit. He is able to walk a little and to talk, although as yet he uses only the few simple words such as a child beginning to talk would know. He is said to resemble his father as to hair, but his eyes and facial features are those of his mother, allowing for the chubbiness of a baby face. He has a dimple in his chin."

Television, which was in its infancy, was also used in the search. At Station W2XAB, atop the Columbia Broadcasting System's building on Madison Avenue, the child's picture was broadcast continuously from 2:00 until 6:00 P.M. and at fifteen-minute intervals during the evening. The signal carrying the image had a one-thousand-mile radius. There were several thousand television viewers in the area, many of whom reported receiving a distinct, sharp image of him.

When they heard about the kidnapping, pilots in New Jersey and New York, many of whom were personal friends of the Lindberghs, flew above the woods and roads in a wide area around Hopewell, looking for possible clues. Among these flying search parties were the "Quiet

Birdmen," a secret fraternal order of famous fliers, of which Lindbergh was a member.

News about the latest developments in the Lindbergh kidnapping case remained on the front page of every newspaper in the country for days. Newspaper sales in New York, Philadelphia, and Chicago increased nearly 20 percent as soon as the story broke. The Associated Press, the United Press, and Hearst's INS sent out at least ten thousand words daily over their wires. Often lacking real news, reporters endlessly rehashed the already known details of the case, invented outlandish theories, and speculated about new developments, even when it turned out there were none. Desperate for copy, they solicited the opinions of people who had no involvement with it, including Dr. Albert Einstein, on the eve of departing for his home in Germany. Rising to the occasion, the famous scientist commented that he thought kidnapping was "a sign of lack of sanity in social development and not a lack of laws."

Among the wealthy, the fear of being kidnapped or of having their children kidnapped was rampant. Shortly after the kidnapping, 250 bodyguards were hired to protect the wives and children of Morgan partners. According to one historian of the celebrated financial firm, "many of their grandchildren would remember growing up surrounded by opulence and armed guards."

In New York, "little Gloria" Vanderbilt, the richest child in the United States, who had become the object of a titanic custody battle between her beautiful, penniless mother and her fabulously rich aunt, was continuously guarded by detectives at the Sherry Netherland Hotel. According to Barbara Goldsmith, who exhaustively researched the trial, she had "become the target of a kidnap and murder threat." In Goldsmith's opinion, "little Gloria's" frightened, peculiar behavior during the custody battle was the direct result of the Lindbergh kidnapping. She too was scared to death that she would be abducted.

Other members of the Morrow family also feared for their safety. At Smith College, in Northampton, Massachusetts, Constance, a freshman, was kept under constant guard as soon as the family learned that Charlie had disappeared. Three years before there had been a plot to abduct her when she was a student at Milton Academy. The extortioners threatened her with death unless the Morrows paid them fifty thousand dollars. Thwarting the criminals, Lindbergh had immediately flown Constance from the school to the safety of Deacon Brown's Point in North Haven.

Mrs. Morrow, who had received a number of poison-pen letters telling her that "you will be next," also feared for her safety. Next Day Hill was placed under the protection of a large police guard, even though both she and Elisabeth had gone to Hopewell to be with Anne.

But the Lindbergh kidnapping held special significance for people other than the Morrow family and millionaires and their offspring. Many Americans became morbidly obsessed with the kidnapping itself, traveling to Hunterdon County in the hope of seeing the house where the crime had taken place, and then discovering to their utter disappointment that they could not even get close to it. Frustrated, they camped out at the railroad station, airing their theories of the kidnapping to anyone who would listen.

The house also became a tourist attraction for some commercial airlines in the Northeast. Pilots bound for Washington circled over the hilltop and then banked steeply so that passengers might gaze their fill at what was now referred to in the press as "the stricken home."

Governors and other dignitaries flocked to the Lindbergh home to extend their sympathy to Anne, Charles, and Mrs. Morrow. Some, seeking publicity for themselves, posed for pictures next to what they later claimed was the kidnapper's curious ladder.

Letters to Anne and Charles began pouring in to Hopewell by the hundreds, and then the thousands. Some tried to offer advice; others were vindictive, implying that Dwight Morrow, Jr., whose mental instability had now become public, had engineered the crime and that he was aided by Elisabeth and Mrs. Morrow, who were jealous of Anne and her child. Two days after the kidnapping, Anne received a telegram saying that the baby was under the care of a trained nurse and in good health. By April 8 she and Charles had received 38,000 letters, of which 12,000 related dreams, 11,500 extended sympathy, 9,500 suggestions, and 5,000 were from cranks, many of whom, to Anne's dismay, demanded money in exchange for their son or offered their own children as substitutes.

But many of the correspondents were ordinary people who were outraged by the boy's kidnapping and sincerely wanted to help the young couple, including a Florida man who shipped a German shepherd by train to the Lindberghs to protect them in the future. When the stationmaster informed Lindbergh of the dog's arrival, the aviator replied that he could not possibly accept it. The dog was finally adopted by a Western Union official. It was the second guard dog Anne and Charles had received.

The outpouring of sympathy and concern about Charles Augustus Lindbergh, Jr., was perhaps unusual in itself, for he was not the only person of note to be kidnapped in the United States during the 1920s and early 1930s. In fact, during the Depression, when people were financially ruined and desperate, abduction for ransom became a big-money crime, taking its place beside liquor, vice, and drug traffic among the popular rackets. Since 1929, more than two thousand people had been kidnapped for ransom in the United States, and millions of dollars had been extorted from the hapless victims or their relatives. As one observer has pointed out, "The Lindbergh kidnapping was symbolically perfect for the Depression, for it demonstrated that an individual — no matter who he was — could not control his own destiny."

In a crime-ridden era, people simply didn't care when gangsters kidnapped or killed one another. Cynicism turned to outrage, however, in late May 1924 when Nathan Leopold and Richard Loeb, two wealthy, educated young homosexuals, kidnapped and murdered fourteen-year-old Bobby Franks. Although Bobby's father, thinking he was still alive, paid the ransom, money wasn't the reason the two youths kidnapped and killed him. Rather, the motive was the challenge of carrying out the perfect crime, which would prove to the sadistic young men that they were supermen.

Four years later, another sensational kidnapping case shocked the public. In 1928 pretty twelve-year-old Marion Parker disappeared. Soon her father, a wealthy banker, received a note demanding a paltry $1,500 for her release. He immediately paid the ransom, only to discover when his daughter was returned to him that she was not only dead but savagely mutilated — her legs had been amputated above the hips. Later, her killer — an eighteen-year-old bank messenger named William Hickman — confessed to the police that the reason he had kidnapped and killed Marion was that he needed the $1,500 to go to college.

As tragic and gruesome as these two kidnapping-murders were, they did not affect the public as deeply as did the kidnapping of Charles Augustus Lindbergh, Jr. If "Lucky Lindy," with his fame, his wealth, and his guards, could have his child kidnapped right from under his nose, how could the average citizen, with his limited resources, safeguard his own children? Jittery parents cautioned their children never to talk to strangers or accept candy or a ride from anybody. According to Barbara Goldsmith, who herself was a small child during the time of the kidnapping, "Many children of the time felt fear all around them and they assimilated it as their own . . . At night, after I'd been tucked into bed, I would lie awake waiting — knowing that this was the night when the ladder would go thwack against my bedroom window and I'd be *taken away*."

Everyone could not help marveling at the calm, dignified way in which both Anne and Charles seemed to be handling their ordeal. It was reported that Anne was trying to rest but was unable to sleep, that she was still suffering from a cold, and that although a doctor had been summoned, there was no indication that she was on the verge of a nervous breakdown. Ironically, the weather had turned beautiful after the kidnapping, with clear blue skies and a warm sun, but Anne was seldom seen outdoors. From time to time her white, drawn face was seen peering anxiously out of one of the upper-story windows. A state trooper on duty in the house described her as "flitting from room to room like some distracted ghost." Lindbergh, on the other hand, was reported as being continually active and intensely involved with the case. Against the advice of the police, he was personally directing the hunt for his son and was too busy to sleep as he tracked down every lead, every clue that might shed light on his disappearance.

His hyperactivity was understandable under the circumstances. An egomaniac like most crack pilots, this man who five years before had flown the Atlantic alone had been dealt a monstrous blow to his self-image. No longer was he godlike, "a master of the sky," but a man whose vulnerability was clearly apparent to millions of people around the world. Rather than confront his own grief and helplessness about the boy's disappearance and let kidnapping experts conduct the investigation, he usurped their role, much to their frustration, and began to search for his son with the same kind of determination that had once enabled him to fly from New York to Paris. Telling the police they could take no action without his permission, he began to deal with confidence men, gangsters, and charlatans.

When the news of the kidnapping broke, an army of reporters and photographers converged on the Hopewell house. Viewing the press for the first time as allies rather than enemies, Lindbergh personally greeted them and offered them coffee and sandwiches. Shrewdly, he sensed that the reporters whom he had previously despised could now be of assistance to him and his wife. They would print the diet that Anne wanted the kidnappers to feed to the baby, as well as other communications that might aid in the child's safe return.

Flattered by Charles Lindbergh's sudden cooperation, the press portrayed the couple in the best possible light. Thirty-year-old Charles was depicted as living up to his image as the world's most famous hero as he relentlessly pursued the kidnappers, while twenty-six-year-old Anne was seen as "the martyred mother," whose entire life revolved around the well-being of her family, and who, of course, was prepared to go to the ends of the earth to recover her son.

MOTHER MEETS ORDEAL WITH CALM FORTITUDE

If little Charles Augustus Lindbergh, in his strange surroundings, is as gallant as his mother, then he is a very gallant little fellow indeed. Life for Anne Morrow Lindbergh since her marriage to the Lone Eagle of the air has been made up of the things that snarl and snap nerve wires . . . Thousands of camera eyes have been trained on her. Thousands of telegraph wires, of typewriters tapped out the infinite detail of her private and her public life. She has always remained calm, gracious . . .

She keeps a hold on her taut nerves. She keeps her brain clear for whatever direction she may be called to give in the greatest manhunt in history. She keeps her body poised for action. But she has been unable to eat or to sleep. All the first day of her baby's absence she wore a plain navy blue sports frock with a white collar, and she has kept a blue plaid scarf tied about her dark hair so that she will be ready to go — to the end of the world, if need be.

MOTHER KEPT BUSY BY DUTIES IN HOME
FIGHTING SPIRIT ALONE PERMITS MRS.
LINDBERGH TO CONQUER EXHAUSTION
AND DESPAIR.

Never in the history of motherhood has a more gallant fight been waged than is being waged by Anne Lindbergh. She is the same gracious woman she has always been. She has a heart that can and did carry her to her own breakfast table, where she thought of the bodily needs of New Jersey state troopers, determined men who have pledged their lives and their service to the return of her son.

> . . . So she does her woman's job. She feeds them . . . She looks to their comfort . . . Her home is their fortress. . . .
>
> She is physically tired. . . . It is the spirit of her that keeps the machine of her body running — the spirit of the born fighter who does not yield the fight until destiny sounds the gong. . . .
>
> There have been times when the courage of Colonel Charles Lindbergh which carried him to the peak of world acclaim, might have faltered. Anne Lindbergh's courage has not faltered. Somewhere out there in the great unknown is her child. When she finds him, she can think about food and rest and sleep and the things that keep mother-machines in running order for the benefit of their children.

In Anne's case, the press was not resorting to hype. She was in fact handling the nightmarish situation with a dignity and courage that were awe-inspiring. As she herself later described it, the house became now "a bedlam" as it was transformed into a "police station" by the New Jersey State Police, who were in charge of the investigation. Troopers were all over the place, and the telephone rang incessantly. There were mattresses all over the floors at night, and when they ran out, people slept on newspapers and blankets. Planes buzzed overhead constantly.

Often, when Anne would finally manage to rest, detectives would pour into her bedroom to have a conference. Mercifully, the fact of her second pregnancy and the seeming unreality of the situation appear to have had a numbing effect. "It is so terrifically unreal that I do not feel anything," she wrote. She also had the bizarre sensation that time had stopped. "Time has not continued since that Tuesday night. It is as if we just stepped off into one long night, or day."

Immediately after discovering that Charlie was no longer in his crib, Anne had telephoned both her mother and her mother-in-law. Although shaken by the grim news, Mrs. Lindbergh, like her son, chose not to give in to despair. While he was attempting to regain both his child and his sense of power by personally supervising the search for him, his mother was living her life as if nothing had happened. She continued teaching her chemistry classes at Cass Technical High School in Detroit, exactly as she had when Lindbergh had landed at Le Bourget airport five years before.

But Mrs. Morrow, who had just returned from Cleveland, where she had been visiting her own mother, rushed immediately to Hopewell. The only place for her to stay was in Betty Gow's room, and mother and daughter often sat there together, vainly trying to comfort each other. Her mother's presence was soothing to Anne, who appreciated the fact that her mother knew just how to handle her during this tense time of waiting and hoping. Mrs. Morrow never tried to comfort her when she felt as if she might burst into tears and made sure that she got sufficient rest. Since the afternoons were particularly long and tedious, the practical Betty Morrow also suggested that she and Anne take a nap every afternoon to help pass the time. Although holding in her own feelings, Mrs. Morrow did on one occasion succumb to her emotions, confessing to her daughter that she desperately wanted her first and only grandchild to be returned on a Monday, the day of her husband's death — it would take "the sting" out of it, she said.

Later, Anne expressed her feelings of gratitude to her mother in a heartfelt letter:

> I can only think of that first week in Hopewell, of you as an ultimate fortress I had, an ultimate source of strength. First: "Well, Mother will be here . . . when Mother gets here . . ." Then morning after morning when there did not seem to be any reason to get up, "Mother is downstairs already": and then those days you went to New York, so terribly long, but "It will be all right tonight, when Mother gets back." And you would always bring back a flurry and breath of life, even in those deathlike days.
>
> I don't know where your ultimate source of strength is, and I feel that I have taken and taken and not given anything back. Perhaps I can't give anything now. It is as though all of us close to this had lost our faith and once it was smashed we were vulnerable — anything could happen. As though your faith, a beautiful shimmering armor of glass, protected you infallibly as long as it was whole. But it's so fragile — once it's gone to pieces you have nothing.

For Anne, her collected, energetic husband, who never ceased trying to find their son, was an almost equal source of strength. "C. is *marvelous* — calm, clear, alert and observing. It is dreadful not to be able to do *anything* to help. I want *so* to help," she wrote to her mother-in-law.

When the baby was first kidnapped, Anne was extremely hopeful about his return. There was a strong tradition of self-control and self-discipline both in her family and in Lindbergh's, and further, the relatives and the police officers tried to buoy her spirits by being optimistic about the chances of the child's recovery. Anne, in turn, tried to keep up their spirits by not succumbing to despair. "In a survey of 400 cities, 2000 kidnapped children returned," she wrote to Mrs. Lindbergh. "Never in the history of crime has there been a case of a gang bargaining over a dead person."

At this point she still believed that gangsters had stolen her child, brushing aside police theories that someone within her own or her mother's household had aided the kidnappers, even though the facts of the case suggested that a person or persons close to the family had been part of the conspiracy. Incredibly, she and Charles and her mother continued to have utter faith in every one of the thirty-two people who worked for them. In fact, this couple who had become so mistrustful of the press and the average American that they often used disguises when they went out in public chose not to have their prospective servants investigated by a private detective agency before hiring them. Instead, they trusted their own impressions after a brief interview. When the baby was kidnapped, Anne stubbornly refused to believe that a member of her or her mother's staff had anything to do with it. Her conscious mind rebelled against the thought of anyone in their employ betraying them. However, as the following diary excerpt shows, she was at least dimly aware that the facts of the crime suggested an inside job:

> Their knowledge of our being in Hopewell on a weekday. (We have not done it since *last* year and only stayed down because the baby had a cold. However, Tuesday and Monday too, he had *no* temperature and was *cured* Tuesday really. We planned to take him to Englewood Wednesday.) Their knowledge of the baby's room, the lack of fingerprints, the well-fitted ladder, all point to *professionals,* which is rather good, as it means they want only the money and will not maliciously hurt the baby.

It was, of course, far easier for her to believe that the knowledge of precisely when to act had come from total strangers, hardened criminals, and not from a trusted servant who she had every reason to think was very fond of them. Both she and Lindbergh became convinced that through underworld connections, they could make contact with the gangsters whom they continued to believe had kidnapped their child. As their go-betweens they appointed Salvy Spitale and Irving Bitz who owned several speakeasies in New York. The Lindberghs issued a statement to the press, which read: "If the kidnappers of our child are unwilling to deal direct we fully authorize 'Salvy' Spitale and Irving Bitz to act as our go-betweens. We will also follow any other method suggested by the kidnappers that we can be sure will bring the return of the child." Although many Americans deplored the couple's decision to appoint racketeers and thugs to represent them, Anne was impressed by the two men. "I met the two underworld kings last night," she wrote in her diary. "Charles, Col. Henry and I feel convinced they are sincere and will help us. Isn't it strange, they showed more sincerity in their sympathy than a lot of politicians who've been here."

Despite their numerous underworld connections and their assurances that they would return the baby alive, Spitale and Bitz failed to make contact with the kidnappers. Finally, after many days of seeing their names on the front page of every newspaper in the country, Spitale admitted to the press that his mission was hopeless: "If it was someone I knew, I'll be God-damned if I wouldn't name him. I been in touch all around, and I come to the conclusion that this one was pulled by an independent."

The person who did make contact with the kidnappers was Dr. John F. Condon, a seventy-two-year-old retired schoolteacher and athletic coach who lived in the Bronx. Tall, with snowy hair and a walrus mustache, Condon was a garrulous, sentimental old gentleman who was also intensely patriotic. In his opinion, America was the best country in the world and the Bronx the most beautiful borough in it.

A contributor to the *Bronx Home News,* Condon was among those who were upset that the Lindberghs had authorized two underworld figures to act as go-betweens. He wrote a letter to the editor, saying that he was prepared to act as an intermediary between Lindbergh and the kidnappers and would also add his own savings of a thousand dollars to the fifty-thousand-dollar ransom money. The editor ran his offer on the front page of the *Bronx Home News* on March 8.

To his surprise, Condon received a note from the kidnapper the following day. Written in the same indecipherable handwriting as the ransom note Lindbergh had received and clearly the work of someone of Germanic descent, it said:

> Dear Sir: If you are willing to act as go-between in Lindbergh cace pleace follow stricly instruction. Handel incloced letter *personaly* to Mr Lindbergh. It will explan everyding. Don't tell anyone about it. As son we find out the Press or Police is notifyd everyding are cansell and it will be a further delay. Affter you gett the mony from Mr Lindbergh put these 3 words in *New York American*

Mony is Redy

Affter notise we will give you further instruction. Don't be affrait we are not out fore your 1000 $ keep it. Only act stricly. Be at home every night between 6–12 by this time you will hear from us.

As soon as he read the note, Condon dashed to the phone and somehow managed to get through to Hopewell. When he read the note on the phone to Henry C. Breckenridge, Lindbergh's friend and adviser, and described the strange interlocking blue and red circles that served as the kidnapper's signature (this information had never been printed in the newspapers), he was told to drive down immediately.

Condon later wrote a heavily embroidered account of his experiences as an intermediary in the case. In it, he claimed that he reached Hopewell shortly after two in the morning, and that after Lindbergh had examined the notes from the kidnappers and was convinced of their authenticity, Condon was invited to spend the night. Although it was nearly three in the morning, he asked Lindbergh if he might not meet his wife. According to Condon, Lindbergh, unmindful of the hour, ushered him into their bedroom, where he saw "a tiny, childlike pretty creature, sitting on the edge of the bed . . . dressed in a simple dark frock of some sort."

Lindbergh introduced him to Anne, who, Condon insisted, "stretched out her arms towards me instinctively in the age-old appeal of motherhood."

"Will you help me get back my baby?"
"I shall do everything in my power to bring him back to you."
As I came closer to her I saw the gleam of tears in her soft dark eyes. [Anne's eyes were blue.]
. . . I smiled at her, shook a thick reproving forefinger at her. With mock brusqueness I threatened Anne Lindbergh.
"If one of those tears drop, I shall go off the case immediately."
She brushed away the tears. When her hands left her face, she was smiling, sweetly, bravely.
"You see, Doctor, I am not crying."
"That is better," I said. "That is much, much better."

In *The Airman and the Carpenter,* his best-selling book about the kidnapping in which he claims that Bruno Hauptmann, the man executed for the crime, was innocent, BBC journalist Ludovic Kennedy doubted whether such a meeting ever took place: "Or was it a scenario etched by Condon to portray himself as the father figure in whom all might trust, the humble teacher who would bring peace and comfort to the nation's hero and his anguished wife? Condon was so great a self-deluder that neither then nor now can one believe without confirmation anything he says."

Anne herself made no mention of the encounter in her published diaries and letters. Her only reference to Condon was in an April 13 letter to her mother-in-law in which she wrote about the negotiations that were being carried on "through letters and through the go-between who was chosen by the kidnappers." Since Anne's diaries and letters often contained her impressions of people she had just met, it seems odd that she did not include her feelings about Condon, especially since he was to become such a crucial figure in her and her husband's lives. Possibly she and the elderly gentleman had only a brief, perfunctory contact. But it is also possible that Anne had her own doubts about Condon's strange role in the kidnapping and has been hesitant to publish them out of fear that they might give credence to a theory that was widely circulated at the time. This theory holds that Condon himself was part of the gang that kidnapped the Lindbergh baby. His bizarre correspondence with the kidnapper in the Bronx newspaper was, in this theory, part of a preconceived scheme to get Charles Lindbergh to hand over the ransom money, which he would share. Although many people were skeptical of Condon's veracity, and he did begin to receive hate mail and phone threats, Lindbergh himself appears never to have doubted him. He once described Condon as an "old and kindly professor in the Bronx," and wrote a letter to him when he was under fire expressing his "sincere appreciation for your courage and cooperation." His words of support, which were later published, were of inestimable help to Condon, who by this time was regarded by the police as a prime suspect. He was eventually cleared, but even though many law enforcers no longer thought him part of the kidnap gang, they considered him "a screwball."

Lindbergh and Breckenridge authorized Condon to proceed with the delivery of the ransom, and on March 11, the following ad appeared in the *New York American:* "I accept. Money is ready. Jafsie." (The name "Jafsie" came from the teacher's initials, J.F.C., and was used because it was believed that no one but the kidnapper would recognize it.)

On April 2, after making contact in Woodlawn Cemetery with the presumed kidnapper, who called himself "John" and had a German or Scandinavian accent, Condon had Lindbergh drive him, as instructed, to another cemetery — St. Raymond's, in the Bronx. Following "John's" orders, Condon got out of the car. Soon a man appeared on the side-walk next to the cemetery. In a low voice, he said, "Hey, Doctor!" which Lindbergh was later to maintain that he heard clearly, even though he was still in the car parked across the street.

Condon exchanged the fifty-thousand-dollar ransom across the cemetery wall for a note promising that the baby was on a "boad Nelly" (meaning "boat *Nelly*"), which could be found near the Elizabeth Is-lands between Martha's Vineyard and Cape Cod. The ransom was paid in gold banknotes from Lindbergh's bankers, J. P. Morgan and Com-pany, the number of each one having been recorded as a means of later apprehending the kidnapper.

Lindbergh was jubilant when he read the note. His happiness, how-ever, swiftly turned to disappointment. He made two flights to the Eliz-abeth Islands but found no trace of the boat. Although both he and Anne were deeply upset that they had been duped, they still remained optimistic that they would recover their son alive.

Charles's spirits were raised by yet another lead. A Norfolk boat builder named John Hughes Curtis stated that he was in touch with the kidnappers. He claimed that the baby was being kept on a boat called the *Mary B. Moss,* which was anchored somewhere off the Jersey coast. That earlier night at the cemetery, the man who took the ransom money had said the baby was on a boat called the *Nelly.* Perhaps the kidnappers had changed the name to throw the police off the track. Al-though Anne, like many of the detectives, thought the lead would amount to nothing, Lindbergh thought it was worth pursuing. He be-gan to search for the boat by air and later by sea.

On Thursday, May 12, almost nine weeks after he had been kid-napped, the search for Charles Augustus Lindbergh, Jr., ended. A truck driver named William Allen stopped along the road from Hopewell to Princeton, and when he stepped into the woods to relieve himself, he made a horrifying discovery. Lying face down in a shallow ditch under a scattering of leaves and dirt was the badly decomposed body of a baby half eaten by wild animals. The left hand, right arm, and left leg from the knee down were missing, as were all the major organs except the heart and liver. Under the leaves beside the body was a burlap bag. A later postmortem disclosed that this partially skeletonized corpse was the body of Charles Augustus Lindbergh, Jr., and that he had died more than two months before, undoubtedly on the night he had been kid-napped. The cause of death was a fractured skull. Doctors and the po-lice speculated that this mortal injury might have occurred when he was being carried down the ladder by the kidnapper in the burlap bag, into which he had been shoved to keep him from crying and alerting the household. As the kidnapper was making his way down the ladder, the extra weight caused the ladder to break at its weakest point, and he dropped the child, who struck his head on the cement windowsill. Realizing the baby was dead, the kidnapper quickly got rid of the body, half burying it in the woods only a mile or two from the Lindbergh home.

In Hopewell, on a late spring afternoon, Anne knew nothing of this discovery until her mother quietly took her aside and told her. She was still waiting and hoping for her child's safe return. Lindbergh was not at home — he was still out on the Atlantic Ocean searching for his son — and it became Mrs. Morrow's sad duty to break the news. "Anne, the baby is with Daddy," she said simply.

For Anne, suddenly faced with the reality of her little boy's death, it was a relief at first to know that the long period of waiting and uncertainty had come to an end. "I feel strangely a sense of peace — not peace but an end to restlessness, a finality, as though I were sleeping in a grave. . . . To know anything definitely is a relief. If you can say 'then he was living,' 'then he was dead,' it is final and finalities can be accepted."

The police managed to notify Lindbergh at sea, and he returned immediately to Hopewell, arriving around two o'clock in the morning. Both he and Anne were far too agitated to sleep. They stayed up all night, and Lindbergh talked to his wife "beautifully" and "calmly" about death, which gave her courage.

The next morning the full horror of what had happened descended on them. Lindbergh and Betty Gow drove to a mortuary in Trenton where they were asked formally to identify the baby's remains. Holding in his emotions, Lindbergh, looking exhausted and suddenly middle-aged, was ushered into a room where a small form lay on a table covered with a sheet. He asked that the covering be removed. Then, his face flushed, he gazed down at the skeletal remains of his son for a few seconds. He bent over and looked into the corpse's mouth, counted its teeth, and then inspected the right foot with the two small overlapping toes. Finally, answering an official's question, he confirmed the almost completely decomposed corpse's identity. "Yes, I am perfectly satisfied that it is my child," he said. Then, without further comment, he left the room.

Later that day the body of Charles Augustus Lindbergh, Jr., was cremated at the Rose Hill Cemetery in Linden, south of Elizabeth, New

Jersey. Charles Lindbergh attended the cremation alone. At his and Anne's request, there was no religious service. He watched as the tiny oak coffin was rolled through the glass doors of the cremation chamber and the flames devoured his son's body.

While Lindbergh was en route to New Jersey, after learning about the discovery of the baby's body, newspaper photographers broke in through a window of the Trenton morgue, opened the casket, and photographed the remains. For that act Lindbergh never forgave them. It confirmed all his worst suspicions about reporters, that they were all loathsome human beings.

Although Anne was spared the gruesome sight of her son in death, it did not make the tragedy any less horrible for her. Her grief only intensified as the days passed. The only way she was able to vent her feelings of sadness and loss and to begin the slow process of healing was by writing in her diary, which she had begun keeping again on the day before the baby's body was discovered, on May 11, 1932, after a lapse of more than three and a half years. The entries she made at this time were heartbreakingly intense and personal. Together, they form a vivid and moving testimony to a sensitive young woman's supreme tragedy. Reading her diary today, sixty years later, is to be swept back in time to the late spring of 1932 and to experience with a grief-stricken mother her terrible sense of loss. In a sense, the immediacy and eloquence of Anne's writing about the death of her son would become his most enduring memorial. For her portrayal of her anguish is so poignant, so beautifully written and strongly communicated that the reader may feel as if the tragic passing of Charles Augustus Lindbergh, Jr., is a death in his or her own family.

Friday, May 13, 1932. He has already been dead a hundred years.

A long sleepless night with C. sitting beside me every hour, and I could see it all from a great distance . . .

Then a long day when everything personal flooded back over me, a personal physical loss, my little boy — no control over tears, no control over the hundred little incidents I had jammed out of sight when I was bargaining for my control . . .

I am glad that I spoiled him that last weekend when he was sick and I took him on my lap and rocked him and sang to him. And glad that he wanted me those last days. . . .

Impossible to talk without crying.

Immortality perhaps for the spark of life, but not for what made up my little boy.

Anne Spencer Morrow in 1928, after her engagement to Charles Augustus Lindbergh, Jr., "the most worshipped man in the world."

There is nothing of the shy, modest, "unheralded boy" who captured the imagination of millions in this photograph of Lindbergh, taken one month after his 1927 transatlantic flight. Here he is the epitome of the heroic aviator: daring, virile, and romantic.

Lindbergh with his future in-laws, Ambassador and Mrs. Dwight Morrow and their youngest daughter, Constance, at the American Embassy in Mexico City in 1927. The aviator had not yet met Anne, who was still at Smith College and unimpressed with his celebrity.

"COME!"

"Lindy, I didn't know you cared!"

How Everygirl would like to have her engagement broken.

Lindbergh's effect on women is apparent from this cartoon, which appeared in a 1928 issue of *Judge*, a popular humor magazine.

Lindbergh with the *Spirit of St. Louis*, 1927.

Lindbergh's father, the Republican congressman Charles Augustus Lindbergh. Perhaps the ultimate stoic, the elder Lindbergh once insisted on undergoing an operation without any anesthetic.

Lindbergh and his mother, Evangeline Lodge Land Lindbergh, with the *Spirit of St. Louis.* Until Lindbergh married, his favorite flying companion was his mother.

Next Day Hill, Dwight Morrow's mansion in Englewood, New Jersey, where Anne and Charles were married in great secrecy on May 27, 1929.

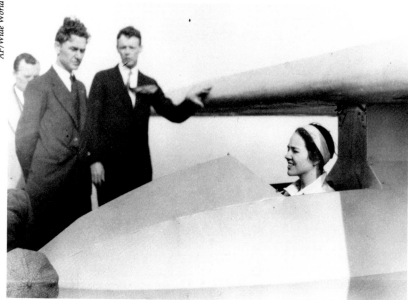

Anne Morrow Lindbergh in the cockpit of a Bowlus glider, minutes before winning her first-class glider pilot's license in San Diego. Charles is standing beside her, his hand on the wing.

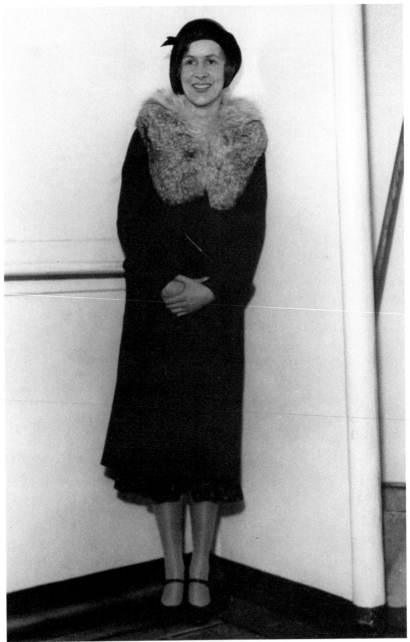

Elisabeth Morrow, Anne's older sister, whom Lindbergh once dated, aboard the *S.S. Aquitania* in 1930. Suffering from a weak heart, Elisabeth was bedridden for a good deal of her life, but here she appears happy and healthy.

Amelia Earhart, the world-famous aviator whom the press dubbed "Lady Lindy" because of her resemblance to Lindbergh, and her husband, the publisher George Palmer Putnam. Of Anne she wrote, "Under her gentleness lies a fine courage to meet both physical and spiritual hazards with understanding."

Recovering from their injuries after a plane crash caused by a marital spat, bandaged British aviators Amy Johnson and James Mollison are flanked by Joseph and Mary Haizlip, another famous husband-and-wife flying team.

Anne and Charles Lindbergh in front of the *Sirius*, the dual-cockpit plane in which they set a coast-to-coast record when Anne was seven months pregnant.

Saturday, May 14. I am very tired from not sleeping and the drugs. But I feel that perhaps he gave enough in his short life, amazingly — to Daddy for a year, to Mother when Daddy went, those first three or four months, to me, to Mrs. Lindbergh, to C., to my grandmother. C. and I have never been so close as at his birth, except now, at his death. He has made something tremendous out of our marriage that can't be changed now. And for the world, too, perhaps, the sacrifice will bring something.

Sunday, May 15. I am glad he did not live beyond that night. He was such a gay, lordly, assured little boy and had lived always loved and a king in our hearts. I could not bear to have him baffled, hurt, maimed by external forces. I hope he was killed immediately and did not struggle and cry for help — for me.

Tuesday, May 17. C.'s grief is different from mine and, perhaps, more fundamental, as it is not based on the small physical remembrances. There is something very deep in a man's feeling for his son, it reaches further into the future. My grief is for the small intimate everyday person.

Wednesday, May 18. I thought I would lead him and teach him and now he has gone first into the biggest experience in life. He is ahead of me. Perhaps when I have to go through it I will think of him — my gay and arrogant child going into it — and it will not seem so terrifying, so awesome, a *little* door . . .

To reconstruct his murder, to try to understand, I will never climb out of this hell that way. And yet perhaps it is better, more unreal here. Englewood will be a place every corner of which will bring back the physical dearness of my boy. But I want the image of my boy, a spiritual thing. I don't want to get any nearer to his murderers, to see their faces, the weapon they killed him with, the place where he was killed. It must be discovered, but not by me, not every night.

Thursday, May 19. If this is true he died before he really woke up, I would like to think that. I hope they will not go through it all again for a while. C.'s mind works on it incessantly. But I am sick of this police-case end of it. Is this going to be the realest thing in my memory of my boy? This picture of his mutilated body and how it happened? I must go back to Englewood and find him again. Even though I am afraid of it. Decent grief, no matter how great, is better than this distorted, prolonged, unreal horror. There is no reconstruction until this is over. We are building backwards, not forwards. I feel as if it were a poison working in my system, this idea of the crime. How deep will it eat into our lives?

On Friday, May 20, Anne ventured into the nursery and opened Charlie's closet.

His blue coat on a hook, his red tam, his blue Dutch suit, the little cobweb scarf we tied around his neck. . . . In the pockets of his blue coat I found a shell, a "tee," and his red mittens. It was like touching his hand. In the drawers I found all the Hänsel and Gretel set he played with that last day and the little pussycat I pushed in and out of a little toy house for him. It delighted him so. It gave me a pang of happiness to find it again. Oh, it was so good to feel that intimacy of that memory. It was grief; but it was for my own boy — real, alive in my memory, not a police case.

The following day was the fifth anniversary of Lindbergh's historic flight. Anne was still too absorbed by the tragedy even to refer to it in her diary, although she did note with some enthusiasm that Amelia Earhart had landed in Ireland — she was the first woman to fly alone across the Atlantic Ocean. That afternoon she and Charles finally left Hopewell and went to Falaise, the Guggenheims' estate on Long Island. It was a rainy, late spring day. Lilacs were in bloom, and the sea was pearly gray. The quiet sound of the ocean and the cloistered atmosphere of the house reminded Anne of the time she and Charles had visited Falaise after their honeymoon, three years before. "It is so peaceful, like that evening — only I am old, old, but I understand nothing more," she wrote in her diary. "We are starting all over again — no ties, no hopes, no plans . . . So many people have lost children, I must remember."

In the weeks that followed, she tried to hold the baby close in her memory by having an artist friend paint his miniature from a photograph and by bringing his record up to date. Often she would sit alone in his nursery at Englewood, looking at his toys and the small Swedish rocking horse, as well as his crib, which now held only the linen dog and a toy gray cat with a bedraggled tail that had been his favorite playthings. But with each passing day, as the new baby grew bigger within her, her first-born was moving farther and farther away. Soon she stopped going to the nursery and sitting among his things. "He is gone," she wrote forlornly in her diary. "I can't get him back that way or any other way. He is just gone. There is nothing to do."

CHAPTER 9

Victims

Shattered by her son's death, Anne struggled to rebuild her life, although in a sense both she and Charles never fully recovered from their terrible loss. Instead, their life from 1932 on was more or less an effort to work out their feelings about Charlie's senseless murder. Rigidly self-controlled and walled off from his emotions, Lindbergh escaped from his grief through flying and through his work with Alexis Carrel at the Rockefeller Institute. Since childhood, the godlike world of flight and the precise, controlled world of science had been his escape from emotional trauma, and once more he fled to them. But for his acutely perceptive and emotional wife, the outside world and its activities offered no panacea.

Nor could organized religion provide her with any comfort. Although she had regularly attended services at the Presbyterian church as a child and young adult, part of her had died with her son, and even worse, so had her faith in the comfortable, reassuring religion of her parents. After Charlie died, she struggled to regain her belief that the world was orderly and just, but it was impossible. For she had learned firsthand that intelligence and civility, as well as fame and great wealth, were no match for the threatening, brutal forces of evil. Without her childhood faith to sustain her, she felt fearful and defenseless, "as though once you had lost your faith, you were vulnerable and nothing you did could stop evil and sorrow and misery from pouring in."

Conditioned since childhood to be polite and diplomatic, she had always found it difficult to express rage and hatred. A different kind of

woman might have gained some measure of relief by inventing elaborate fantasies of revenge on her son's murderers. But Anne was too well-
bred and civilized to permit herself such an outlet, and so, not surprisingly, she turned her suppressed vengeful feelings inward. Her thoughts
became morbid and depressed, and she was obsessed with death. She kept
reminding herself that a year ago, Charlie and her father had both been
alive. Now they were gone, and she wondered who in her family would
be next. Her anxieties soon focused on Elisabeth, whose health had recently taken a turn for the worse. At Lindbergh's insistence, her sister
had gone to the Rockefeller Institute for a medical evaluation. After the
tests were finished, the doctors took Mrs. Morrow aside and told her
that one of her daughter's heart valves had been so severely damaged by
childhood rheumatic fever that they doubted whether she would live
another five years.

Unaware of this poor prognosis, but despondent over her continuing poor health, Elisabeth decided to spend the summer in Somerset,
England. She hoped that the house where she would be staying would
be peaceful and quiet, in contrast to the frenetic pace of Next Day
Hill, with an atmosphere that would be beneficial for her health. Every
time Anne looked at her older sister, with her delicate pre-Raphaelite
beauty, she was struck anew by the transitoriness of life. "I look at her
and think, Life is captive here — now — soon it will go. Why can't we
hold it, why can't we help it?"

She also worried about Lindbergh, who, in her opinion, was still too
obsessed with the case and the capture of the kidnappers. To Anne, it
was obvious that the ordeal of the last several months had taken its toll
on him, despite the impression he liked to give of always being in command of his emotions, a tower of strength to everyone. Watching him
play tennis one June afternoon at Falaise, she noted with some relief
that he suddenly looked like himself again — "youthful and golden"
— the way he had looked shortly after their marriage, when life had
been like a dream of perfect bliss and he was at the zenith of his power
and glory, a man who had conquered both the sky and the Atlantic
Ocean.

Hoping that writing, long a joy and an escape, might lift her out of
her despairing mood, Anne forced herself to resume working on her
manuscript about their trip to the Orient. But she could find little enthusiasm for it within herself, and the few words she managed to set
down on paper were flat and lifeless, in her opinion. Her emotions, she

realized, were still centered on Charlie's death. As she noted in her diary,

> `I think, analyzing it, that women take and conquer sorrow differently from men. They take it willingly, with open arms they blend and merge it into every part of their lives; it is diffused and spread into every fiber, and they build from that and with that. While men take the concentrated bitter dose at one draught and then try to forget — start to work at something objective and entirely separate. So C. says, "Write about Baker Lake — that has no connection."
>
> But that is just it — it has no connection; my heart is not in it. I can only work from the one strong emotion in me; my love for that boy, and the things that grow from it — wanting a home, wanting children, things to give and do for them, for Charles and my home. I will get beyond this almost animal feeling and want more, but not yet.

Only her piano lessons, which she had resumed, seemed to bring her pleasure, even though she was a beginner and her fingers felt "like old ladies going up and down stairs." But she soon found that she did not really want to learn to play for herself, but for the little boy who was no more. Whenever she practiced the piano, she remembered how much fun it had been to bang out simple tunes, while Charlie danced beside her.

Adding to her melancholy was the problem of what to do about the Hopewell house, which had once seemed so safe and impregnable. Both Lindberghs had mixed feelings about continuing to own it. On the one hand, they adored its beauty and seclusion; on the other, they knew they would always be reminded of the crime that had occurred there. Even more troubling was the thought that if they decided to live there again with the new baby, some crazed person might try to kidnap him too.

Another problem was the crowds of people who were always trying to invade their privacy. Some were simply morbid curiosity seekers who wanted to gaze at the place where the crime had been committed; others felt sincerely sorry for the young couple and naively thought that their presence might be helpful. For Anne, the constant sight of curiosity seekers in the town of Hopewell was profoundly unsettling. Among these anonymous hordes, who might be another kidnapper, another killer? But these crowds of obsessed visitors unnerved her for another reason. Their fascination with the crime aroused her own guilt about the baby's death, a dark, secret tortured feeling, for in her heart, she knew that her child might have lived a normal life had he not had the misfortune to have been born to such famous parents. "If it were not for the publicity that surrounds us we might still have him," she noted remorsefully in her diary.

One afternoon at Falaise, the Lindberghs' close friend Harry Guggenheim tried to counsel them on the necessity of learning to live with fame and the press. "As long as you do anything constructive all your life, you will have to meet it, you can't get away from it," he advised them. "The only thing to do is to change your whole attitude. Conquer it *inside* of you, get so you don't mind."

But the Lindberghs *did* mind the magnesium flash lamps, with their blinding light and noxious odor, exploding in their faces every time they stepped out the door and the constant intrusion of reporters and photographers into their personal lives. The subject of the press was such a touchy one that they were "too sore and hurt" even to listen to any of Guggenheim's practical suggestions.

And they were just as angry and defensive when their names were thrust again into the headlines on June 10, when Violet Sharpe, a twenty-seven-year-old English waitress in Mrs. Morrow's employ, committed suicide.

At the time of her death, Colonel H. Norman Schwarzkopf, the commanding officer of the New Jersey State Police (and the father of the general who later led the coalition forces in the Gulf War), stated his belief that Violet Sharpe's suicide proved that she was in fact involved in the crime. "The suicide of Violet Sharpe strongly tends to confirm the suspicions of the investigating authorities concerning her guilty knowledge of the crime against Charles Lindbergh Junior," he told reporters. Other detectives involved in the investigation stated publicly that Violet was "the informant and agent for the kidnappers." But many members of the press in both the United States and Britain had a different theory about Violet's suicide. They believed that she had been grilled so mercilessly that she had swallowed poison.

For once, Anne agreed with the press. The servant girl, she believed, had had nothing to do with the kidnapping, but had become so agitated by the thought that she was going to be implicated in the crime that she killed herself. Trusting to the point of incredibility, Anne continued to maintain a blind faith in the loyalty of her household staff as well as her mother's, even though the fact that the kidnapper or kidnappers had known precisely when to snatch her child from his crib made it altogether possible that someone with a knowledge of her plans had either masterminded the crime or had been an accomplice. Refusing to speculate on the sinister implications of Violet's death, she was more concerned with its emotional impact on her mother, who had been with her servant girl when she died on the floor of the butler's pantry at Next Day Hill, after swallowing some crystals of cyanide chloride, which she used for polishing silver. It was one more tragedy that Mrs. Morrow had to weather. Although Anne knew that her mother would deal with it with her usual courage and fortitude, she was nevertheless happy that Mrs. Morrow and Dwight, Jr., would soon be leaving for the "peace and beauty" of Europe and England. On this trip, they planned to visit Elisabeth, who, in contrast to the rest of the family, seemed to be having a tranquil summer and, moreover, had apparently fallen in love.

Anne had always loathed the "police aspect" of the case, but that summer there was no escaping it. In late June, the Lindberghs returned to the house in Hopewell after a long absence so that Lindbergh could testify at the trial in Flemington of John Hughes Curtis for obstruction of justice. In a case noted for revealing the worst in humanity, Curtis proved merely to be one of many people who had set out to dupe the desperate young couple for personal gain. While vainly searching for the boat *Nelly* after paying the ransom money in April, Lindbergh had been approached by Curtis, who convinced him that the kidnappers had hidden Charlie on a boat named the *Mary B. Moss* off the New Jersey coast. After the child's body was discovered, Curtis immediately broke down, confessing that he had concocted the cruel tale, not for money but so that he could become famous. He tried to take Lindbergh's hand, but the aviator backed away in horror and disgust.

As usual, Anne's preoccupation was less with the people who had perpetrated these cruel deceptions against her and her husband, and more with her own continuing grief about Charlie, which she felt certain would become even more intolerable on her return to Hopewell. She dreaded entering the house that had once seemed such a happy place but now was blighted. "To live there in no hope, where I lived so long *just* on that."

It was a stifling hot day when she and Lindbergh traveled from Englewood to Hopewell; to her surprise, however, Anne found the house "cool and peaceful," a home again, with little to remind her of the crime. When she climbed the stairs to the baby's room, she found it "still and peaceful, the big French windows wide open, just the same

secure intimate room it was in that other world. I left the door open."
In her diary she wrote,

> This place does not suggest crime now, but I realize here intensely what
> I am realizing at Englewood more and more: that the new baby will not
> make any difference to me in this feeling I have for Charlie. I thought
> vaguely that it would be better after the baby came, but it won't be at all.
> It won't change things. I'll miss him just as much. The feeling for the
> new baby will grow up separately, a lovely, different thing, alongside of
> this feeling. I'll live with that always, always all my life, only it will be
> perhaps easier to live with because it will be more and more separate
> from my daily life. I don't want it to be otherwise.

Inevitably, her sadness and depression intensified once they began
living in the house where such horror had taken place. Her dreams became filled with vivid images of the dead: Charlie, "condemned to die,"
running toward her, with his golden curls tangled; herself, in a rare show
of anger, raging at the people who were about to take him away; her
father, sitting in his chair, humorously demanding a kiss. In the dream,
she started toward her father reluctantly as she had as a young girl, but
soon realized that she wouldn't always be able to kiss him — that all
too soon he would be dead. "And I went towards him lovingly and
looked at his eyes and thought how beautiful they were — how they
were *His Eyes,* brimming over with blue and twinkle (that brimming
over quality I had forgotten) — and I loved him and kissed him."

During the next few days, her feelings about the house grew even
darker, and she realized that she would never be able to live there again
because she would always be reliving in her mind the fateful night
when her son was killed. And yet, she kept telling herself, it was such a
wonderfully planned house, with such beautiful surroundings, and she
wondered whether she and Charles could ever bring themselves to
leave it. She tried to convince herself that "this is another house now —
one in which there was tragedy years and years ago."

From a practical point of view, there was still their safety to consider,
and this question continued to prey on Lindbergh's mind. He toyed
with the idea of hiring an armed guard or obtaining trained police dogs
to guard the property. Although earlier he had refused to accept the
two guard dogs that had been sent to him, one Sunday he and Anne
traveled to Princeton to visit Joseph Weber, a breeder and trainer of
German shepherds. After looking over the Weber kennels, Lindbergh
fell in love with a big, ferocious animal that Weber said hated strangers.

To test the dog, Lindbergh tried to pat him and, to his delight, was greeted by a growl.

Anne and Charles bought the dog, and a few days later the trainer brought him to Hopewell. After working with Weber for several days, Lindbergh was able to persuade the dog to accept him as his master. But Anne was the member of the family to whom the dog, eventually named Thor, was the most devoted. He never let her out of his sight. "The devotion of this dog following me everywhere is quite thrilling, like having a new beau," she observed.

In July the trial of Curtis ended. The boat builder was found guilty of obstructing justice and sentenced to a year in jail and a one-thousand-dollar fine. (Later, his jail sentence was suspended and he only had to pay the fine.)

As soon as the trial was over, the Lindberghs left Hopewell and returned to Englewood. Even though they now had Thor to protect them, Lindbergh was still uneasy about his family's security at their country retreat. He decided it would be best for them to reside again at Next Day Hill, where they would be safe from intrusive reporters and the prying public. For the aviator, who had flown alone across the Atlantic but now could not guarantee his family's safety, it must have been a humiliating prospect to have to retreat to his mother-in-law's home.

Late on Monday night, August 15, 1932, Anne's labor pains started. She, Lindbergh, and her mother were driven from Englewood to her family's magnificently appointed apartment overlooking Central Park. They arrived there at around 4:30 in the morning and were soon joined by an obstetrician, an anesthetist, and a nurse. In a remarkable diary entry, Anne conveyed her feelings about giving birth for the second time under such bizarre circumstances, and about her quest for the meaning of existence. Crying uncontrollably, in physical pain when she wasn't rendered unconscious by the gas, Anne was sustained throughout her labor only by the presence of her husband and her overwhelming love for him.

> I always knew whether C. was in the room or not, a second or two before I woke and found my eyes drawn inevitably to his. I *had* to turn to him; it was the one compelling thing in me, like Thor leaping pell-mell over things to get to me — a blind instinct. Sometimes my hand in his was the first thing to come back to life — my hand in his; while I was still blind and deaf and dumb, I could feel his forefinger stroking my wrist. Like the first tip of rock rising above the receding flood of unconsciousness.

Anne was in labor for four hours, a much shorter labor than she had had with Charlie. When she woke from the anesthetic and learned that she had given birth to a boy, her first thought was that the infant might be defective. After being assured by the nurse that he was perfectly normal, she murmured something about always having wanted Charlie to have a brother, breaking down in tears when the nurse brusquely reminded her that Charlie was dead and that she should start concentrating her attention on her new baby.

To her disappointment, the infant, who had inherited her rather large and fleshy "Morrow" nose, seemed not half as handsome as Charlie. Yet, gazing at the same Lindbergh dimple in his chin that Charlie had possessed, she suddenly felt as if "a door to life opened. I *wanted* to live, I felt power to live. I was not afraid of death or life; a spell had been broken, the spell over us that made me dread everything and feel that nothing would go right after this. The spell was broken by this real, tangible, perfect baby, coming into an imperfect world and coming out of the teeth of sorrow — a miracle. My faith had been reborn."

But her new faith wasn't as easy to sustain as she had hoped. Comparisons of the living second son with the dead first one were inevitable, and she alternated between love and adoration for her new son, and grief and despair for her lost one.

Anne tried to keep the two children separate in her mind, but it wasn't easy. Her nickname for Charlie had been "the fat lamb"; for the new baby, it was "my little rabbit," inspired by his soft brown hair and rabbit's nose. Still, sometimes she and Mrs. Morrow slipped and called him "Charlie."

"I find I am thinking of this baby as though he *were* the other baby starting again," she noted in her journal. "And sometimes think half-madly, 'How lovely it will be when he is big again. . . . How lovely when he knows me again.' Then I fight it and say, 'No, this is another child. I must not try to see Charlie in him.' "

Although Anne wrote in her diary and to her correspondents about the new baby's development, she did not mention him with the same kind of maternal delight that she had in describing Charlie's progress as an infant. There was a guarded quality to her entries and letters, as if she were afraid that if she wholeheartedly accepted her new son, not only would she be betraying Charlie but her second child would die too. At the same time, she desperately wanted to love the baby for himself, to treat him as an individual, his own person.

The Lindberghs did not name their second son until the middle of October, two months after his birth. They called him Jon. The regular contraction of "Jonathan," Jon was a name they had come across in a Scandinavian history book and decided would be perfect for their son, after rejecting John, because it was too common a name, and Carl, which they felt sounded too much like Charles. In addition, Carl was a name they had called Charlie for a few months. In an attempt to free both themselves and their new son from the cruel, overshadowing past, they deliberately chose a name with no associations.

But the murder of their son continued to haunt them, and they remained fearful that Jon would be doomed by the same kind of publicity that had killed Charlie. In a plea for his family's privacy, Lindbergh issued a statement to the press shortly after the baby's birth:

> Mrs. Lindbergh and I have made our home in New Jersey. It is natural that we should wish to continue to live there near our friends and interests. Obviously, however, it is impossible for us to subject the life of our second son to the publicity which we feel was in large measure responsible for the death of our first. We feel that our children have the right to grow up normally with other children. Continued publicity will make this impossible. I am appealing to the Press to permit our children to live the lives of normal Americans.

Yet, even as he was making this statement, Lindbergh realized that it was impossible for reporters and the public to let them alone. When she went to buy a hat at Macy's, Anne was mobbed by shoppers offering condolences and suggestions on how to catch the kidnappers, who still remained at large. The Lindberghs, as well as Mrs. Morrow, continued to receive crank letters, and some unbalanced people, though harmless, tried to gain access to them through their servants — one demented soul even managed to call up at the baby nurse's window late at night.

As for the Hopewell house, the Lindberghs soon came to the sad conclusion that it would be unsafe for them to live there again, and Lindbergh began toying with the idea of turning it into a children's home. He broached the subject to Anne and Mrs. Morrow, who were both excited by the idea. They would form a nonprofit organization to benefit children, with themselves and several other prominent persons, including Mrs. Morrow, as trustees. Lindbergh's resolve was strengthened when he and Anne began receiving anonymous letters threatening to kidnap Jon. The house where Charlie had spent many happy hours was to "provide for the welfare of children, including their education, training, hospitalization, and other purposes, without discrimination in regard to race, color or creed." Their country retreat had never had a name, but now they decided to call it "High Fields," which Anne wrote to her mother had "a secret second meaning," possibly referring to Charlie's pet name for his father, "Hi."

Aside from Jon's birth, the only bright spot during this turbulent period was Elisabeth's engagement in November 1932. During her summer visit to England, Elisabeth had met and fallen in love with Aubrey Niel Morgan, a man who was in many ways the antithesis of her brother-in-law. Tall and plain, Morgan was a middle-aged Welshman whose family owned David Morgan, Ltd., a large department store in Cardiff. His appearance notwithstanding, Morgan was intelligent and charming. Mrs. Morrow adored him, and even Lindbergh, who thought most of the British overcivilized and effete, liked him immediately.

In late August 1932, Elisabeth returned home to Englewood. Gazing at her sister, with her healthy-looking tan and new Greta Garbo–like coif, Anne could not help thinking how well she looked. The doctors' grim prognosis seemed unreal. Despite their past competitiveness, Anne was genuinely delighted by the news of her sister's approaching marriage. In her opinion, Elisabeth was "made" for marriage and domesticity. "No career would ever satisfy her," she reported to her mother-in-law, a remark that perhaps revealed more about herself than her sister.

Undoubtedly, for Anne, Elisabeth's impending marriage came as a relief, for a variety of reasons. Although still in desperately poor health, despite her tan, Elisabeth was not going to be denied a woman's life. If the doctors were correct and she was soon going to die, at least she would go to her grave knowing what life was all about — as it did for Anne and many women of her generation, this meant being married and having children. A career, although considered a noble pursuit, took second place.

Elisabeth's marriage also meant that she would no longer pose as much of a threat to Anne and her relationship with Lindbergh. Presumably, the fulfillment the older woman would experience in her own marriage would make her less envious of her sister's good fortune, and, as a safely married woman, less likely to be attractive to her brother-in-law.

Three days after Christmas, on December 28, 1932, Elisabeth married
Aubrey Morgan at Next Day Hill. All the surviving members of the Mor-
row-Lindbergh families were present, although it is unclear whether
Charles Lindbergh attended the ceremony.

That morning Anne breakfasted in her sister's bedroom. It was Elisabeth's last morning as a single woman. What the two sisters talked
about we do not know, but we do know that the bride-to-be was in such a
state of high excitement and nerves that she petulantly refused to eat
the breakfast that had been specially prepared for her.

That afternoon, seemingly collected, Elisabeth placed her pale, slender hand on the arm of her brother, Dwight, who was to give her away.
Together, brother and sister glided into an enormous room of the Morrow mansion, which had been tastefully decorated for the occasion with
potted trees and ferns. Among the distinguished wedding guests were
J. P. Morgan and Jean Monnet, the French political economist. In a
compellingly written diary entry, which would serve as the basis for one
of her later books, *Dearly Beloved,* Anne described not only the wedding scene but her conflicting thoughts about the sister who bewitched
and bedeviled her:

> This was the old Elisabeth as I thought of her — her straightness and
> her clarity and her radiance. This was the sharp blue flame of Elisabeth. I
> remember as a child watching the flame of a candle suddenly soar to a
> height two or three times its normal size, a strong smooth spear of flame
> soaring, and I would watch with bated breath. And this was Elisabeth.
> Here and now, this beauty, this radiance — this is the essence of Elisa-
> beth; not as with most brides one says, "Doesn't she make a lovely
> *bride!*" I wanted to say, "Doesn't she make a lovely Elisabeth!" This was
> the *real* Elisabeth — not that person we had watched at the table, fuss-
> ing over food, refusing eggs. This was the real Elisabeth. The veil, the
> train, the band of orange blossoms in her hair, the color in her cheeks,
> her slim body in a sheath of satin.

Next Day Hill was crowded with wedding guests, and there was music, gaiety, and laughter. Despite her cold, Elisabeth seemed the picture
of good health, but when Anne gazed at her sister's radiant face, she
was reminded of a painting that had hung in their previous home in
Englewood. It was of a young woman who had died shortly before she
was to be married.

Despite Jon's birth and Elisabeth's wedding, Anne continued to be
plagued by morbid thoughts. By January 1933 she was close to a nervous

breakdown. Although she continued to write in her journal, her entries were disjointed and emotionless, the thoughts and impressions of a deeply depressed person. At night, her despair worsened. She suffered recurrent nightmares about the kidnapping. On awakening, her immediate thought was, if only she had been able to prevent it.

> *It did not happen* and *It Happened.* For I go over the possibilities of its not happening — so close, so narrow they are. So hard do I think about it that almost I make it unhappen. . . . Then, at last, back to the only comfort — Death: We will all have it. In a century this distance between him and me will be nothing.
> And then: He did not suffer, he did not know, a blow on the head.
> But I want to know — to know just what he suffered — I want to see it, to feel it even.

The first anniversary of Charlie's death, March 1, 1933, was agony. The passage of a year made the baby seem so far away, and she wanted to keep him a tangible presence, not have him fade further and further away into memory. "The punctuation of anniversaries is terrible, like the closing of doors, one after another between you and what you want to hold on to," she mourned in her diary.

Anne's unremitting anguish, coupled with guilt and remorse over her son's death, and Lindbergh's rigid control over his emotions were not unusual under the circumstances. Today we know that many other victims of violent crime suffer the same symptoms, which may include a sense of helplessness, rage, persistent preoccupation with the crime, and loss of belief that the world is a safe and just place. In Charles Lindbergh's case, the murder of his son must have had the devastating effect of making him feel powerless, an uncomfortable feeling for most men, but in his case magnified by the fact that he was so famous and that he had always prided himself on his vigilance in the air, his ability to foresee disaster and to take preventive measures against it. In a matter of minutes, one of the United States' most celebrated heroes had become its most memorable victim, and Lindbergh must have felt like a supreme failure. On that fateful March night, he, who was so invincible in the sky, had been unable to protect his own family. A stranger had entered his house and stolen his son while he was conversing downstairs with his wife about the day's trivial events. It was no wonder that Lindbergh, a self-absorbed individual as well as a loving father, attempted to solve the case himself, often interfering with police efforts. It was not only his son he was trying to regain, but his own sense of mastery.

In Anne and Charles's day, there were no psychiatrists who specialized in the therapy of victims of violent crime, no nationwide groups like Parents of Murdered Children or the National Organization for Victim Assistance in Washington, D.C., to offer counsel and advice. But even if such organizations had existed, it is unlikely that Anne and Charles, given their unique station in life, would have availed themselves of their services. For comfort and support, they had to look to their families and a few close friends, whose love and understanding, Anne said later, helped her achieve her own eventual recovery. She also had her own emotionally strong husband to lean on, for throughout the tragedy, she and Lindbergh supported and strengthened each other. The couple was unusual in this regard. Today, we know that many marital relationships collapse after a family member becomes the victim of a violent assault. At precisely the time when they should be closest, men and women begin to experience severe conflicts in their marriage. Often; they separate or divorce. Many factors are responsible, but in some cases one partner blames the other for not preventing the crime or for not openly confessing his or her deepest feelings about the fate that both have shared. In other cases, one partner may become obsessed with what has happened, while the other wants to forget the catastrophe as soon as possible. Sometimes, in order to make sense of the tragedy, a crime victim will invent a new personality as well as a new set of values, so that a husband or wife has trouble adjusting to the changes.

Anne vented her feelings in her diary and her letters to her mother, sisters, and mother-in-law, while Charles, by nature stoical and reticent, kept a tight rein on his emotions. No evidence exists that he ever broke down and wept over the death of his son. Instead, he appears to have been a pillar of strength to his grieving, heartbroken wife. It was he, and not she, who had both the fortitude and sense of detachment that enabled him to identify their child's decomposed body by examining the teeth. As his daughter Reeve commented many years later, "I thought, my God, how could you do this at such a time, and then I thought immediately, that's exactly what he would do . . . He wouldn't be able to dissolve in grief, or weep and wail, or even talk about it, but he could examine carefully and clinically, and that was his strength and, some people felt, his weakness, but that was certainly the way he got through his life."

For many men and women forced to confront a tragedy, this difference in expressing their emotions ultimately wedges them apart. Fortunately, for the Lindberghs, this did not happen. In fact, the death of their child appears to have drawn them even closer. Possibly, their continued, deepening affection for each other was made possible by their ability, from the beginning of their relationship, to accept the differences in their emotional makeup and draw strength from them.

But even their abiding love for each other could not heal the festering wound. Essentially, Anne and Charles Lindbergh would remain victims for the rest of their lives. Like other victims of violent crime, they would try to invent new personalities for themselves and embrace new values that their friends and the world would find strange and puzzling. And they would experience a similar degree of horror, rage, and helplessness, leading to a messianic sense of historic mission, whenever they were confronted with any global event that reminded them of their own devastating loss.

CHAPTER 10

"Where Is My World?"

SINCE HER SON'S KIDNAPPING, Anne had not had the heart to go flying. However, in late March 1933, a little more than a year after Charlie's death, she left seven-month-old Jon in the care of her mother and a detail of the New Jersey State Police and flew with Lindbergh to California to pick up their Lockheed monoplane *Sirius*, which had been repaired at the Lockheed factory in Burbank. The plane had undergone a transformation since they had last seen it in the fall of 1931, ignominiously flipped over on its side in the Yangtze River. It was now smartly repainted red and black, and boasted a bigger and more powerful engine.

Another purpose of the Lindberghs' flight to California was to confirm a route for a cargo plane service that Transcontinental Air Transport was inaugurating.

In the past, flying had had a calming and inspirational effect on Anne, and this journey was no exception. "And over the earth a clear calm light, quiet. One could sit still and look at life — that was it. The glaze on life again, the glaze that art puts on life. Is that the fascination of flying?" she noted en route in her journal.

A few months later, on July 9, 1933, Anne and Charles were in the air again, taking off from Glenn Curtis Airport on Long Island on a second survey flight, which was to last five months, three times longer than the first one in 1931 and which would prove to be one of their most challenging adventures. When it was over, Lindbergh would comment that both these trips had been far "more dangerous" than flying the Atlantic solo.

The Lindberghs were to survey possible transatlantic air routes and bases for Pan American Airways, with the hope that the data they collected would enable Juan Trippe to open up a regular passenger service. Their thirty-thousand-mile route took them to four continents and thirty-one countries and colonies, including Greenland, Iceland, Denmark, Sweden, Russia, England, Spain, Africa, and Brazil. From a technical viewpoint, the trip was an unqualified success; as an aviation expert commented recently, "Not only had they joined together the continents of the world for commercial aviation, but they had gone faster and farther than any other explorers in history." At its conclusion Lindbergh was able to advise Trippe that a transatlantic air route via Greenland and Iceland was in fact possible and could be successfully operated even in the summer months with the use of seaplanes. And Anne's skills as a navigator and radio operator were tested to their limits. During the trip, en route to the Cape Verde Islands, off the coast of West Africa, she made contact with a ground station at Sayville, Long Island, establishing a world record of over three thousand miles for radio communication between an airplane and a ground station.

By this time, the Lindberghs were not the only married flying couple to capture the imagination of the public. On July 23, 1933, almost two weeks after the Lindberghs departed on their second survey flight, Captain James A. Mollison and his wife, Amy Johnson, two famous British aviators who individually had set many records, took off in their plane, *Seafarer,* to fly nonstop from Pendine, Wales, to New York. Although they crossed the Atlantic successfully, they were forced down after thirty-nine hours in the air at Bridgeport, Connecticut, almost in sight of Floyd Bennett Field, their objective. The plane, with Jim Mollison in control, overshot the landing field and nosed over in a ditch. For an experienced pilot who had successfully crossed the Atlantic, it was an ignominious end to what should have been a victorious trip. In the crash, their plane was demolished, and both flying Mollisons, as they were called, were injured. They were taken by airplane to a local hospital and then recovered in style at New York's Plaza Hotel in twin beds that had been pushed together.

Unlike the Lindberghs, the Mollisons were highly competitive with each other, and their crash was the result of an argument. As the flight neared its end, the couple began to disagree about the best way to land, and Jim, who refused to relinquish the controls to Amy, became so distracted that he bungled the landing. Later, there were rumors of heavy drinking, mutual infidelity (Mollison, whose nickname was "Brandy Jim," numbered among his lovers their good friend the aviator Beryl Markham), and terrible arguments that culminated in Mollison's beating up Amy so badly that their bathroom resembled "a slaughterhouse." Divorced in 1937, the two pilots went their individual ways, with Amy preparing for an around-the-world flight, which she never had the opportunity to make. In 1941 the plane she was delivering for the RAF developed engine problems above an estuary of the Thames, and she parachuted out and drowned.

In contrast to the volatile Mollisons, James and Mary Haizlip had a far more harmonious flying partnership. Like the Lindberghs, the Haizlips were madly in love with each other and with flying. Each was a speed demon, Jim winning the Bendix Trophy in the 1932 National Air Races when he flew from Los Angeles to New York in a record-breaking ten hours and nineteen minutes, Mary when she broke the women's world speed record in a Wedell-Williams race plane in 1933. Her plane was filled with 100 octane gasoline, which no pilot had used before, and the reporters and the crowd gathered on the airfield to see her off were convinced that it would explode. Like Charles Lindbergh, Jim Haizlip was a crack pilot who taught his wife how to fly. There was an important difference between the two flying couples, however. Lindbergh trained Anne to become his copilot and navigator so that she would be able to take over if anything happened to him in the air, while Haizlip turned Mary into a first-class pilot who broke records on her own. He was so obsessed with improving her racing speed that he continued to drill her long after they had left the airfield. As Mary later admitted to a reporter, "I may have been the only bride ever to learn about racing airplanes in the bedroom. Using a length of string looped around our bedpost, Jim would go over his strategy clearly and precisely, using the bedpost as the pylon."

Although the Mollisons and the Haizlips were well-known flying couples, neither boasted the Lindberghs' enormous fame and popular appeal. This was something of an oversight, because, as pilots, both Amy Johnson and Mary Haizlip were far more technically skilled and experienced than Anne. As Anne herself was the first to admit, it was her association with the world's most famous pilot that boosted her status with both the public and the aviation community. Nevertheless, by helping her husband chart new transatlantic air routes, which paved the way for commercial airline passenger service (and are still in use today), she herself was also regarded as an aviation pioneer. On March 31, 1934, the National Geographic Society honored her with its highest award, the prestigious Hubbard Gold Medal, for her achievements as copilot and radio operator during the 1933 intercontinental survey flight. Anne was the first woman to receive this award, which had previously been given to nine men, among them her husband and Admiral Richard E. Byrd, for their geographic achievements.

During the many months they were gone from home, Anne did not see Jon, who at the time of her departure was not quite a year old. Before she left, she sequestered the child at the Morrows' summer retreat in North Haven, where his every move was constantly monitored by Betty Gow, an armed guard, and Charles's mother, who had come east to help.

Why would a mother whose son had been murdered allow herself to be parted for so many months from her second child, especially when she knew his life might be in jeopardy? Since Anne was a caring, thoughtful mother, the only explanation that seems plausible has to do with her reluctance to be separated from her husband for such a long period. Clearly, Lindbergh's career, with which she was now closely associated, and their own private relationship took priority over caring for her new son. But there was also another possible reason why Anne chose to entrust her child to the care of others and accompany her husband on so long and distant a journey. Still deeply depressed about Charlie's death, she may have hoped that the trip, with its technical involvements, fast-paced schedule, and exposure to new places and people, might take her mind off the tragedy.

In the past Anne had always felt that there was "something binding about flying together, because it is such a lonely thing. One is so dependent on the other person, the experiences are so *peculiarly* one's own." But on this occasion, being in the air with her husband failed to work its customary magic. She brooded unceasingly about Charlie, becoming engulfed by despair in Greenland when she lost a small comb with which he had played, and she keenly missed Jon whenever her mother or Betty Gow wrote or sent pictures of him. Most of these maternal yearnings she was forced to keep to herself, for Lindbergh was too preoccupied with the technical aspects of the trip to empathize. When a relative sent Anne some photographs of Jon, he dryly commented, "Very bad for you to look at these."

Although Anne's marriage still remained the center of her life, some aspects of her relationship to Charles had begun to rankle her, especially the fact that many people were nice to her only because they wanted to meet the world-famous aviator. "Damn, damn, damn! I am sick of being this 'handmaid to the Lord,'" she wrote in her diary. "They think they can wangle *me,* if they can't get at him, make up to me. . . . Where is my world and will I ever find it?"

Struggling to find her own identity, she was nevertheless aware that she could never be fulfilled by a career in aviation. Even if it had been her ambition to become a pilot, she knew that she did not possess the talent or skill to compete professionally with her husband or with any of his famous female colleagues, such as Amelia Earhart, Amy Johnson, Mary Haizlip, or Ruth Nicols, who flew solo or were breaking world records for distance flying. "But in C.'s world I would *not* survive, except for him, and I am afraid of being exposed. I feel insecure. I would like to stand alone once, in that world. I don't know why I want to prove I can. I indulge in dreams of saving the situation, but of course I could not. I would be the first to have to be pulled out, the weak link."

By "weak link," Anne meant the sheer physical terror she had begun to experience in dangerous flying situations. Although she had formerly been fearless in a plane, after her son's murder the hazards of flying became all too real for her. No longer was she shielded by the "magical thinking" that both she and her husband were invulnerable.

As far as dangers went, the Lindberghs' second survey flight was especially taxing. Often the weather was extremely hazardous, and the couple had to cope with every kind of atmospheric condition, from hurricanes to snowstorms. For Anne, dense fog, which was considered the pilot's nightmare, was especially frightening, and on this particular trip, there were many times when they were flying blind. "I . . . am in a panic the whole time, and every time we go through a day like that I think I cannot go on with that kind of life. Of course, when we get down C. says we never were in a bad position. I do trust him perfectly and know that he is very careful and does not take chances, but it is a kind of uncontrollable physical terror, exaggerated by imagination."

In reality, Anne's fear of flying was well founded. In the late twenties and thirties, pilots were still dying in crashes with depressing regularity. Florence Klingensmith, a willowy Grace Kelly–type blonde, crashed and died when the fabric suddenly ripped off her wing during a traditionally male air race in Chicago in 1930. Officials may have blamed her death on the fact that she was a woman — from then on, female pilots were barred from participating in the race — but sex had nothing to do with the tragic demise of William ("Big Bill") Hopson. A man with a physique like a Mack truck, Hopson had joined the airmail service in 1920 and pioneered the transcontinental route, only to die in a crash in Pennsylvania before the decade was finished. Many other adventurous men and women shared Klingensmith's and Hopson's untimely, fiery end, as aviators in fragile machines, equipped with primitive instruments, strove to fly farther and faster.

Lindbergh appears to have brushed aside his wife's fears. He merely looked annoyed when she passed one of her frantic notes to him where he was seated in the first cockpit. The irritated look on his face implied that he felt she was questioning his skill as a pilot, which made her feel more unworthy and guilt-ridden than usual. "I can't have him feel that way. No, he smiles now — that is better. I feel better. I will shut my eyes and have faith in him."

En route Anne and Charles received the news that Elisabeth, who was living with Aubrey in a rented house in Wales, was again in poor health. She had suffered another heart attack, and her British physicians were advising that she spend at least a year in a more clement climate. Elisabeth was debating whether she and Aubrey should move to Bermuda or to California. In a letter mailed during a stopover, Anne advised her sister to choose California, in particular the area near Santa Barbara, which she felt would be near not only many first-rate physicians in Los Angeles but also many beautiful, interesting places. The Morgans decided on Pasadena, however, which Anne privately thought was a mistake, as, in her opinion, the city wasn't nearly as scenic as Santa Barbara.

The Morgans were soon to set sail for the United States, but before they departed the Lindberghs visited them in Wales in early October. Anne was relieved to find Elisabeth in better health than she had imagined, although she was alarmed by how much weight her older sister had lost. However, during their visit, the doctors informed Elisabeth that she was dangerously ill. In an attempt to ease the stress on her severely damaged heart, they confined her to complete bed rest. Anne was deeply upset by the thought of her sister's having to spend a year in bed and not being well enough to move to California. In her mind, it spelled Elisabeth's death sentence. "All this visit I felt as though something were hanging over us. I couldn't let go. Not only our trip back, which I have been dreading, but Elisabeth's. If she can get to California — if she can just get there all right. We are *always* saying that," she confided despairingly to her diary.

Her mood did not improve upon their return home, when social obligations again crowded in on her, as did concerns about Jon, who was proving to be a headstrong, difficult child. One glance at the avalanche of toys he had collected during her absence convinced her that, contrary to her instructions, he had been spoiled and indulged by his caretakers. By then she had formed a definite plan for his upbringing — she wanted him to become as independent and courageous as his father and grandfather — but whenever she tried to broach the subject to her mother, Mrs. Lindbergh, and Betty Gow, they all made it plain that they knew far more about child-raising than she.

In the winter of 1934, she and Charles, in yet another attempt to break free of their dependence on Mrs. Morrow, rented a small penthouse apartment in New York. Although both Lindberghs disliked the fast pace as well as the confinement of city life, for Anne it was a time of stimulation and creativity. Not only did she complete the first draft of her book about their first survey flight to the Orient, but she also began working on an article about their recently completed survey flight for the *National Geographic.*

During this period, when she spent a good deal of time caring for him, Anne finally accepted Jon as an individual. No longer did she constantly compare him to Charlie or confuse him with his deceased brother. Obviously now doting on him, she wrote to one of her correspondents, "Jon seems so wonderful to me that I can hardly believe it. I am more thankful every day to have him." Undoubtedly sensing for the first time that his mother truly loved him for himself, Jon responded by becoming calmer and less clinging.

After returning from their second survey flight, the Lindberghs donated the *Sirius* (which they had renamed the *Tingmissartoq,* Eskimo for "the one who flies like a big bird") to the American Museum of Natural History in New York. As a replacement they decided to purchase a single-engine, high-wing monoplane from the Monocorpe Corporation in St. Louis. In September they flew to the Midwest to pick it up and then to California for a visit with Elisabeth and Aubrey, who were staying for several weeks at Will Rogers's ranch.

When she saw her sister, Anne was relieved to see how well she looked. In fact, Elisabeth's health had improved to the point where the doctors thought she might be able to visit her mother in Cuernavaca, where Mrs. Morrow was planning to spend part of the winter.

On the evening of September 19, while the couple was still visiting Elisabeth and Aubrey at Will Rogers's ranch, Lindbergh was summoned to the telephone. His caller was Colonel Norman Schwarzkopf, head of the New Jersey State Police, and the colonel gave him some incredible news. A man named Bruno Hauptmann, a thirty-six-year-old German-born carpenter who lived in the Bronx, had just been arrested and charged with the kidnapping and murder of the Lindberghs' son.

Hauptmann, Schwarzkopf said, had been arrested several days after giving Walter Lyle, an attendant at a Warner-Quinlan gas station in the Bronx, a $10 gold certificate. The use of gold certificates was then illegal, for President Roosevelt on April 3, 1933, in an attempt to combat the Depression, had ordered all persons possessing gold notes to exchange them for silver certificates. Both the management of Warner-Quinlan and the New York police had asked the attendants to be on the lookout for gold notes and to write down the license number of every customer who paid with a suspicious bill. When the owner of the dark blue Dodge sedan paid Lyle with a $10 gold note, the attendant jotted down the license plate number, 4U-13-41, on the back of the bill.

Another attendant, John Lyons, then took the $10 gold note, along with other receipts, to the Corn Exchange Bank at 125th Street and Park Avenue, where an alert teller compared its serial number to those on the Lindbergh ransom list, which had been sent to all banks in the country. Discovering that it did in fact match one of the numbers on the published list, he immediately contacted the Justice Department's Division of Investigation in New York.

When agents called the New York State Motor Vehicle Bureau, they learned that the car belonged to a Richard Hauptmann, 1279 East 222nd Street, in the Bronx. Searching the small frame-and-stucco house, police found $13,760 more of the ransom money bundled up in newspapers behind the walls of the garage.

When he was arrested, Hauptmann insisted that he had had nothing to do with the crime — the money had been given to him in a shoebox by one Isidor Fisch, a fellow German who was a fur trader and with whom Hauptmann had been a partner in several fur deals. Fisch, he said, had left the shoestring-tied box with him for safekeeping when he went to visit his parents in Germany. And where was Fisch now, the police asked? His health wasn't very good, Hauptmann told them, and he had died of tuberculosis in Leipzig six months earlier. Hauptmann also maintained that he had not learned what was in the shoebox until recently. When Fisch first gave it to him, he kept it in a closet in his house. He had forgotten all about it until one day he accidentally hit the box with a broom, and when gold certificates fell out he took the money out and wrapped it in newspapers and hid the bundles behind the walls of his garage. A few days later, however, he started to spend some of it. Fisch, he maintained, still owed him some money from two loans Hauptmann had given him when he had had some bad luck in the stock market. Despite Hauptmann's protestations that he hadn't known it was the ransom money, Schwarzkopf assured Lindbergh that they had the right man.

Although they had only been in California for four days, Anne and Charles cut their trip short and immediately returned to Englewood. Eleven days later, on September 28, Anne dashed off a note to her mother-in-law, which merely stated, "This is just a note at midnight to tell you that this man you read about in the papers is beyond doubt one of the right people. What may develop we don't know." It was the only mention she made in her diary of Bruno Hauptmann's arrest.

Her lack of curiosity about the man whom the police had charged with the murder of her son seems puzzling. Most parents of murdered children are obsessed with knowing everything about the killer and his motives. In contrast, Anne seems to have preferred to know as few details about Hauptmann as possible, although it is important to point out that, judging from the contents of her note, she seems to have believed that he had not committed the crime alone.

In late August 1934, with the trial of Bruno Hauptmann only five months off, the Lindberghs left their Manhattan penthouse and once more retreated to Next Day Hill. When Anne's friends asked her why they had given up the apartment, she replied that it was because their landlord had raised the rent, a lame excuse, considering that they could well afford it. The truth of the matter was that at the respective ages of thirty-two and twenty-eight, Charles and Anne were still emotionally dependent on Mrs. Morrow. Despite Lindbergh's daring aerial exploits and Anne's literary pursuits, they both had trouble coping with daily life and family responsibilities. And as is so often the case with people who cannot seem to establish an independent life for themselves, they began to resent the person on whom they were dependent. Anne began to use her diary as an outlet for her feelings of irritation with her mother, whom she felt could never be alone and had to fill her days with incessant good works and socializing. It was a shame, she thought, that Mrs. Morrow couldn't be quiet and reflective like her and Charles, and that she had permitted Next Day Hill, with its constant stream of visitors, to become more like a hotel than a home.

But Anne's conflicts with her vivacious, on-the-go mother had a more profound basis than a mere difference in their personalities and lifestyles. The indefatigable Mrs. Morrow, who had started writing poetry and children's books after her husband's death, remained an influential figure in public affairs, one whom her daughter wanted both to emulate and to compete with, and yet simultaneously break free of. By marrying Charles Lindbergh, Anne had hoped that she would at last be able to break away from her loving but dominating family and find her own identity, yet she discovered after several years of marriage to an equally supportive but controlling man that she was still bedeviled by many of her old conflicts. Like her family, he both sustained and trapped her. This inability to find and maintain her own identity was summed up in a brief diary entry in which she noted that her life was an "eternal struggle of what I must be for C., and what I must be for Mother, and what I must be for myself."

This constant inner struggle not only affected her relationship with her husband and her mother, but would animate much of her future literary work.

CHAPTER 11

"The Geisha"

IF IT WAS PEACE AND SECLUSION the Lindberghs were seeking at Next Day Hill, they could not have picked a worse time to visit. The mansion resounded with the noise of servants rearranging the furniture, vacuuming the hallways, and cleaning the silver, as the usually unflappable Mrs. Morrow rushed around, snapping out orders. When Anne asked her mother what was going on, she was told that Harold Nicolson, the well-known English biographer and diplomat, was coming to stay at Next Day Hill for the next several months.

That past June, Mrs. Morrow, through Teddy Grenfell, of Morgan, Grenfell and Company, the London financial house associated with J. P. Morgan in New York, had written a letter to Nicolson, the author of well-received biographies of Alfred, Lord Tennyson, and Lord Carnock, his distinguished diplomat father, asking if he would be interested in writing a biography of Dwight Morrow. According to Nicolson's son, Nigel Nicolson, Harold, although a well-known biographer, was not a very good choice. He had met Morrow only once, at the time of the London Naval Conference in 1930, and he had never met his widow, who still cherished her husband's memory and wanted the public to remember his achievements. "It was a brave gamble on her part to commission an Englishman," Nigel Nicolson later wrote,

> and Harold Nicolson was well aware of the double pitfall of misinterpreting American sentiment and upsetting his widow-patron. Besides, Morrow had spent much of his life with the firm of J. P. Morgan and Co., and finance had never been among Harold Nicolson's strongest sub-

jects. It would also mean a long absence in the United States. But he was attracted to the idea for precisely the same reason as had prompted Mrs. Morrow to invite him: it would give him a splendid opportunity to write about American diplomacy, and add a fourth volume to his diplomatic trilogy.

The Lindberghs departed for California in the midst of these frenzied preparations for Nicolson's visit, and when they returned to Englewood at the end of September they found the biographer already in residence. Although at first Anne felt shy and inferior, like a "country bumpkin," in the presence of the distinguished, cultured Englishman, she soon found that he was not as formidable as he appeared. "He is a quiet man, a little hard to tell whether he is shy or bored — perhaps a little of both. However, he has turned out to be kind and understanding. . . . [He] gets on with every member of the household with the utmost tact. I think he is getting a little tired of the intensity of the household. C. is the only person who is not intense."

This was not Nicolson's first exposure to the celebrated couple. He and his wife, the novelist and poet Vita Sackville-West, had come to the United States on a lecture tour in January 1933 and had met the Lindberghs at a party at the Waldorf Astoria.

For Nicolson, who had heard the rumors that Lindbergh was a stupid, uneducated, boorish, and difficult man, his first meeting with the aviator had come as a delightful "surprise." Writing down his impressions, he described Lindbergh as a man with

> much more in his face than appears in photographs. He has a fine intellectual forehead, a shy engaging smile, wind-blown hair, a way of tossing his head unhappily, a transparent complexion, thin nervous capable fingers, a loose-jointed shy manner. He looks young with a touch of arrested development. His wife is tiny, shy, timid, retreating, rather interested in books, a tragedy at the corner of her mouth. One thinks of what they have been through and is shy to meet them.

At his second meeting with the couple, Nicolson sharpened his observations:

> Anne like a Geisha — shy, Japanese, clever, gentle, obviously an adorable little person. Charles Lindbergh — slim (though a touch of chubbiness about the cheek), school-boyish, yet with those delicate prehensile hands which disconcert one's view of him as an inspired mechanic. They were smiling shyly. Lindbergh's hand was resting upon the collar of a

dog. I had heard about that dog. He has figured prominently in American newspapers. He is a police dog of enormous proportions. His name is Thor . . .

But Nicolson rapidly discovered that Lindbergh, despite his unaffected manner, could be quite dull and prosaic. When asked a casual question during a conversation, he was often tediously laborious in his response, delivering what amounted to a treatise on the subject. Nevertheless, Nicolson managed to overlook this fault and continued to find him charming. In his opinion, the aviator was quite the opposite of his aloof and uncooperative public image.

"He [Lindbergh] is a very decent man," Nicolson wrote to Vita. "His reputation of sulkiness and bad manners is entirely due to his loathing of society. 'What I loathe most,' he said, 'is the silly women who bring their kids up to shake hands with me at railway stations. It is embarrassing for me and embarrassing for the kids. It makes me fair sick.' "

Yet there was something about his personality that eluded the biographer, that he could not easily sum up. "He amuses and puzzles me," Nicolson confided to his wife in another letter.

On the one hand he is a mechanic and quite uneducated. On the other hand he is shrewd and intelligent. He has also got a sense of humour. Mrs. Morrow mentioned that Mrs. Lamont, who is not air-minded, said that she would only fly if he took her up. "Now isn't that just like those old dames," he said. "Just because I flew alone to Purris [*sic*], they think I'm a safe pilot. That is just silly." He has an obsession about publicity and I agree with him. He told me that when Coolidge presented him with a medal after his Paris flight, he had to do it three times over — once in the President's study, which was the real occasion; and twice on the lawn of the White House for the movie cameras. "The first time," he said, "I was kind of moved by the thing. After all I was more or less of a kid at the time and it seemed sort of solemn to me to be given that thing by the President of the United States. But when we had to go through the whole damned show over again on the lawn — me standing sideways to the President and looking like an ass, I felt I couldn't stand for it. Coolidge didn't seem to care or notice. He repeated his speech twice over just in the same words. It seemed a charade to me . . ."

An odd thing. We have breakfast together. The papers are on the table. The Lindbergh case is still front-page news. It *must* mean something to him. Yet he never glances at them . . . It is not a pose. It is merely a determined habit of ignoring the Press. I like the man. I dare say he has his faults, but I have not yet found them. She is a little angel.

Later Lindbergh "opened his heart" to Nicolson about his and Anne's hatred of publicity, confessing that the worst aspect of the Hauptmann trial was that he was again in the news and that reporters were "persecuting" him.

On October 8, 1934, Lindbergh identified Hauptmann's voice as the one he had heard in early April at St. Raymond's Cemetery in the Bronx, when Dr. Condon had handed over the ransom money to the kidnapper. Still working on his biography in Englewood, Nicolson was astounded to note that

> this dramatic event did not record itself upon the life here. Lindbergh was at breakfast as usual and thereafter helped me to unload my Leica camera. He is very neat about such things and I am clumsy. He then said, "Well, I have got to go to Noo Yark [*sic*] — want a lift?" I said no. Then I worked hard at my files and at luncheon there was only Anne and me as Mrs. Morrow had gone to some charity committee. Towards the end of luncheon, Lindbergh arrived and we chatted quite gaily until coffee came. We had that in the sun parlor, and when it was over I rose to go. The moment I had gone I saw him (in the mirror) take her arm and lead her into the study. Obviously he was telling her what happened in the court. But they are splendid in the way that they never intrude this great tragedy on our daily lives. It is real dignity and restraint.

At one point during his visit, Harold Nicolson read Anne's article about the couple's second survey flight, "Flying Around the North Atlantic," which had been published in the September 1934 issue of the *National Geographic.* Prepared to read a dry, prosaic account of the trip, he was astounded by the vividness and sensitivity of her prose and voiced his enthusiasm to both its author and her husband.

"You should take another trip so that she can write another story, for the writing instinct, once it is started, is much stronger than the flying one," he told Lindbergh.

When she heard Nicolson's opinion of her work, Anne was so excited that she couldn't sleep that night. A distinguished English writer had just told her that she had real talent! Although she was loath to admit it, what a contrast his comments were to her husband's. Lindbergh may have encouraged his wife to write, but he frequently chastised her for frittering away her talent in long letters to her family and friends. In his opinion, she should be writing something more substantial that could be published. A college dropout, while Anne had been a prize-winning English student, he also insisted on editing her work. Although Anne often resented seeing his black pencil marks through her carefully chosen words, she characteristically never worked up the courage to tell him so. But here was Nicolson, a highly educated man and an excellent writer himself, not only encouraging her but, unlike her husband, not criticizing her effort. In her journal, she recorded her ecstatic reaction:

> It was a sudden recognition of something inside of me that I have believed in, from time to time, that has sometimes been coaxed out, often crushed, raised its head in rebellion, been forgotten about, hurt, smothered with false attention, that I have tried to ignore for fear of being hurt. "I can't write. Someone should kill this thing in me. Someone should tell me bluntly I can't write, send me back to children."
>
> But Mr. Nicolson said — implied — that it existed, that I should go on. And the Thing rose up inside of me and possessed me. For twenty-four hours I felt young and powerful. I felt life was not long enough for all I wanted to do, and I lay awake all night, my mind racing and my heart pounding.

Obviously, at this stage of her marriage, being the wife of Charles Lindbergh was not enough to sustain her. Although he remained the pivotal figure in her life, Anne longed to achieve something of her own. Writing might be the answer, her secret rebellion against being married to one of the most famous men in the world. Although she had always been unsure of her literary ability, despite winning all sorts of prizes in college, for the first time she felt that she possessed enough talent to become a professional writer.

Nicolson sent Anne's article to Sackville-West for her literary opinion, with the following astute description of its author:

> Anne is so modest and diffident, and was so anxious to appear scientific and geographical and un-stuntish. But underneath her modesty pierces, I think, something very real and literary. I want your opinion as I am urging her to write it up into a real book plus her other journey. (To China via Alaska in 1931). She says "Oh, yes, but the papers here would take it up as a Lindbergh stunt and spoil it all for me — and it was so lovely; you can't think how free one felt." . . . Please read it, first from a narrative point of view, and then more carefully from a literary point of view. And please send me your views as frankly as you can . . . I mean really frankly. . . . The question I want you to answer is "Do you not think this article ought to be expanded into a book and is of sufficient literary merit to justify Anne in writing a book and conquering her publicity complex?" I am sure that the answer is YES. But I may be under the

glamour of that mouselike modesty of Anne and that Staglike modesty of Charles. But oh my god what charming people!

To Nicolson's disappointment, Sackville-West did not share his enthusiasm.

> I've read Anne Lindbergh's article, and do you know I am afraid I can't see why you got so excited about its literary value? Of course, as a *story* it is thrilling, but even so I am not sure that it would stand being expanded into a book. I do not think one wants to read too much of adventure, unless it is written as well as, say *Brazilian Adventure;* and her style is in no way comparable. It seems to me just an adequate style, but rather flat and without much vividness. . . . Apart from this, the simplicity and modesty are of course most endearing.

In the middle of November, while Nicolson was still at Englewood, Elisabeth developed acute appendicitis as she was flying from California to Mexico for a winter vacation with her mother. The plane had to make an emergency landing in California, and she was rushed to a nearby hospital. Her appendix was removed, and she seemed to be making an uneventful recovery, when suddenly, a short time later, she contracted bronchial pneumonia.

When Elisabeth's husband, Aubrey, called Mrs. Morrow, still in New Jersey, to tell her of her daughter's critical condition, a violent autumnal storm was brewing on the East Coast. But the stalwart Mrs. Morrow could not be dissuaded from flying from Newark to Pasadena to be with her eldest daughter, who was fighting for her life in an oxygen tent.

It was one more tragedy for this seemingly doomed family to endure, and Nicolson detailed his admiration for Mrs. Morrow in a letter to his wife, dated November 23, 1934:

> Some terrible fate does certainly hang over this family. Elisabeth, who had survived her appendicitis, has now developed pneumonia. They have telephoned for Betty Morrow to fly there. She leaves in an hour. I feel quite bruised with pity for her. She seems so lonely in her misery, poor little thing. I do admire that woman. She never breaks down under these blows. For the first time tonight she mentioned the baby and in such a pathetic way. I said something about her control and courage. "Courage?" she said. "Do you know that I cry about that baby of ours every night even now. That is not *courage!*"
>
> I wrote the above last night . . . but I was really upset by this tragedy. Lindbergh got back and started telephoning to air companies. His own

company did not think it safe to fly (TWA), and in fact there was a gale and wind. But another company offered to fly her. Lindbergh was really fussed but thought she ought to risk it. So at 8 P.M. poor little Betty was bundled into the car and driven to Newark. I shall always think of her in the doorway with her little hat and bag. A gale outside and the rain lashing down. There she was about to fly three thousand miles in the night. And she loathes flying in any conditions. So small and pathetic she looked. But what guts that woman has got! She is the real pioneer type. I confess that I was deeply impressed.

Charles and Anne drove off to the aerodrome with her. I dined with Springer the secretary. . . . [They] got back after I had gone to bed. They sat up till after midnight by which time Betty had passed Cleveland and was out of the bad weather zone. They telephoned to Charles all along the route as her aeroplane passed over — one of the few advantages of his national fame. It must have been an odd feeling sitting in that gay little sitting room with the fire and the latest magazines — and thinking of poor little Betty with her bag and her little coat bumping away through the rain and storm.

God! How I admire courage — I have none myself. Would I face a thing like that with her superb dignity? I hope so. I know you would but then you are also magnificent.

For some time Anne had known that Elisabeth did not have long to live. Recently she had even begun to accept the fact of her sister's premature death. Still, she was paralyzed by the thought of her mother having to fly to California alone in such hazardous weather. She had not accompanied her mother because Lindbergh thought that with the Hauptmann trial only two months away, she would be mercilessly hounded by reporters and curiosity seekers once she arrived at the Pasadena airport. Rather than becoming angry with her husband for not allowing her to be with her mother and sister at such a crucial time, she focused her attention on her mother's safety, trying to convince herself that nothing would happen to her. "I feel terrified and yet feel that fate *couldn't* strike at her — such a courageous figure. She *will* get there all right."

Fortunately, despite the terrible weather, Mrs. Morrow landed safely in California. While they waited for news of Elisabeth's condition, Nicolson and Anne went through some notes the biographer had asked her to write about her father, who, from the biographer's viewpoint, was proving a highly frustrating and elusive subject. As Anne read her notes to him, the literarily snobbish Harold was again struck by Anne's writing talent. As he later wrote to his wife,

You know, Viti, there is a great difference between an observant and a non-observant person. An observant person is a person who observes. An unobservant person is a person who does not observe. 97 per cent of humanity belong to the second category. Anne belongs to the first. She noticed every detail about her father and remembered it. She sat there graceful and shy upon the large chintz sofa reading her notes slowly with precision. "He would rub his right forefinger over the back of his left hand as if feeling a lump." "When he threw away his newspaper it never fell flat upon the carpet but always remained standing upwards." "He would tear off little bits of paper while talking, roll them into spills, and then work the spills into his ear. These spills would lie about the floor. We hated them." "On Sunday evenings we used to have family prayers. As we got older these prayers became more and more embarrassing and therefore fewer." And then there was a description of family breakfast which was so good that I told her to write it down and I shall produce it in the book . . . Whatever you say, that girl has real literary ability.

Ironically, this encouragement for Anne's writing coincided with yet another terrible personal loss. Despite the best medical care in the world and the presence of her mother and her new husband at her bedside, Elisabeth died on December 3, 1934. She was thirty years old.

When the Lindberghs were notified of her death in the early morning hours, Lindbergh started to reach for his wife, but Anne broke free of his embrace. She wanted to mourn her sister alone.

All life ahead of me telescoped. I would fill it up with things. It would pass quickly. In that leap of the mind I seemed to jump to the end of my life and not even fear death. Oh, I prayed Elisabeth was not afraid. After all, I felt, the big things in my life had happened. Nothing important was going to happen to me again. Elisabeth had been with me through all of them: love and marriage (though that is still to do) and birth, children, and death, and evil, and now the loss of Elisabeth herself. There did not seem to me anything to fear in life any more, or anything to want. And I decided that I must write. I must write about Elisabeth, all of her I had — all I remembered. I must write about her as long as I lived.

It was the same promise that Anne had made to her dead child less than two years before. Forced to endure one tragedy after another, she found solace in writing, which had become for her a compensatory act, providing a means both to explain and to escape from her complex, extraordinary life. In addition to offering her a way out of sorrow and disillusionment, it was a release for the intense, bottled-up feelings that at times threatened to engulf her. Although she was loath to admit it, writing had become even more important to her during this period of her life than her relationship with her husband. "I must write it out, at any cost. Writing is thinking," she told her diary. "It is more than living, for it is being conscious of living."

She longed to spend her days quietly, writing about Elisabeth and about her deepest feelings regarding the meaning of existence and nature, and to discover who she was, aside from being the wife of a very famous man.

But the days of peace for which she longed were still far in the future. The trial of Bruno Richard Hauptmann for the murder of Charles Augustus Lindbergh, Jr., was about to begin on January 3, 1935, at the Hunterdon County Courthouse in Flemington, New Jersey. Anne dreaded the proceedings. She knew that she would have to relive before the entire world that windy March night when she had rushed into her son's nursery and gazed with horror at his empty crib. Although Charles abhorred the idea of the public's knowing any detail of their private life, Anne knew that he would be in total command of himself on the witness stand. But could she, a far more emotional person than he, control her feelings as well? Or would she humiliate them both by breaking down? Whatever probing, personal questions the defense might ask, she must maintain her dignity, and in her diary she vowed "not to disappoint C. at the Trial." Her other self-sacrificing goals were "to finish the book for him, to give him a home and a sense of freedom and power and fulfillment."

Still devastated by the deaths of her little boy and her sister, but for the first time confident about her future as a writer, Anne was determined not to let violence, horror, and sadness reign triumphant over her. Somewhere in the future lay happiness and hope. And she must do her best to regain them.

CHAPTER 12

Witness

ALL EYES were focused on Anne as she took the stand in the small, drab courtroom in Flemington, a tiny, childlike figure dressed in a black silk suit and a hat with a bow across the front, the mournful color of her clothes lightened only by the soft pink of her blouse. Her youthful, delicate face was pale and composed, the face of someone who had adjusted to living with deep sorrow.

The stillness of the packed courtroom was in sharp contrast to the frenzy outside. In the words of one observer, the formerly sleepy little town of Flemington, New Jersey, population 2,700, "looked like a frosted picture postcard gone mad." People were jostling one another on the small steep flight of stone steps leading into the old courthouse, with its white stucco facade and quartet of Grecian-style columns. As the entrance doors swung open and closed, the crowd was desperately hoping for a glimpse of Anne and Charles or Bruno Hauptmann, the accused, with his ashen, curiously cadaverous-looking face.

There was an even larger crowd across the street, tightly packed in front of the old Union Hotel, a four-story building with a capacious porch and balconies, where many newspaper and radio reporters and members of the jury were staying. Although small and cramped, with only one bathroom, the Union had suddenly become the most famous hotel in the world. Day and night, its two bars, known as Nellie's Taproom because of a large dog who parked herself in front of the entrance, were crowded with reporters and the famous people who had flocked to Flemington to attend the trial. There were a great number of celebrities, for in some circles of fashionable society, the Lindbergh trial was regarded as one of the prime social events of the season. People felt it gave them a certain cachet to be able to tell their friends that, yes, they had been to Flemington and actually been only a few feet away from modest young Lindy, the idol of America, and his grief-stricken, courageous wife, not to mention the man with deep-set blue eyes, high cheekbones, and a pointy chin who without question had killed their baby.

At noon, when the court recessed for lunch, the streets of Flemington became even more crowded, as people headed into the Union Hotel's dining room or the lunchroom in the basement of the church just across from the courthouse. There, bustling matrons served up wholesome American home-style cooking, complete with apple pie, for seventy-five cents to both celebrities and ordinary people alike. Those who couldn't find a place to eat were forced to mill around until the lunchtime crowds thinned out. Their wait was not dull. Vendors hawked not only miniature replicas of the kidnap ladder, but fake locks of the murdered baby's hair, as well as forged autographed photos of Colonel Charles Lindbergh, a man in fact known to duck every time he was approached by autograph seekers or photographers. Prostitutes were also working the streets, with some of the more enterprising promising would-be customers kinky thrills, which they advertised via transfer pictures of the *Spirit of St. Louis* flying over certain parts of their anatomies. Fortunately for everyone concerned, Judge Thomas Whitaker Trenchard, the elderly, dignified judge who conducted the trial, managed to keep this carnival atmosphere from permeating the courtroom.

Inside the hushed room, David Wilentz, a darkly handsome young man who was New Jersey's attorney general, began his direct examination of the witness.

"Mrs. Lindbergh, you are the wife of Charles A. Lindbergh."

"I am" was the soft, firm answer.

Wilentz then began to question his witness about the events of Tuesday, March 1, 1932, asking in particular who was living in the Hopewell house on that date.

"I was there myself and my son, Charles A. Lindbergh, Jr., Mrs. Elsie Whateley, her husband, Oliver Whateley, and later in the afternoon, Betty Gow."

"So that the household on that date consisted of yourself and also Colonel Lindbergh in the evening?"

"In the evening," Anne repeated.

"And Mr. and Mrs. Whateley and Betty Gow and your infant son."

"Yes."

"How old was he?"

"Twenty months."

"He was born in June 1931?"

The moment had now come that Anne had dreaded for weeks, as Wilentz began to question her about Charlie. But, to her relief, she was able to answer him calmly.

"June 22, 1930," she gently corrected Wilentz in her pleasant, even voice, which could be heard in the far corners of the courtroom.

With Wilentz as a sympathetic guide, Anne recalled her last afternoon with her son: How Betty had brought him to the nursery window after she had thrown a pebble against it when she returned from her late afternoon walk; how they had played together in the sitting room in the fading light of the late afternoon; and how the baby had run happily off into the kitchen and she had not seen him again until she went up to the nursery at around 6:15 P.M. when he had almost finished his supper.

"Will you tell us about the child, about his playfulness that day. Was he a normal child?" Wilentz asked.

"He was perfectly normal," Anne replied, her blue eyes suddenly shining with pride. Undoubtedly, her emphatic answer was intended to dispel once and for all the malicious gossip that had circulated after the baby's death. One particularly vicious rumor had it that her enchanting, lively, and curious child had been born hopelessly retarded, and that rather than be burdened with his lifelong care, his cruel, uncaring parents had secretly arranged for his death.

Anne emphasized that Charlie had been a very normal and healthy child who knew enough words to carry on a conversation. His hair was light golden and curly, she said, and his eyes were blue.

Wilentz handed Anne a photograph of her son.

"I show you a picture and ask you if that is a picture of the child," he asked.

"It is," she answered firmly.

After offering the photograph into evidence, Wilentz then asked Anne to describe how her son's nursery had looked on the evening of March 1. As she began to discuss the box under the French window in which all his toys were kept, a murmur swept through the courtroom. The spectators were excited now. They knew that in a few moments they would hear firsthand how Anne had felt when she discovered her baby was missing, and they wondered if she would cry on the stand. Highly irritated by the outburst, Judge Trenchard called for silence.

When the courtroom was again quiet, Anne resumed her testimony about the nursery and its furnishings. And then came the moment that everyone in the packed courtroom had been waiting for . . .

One by one Wilentz handed Anne the articles of clothing that Charles Augustus, Jr., had worn on the last night of his life and asked her to identify them. The first two items had been found on his badly decomposed body, which had been half-eaten by wild animals, and were in deteriorated condition.

And one by one Anne held the small garments in her hand and said in her soft measured voice that, yes, they had belonged to her son: the homemade flannel shirt with the blue Silko thread which, hours before his death, Betty Gow had cut out and made for him from Elsie Whateley's old nightgown; the sleeveless woolen shirt, marked B. ALTMAN CO., NEW YORK, which was cut very low in the front and back; a wire thumbguard, which had been fastened around the wrist of the sleeping suit he was wearing and was discovered a month later on the grounds of the Lindbergh home; and the laundered woolen sleeping suit itself, which "John" (the man in the Bronx cemetery whom Lindbergh later identified as Hauptmann) had mailed to Dr. Condon in mid-March 1932 to substantiate his claim that the Lindbergh baby was alive and being well taken care of.

"Did you buy that sleeping suit yourself?"

"I did," Anne answered.

"I show you what purports to be a sleeping suit, No. 2, Dr. Denton, and ask you whether or not you recognize that sleeping suit."

"I do."

"What sleeping suit is that, Mrs. Lindbergh?"

"It is the sleeping suit that was put on my child the night of March 1."

"1932?"

"1932."

"And it is the sleeping suit then that your son wore that night as he went to bed?"

"It is."

After her son's clothing was placed in evidence, Anne was asked to recount her movements after she had left him in the care of Betty Gow at around 7:30 P.M. Then Wilentz had no more questions, and it was Edward J. Reilly's turn to examine the witness. But Reilly, the chief de-

fense lawyer for Bruno Hauptmann, declined the opportunity. Undoubtedly he felt that questioning such a sincere and believable witness would
only prejudice the jury further against his client.

"The defense feels that the grief of Mrs. Lindbergh requires no cross-
examination," he said.

"That is all, thank you, Mrs. Lindbergh," Wilentz dismissed his witness.

All eyes followed her as she carefully descended from the stand, a petite, ethereal young woman whose fragility was deceptive. In reality, as
everyone in the courtroom now knew, she was iron-strong, the epitome of self-control and courage.

Betty Gow, the baby's nurse, was being called to the witness stand, but
the attention of the courtroom spectators was not yet focused on her.
They were still absorbed by Anne's bravery and grace. Even the reporters in the courtroom were deeply impressed by what they had seen.
There were more than three hundred of them in attendance that day in
Flemington, and they had come from all over the world to cover the
trial. Some were almost as famous as Charles and Anne Lindbergh them-
selves, household names such as Damon Runyon, John O'Hara, Walter
Winchell, Fannie Hurst, Alexander Woollcott, Edna Ferber, Arthur Bris-
bane, Ford Madox Ford, Adela Rogers St. Johns, and Sheilah Graham.
Also there were veteran reporter Jim Kilgallen and his young daughter,
Dorothy, who was just starting out in the newspaper business and
scrambling to compete with the far more experienced Graham and St.
Johns for exclusive interviews with the witnesses.

The undisputed queen of this motley group was Adela Rogers St.
Johns, a veteran reporter who had been hand-picked by her boss, William Randolph Hearst, to cover the trial for his newspapers. As St. Johns
later remembered it, Hearst had called her one night from his gloomy
San Simeon castle, which was cluttered with priceless paintings, statuary, and bizarre objets d'art, and intoned, "Mrs. Lindbergh will take
careful handling in this trial. I hope you are free to be there for us."

"We cannot endure the kidnapping of our children," he continued
in what could hardly have been a casual business conversation. "In this
trial I am sure we can produce a flame of indignation that will deter other
criminals. As you know, crime is the most dingdong repetitive thing in
the world, we must not allow this to become a *wave*."

Armed to conduct her own personal battle against the nation's would-
be kidnappers in chic Hattie Carnegie outfits, which she charged to her

expense account, St. Johns was every bit as much a star in the proceedings as the Lindberghs and Hauptmann, whose entire defense was paid for by Hearst on the condition that the accused man give interviews only to his reporters. The courtroom staff did errands for her, and even the judge seemed in awe of her. St. Johns was a flamboyant presence in the courtroom, and her coverage of the trial in the New York *Journal* was yellow journalism at its most sensational best. Some typical samples:

ADELA ROGERS ST. JOHNS SAYS:
Somebody kidnapped that baby, somebody killed him and left Lindy and Anne to those nights and days of hell and crucifixion. Who was it?
    Today we begin the trial of Bruno Hauptmann for that crime.

ADELA ROGERS ST. JOHNS SAYS:
In this small, drab old courthouse packed with humanity, we are again living every horror, every anguish, every suspense, every dastardly step of the murder of our Little Eagle.

ADELA ROGERS ST. JOHNS SAYS:
Not one person in that courtroom would have been surprised if suddenly Lindy had risen from his seat and grasped Hauptmann by the throat . . . we were waiting for it.

ADELA ROGERS ST. JOHNS SAYS:
KEEP YOUR HANDS OFF OUR CHILDREN

A hard-bitten realist, with an intensely dramatic writing style, Adela Rogers St. Johns was the opposite of Anne Morrow Lindbergh in both personality and attitude toward the printed word. Yet Hearst's star reporter was plainly moved and inspired by Anne's testimony. "I carried Anne Lindbergh out of the Hauptmann trial with me," St. Johns later wrote. "No one I had ever met made so profound an impression on me as this girl whose voice I never heard, whose face I never saw except from the witness stand."

This was stretching the truth a bit, for many years later St. Johns was to reminisce about the time she had met Anne and Charles *before* their child was kidnapped.

"I only saw them once in those days," she wrote.

I was writing in a little house in Carmel when they came to be guests of Samuel F. B. Morse, whose great-grandfather invented the telegraph. I went to a party given for the Lindberghs at the Morses' dream house on the shore at Pebble Beach and they were beyond what I had expected. My first thought was, How tiny she is! Beside him, of course. The plain one?

I found her, then and always, beautiful. As the hand of God had created her you were more aware of the light shining through than of the lamp. I was to think this again when I saw her next on the witness stand in the courtroom at Flemington.

For St. Johns, Anne's testimony was the trial's most unforgettable moment. "Everyone I have asked for the Great Moment of the trial has, without one exception, said Mrs. Lindbergh on the witness stand. She gave us a new dimension."

> We who sit in this courtroom have seen something we will never forget. When Anne Lindbergh sat on the witness stand we saw a slim young thing in black who will never be entirely happy again but who, a great woman and a great lady, was courageous in sorrow and gallant in grief.
>
> Anne Lindbergh didn't break, she didn't faint. None of the things movie actresses do in big scenes.
>
> I would rather have seen her break than to behold that brave smile. I would rather have seen her faint than watch those pauses when her face grew whiter and whiter and it took every drop of her courage to speak at last. I would rather have seen gallons of tears than the blue eyes looking blindly for help . . .
>
> You knew how effective she had been as a witness when Mr. Reilly let her go without one word of cross-examination. He wanted to get her off that stand, he knew he couldn't make anybody doubt her.

Another equally famous writer of the period, Alexander Woollcott, who considered himself a connoisseur of crime, was also present in the courtroom on the day Anne gave her testimony. Even though he was incorrect about who had made the sleeping garment, his admiration for her was obvious:

> Hauptmann's trial was the climax of the world's greatest manhunt and therefore the prevailing atmosphere in the old courthouse at Flemington, N.J. was not inappropriately that of a sporting event. There was, however, one unforgettable moment when all the hubbub ceased.
>
> That was when Anne Morrow Lindbergh took the witness stand and identified the sleeping garment which her own hands had sewn for her small son. In that hushed moment the case, stripped to its essentials, was revealed for what it really was — evil incarnate standing accused by every American hearth.

Although Anne was in the habit of sharing her innermost thoughts with her diary, she was curiously silent on the subject of her testimony, making no entry on that day, nor did she record her husband's reaction. Presumably, he was not "disappointed" but praised her for conducting herself in a manner that brought credit to them both. It would be more than a month later, in February, before she was finally able to confide to her journal that her day in court had in fact been an ordeal, although not as traumatic as she had imagined. In order to maintain a grip on her emotions, she had steadfastly gazed at a triangle of blue sky through the courtroom window. No reference was made to seeing Bruno Hauptmann for the first time. Nor was any mention made of whether she agreed with her husband that he was guilty of kidnapping and murder.

When Lindbergh later testified that it was Bruno Hauptmann's voice that he had heard in St. Raymond's Cemetery, calling, "Hey, doctor," with a foreign accent, Anne was not present in the courtroom. Unlike his wife, Lindbergh was the prosecution's star witness — his testimony directly implicated Hauptmann in the crime. Considering Anne's devotion to her husband, it seems strange that she wasn't there to lend her support, for many people were skeptical that Lindbergh could identify a voice after the passage of two years which he had heard from a distance. Perhaps Lindbergh had specifically asked her not to come, feeling that the spectacle of his undergoing a brutal cross-examination by Hauptmann's lawyers would be traumatic.

Although Anne did not hear her husband's lengthy testimony, in which, among other things, he emphatically reaffirmed his belief in the integrity of Condon, as well as Betty Gow and the other servants in his and his mother-in-law's employ, she wrote in her diary that he had made an excellent witness and was so convinced of the truth of what he was saying that it was impossible for the defense to poke holes in his story. Yet she also felt resentful about his being subjected to such an ordeal. "I read the papers and feel bitter to think of how they *use* C. Dangle him and his life in front of the stage for their own ends. And he has to sit quiet and watch."

Ironically, Adela Rogers St. Johns, who observed Lindbergh daily during the trial, was more attuned to its impact on the aviator's modest, yet secretly power-driven personality. Years later she wrote:

> On top of his sorrow he was going into an unbottomed boundless Valley of Humiliation . . .
>
> As a young hero he had abhorred the glory spotlight, even when he was their idol he had never been at ease with crowds. Now this vast and terrible spotlight would show him flying not for worlds to conquer but at the orders of a criminal, in a senseless horrid hoax . . .

Tomorrow and tomorrow and tomorrow would find him a few feet from this man whom the state charged had killed his son, dire and dreadful enough but under the vast spotlight his pride would burn to shame; he had not been able to protect or save his son. Laying bare his soul, his agony, the sympathy of the multitudes was something he did not want.

All during the bleak months of January and February, while an obsessed Lindbergh sat mesmerized in the Flemington courtroom, Anne tried to forget her inner pain by writing about a happier time, when Charlie had been alive and she and Charles had made their first survey flight to the Orient.

But the brutal reality of her life descended again on Saturday, February 9, when she put aside her writing and accompanied her mother to Flemington, where Mrs. Morrow was to testify about the character of her deceased servant Violet Sharpe.

To Anne's surprise, her second appearance in court was far more upsetting than the time she herself had testified. By her own admission, she felt "freer to feel." And, one might add, to observe. For the first time she appeared aware of Hauptmann and his distraught wife, Anna: "That pale profile of Hauptmann startling one through a gap in the heads. The pathetically bedraggled thin face — tired, bewildered — of Mrs. Hauptmann."

That morning Ewald Mielke, who owned a Long Island mill-working plant, was being quizzed by Edward Reilly about a rail from the strange ladder used in the kidnapping and about its connection with a floorboard that the police had later taken from Bruno Hauptmann's attic. In Mielke's opinion, the two pieces of wood were not part of the same board, which was a direct contradiction of the earlier testimony of state witness Arthur Koehler of the United States Forest Products Laboratory in Madison, Wisconsin, who was convinced that one of the rails of the ladder had been cut from the same piece of the floorboard in the defendant's attic. In his testimony, Koehler, a leading wood expert, said that he had laid a board on a joist in the attic and found that the nail holes in the board matched those in the joist. Under cross-examination, Mielke admitted that, in comparison with Koehler's laborious analysis, he had spent about five minutes examining the two wood samples; as he was testifying to this fact, Anne thought with a pang, "How incredible that my baby had any connection with this!"

After lunch, Mrs. Morrow was called to the stand to testify as to the whereabouts of Violet Sharpe on the evening of March 1. During her mother's testimony, in which Mrs. Morrow stated that Violet had served her and Elisabeth dinner that night at Next Day Hill, Anne continued to regard Bruno Hauptmann in a curiously detached manner, in fact as if the man who stood accused of cold-bloodedly killing her son and dumping his body in the woods were not even present in the courtroom. Whatever anger she had toward him appears to have been transferred to his lawyer, Edward Reilly, who offended her by disdainfully referring to Violet as "just an ordinary servant girl," although a reading of the trial transcript reveals that Reilly never described Violet Sharpe in such terms.

The spectacle of her elderly mother being asked to remember the evening when both her grandchild and her favorite daughter, Elisabeth, had both been alive was more than Anne could bear. Suddenly she felt the blood rush to her face and heard a pounding in her ears. It was all she could do not to cry.

She was relieved when Reilly's cross-examination of her mother proved mercifully brief and they were free to leave Flemington, with its awful, gaping crowds and unreal, cardboard-like "gingerbread houses." A short drive away lay the cavernous safety of Next Day Hill, which, even if it seemed like a hotel, at least made her feel protected and secure.

Behind her lay confusion and controversy, as "the trial of the century" was reaching its final stages. In fact, the trial of Bruno Richard Hauptmann, an illegal alien from Germany with a record of petty crime, was one of the most controversial proceedings in the history of American jurisprudence. Today, sixty years later, grave doubts still linger about the verdict. Though many people are convinced that the jury decision was a wise one and that justice was served, others believe that it was a grave miscarriage of justice and that all the pieces of physical evidence the state introduced against Hauptmann were either manufactured by the police in their eagerness to obtain a conviction or were falsely interpreted by so-called expert witnesses.

Part of the reason for this seemingly endless controversy is that the case against Hauptmann was based overwhelmingly on circumstantial evidence. This evidence included the misspelled ransom notes, which several handwriting experts testified were in his hand; the ladder rail, which a state witness, Arthur Koehler, testified had been part of a floorboard in Hauptmann's attic; the fact that some of the ransom money was found in his possession (the state claimed that no more gold notes were recovered after his arrest); and finally, a board that the police later discovered inside Hauptmann's closet on which was scribbled Dr. Condon's telephone number.

In defending their client, the Hearst-paid lawyers argued that Hauptmann could not have committed the crime because Condon's phone number had been written on the board by the New York City police as part of a scheme to frame him. Moreover, how could Hauptmann, a simple carpenter from the Bronx, possibly have known the whereabouts of the Lindberghs and their child on the night of March 1, 1932? Normally, they would have been at Next Day Hill and were at their country retreat in Hopewell, New Jersey, only by accident. Could any member of the jury really believe that Hauptmann, a man unfamiliar with the area, had managed to walk almost a mile through dark woods, carrying a ladder, and then set it up against the wall of a strange house, which was occupied by four adults whom he might encounter at any moment, and then scurry up the ladder, push open a shutter, and walk into an unfamiliar room? As Edward Reilly stressed to the jury, it seemed far more likely that Anne and Charles had been betrayed by someone who worked for them. If a stranger like Hauptmann had been the kidnapper, he pointed out, why then had their dog, Skean, a little fox terrier, not barked? And why had the child not cried out when he had been snatched from his crib? Was it because he felt comfortable with the person who was taking him?

If it had not been an inside job, why had Violet Sharpe committed suicide? Didn't it seem reasonable to assume that she had killed herself because she did in fact have what the police called "a guilty knowledge of the crime"? As for the ransom money, it was important for the jurors to keep in mind that Hauptmann was only holding it for his ex–business partner Isidor Fisch, who had given it to him for safekeeping before he returned to Germany. Finally, as for the rail from the ladder matching the board in Hauptmann's attic, could anyone really believe that Hauptmann, a professional carpenter who had access to a lumberyard around the corner, would crawl up to his own attic, yank up a board, and then saw it into pieces to make the side of a ladder? And why would a man whose profession was woodworking make such a shoddy ladder in the first place, one that was not only crudely built but which collapsed under the slightest strain? When Hauptmann was shown the ladder during the trial and asked if he had made it, he shook his head contemptuously and said, "I am a carpenter."

In his charge to the jury, Judge Thomas Trenchard, noting the preponderance of circumstantial evidence in the case, pointed out that "the crime of murder is not one which is always committed in the presence of witnesses, and if not so committed, it must be established by circumstantial evidence or not at all."

Anne was still at the mansion on February 13, 1935, the day Judge Trenchard began to instruct the jury. As he was doing so, an enormous group of people began to gather in front of the courthouse. As the day wore on, the crowd became increasingly rowdy and menacing. Many were drunkenly shouting that they would take the law into their own hands if the jury did not render a satisfying verdict. Still others in the mob were making bets about Hauptmann's chances for acquittal, although few believed him to be innocent. In their opinion, the only question for the judge to decide was whether the German carpenter would die in the electric chair or spend the rest of his life in prison.

The bloodthirsty attitude of the crowd did not extend to the reporters covering the trial. Years later Adela Rogers St. Johns recalled that shortly after Hauptmann was convicted of murder and sentenced to die in the electric chair, "Mr. Hearst took a poll of our reporters who had covered the kidnapping and the trial and those who had done editorial work on it at city desks and copy desks. Without exception, we agreed that Hauptmann had not done it alone, that he should be kept alive to find the other guilty parties and to resolve the unanswered problems."

Lindbergh was present during the trial's final moments, only managing to tear himself away from the courtroom after Judge Trenchard had concluded his summing up. Somehow he managed to slip past the crowd unnoticed and duck into a car parked by the side door.

As soon as he returned to Next Day Hill, Anne, her mother, her sister, Constance, and Harold Nicolson rushed to meet him. That day, Nicolson had just returned from England where he had finished a good portion of his biography of Dwight Morrow, and he wanted to discuss it with Mrs. Morrow and other members of the family. It was obvious to him that everybody was nervous and on edge. Nicolson had just read Judge Trenchard's summing up in the newspapers, which he thought he did "very well," although Lindbergh told him "that it reads more impartial than it sounded. For instance, he kept on saying to the jury, in going over some of Hauptmann's evidence, 'Do you believe that?' Now that sounds all right when read in print. But what he actually said was, 'Do *you* believe THAT?' "

When they sat down to dinner, the jury had been out for five hours and a verdict was expected at any moment. As Nicolson later described it to Vita, the occasion was rather "strained." Two radios were on in the house, one in the pantry next to the dining room, and one in the drawing room. "Thus there were jazz and jokes while we had dinner, and one ear strained the whole time for the announcer from the court-house. Lindbergh had a terrible cold which made it worse. 'A-tishoo,' he kept on saying."

After dinner they all went into the library, which was next to the drawing room, so they could hear the radio. "They were all rather jumpy. Mrs. Morrow, with her unfailing tact, brought out a lot of photographs and we had a family council as to what illustrations to choose for the book. This was just interesting enough to divert, but not to rivet, attention."

Around 10:35 P.M., Dick Scandrett, a nephew of Dwight Morrow, came to see Nicolson, and Mrs. Morrow, the Morgans, and the Lindberghs left them alone. As they were discussing Dwight Morrow,

suddenly Betty [Morrow] put her head round the huge Coromandel screen. She looked very white. "Hauptmann," she said, "has been condemned to death without mercy."

We went into the drawing room. The wireless had been turned on to the scene outside the court-house. One could hear the almost diabolic yelling of the crowd. A-tishoo! A-tishoo! from Lindbergh. They were all sitting round — ... Miss Morgan [a relative of Aubrey Morgan] with embroidery, Anne looking very white and still. "You have now heard," broke in the voice of the announcer, "the verdict in the most famous trial in all history. Bruno Hauptmann now stands guilty of the foulest . . . " A-tishoo! A-tishoo! A-tishoo! "Turn that off, Charles, turn that off." Then we all went into the pantry and had ginger-beer. And Charles sat there on the kitchen dresser looking very pink about the nose. "I don't know," he said to me, "whether you have followed this case carefully. There is no doubt at all that Hauptmann did the thing. My one dread all these years has been that they would get hold of someone as a victim about whom I wasn't sure. I am sure about this — quite sure. It is this way . . . "

And then quite quietly, while we all sat round in the pantry, he went through the case point by point. It seemed to relieve all of them. He did it very quietly, very simply. He pretended to address his remarks to me only. But I could see that he was really trying to ease the agonised tension through which Betty and Anne had passed. It was very well done. It made one feel that here was no personal desire for vengeance or justification; here was the solemn process of law inexorably and impersonally punishing a culprit.

The main points were (1) The handwriting. Five separate experts stated that there could be no doubt at all that the ransom notes were in Hauptmann's writing. The only expert who doubted this one was produced by the defense and he was proved to have paid to say it. (2) The ladder. That was the most brilliant piece of detective work. They traced the wood from which it had been made to a lumber yard in which Hauptmann had worked. They also proved that one piece had come from his own attic. The section cut from the attic roof fitted exactly into the timbers. (3) Condon's telephone number scribbled on the wall of Hauptmann's room. He was never able to explain that. (4) His possession of the notes and the fact that he began to invest money in April 1932. (5) Recognition of his voice by Condon, Lindbergh and the taxi driver [Joseph Perrone, who was hired by the kidnapper to deliver one of the ransom notes to Dr. Condon]. Lindbergh says that Hauptmann had a very strange voice and that it was unmistakable. (6) The fact that his alibis were all proved fraudulent.

Then we went to bed. I feel that they are all relieved. If Hauptmann had been acquitted it would have had a bad effect on the crime situation in this country. Never has circumstantial evidence been so convincing. If on such evidence a conviction had not been secured, then all the gangsters would have felt a sense of immunity. The prestige of the police has been enormously enhanced by this case.

Poor Anne — she looked so white and horrified. The yells of the crowd were really terrifying. "That," said Lindbergh, "was a — A-tishoo! — lynching crowd."

He tells me that Hauptmann was a magnificent-looking man. Splendidly built. But that his little eyes were like the eyes of a wild boar. Mean, shifty, small and cruel.

Nicolson astutely observed that the sounds of the mob upset Anne. That night and the following morning she made the following entries in her diary:

That howling mob over the radio — how incredibly horrible and bitter to realize that this has to do with us. That C. should have to bear it.
 Incredible as that first night.

The trial is over. We must start our life again, try to build it securely — C. and Jon and I. It is I, really — I must start again, without Elisabeth, with my eyes open, without confusion or fooling myself, honestly and patiently, keeping clear what matters. Charles and a home and Jon — and work.

Hauptmann was executed at the state prison in Trenton, New Jersey, on April 3, 1936. During the many years since, Anne Lindbergh has remained silent about the question of his guilt or innocence. In recent interviews, whenever the question of the celebrated case has been raised, she has brushed aside the reporter's query, saying that it was decided "a long time ago." And she has declined to be interviewed by the authors of several recent books defending Hauptmann, or by a producer of a public television documentary on the continuing controversies surrounding the crime. With Ludovic Kennedy, the author of a best-selling book about the kidnapping entitled *The Airman and the Carpenter,* which makes a compelling case for Hauptmann's having been framed, she was a bit more cooperative, answering the two letters Kennedy sent her during the writing of the book. "I got the impression — and it was no more than an impression," Kennedy says, "that she had some reservations as to whether Hauptmann was really guilty of the kidnapping and murder. My general feeling was that at her age she did not wish to be reminded of what must have been a very upsetting period in her life."

Whatever lingering doubts Anne Lindbergh may have about Hauptmann and whether his execution was a grave miscarriage of justice have remained her secret, something she has never cared to discuss publicly.

CHAPTER 13

Interim

A NEW LIFE for Charles, Jon, and herself — this was Anne's fervent wish as soon as the trial ended. And for a few months it did seem possible that she and her family could live peaceful, ordinary lives unmarked by violence and sensationalism.

Anne spent that spring quietly, finishing *North to the Orient*. As soon as the manuscript was completed, she began looking for a publisher. During his recent visit, Harold Nicolson had suggested that his publisher, Harcourt, Brace and Company, might be receptive to publishing the manuscript. To her delight, he had recommended her writing talent to Samuel Sloan, one of the editors. Yet despite Nicolson's glowing endorsement, Anne was suddenly dubious about the book's chances. In her estimation, it was far too slender a work — only forty-two thousand words — to be published. And on rereading it, she had come to the conclusion that only three chapters had any merit. And what was worse, if Harcourt decided to publish the book, people would say that it was only because the author was married to Charles Lindbergh.

In late April, Anne, for once not mindful of who gawked at her, entered the Madison Avenue offices of Harcourt, Brace and Company. A short time later she emerged, feeling elated — Alfred Harcourt, the president, as well as Samuel Sloan, the editor, had both assured her that they would be more than happy to read her manuscript.

As soon as she returned to Next Day Hill, Anne threw herself into a frenzy of work, with Lindbergh supervising the revisions. Bluntly he told her that the preface was boring, which deeply hurt her feelings although she never told him so. In the next few days, he carefully edited each chapter, changing words and phrases that were not to his taste.

Within a week, the couple had arrived at a final draft, and instead of mailing the manuscript or having it sent by messenger, Sloan was summoned to Next Day Hill to fetch it in person.

As soon as he had departed, Anne was assailed by self-doubt. She told herself not to become excited about the book's chances for publication because even though she and Charles had worked hard on it, it still seemed rough and unpolished. Although she knew that she alone would be credited with authorship, she feared that a poorly written account of their flight by Anne Lindbergh might undermine her husband's reputation, and she asked herself, "What justifies letting it go out under C.'s name?"

Her mood swiftly changed the following Monday when Alfred Harcourt himself called to convey the good news that, in his opinion, the book was wonderfully written and deserved publication. "It's a good story," he said. "It's moving, it's well constructed, and parts of it border on poetry." Anne was ecstatic as she listened to his comments. For the first time since the kidnapping she felt completely happy. Suddenly she felt as if "there is a place for me. There is some reason for my living. I can hold my head up."

The minute Lindbergh came home, she rushed to tell him the wonderful news. One look at his suddenly youthful face, beaming with pride, made her feel that all her work had been worthwhile.

Still, doubts about her creative talent continued to plague her as she tried to sleep that night. She could not help thinking that Harcourt was well aware that any book written by the wife of Charles Lindbergh would enjoy brisk sales, even if it were abominably written. Earlier, when phoning to say that she, but not Charles, would be coming in to the office next week to discuss the manuscript, she had thought he sounded disappointed.

Was that the real reason Harcourt had decided to publish her book, Anne asked herself, as she tossed and turned in the darkness, so he could meet her legendary husband?

North to the Orient, which contained maps made by Charles Lindbergh, was published on August 15, 1935, and it immediately became a best seller. Still in print nearly sixty years after its first edition, it is one of Anne's most enduring works, fascinating generation after generation of readers with its poetic and absorbing account of what it was like to fly halfway around the world in a small monoplane.

Any doubts Anne may have had about her ability as a writer should have been erased by the reviews, which were uniformly glowing. Noted one critic:

> Anne Lindbergh has a sense of drama, and she knows how to tell a story, to tell it with simplicity of style and an exquisite feeling for words. Every page is a pure delight. And since Anne Lindbergh happens to be Anne Lindbergh, it should be said that her book stands firmly on its own feet, independent of any interest in other Lindbergh achievements; it would have lost nothing of its charm had the story, as she relates it, been concerned with a similar flight made by obscure Smiths, Joneses, or Browns.

This estimate was echoed in many of the other reviews. The *Saturday Review of Literature* noted that "Mrs. Lindbergh has the seeing eye and the singing heart, and of whatever befalls she presents an account glowing with animation and emotion . . . This is a thoroughly charming book." And Lewis Gannett of the *New York Herald Tribune* observed, "*North to the Orient* has a rare and delicate intimacy and a winning girlish charm, and it reveals Mrs. Lindbergh as far more than a wife and a daughter. The girl can write."

After years of uncertainty about the merits of her work, Anne was finally receiving the recognition that she deserved. She was a writer, and an excellent one at that, for her prose was not only exquisitely delicate and graceful, but she was able to bring a poet's sensitive vision to a scientific and technical achievement, which added to its historical importance. She who had always deferred to her celebrated husband now found herself alone in the spotlight. Leading literary critics were applauding her first major effort, and her friends were all offering their congratulations. These included such well-known literary figures as Mina Curtiss, Vita Sackville-West, and Harold Nicolson, who liked the book so much that he personally gave a copy to Virginia Woolf — one of Anne's favorite authors and a major literary influence on her.

Yet despite the enthusiastic reviews and the accolades from her friends, Anne still did not completely believe in her talent. Perhaps the reviewers were being kind to her because she had written about the daring achievements of Charles Lindbergh, aviation pioneer and a very great man. If she hadn't been married to him, undoubtedly her writing would still be unpublished, or sitting on some dusty shelf. Her persistent lack of faith in her ability became apparent in her reaction to the news that Smith College, her alma mater, planned to give her an honorary master of arts degree at its commencement exercises in June. Although thrilled by the honor, she could not help feeling that she was unworthy of it, that it should have been given to a woman with a career of her own. "They ought to give degrees to people who have done things in their own rights, on their own responsibilities — women who have held a career by themselves," she wrote to a friend. "After all, what *are* they giving it to me for? Flying around the world with my husband? I certainly have no career as a pilot or a radio operator. C. could have got a better copilot, a better navigator, and a better radio operator. I don't know whether he could have got a better wife — although even so, I was only a moderately good one, I kicked a lot and was afraid most of the time."

Still, it was an exciting moment in her life when she was honored by her alma mater in June 1935. In conferring the degree, her old friend and mentor, President William Allan Neilson, said:

> Anne Morrow Lindbergh, B.A., Smith, 1928, Hubbard gold medalist of the National Geographic Society, poet, pilot, navigator, radio operator, co-explorer with her husband of the unflown air routes of five continents and two oceans, who has proved to an admiring world the compatibility of imagination and practical dexterity; of sensitiveness and fortitude; of modesty and daring; the pride of her college; the glory of her country.

At the same commencement exercises, Mrs. Morrow, in her capacity as a trustee of the college, bestowed a bachelor of arts degree on Constance, who was graduating from Smith with the highest honors. But for once Anne did not feel diminished by the presence of her vibrant, dominating mother or her charming, far more confident and relaxed younger sister. Standing on the podium that summer day, with the flushed young faces of the Smith graduates gazing expectantly up at her, she suddenly knew what her life, in all its glory and heartbreak, meant to many other women.

Despite these personal triumphs, Anne was still haunted by Elisabeth's death. For a time the only thing she wanted to do was gaze at the dead woman's photographs and reread her journal, which Aubrey had recently given to her. It had come as something of a shock to discover that Elisabeth hadn't thought about her half as much as she had about

Elisabeth. Feeling guilty about being alive while Elisabeth was dead, Anne berated herself whenever she felt her sister growing "faraway" from her. These feelings were intensified whenever she thought about the effect of Elisabeth's death on her mother. For Mrs. Morrow had made no effort to disguise the fact that of her three daughters Elisabeth had been the favorite. Sadly, Anne realized that she could never offer her mother the same kind of emotional closeness and companionship. Although she never mentioned feeling hurt or jealous, it must have pained her to realize that her mother would never love her in the way she had her sister.

During this period Anne formed a close friendship with Margot Loines, a friend of Constance who was dating Dwight, Jr. The kidnapping had been an especially difficult time for her emotionally fragile younger brother. The press had gotten wind of Dwight's mental problems, and some of the tabloids had made the cruel allegation that it was he who had kidnapped and killed his nephew. It was claimed that because of his chronic mental illness, his father had deliberately cut him out of the will, leaving him only one dollar, while bequeathing his entire share to Charles Augustus Lindbergh, Jr., and that Dwight had killed his nephew out of spite. Although this rumor was untrue (aside from several large bequests to relatives, various institutions and charities, Morrow had left his entire estate to his wife, Betty, with the provision that she "provide for herself and my children") and no one close to the investigation took it seriously, Dwight had become overwrought when he learned that some people suspected him of the crime, and Anne was grateful to Margot for helping her brother recover his equilibrium. She was also indebted to her for another reason. Like Elisabeth, Margot was a vibrant, outgoing woman, and her friendship helped fill the void created by Elisabeth's death.

That fall Harold Nicolson's biography of Dwight Morrow was published. When she read it, Anne found herself stirred by many of the old conflicts about her relationship with her father, which in retrospect had been almost as complex as the one she had with her husband.

On the one hand, she felt intensely proud of what her father had been able to do with his life, despite the obstacles confronting him. "I suddenly feel my heritage, feel him in me," she wrote. "It is mine. . . . It is in me, *some* of that strength and tolerance and vision, and the ability to make something out of my life, my marriage, my work. I am challenged by it, and I feel a great wall of strength behind. My mind is challenged when Harold Nicolson talks, about peacemaking, about governments, about history. Something of my father rises in me, is pulled by it, finds itself fascinated, finds it can understand and grasp and wants more!"

But there was also something about her father's treatment of her that continued to feel repellent, although characteristically she did not delve deeply into it. During a family gathering following his wife's funeral, her father's brother, Jay, a former governor of the Panama Canal Zone, had insisted on resting his hand heavily on Anne's shoulder. Although Anne realized that her uncle, by then a quite senile old man, was only reaching out for comfort, she could not help remembering that her father had had the same habit, and it had outraged her. Unprotesting whenever he had put his hand on her shoulder, she had nonetheless felt like his chattel, someone who "wasn't worth talking to, or even looking at, but nice to stroke, like a spaniel's ear."

Despite the conflicted feelings that reading the book evoked, Anne genuinely liked the biography. She told Nicolson that it was a wonderful portrait, a response deeply appreciated by the biographer who privately thought that *Dwight Morrow* was the worst book he had ever written. As Nicolson was only too well aware, he had never really been able to get a fix on his subject, a fascinating man who had done dull things, and his writing style had succumbed to "American sentimentality," with the result that the biography was not only "sugary sort of stuff" but "heavy as lead." Some of the book's problems, he felt, also resulted from his fear of hurting Mrs. Morrow's feelings if he had revealed anything negative about her husband. And it hadn't helped that the powerful J. P. Morgan, Jr., himself had been personally offended by many passages discussing Dwight Morrow's long association with the banking dynasty. To assuage his anger, Nicolson had been forced to delete any passages that revealed the firm in a less than glowing light. These excisions, as he bluntly wrote to Sackville-West, "removed from the book any tang it may have had."

Although she had nothing but praise for Nicolson's work, Anne had mixed feelings about the biographer himself. On Nicolson's return to Englewood in February 1935, she had the opportunity to study him more closely, noting that he shied away from intimacy and withdrew from her whenever she tried to engage him in a serious discussion. "It baffles me like sitting in a theatre and looking always at a beautifully painted curtain," she observed. "I keep waiting and waiting for the curtain to rise and show the real play."

But she also acknowledged that one reason Nicolson unsettled her was that he made her painfully aware of her own inadequacies. His sophisticated, brittlely entertaining manner immediately reduced her to feeling like a shy, awkward, and unattractive teenager. In a flash, she became her mother's pale, tired "little girl." Of course, in contrast, her dynamic, self-possessed mother more than held her own with the biographer.

But Nicolson wasn't the only visitor at Next Day Hill to get on her nerves. The ceaseless stream of people coming to see her mother not only had the effect of irritating Charles, who hated the inevitable fuss that strangers made over him, but also made it impossible for her to write. To escape the constant noise and interruptions, she decided to rent a small one-room apartment in New York for the winter. At last she had found her own place, "my own room," as she called it. Clearly she was influenced by Virginia Woolf's trenchant essay, *A Room of One's Own,* first published in 1929, in which the English novelist stressed that the only way for women writers to create works of genius would be by having a fixed income and privacy. Anne had never had to think about money, the first of Woolf's requirements, and now, by renting the studio, she possessed the second. Every time she unlocked the door and stepped into the silence, she felt peaceful and happy. In her studio, decorated with a large Orozco reproduction over the mantel, she could daydream and write, free from interruption and from her husband's scrutiny, for he continued to look askance whenever he discovered her writing letters and had even tried to dissuade her from replying to her friends' letters of congratulations about her book.

At Next Day Hill, whenever Anne heard his familiar whistle outside her window, she knew she would have to drop her writing immediately and do what he wanted — otherwise, he would be cross with her. But here in her small studio, with its serene atmosphere and soothing pictures, which she had personally selected, there was no one to answer to but herself.

This rented studio would be the first of many places to which she would retreat during the coming years, a place of her own where she could be free to think and write undisturbed.

No sooner had Anne settled into her new studio and writing routine, however, when she and Lindbergh began receiving numerous threatening letters. Ordinarily, they would not have paid much attention to them. Ever since Lindbergh's famous flight, he had received crank mail.

But when Jon was born, the volume of sinister letters increased alarmingly. The threat was usually the same: the new baby would be kidnapped and killed, like his brother, unless money was handed over. There was just a trickle of mail at first, but because of the murder of Charles Augustus Lindbergh, Jr., the police took the threats seriously. A number of the writers were tracked down, and at least a dozen people were arrested for extortion. Extremely anxious about Jon's safety, Anne and Charles, who had always refused to have personal bodyguards, hired an armed guard to watch their son.

According to the police, the great increase in their threatening mail was caused by the circumstances surrounding Hauptmann's impending execution. Recently New Jersey governor Harold G. Hoffmann had made the sensational disclosure that he had secretly visited Hauptmann on death row at the state prison in Trenton. Hoffmann stated that he was not at all convinced that Hauptmann was guilty of the crime, which in his opinion could not have been committed by just one person, and that he personally wanted to review the evidence that had led to Hauptmann's conviction.

Hoffmann's critics — and there were many — accused the governor of being motivated more by politics than by a sincere belief in Hauptmann's innocence. They pointed to the fact that Hoffmann, a Republican, had tried to fire David Wilentz, the Democratic attorney general who had prosecuted Hauptmann. When this proved impossible because of the length of term of Wilentz's office, Hoffmann had dismissed Colonel Norman Schwarzkopf, a Democrat, who had headed the investigation for the New Jersey State Police.

For Anne and Charles, Hoffmann's interference in the case had profound repercussions. In addition to the increase in their threatening mail, the firing of Norman Schwarzkopf was deeply upsetting to them. The police chief, whom many other people disliked because of his controlling, abrasive personality, had become a good friend, and there was no question in their minds that he had done his job well.

But then something happened that convinced them that Jon's life would be in jeopardy if they remained in the United States any longer.

As the three-year-old boy and his teacher were being driven by automobile from the Little School, the nursery school that Elisabeth had founded, to Next Day Hill, a large vehicle cruised dangerously close to the car and then crowded it to the curb, forcing it to stop.

As little Jon quivered with fear in the back seat, several men jumped out of the vehicle. Cameras were thrust against the window of the car, and a series of clicks was heard. Then the men jumped back in their car and sped away.

These men were not kidnappers or extortionists but Hearst photographers. Jon's picture was published in the New York *American* and in other Hearst newspapers, and then offered for sale to many other papers throughout the country. The man who took the photo was paid a sizable bonus.

There had been other similarly terrifying incidents involving photographers attempting to snap the little boy's picture, but when Lindbergh learned of this latest intrusion on his family's privacy, he decided to take swift action. Although he, Anne, and Jon would not relinquish their American citizenship, they would give up their residence in the United States and go to live in England, perhaps permanently if the press and the public would not let them alone. The reason Lindbergh chose England was that of all the countries he had visited since his celebrated flight, its people, he believed, "have a greater regard for law and order in their own land than the people of any other nation in the world."

After secretly obtaining passports for himself and his family in Washington, he booked passage on the *American Importer,* a small passenger-freighter. No one, with the exception of his mother, Anne's family, and a few government officials in both the United States and England who were sworn to secrecy, knew the name of the ship on which they would be sailing from the United States. Even the port police were not informed.

With his customary precision, Lindbergh had the plan all worked out. When they arrived in England, they would be met by their brother-in-law, Aubrey Niel Morgan, who would take them to his family home in Cardiff until they found a suitable place to live. Like the Lindberghs, Aubrey appears to have been seduced by the splendor and protective atmosphere of Next Day Hill — he had been living there with Mrs. Morrow and the rest of the family since Elisabeth's death. However, when he learned of the Lindberghs' plight, he immediately offered to sail for Britain at the same time, on a faster ship, so he could be of help to the family when they arrived.

On December 7, Lindbergh told his wife that they would no longer be able to live in the United States, and he instructed her to start getting their things together. She must be ready to leave for England by the end of the week. When they would return, he did not know. Although his order threw Anne "in a turmoil," she quickly convinced herself that leaving their native land would be yet another "exciting" adventure in their lives. As a loving wife, wasn't it her duty to "jump into anything" with Charles "at any moment"? Still, she had some regrets about leaving her family and her newly decorated studio. She realized it would not be easy to write in a new, unfamiliar place. "All my life seems to be trying to 'get settled,' and C. shaking me out of it. But you like it? Yes."

They sailed on the freighter from New York to Liverpool, England, in the early hours of December 22, 1935. They were the only passengers on board. During the nine-day voyage, Anne spent most of her time caring for Jon. In Englewood, there had been many servants to help watch over him, but on this rough crossing she was solely responsible for his care. Although being with her son absorbed her entire attention, she was grateful for the opportunity to spend time alone with him. Jon, she knew, had been deeply affected by the emotional turmoil of the household in the past several years, and she desperately wanted to make his life happier and calmer. As she watched her son play with a kitten on the ship, she prayed that their new life in England would do him good.

At night she and Jon ate dinner together, while Lindbergh, who seems to have been too preoccupied with other matters to help with his son, dined separately with the captain. On Christmas Eve, Anne sat alone in their cabin, opening the presents her family had given her before she sailed for England.

There was so much to think about, and on many nights of the voyage she had trouble sleeping. The sea was rough, and as she lay awake, listening to the crash of the waves against the porthole, she thought about the future and what it would hold for the family.

On New Year's Eve the Lindberghs arrived in Liverpool, amid much hullabaloo, for the news of their self-imposed exile had been published in the *New York Times* shortly after they sailed from New York. As they walked down the gangplank — a small, unsmiling woman in dark clothing followed by a tall grim-faced man holding a bewildered little boy in his arms — newspaper photographers rushed forward to take their photographs. On the streets newsboys were shouting the story of their arrival. Soon, they would learn the reaction to their departure in the United States and read some of the mostly sympathetic newspaper editorials, which blamed yellow journalism and in particular the Hearst press for the cruel hounding that had forced the Lindberghs to leave their native land.

The next day would be the start of a new year as well as a new life. Although Anne told herself that this fresh start in another country would do them all good, she could not help thinking, as she was driven through the drab streets of Liverpool, about the land they had deliberately left behind.

CHAPTER 14

Days of Heaven

Charles's decision had proved a wise one. In England, in an old country house named Long Barn in the Weald of Kent, the Lindberghs found the peace and marital happiness that had long been denied them. That they found such bliss in this house was ironic, for it was owned by a couple whose idea of love and marriage was very different from their own.

Like its owners, Harold Nicolson and his wife, the novelist and poet Vita Sackville-West, Long Barn had an unconventional history. Built in the fourteenth century, it was rumored to have been the birthplace of William Caxton, the first English printer, whose ghost, it was said, still haunted the place.

When the Nicolsons discovered the property in 1915, the cottage itself was in ruins. According to their son Nigel,

> The floors sloped crazily, so that every piece of furniture appeared crippled, and the roof was held together less by construction than by natural angles of repose. In place of a garden there was a chute of rubble and a tangle of briars and nettles. They restored the cottage, transformed it into a house by adding a new wing at a right angle (the timbers coming from an old barn that lay askew at the foot of the hill), and made a garden in a series of lawns and walled terraces, leading by gradual descent from formality to the artlessness of the surrounding copses. Long Barn was not simple. There were seven main bedrooms, four bathrooms and a sitting-room fifty feet long. There were always at least three domestic servants and two gardeners. It could put up three or four guests at a

time, and was sunny, pretty, romantic and comfortable. But it retained an atmosphere of fourteenth century rusticated innocence.

As soon as Anne saw the rambling ancient house, with its wildly sloping floors, slanted walls, exposed beams and warm, inviting rooms filled with beautiful, though worm-eaten, English antiques, she fell in love with it. There was something about Long Barn that gave her a feeling of "peace and security," as if the house itself had wrapped its arms around her. Equally soothing to her spirits were the breathtakingly beautiful gardens, which Harold had designed and Vita herself had planted.

Harold and Vita had bought Long Barn shortly after they were married. It always held a special place in their hearts, not merely because of its antiquity but because it was their first home, and it was there that they first began to garden seriously, beginning by replanting on the property some primroses they had dug up in the woods. After living at Long Barn for fifteen years, they had moved to an Elizabethan castle near Sissinghurst, Kent, some twenty miles away. But their new home was in total ruins, and to pay for its extensive restoration, as well as a new garden (which later would become one of the most famous in the world), they sadly concluded that they had no choice but to sell their former home. It was not an easy decision on their part, as both Vita and Harold were deeply attached to it. But the sale of Long Barn soon became unnecessary. With the death of her mother, Lady Sackville, in 1936, Vita became an heiress and did not need additional sources of income. An excellent businesswoman as well as a writer, however, she still thought it a wise idea to rent it out.

Although the Nicolsons had not been living full-time at Long Barn for three years, Anne sensed the couple's electric presence as soon as she moved into the house, which was filled with many of their belongings. Dominated for too long by her mother and her luxurious tastes, she was determined not to let Harold and Vita hold sway over her, so the first few days she spent rearranging the furniture in an attempt to assert her own identity in the house. Soon, convinced that the presence of its former inhabitants had been eradicated, Anne began referring to Long Barn as "our own home."

Yet Long Barn's owners continued to fascinate her, in particular, Vita, whom Anne had met briefly in early January 1933 at the Waldorf Astoria when the Nicolsons had come to the United States for a lecture tour. By then, Vita was an important literary figure, who was also known as an outspoken advocate of women's independence. Her striking appearance created a sensation wherever she went, for she was a tall, beautiful woman with fine dark eyes, carmine red cheeks, and a deep caressing voice, and she liked to dress in mannish clothing, which she offset with such feminine touches as long earrings, ropes of pearls, and lacy shirts.

As the writer Peter Quennell, who met Vita in 1937, observed many years later, "Larger and a little taller than her husband, who, beside her, with his fresh pink face, briar pipe and conventional tweed coat, had a somewhat boyish or under-graduateish air, she resembled a puissant blend of both sexes — Lady Chatterley and her lover rolled into one, I recollect a contemporary humorist observing."

Anne's curiosity about this extraordinary woman was soon satisfied. Not long after she and Charles had moved into Long Barn, Vita herself came to call on them. At first, Anne was nervous in her presence, but soon the writer's "nice and natural and easy" manner put her at ease. Although they mainly discussed business, Anne could not help imagining that Vita was deeply impressed with Charles. It made her feel happy that someone of Vita's reputation and caliber respected and admired her husband. "It is like metal meeting metal, almost as though I could hear it ring!"

Indulging in one of those comparisons in which she invariably came out the loser, Anne concluded that Vita had "suffered much more and learned much more" than she (a strange remark, considering her own profound grief over the deaths of her son and sister). She couldn't help but wonder why Vita made her "feel like a child," since she usually felt older than most of the women she met. But there was something about Vita, in her riding trousers and velvet doublet, that made Anne feel "curiously feminine, terribly frivolous and feminine, and half the time as if she [Vita] weren't a woman at all."

Although Anne was often naive about people, this was an astute observation on her part, for Sackville-West loved many of her own sex. Her most famous lover was the sexually timid Virginia Woolf. In fact, Woolf's *Orlando*, a charming fantasy about a young nobleman with literary aspirations who changes sex, was not only a portrait of Vita but a love letter to her. It is unclear from Anne's diaries whether she guessed Vita's sexual orientation, or, for that matter, Harold Nicolson's — he too had many homosexual liaisons within the context of his marriage. (Anne once described him as being "slightly effeminate" but never publicly discussed his sexuality.)

Given Anne's tolerant nature, it is unlikely that she would have been shocked by Harold and Vita's sexual preferences. More disturbing would have been Vita's abhorrence of marriage, which she felt limited a woman's freedom, and her insistence on living a private life that excluded her husband. She and Harold were apart more than they were together, yet, according to their youngest son Nigel, "their marriage not only survived infidelity, sexual incompatibility and long absences, but it became stronger and finer as a result." Vita and Harold's marriage, which was essentially sexless, was the opposite of Anne and Charles's, which had its basis in sexual passion, a constant, almost cloying togetherness, and traditional sexual roles.

Although their attitudes toward marriage could not have been more dissimilar, the two women had much in common. Both loved solitude and detachment, to the point of reclusiveness; both were married to men who were undemonstrative, with a strong distaste for emotional display; and they both had experienced the devastating loss of a child, which had brought them closer to their husbands. When Vita's second son was born dead in 1915, she was inconsolable and wrote to her husband, "Harold, I am sad. I have been thinking of that white velvet coffin with that little still thing inside. He was going to be a birthday-present to you next Sunday. Oh darling, I feel it is too cruel. I can't help minding, and I always shall."

This heartbroken letter could have been written from Anne to Charles about the death of their son.

If Vita was impressed by Lindbergh, as Anne fondly imagined, she did not record her feelings of admiration. However, it is not unreasonable to speculate that she did not respond to him as a male. According to her biographer Victoria Glendinning, Vita "could not relate easily to strong silent masculine men." She loved Harold, who, like the other men who attracted her, was an "over-civilized, articulate, non-masculine man."

As for her impressions of Anne, it appears that, having dismissed her as a literary talent, Vita mainly regarded her as a source of future income. After meeting Anne and Charles, she wrote to Harold, "The Lindberghs take Long Barn for one year, with option of giving two weeks notice, in which case they pay a penalty. They *insisted* on this clause being put in, though I protested. They were charming and more muddle-headed than I could have believed possible. I arranged everything for them, even to ordering their coal! They obviously love the place already."

It was the view of a practical landlady, and Vita continued to keep the relationship on a businesslike level, although naturally she was curious about her famous tenants. Some time later, when she returned to Long Barn to see how the couple was doing, she was disappointed to find them not at home. But, as she reported to Harold, she was told by their servants that

> they might be arriving this evening with Mr. Morrow, Con, and Aubrey Morgan. Evidently they preserve their policy of secrecy even towards their household! . . . But what interested me most, was that the hall was stacked with packing-cases from America, "because Mrs. L. has never had a home before, and she loves this so much that she wanted to have all her own things round her," so evidently they mean to stay for some time. And not only that, but they have sent for Thor, who came over on the Queen Mary, and is now in quarantine at Croydon. So it looks hopeful."

Anne's happiness at Long Barn did not come only from at last having a home of her own. For the first time, she was now able to live like an average woman, something she had been unable to do since relinquishing her life as a private citizen to marry Lindbergh. For years, whenever they had appeared in public, she and Charles were mercilessly hounded by the press, but now they could go for a stroll in the Weald undisguised or Anne could take Jon shopping and no one would even stare at them. No doubt English politeness and respect for privacy were to a large extent responsible for their being left alone, but it also seems that Harold Nicolson had something to do with it. Before their arrival, he had telephoned Mrs. Woods at the Weald Post Office and asked her to instruct the local residents not to disturb the Lindberghs. "No sir, we shall not stare at the poor people," she had assured him.

Unlike their American counterparts, members of the British press had come to an unwritten agreement not to pester the celebrated couple, and so on April 3, 1936, Anne and Charles were left to the privacy of their own thoughts when Bruno Hauptmann, still firmly maintaining his innocence, was executed in Trenton for their son's murder. Newspapers in Britain and all over the world reported that the prisoner had gone to his death stoically. In fact, he had walked rapidly toward the electric chair and sat down in it eagerly, as one account gruesomely put it, "as if inviting the lightning and held on to the arms with a strong grip."

Bruno Richard Hauptmann was pronounced dead at 8:47 ½ in the evening. In England, it was almost two o'clock in the morning, and Anne and Charles were undoubtedly asleep.

Anne's reaction to Hauptmann's execution remains unknown, as she has neither chosen to make public her diary entries during this period nor confided her feelings about the controversial crime in recent interviews. In fact, her published diaries and letters for 1936 make no mention of either Hauptmann's execution or the crime that led up to it.

Given Anne's reverence for life, it seems unlikely that she would have been overjoyed by the news of his death, a common reaction among the survivors of murder victims, many of whom believe that justice has been finally served when the killer of a loved one is executed. More likely, his execution triggered within her a multitude of emotions — a sense of relief that he was dead, coupled with horror at taking a human life, as well as profound sadness that nothing could bring back her little boy, including the death of his killer.

Strangely, although Anne did not refer to her murdered son in her published diaries and letters, she continued to obsess about her sister's death. In fact, the ghost of Elisabeth, whose death had occurred only four months before, seemed to haunt Long Barn, as if at times the house belonged to her instead of to Anne. "I have a strange feeling, going around the rooms, that it is Elisabeth's house, that I am getting it ready for a visit from her," Anne told her diary. She continued to be plagued by nightmares in which Elisabeth was still alive, although in her dreams Anne was always painfully aware of her sister's impending death.

Yet, even though Elisabeth was gone, Anne refused to believe that their relationship had ended. "It isn't really time or space that separates people but states of mind. We never were separated from Elisabeth, were we?" she wrote to her mother.

Unwilling to part with Elisabeth, Anne tried to keep her memory alive by wearing her fashionable, pretty clothes to social functions. Since the two sisters were not of the same height or build, many of the dead woman's dresses had to be altered to fit, but Anne did not seem to mind the bother. Wearing a suit Elisabeth had liked or carrying one of her favorite purses to a glamorous social occasion was perhaps her way of trying to incorporate within herself the personality of her vivacious, confident sister. Not only did it make her feel more socially adept, it also provided a way for her to deal with her guilt at being alive and continuing the adventure of her life while Elisabeth was dead.

Spiritually, Anne had come to believe that one did not recapture the "reality" of the dead by rereading their letters or looking at old photographs, or even by remembering them. On the contrary, she felt that the best way to hold on to feelings about a lost loved one was to look inward. "But it is something undefined in me . . . something that goes along with me and has — this is the shock — *grown with me.* The Elisabeth I carry around with me every day is much much older than the Elisabeth of those letters. It is she *in me* growing old along with me. Is that possible?"

Not too long after Elisabeth's death, her husband, Aubrey Morgan, fell in love with Constance, the youngest of the Morrow daughters. More than a year later, he proposed marriage. Although she had adored Elisabeth, no one was more delighted with this somewhat unusual turn of events than Mrs. Morrow, who had always been very fond of Aubrey. When Anne heard the news of her younger sister's and brother-in-law's engagement, she was shocked, possibly because their relationship reminded her of the triangle that had once tied together Lindbergh, Elisabeth, and herself. Ironically, it was now the memory of Elisabeth, her former rival, that she felt was in danger of being obliterated. Nevertheless, she tried her best to view their forthcoming marriage not as a betrayal of her sister but as a union between two people who had both loved her. "I had foreseen it, but I had not expected it so quickly. I felt, Yes it is right — right for her, right for him. It is wonderful — perfect," she wrote in her diary. "And yet a jolt to my whole picture of life at the moment."

It was at Long Barn that Anne was able to work in earnest on her second book, *Listen! the Wind,* an account of the ten-day 1933 survey flight she and Lindbergh had made to study air routes between Europe and the United States. Yet even in this secluded, idyllic setting, writing was difficult. Although she had three live-in servants, including a nurse for Jon, her son's inexhaustible energy and constant need for attention interfered with her writing schedule to the point that she became irritated with him and then angry at herself for becoming annoyed. Frustrated and depressed, she had begun to question whether she should give up writing and concentrate on being a mother, which she had come to appreciate as an enormous undertaking in itself.

But Jon wasn't the only member of the family who required constant attention. No sooner had they moved into Long Barn than the ever restless Charles, who had become interested in primates as experimental animals as the result of his research on organ culture with Alexis Carrel, announced that he wanted to visit Africa, a trip that, fortunately for Anne, did not materialize. However, as soon as he mentioned his plans, her old conflicts resurfaced about her need to work versus her need to be with her husband. Should she stay at home and write her book, or drop her writing to travel with him? As usual, she saw his life as significantly more important than her own. "Who am I to say No, I want my own life, No, I want my own work. No, I will not go to Africa because I want to finish a book," she wrote in her journal. "Of what value would that book be? A personal account of hashed-over, dead experiences. Of what value, next to the vision, the new ways that C. can give, and I by keeping him happy, by doing what he wants? And yet, he does not want that. He wants me to have my own life — to write."

Yet even though Lindbergh was strongly encouraging her to pursue her own interests, Anne was still uncertain about continuing to write professionally. On the one hand, she longed to become a first-rate writer, but on the other, she did not want her writing to become the most important aspect of her life. Whether this was due to cultural conditioning or fear of failure on her part is an interesting question, but in any event, she decided that a career, if she pursued one, should be secondary to marriage and motherhood.

On July 4, 1936, Independence Day in the country she had left behind, Anne outlined in her journal her own rules for her future happiness:

> That marriage is the most interesting, difficult and important thing in life.
>
> That everything that I am trying to live and be and do is nothing if I cannot somehow give it to Jon.
>
> That living is a more important art than any other one. That writing is only important in that it gives me the balance required to live life as an art. Something more, too, intangible, difficult to analyze. It is important to me not because I think I can write great things and give them to the world, but because it happens to be the lens of me, clarifying me, enabling me to see things and to think, and to concentrate what's in me and therefore to live better....

To speak of living life for life itself was very different from her attitude as a sheltered, timid young woman, when she had felt that her experiences only became meaningful when she wrote about them. That had all changed when she met and married Charles Lindbergh. Their passionate sexual relationship and the tumultuous joys and sorrows they shared together had catapulted her into life. No longer was she an unawakened girl but a mature woman with a husband and son who had experienced life in all its sweetness and bitterness. Despite her personal tragedies, her new life remained enthralling, and her husband and second child were at its core, the two people who gave it meaning. By comparison, writing, though she still depended on it as a vehicle to explore her feelings, seemed a lifeless occupation.

Anne continued to view marriage as the cornerstone of a woman's life. She believed it was so crucial to a woman's emotional and physical development that only in marriage could a woman attain psychological maturity. "I feel that you have done so much piecing [*sic*] already without ever being married," she wrote to Margot Loines, who had recently become engaged to Dwight, Jr. "I felt that the first time I met you. 'How did she get as far as that, without being married?' "

Perhaps because she was married to a dynamic, famous man with whom she was living such an exciting, fulfilling life, Anne had by now thoroughly convinced herself that she didn't really want to be a "woman writer" any more than she had wanted to be a "woman aviator." Although her amateurishness "disgusted" her, she tried to justify it by telling herself that she had never been prepared to make the necessary sacrifices to become a serious writer. At this point in her life, the idea of writing as a secret "rebellion" against her overbearing husband and family no longer held any appeal for her. In fact, even the thought of combining a career with her all-absorbing domestic life was threatening, although intellectually she knew that it was possible for women to combine a home life and a career. "But I think they [women] do it (if successfully) at the price of a pigeonholed life — a man's life. Because in order to compete with men they must concentrate their energies into a narrow line. And I think in doing that they deny themselves the special attributes and qualities of women."

It is debatable whether Anne arrived at these conclusions about her own sex independently, for by this time she, as well as Charles, had fallen under the spell of Alexis Carrel, with whom Charles was developing a pulsatile perfusion pump to keep organs alive outside the body. In fact, as Lindbergh had predicted, the famous French surgeon had become his philosophical mentor. This was perhaps not surprising, since Lindbergh, after the murder of his son, may well have been in need of a father figure, especially one like the charismatic older Carrel, who had much in common intellectually with Lindbergh's father and grandfather. Both the elder Lindbergh and Dr. Land had been social Darwinists, but Carrel carried his fascination with eugenics to an extreme. In

1935 he published a book called *Man, the Unknown*, which shocked many readers because of its sensational theories regarding the superiority of the Nordic races and the euthanasia of criminals and other "undesirable" people. In his book, Carrel suggested that future generations should put "undesirable" people to death to improve the race. He also believed that hardened criminals as well as insane people guilty of a crime should be executed.

> Those who have murdered, robbed while armed with automatic pistol or machinegun, kidnapped children, despoiled the poor of their savings, misled the public on important matters, should be humanely and economically disposed of in small euthanistic institutions supplied with proper gases. A similar treatment could be advantageously applied to the insane, guilty of criminal acts. Modern society should not hesitate to organize itself with reference to the normal individual. Philosophical systems and sentimental prejudices must give way before such a necessity.

As Leonard Mosley, one of Lindbergh's biographers has pointed out, though Carrel was not an anti-Semite, his ideas nevertheless "bore an uncanny resemblance to those which National Socialism was beginning to follow in Germany. He already shared with Nazi theorists the assumption of the superiority of the Nordic race, his explanation of this being that lesser races — blacks, Latins, Indians, and Asiatics — had been 'burned' into inferiority by generations of too fierce light grilling down upon them."

But it wasn't merely Alexis Carrel's racist views that attracted Lindbergh, himself a confirmed social Darwinist and a man whose life had been irreparably damaged by a criminal act. Temperamentally, the two men were very much alike. According to one of their colleagues at the Rockefeller Institute, both men were extremely rational in their thinking, although the French surgeon was even more logical than the aviator. "Neither Carrel nor Lindbergh was an intensely feeling individual," the scientist recalled. "A prima donna as well as the most intelligent scientist I have ever known, Carrel was an essentially cold-hearted man, which was why he had a number of enemies at the Rockefeller Institute who wanted him ousted . . . while Lindbergh was not cold in the same degree." In the colleague's opinion, Lindbergh was "not a heartless man at all." He remembers him as being "overwhelmingly an engineer in his way of thinking," adding that he was "a very educated engineer who was largely self-taught about science, as were many scientists of his generation. He was a chap who loved things that had never been done, that potentially could be done, and that he could try to do."

Anne seems to have been less impressed by Carrel's beliefs than was her husband ("Of what use is it?" she wrote after reading *Man, the Unknown*. "Is the emphasis correct? Is the spiritual and mental up to this? Or will it breed a race of tall soft-headed athletes?"). Nevertheless, it seems that she was more influenced by the doctor's theories about women and their societal role than she cared to admit. For Carrel had stressed in *Man, the Unknown* that "women should develop their aptitudes in accordance with their own nature, without trying to imitate the males," also emphasizing that "women should receive a higher education, not in order to become doctors, lawyers or professors, but to rear their offspring to be valuable human beings." In fact, Anne's letter to Margot Loines, praising her emotional maturity, which Anne thought was remarkable for an unmarried woman, could have been written by Carrel himself, who believed that "females, at any rate among mammals, seem only to attain their full development after one or more pregnancies. Women who have no children are not so well balanced and become more nervous than the others."

Personally, Anne was in awe of the theatrical, eccentric surgeon, a tiny man who wore a pince-nez and Nehru-type jackets and who insisted that he and his assistants, as well as his operating room at the Rockefeller Institute, be draped in black to prevent contamination by germs. A rugged individualist with a terrible temper, Carrel was heartily disliked by many of his colleagues at the institute because of the disdainful way he treated them. But Anne was deeply impressed by the doctor, who believed that women should not make excessive demands on men of genius. Deferential toward unusual and powerful men, she once described him as "compact, alert, trigger-pulled," adding reverentially, "terrific force, under control."

Equally impressive to Anne was Carrel's wife, a solidly built Breton nurse who fancied herself blessed with psychic powers. Carrel had married her when he was forty. In Anne's opinion, Madame Carrel was "an incredibly strong, beautiful person," combining the intuition and compassion of a woman with a man's "breadth of view, clarity of vision, impersonality of attitude (the scientific attitude)."

However, this opinion was not shared by many of Carrel's scientific associates, who wisecracked behind his back that they never knew "why there was a Madame Carrel" and thought her to be anti-American, feigning poor health so she would not have to travel with her husband to the United States. (In reality, Madame Carrel was in excellent health and outlived her husband by some thirty years.)

Eventually, Anne's old feelings of inferiority got the better of her, and she began to resent the Carrels, whom she imagined found her dull in comparison with her husband. Characteristically, she never voiced her resentment to Lindbergh or the Carrels, but simply blamed herself for being so shy, weak, and fearful that it was no wonder the brilliant scientific couple did not find her interesting. "Seeing their strength, power, health, courage, adventurousness, ability — and the ordeals they have been through — and thinking, Could I go through that? Could I measure up to that?"

During their stay in England, Anne and Charles became intensely politically minded. How this transformation came about is both complex and curious, for hitherto both seemed uninterested in politics and world events. In fact, reading Anne's voluminous diaries, with their myriad details about her daily life and emotional states, one looks in vain for a reference to the Scopes "monkey" trial of 1925, the execution of the Italian-born anarchists Sacco and Vanzetti in 1927, the stock market crash of 1929, and the Great Depression and its devastating effects on Americans in the early 1930s — or, in short, any of the critical events and issues of the late 1920s and 1930s that absorbed most people in the United States and elsewhere. It was as if the Lindberghs' own personal triumphs and tragedies had obsessed the couple to such an extent that, despite their modest public demeanor, they came secretly to believe that *they* were the twenties and thirties.

All this changed, however, during their self-imposed exile in England. Even for cloistered, privileged people like Anne and Charles, who for years had lived a self-absorbed life, it was impossible to ignore the world situation, which was becoming more alarming with every passing day. On the Continent, the Italian dictator Benito Mussolini and the German dictator Adolf Hitler were defying the democracies: Mussolini by invading Ethiopia in October 1935 and overthrowing its monarch, Haile Selassie; Hitler, who had torn up the Treaty of Versailles, by proclaiming German rearmament in March 1935 and, a year later, reoccupying the Rhineland.

Rather than responding with outrage to these acts of aggression, the leaders of many European countries preferred to appease the dictators, or "to look the other way." When Hitler reoccupied the Rhineland, France protested but took no action against him. This was also the case in Britain. Although he did not make British policy, King Edward VIII, who had assumed the throne earlier in the year after the death of his father, King George V, preferred not to know about the brutal excesses of the Italian and German dictators. Far more absorbing to Edward VIII was his affair with Mrs. Wallis Warfield Simpson, a reed-slender, immaculately groomed woman who was not only an American but married.

On May 12 Charles and Anne met the king and Mrs. Simpson for the first time at a U.S. embassy tea given by assistant Air Attaché Martin Scanlon and his wife, Gladys, who were leaders of London's smart set. Determined that the spirit of Elisabeth be present at such a momentous social affair, Anne wore her sister's ten-year-old black silk suit, which she had altered the night before. But not even this costume could transform her into a fluent conversationalist. According to her own account, she became hopelessly tongue-tied when she was introduced to Edward VIII, who, sensing her discomfort, did his best to put her at ease. Undoubtedly, the king was unaware that the shy young woman he was attempting to draw out was coolly sizing him up and would later note in her diary that he had "all the appearance of youth, really — even his face is rather wistful and young like a boy's, only it has hardened. That boy's face drawn tight into the responsibilities of age. Very sad to look at. One feels either he is prematurely old for his looks or else still nostalgically young for his age."

As for the king's American mistress, Anne noted that Mrs. Simpson was "beautifully dressed with the poise and ease of knowing whatever she does is right, and that she is the person in the room that people will turn to, make excuses for, copy, play up to. All she has to do is to play her role and everyone else will follow the cues. But I rather like her. She at least is honest and playing her own part, not someone else's."

It appears that even before this meeting, Wallis Simpson identified with Anne and Charles and their self-imposed exile from the United States. In an emotional letter to her aunt Bessie, written on May 4, 1936, more than a week before she met the Lindberghs, she confessed,

> I have had so much in the last two years in so many different and interesting ways which I won't go into — except to say that I am looked upon here by the majority of people in exactly the opposite way that the U.S.

press presents me. I can't have much respect for a nation that downs its own nationals and thus to belittle them in the eyes of the world. One's countrymen should be loyal. I haven't found them so and therefore like the Lindberghs prefer to live elsewhere, so you mustn't see the situation through their eyes.

The king was charmed by the Lindberghs. Later that month he invited them to be his guests at a royal dinner at St. James's Palace. Also included on the guest list were Mrs. Simpson and her soon-to-be-discarded husband, Ernest, whose official presence at the party, along with that of Prime Minister and Mrs. Stanley Baldwin, soon set tongues wagging all over town. Although there had been a great deal of gossip about Mrs. Simpson's relationship with the king, her association with him had never been formally acknowledged, but now her name — along with her husband's — was appearing in the *Court Circular,* along with the prime minister's.

Anne, however, seemed blissfully unaware of the shock waves the elegant Mrs. Simpson was creating that evening among the distinguished assemblage, including the prime minister, who was so outraged by Mrs. Simpson's presence that he kept announcing that he wanted to "go home," much to his wife's chagrin. Again, Anne was far more concerned with the impression she herself was making on the king, whom she now felt was not only an inherently kind man who tried to put everyone at his or her ease but "the most 'human' Englishman" she had met. On further scrutiny, she realized why she liked him. He reminded her of Charles when she had first met him at the U.S. embassy in Mexico City — "a real person trying to fit the mold of a hopelessly conventional life." As for his impressions of Anne, the king noted to Harold Nicolson that she had been very diffident at first, "but with my well-known charm I put her at ease and liked her very much."

But the king was not the only one to win the Lindberghs over with flattery. A few weeks after the royal dinner, Charles received a letter from a Major Truman Smith at the U.S. embassy in Germany. In the letter, Major Smith extended to him "in the name of General Göring and the German Air Ministry an invitation to visit Germany and inspect the new German civil and military air establishments." Smith continued:

I need hardly tell you that the present German air development is very imposing and on a scale which I believe is unmatched in the world. Up until very recently this development was highly secretive, but in recent months they have become extraordinarily friendly to the American representatives and have shown us far more than to the representatives of other powers. General Göring has particularly exerted himself for friendly relations with the United States.

From a purely American point of view, I consider that your visit here would be of high patriotic benefit. I am certain they will go out of their way to show you even more than they show us.

In closing, Major Smith added that he and his wife were "extremely hopeful that Mrs. Lindbergh will come with you."

Intrigued by the invitation, Lindbergh wrote Smith back immediately, saying that he "would be extremely interested in seeing some of the German developments in both civil and military aviation," and then reporting his findings back to the U.S. government. He also asked Smith to "transmit my thanks and sincere appreciation to General Göring and the German Air Ministry for inviting me to visit Germany and to inspect the new German air establishments." His wife, Anne, Charles Lindbergh added, "would like very much to visit Germany, and we will plan on coming together."

On July 22, 1936, the Lindberghs took off for Berlin in their new Miles Mohawk, which an English aircraft manufacturer had recently built to the aviator's specifications. That same day they landed in Berlin. As Anne watched her husband receive a hero's welcome from American military personnel and German aviation officials, including General Hermann Göring's representative, who greeted them with a Nazi salute, she could not have known that from that moment on his magic and glory would diminish and that the rest of her life would be spent in a stubborn defense of his behavior.

CHAPTER 15

"A Pair of Unicorns"

WHEN ANNE had visited Germany with her family many years before, the country had made little impression on her. But now, driving with the American military attaché's wife, Mrs. Truman Smith, behind the open car in which her husband was being shown off to the German people, she could not help but admire the new buildings and the "neatness, order, trimness, and cleanliness."

In her opinion, Germany was certainly a welcome contrast to the other European countries she had visited, and she found herself considerably impressed with it. There was no sense of poverty here, she noted, and the people she saw on the streets were mainly middle class and nicely dressed. Nazi flags were flying everywhere, as well as the Olympic flag — the games were to begin in August — and the entire city of Berlin had a festive air.

Hitler's home was on their route, and she was surprised to discover that it was a relatively simple building, with only one member of the SS at the gate. Far more impressive, in her opinion, were the uniformed boys who zipped through the streets on bicycles — the Hitler Jugend — and were "tanned and strong-looking."

The next day, she silently cheered Lindbergh on as he read a speech about the perils of aviation to the Air Club of Berlin, where he was the guest of honor at a luncheon attended by many important German aviation experts, including Ernst Udet, the leading World War I ace, and General Erhard Milch, inspector general of the Luftwaffe. "Aviation has brought a revolutionary change to a world already staggering from changes," Lindbergh cautioned in his clear, rather high-pitched voice.

"It is our responsibility to make sure that in doing so, we do not destroy the very things which we wish to protect."

Although Anne shared her husband's deep concern about the air-plane's capacity for destruction, she was nervous as he spoke, for she was well aware that his message criticized air bombing, a military tactic favored by the Nazis, who were building up the deadliest air force in Europe. She was relieved when General Milch told her afterward that he liked her husband's speech.

Later, the Lindberghs were invited to lunch with General Göring, the corpulent, medal-bedecked head of the German Air Ministry, and his wife, a stately blonde, who despite the early hour was gowned in floor-length green velvet, her only adornment a diamond and emerald swastika pin. Although Anne was amused by the spectacle of the flamboyant general and his famous pet lion, who at one point during their visit urinated over his master's lap, she was miffed when Göring ignored her, concentrating his attentions on her husband, whom he peppered with questions through an interpreter.

After meeting other high-ranking Nazis, she discovered that there were many things about them both to dislike and to admire. As she wrote to her mother from Berlin,

> There are great big blurred uncomfortable patches of dislike in my mind about them: their treatment of the Jews, their brute-force manner, their stupidity, their rudeness, their regimentation. Things which I hate so much that I hardly know whether the efficiency, unity, spirit that comes out of it can be worth it.
>
> And yet there they are, a strong, united, physical and spiritual force to be reckoned with — a spirit of hope, pride and self-sacrifice. We haven't got it — or France or England. It bothers me that it seems to be gotten that way — not by democracy.

Although her husband had his own reservations about the Nazis, he justified their policies of aggression by reminding himself that the entire history of the world had been determined by the endless struggle between the weak and the strong. "To me, Nazi Germany was a fascinating country," he wrote later,

> but I disliked its regimentation, its appeal to mass emotions, its restriction of free thought, its fanatical attitude toward race; yet I saw there an aspect of life that was fundamental to life's evolution — the forceful challenge to a status quo. I saw a Western people preparing for aggression

and developing a philosophy to justify such action — as Englishmen had justified building their empire, as Americans had justified wresting a continent from its inhabitants and then throwing out the earlier occupying forces of England, France and Spain.

The Berlin that Anne and Charles visited in 1936 was a deceptive city. According to William L. Shirer, the American newspaper correspondent based in Berlin,

> The Olympic games held in Berlin in August 1936 afforded the Nazis a golden opportunity to impress the world with the achievements of the Third Reich, and they made the most of it. The signs *"Juden unerwuenscht"* (Jews Not Welcome) were quietly hauled down from the shops, hotels, beer gardens and places of public entertainment, the persecution of the Jews and of the two Christian churches temporarily halted, and the country put on its best behavior. No previous games had seen such a spectacular organization nor such a lavish display of entertainment. Göring, Ribbentrop and Goebbels gave dazzling parties for the foreign visitors — the Propaganda Minister's "Italian Night" on the Pfaueninsel near Wannsee gathered more than a thousand guests at dinner in a scene that resembled the Arabian Nights. The visitors, especially those from England and America, were greatly impressed by what they saw: apparently a happy, healthy, friendly people united under Hitler — a far different picture, they said, than they had got from reading the newspaper dispatches from Berlin.

Although Lindbergh declined to be interviewed by American correspondents, Lufthansa, the German state-owned airline, invited some members of the press to a tea party in his honor at Tempelhof on July 23. Shirer was one of the few journalists to receive an invitation. It was the first time he had seen the aviator since covering his arrival at Le Bourget. "I was surprised at how little he had changed in appearance; he still had a boyish air, though I noted that he had become more self-confident," he recalled many years later.

> After tea Lufthansa officials took us for a ride in the then world's largest airplane, *Field Marshal von Hindenburg,* a huge, cumbersome eight-engined craft . . . Göring turned over the controls to Lindbergh somewhere above the Wannsee, and we were treated to some fancy rolls, steep banks and other maneuvers for which the Goliath machine was not designed. I thought for a few moments that the plane would be torn apart and that that would be the end not only of Göring and Lindbergh but of me. Cups of tea and coffee and liqueur glasses careened off our tables on

to the laps of the distinguished guests. It was an unpleasant reminder of something I had heard about Lindbergh shortly after his arrival in Paris; that he was a terrible practical joker. Finally, Göring took back the controls and guided us smoothly back to Tempelhof.

Shirer was baffled by Lindbergh's behavior in Berlin. Although the correspondent was impressed by the flier's speech to the Air Ministry, warning of the new bombers' capability for destroying Europe, he was "disturbed" by the Nazis' boasts that the Lindberghs had become admirers of the Third Reich. " 'The talk is,' I wrote in my diary that evening after the ride in the *Hindenburg,* 'that the Lindberghs have been favorably impressed by what the Nazis have shown them.' "

Hoping to make Lindbergh aware of the truth about Nazi Germany, Shirer, along with some other American correspondents, tried to arrange a meeting. But once again Lindbergh declined an interview.

Two weeks later, at Goebbels's party on the Pfaueninsel to celebrate the Olympic Games, Lindbergh, bowing to the wishes of his host, the Nazi propaganda minister, agreed to meet with the American press.

"Late that evening he sauntered over to our table and greeted us graciously enough," Shirer recalled.

> I thought it was a golden opportunity to enlighten the famous flyer about what lay hidden beneath the surface in Hitler's dictatorship. But . . . Lindbergh proceeded to tell us what the situation was in Germany. He . . . had found a happy, united people, he said. As an airman he was particularly impressed by the German air force and the progress of German aviation in general . . .
>
> That summer in Berlin, the German Nazi leaders were able to sow in Lindbergh's mind, and in that of his attractive and gifted wife, seeds that, when they flowered, would poison their judgment about the course of history and of Western civilization.

Soon after returning to England, Anne discovered that she was pregnant for the third time. Although by now she had no illusions about the effect of motherhood on her writing career, she was thrilled by the prospect of another child — "Charles loves me and I'm going to have another baby," she wrote exultantly in her diary. As had been the case during her previous pregnancies, she had no intention of giving up flying with her husband. She made an extremely arduous trip with him to Italy and India in early February 1937. By then, she was in an advanced state of pregnancy. Jon was left behind in the care of his nurse.

It was on the first leg of this flight, while the Lindberghs were flying from France to Italy, that they were reported missing over the Alps when they did not land on schedule in Rome. But the case turned out to be otherwise. Encountering rough weather, Lindbergh had made an emergency landing in Pisa on February 1. Still filled with contempt for what he regarded as the "irresponsible" press, he had asked the Italian airport personnel not to report their safe arrival.

After spending some time in Rome, Cairo, Jerusalem, and Calcutta, where they attended a conference of the World Fellowship of Religions, the Lindberghs returned to Long Barn at the end of March. A month and a half later, their third son was born on May 12, 1937, the day of King George VI's coronation at Westminster Abbey. As had been the case with Jon, Charles Lindbergh did not make public the news of his son's birth until twelve days later. The couple — it was also announced to the press through a spokesman — had decided to call their third son Land, after Evangeline Lindbergh's side of the family.

At first even Anne disliked the name, thinking it "strange," but soon convinced herself that people would rapidly become accustomed to it. This belief was not shared by Vita Sackville-West, who was appalled by the Lindberghs' taste in names and immediately confided her displeasure to Harold: "Do you see that the Lindberghs have called their baby 'Land'? Is it after *The Land,* do you suppose, because they live at Long Barn? [*The Land,* a sort of English georgic, was Vita's most famous work.] What a name, poor child!"

But nothing could spoil Anne's joy when she heard Jon say "my brother" for the very first time. She was filled with wonder and thankfulness, recording her feelings in her diary: "*My brother.* It was so thrilling, opening up the past and the future, as though I had waited a lifetime for it, waited and waited for my boy to say 'My brother.' " On June 22, her thirty-first birthday, she was still euphoric and grateful for this newfound happiness: "so happy to have on this birthday my two little boys."

Her affection for her two sons did not prevent her from leaving them four months later, in October, to accompany her husband to Munich, where he attended the Lilienthal Aeronautical Society Congress. As she was later careful to emphasize in the introduction to *The Flower and the Nettle,* one of the volumes of her diaries and letters dealing with this prewar period, Lindbergh made this second trip to Germany to continue "his investigation of the growth of the German Air Force for U.S. Army Intelligence."

In her introduction, Anne neglected to mention that she and her husband were the guests of honor of the German government. Nor did she admit that on this visit, Ernst Udet, by showing Lindbergh the new German aircraft and letting him fly the Messerschmitt 109, succeeded in convincing him that it was futile for any European nation to oppose Hitler because the German air force was in fact invincible. As Leonard Mosley, one of Lindbergh's biographers, has pointed out, "The Germans were so obviously friendly and deferential to him that Lindbergh would have found it impossible to believe that Udet was lying to him and would have been even more incredulous had he been told that he was being deliberately used by the Luftwaffe to carry stories of their invincibility back to the democracies and terrorize them." Anne too allowed herself to be swayed by the Germans' flattery. It never seems to have occurred to her why they were being so nice to her.

During this second visit to Germany, the Lindberghs met other powerful high-ranking Nazis. Among them was Walther von Reichenau, then commanding general of the troops in the Munich area, who during the war would remain one of Hitler's leading generals. Anne was quite taken with the general, whom she met at a dinner party, calling him "as balanced and as well-educated a man as one is likely to find." After dinner, she was fascinated by a conversation between Reichenau and her husband about the war in China and military strategies, becoming irritated when some of the other wives began to talk among themselves. In her opinion, their chitchat was boring in comparison with the men's discussion.

The Lindberghs had been back home at Long Barn for a little more than a month when they decided to visit the United States. The reason they decided to return to their native land after a two-year absence was that Charles Lindbergh had some business to attend to in connection with his aviation work. In addition, he was collaborating with Alexis Carrel on a manuscript about the new apparatus and techniques that could be used for the culture of isolated organs.

Before he left for the United States, Lindbergh helped Truman Smith prepare an intelligence report on estimated German air power as of November 1, 1937. In Lindbergh's opinion, military technology in Germany was far superior to that in France and Britain, and should "obtain technical parity with the U.S.A. by 1941 or 1942." The Smith-Lindbergh report was sent to Washington, where it was circulated widely by the General Staff and the War Department.

In December the couple arrived at Next Day Hill. They enjoyed the holidays with Mrs. Morrow and spent the next few weeks catching up with old friends and relatives. Now well into the process of immortalizing themselves, they commissioned Robert Brackman, a well-known American artist, to paint their portraits. Predictably, everyone thought Lindbergh's portrait was a brilliant character study but that Anne's didn't do her justice. They stayed in the United States for four months, and during this period Jon and the new baby were again left in the care of servants. This time, his parents' absence was particularly hard on four-and-a-half-year-old Jon. When he heard that they were not going to be home for Christmas, one of his favorite holidays, he was terribly disappointed, and he asked his mother why she had to be away during the time of year he liked best. "Your father must go, and I must go with him" was her response.

Anne's justification for leaving Jon for such a long period was that "the excitement and nervous tension of Englewood . . . would undo all the good of the last two years." Too many relatives would want to see him, including, of course, her own mother, with whom he had developed a very close relationship while she and Charles had been away on their frequent flying trips. It was better for him to "have his own small family and a life limited by that." Unexplained is her rationale for leaving behind Land, who, at six months of age, was too young to be affected by the fuss that would be made over him. Undoubtedly she was afraid that her two boys might discover life with their grandmother to be a lot freer and happier than the one they lived with their parents, for Lindbergh in particular was a strict disciplinarian. Obviously following in the footsteps of his own stern, emotionless father, he believed that children should become independent at an early age and should never be coddled. He even scolded his own mother for picking up Land when he cried or for protecting Jon.

While the Lindberghs were away, some pipes burst at Long Barn and Vita went down to arrange for their repair. Herself a rather cool and distant mother, Vita was nonetheless appalled by what she perceived as Anne and Charles's neglect of their children. "The Lindberghs, of course, were not there, but only little Jon and the baby," she reported to Harold. "How do they dare to leave them alone like that — with servants and a nurse? The whole place looked dreadfully ill-kept, and is over-run with mice. It was most gloomy."

Nigel Nicolson, Harold and Vita's youngest son, was with his parents on several occasions when they visited the Lindberghs at Long Barn. Many years later, he remembered Charles Lindbergh as being

> very tough with his little boy Jon. He would pick him up by the ankle and swing him around his head, and Anne used to look on white-faced. Sometimes he would put him on a child's swing and swing him very high — he was a very small little boy, only two or three years old — and again, this was to toughen him. Charles would say "he's got to learn, he's got to learn," meaning that he's got to learn that the world is a brutal place and to stand up for himself. That rather shocked my mother.

In Nigel Nicolson's opinion,

> Anne was always very much the child-wife. She has a wonderful personality and is a great writer, but she was terribly dominated by Charles . . . really bullied by him, and she was submissive.
>
> But then after all one must put against that the fact that he did share his later flights with her, and that required some confidence in her and recognition that she was courageous and determined and tough, so she wasn't altogether the sort of down-trodden wife . . .
>
> But in the upbringing of their children, for example, I think his was the dominant voice. I think in a way she wanted that in him. I mean, he was a tremendous figure, a great hero, and you can't be a hero to half the world and a mouse at home.

When the Lindberghs returned to England in the middle of March 1938, Lindbergh decided that it would be beneficial for his work if he lived nearer to Alexis Carrel, who retreated every summer from the noise and congestion of New York to Saint-Gildas, a small island off the coast of Brittany, which he and his wife had purchased in 1922. Illiec, another small island, was to the east of Saint-Gildas, and at low tide it was possible to walk not only to the mainland but from one island to the other.

While they were in England, Charles and Anne had visited the Carrels in their old stone house on Saint-Gildas, which possessed the kind of rugged terrain that immediately appealed to Lindbergh, the loner and adventurer. He wrote to Carrel, "As I told you, I have never been in a place which combines so well all the characteristics which I like. I would rather live on Saint Gildas than any other place I have ever seen." In fact, the only other place the airman loved so much was the farm at Little Falls, Minnesota, where he had grown up.

For once Anne did not share her husband's enthusiasm for a place to live, although no evidence exists that she ever told him about her objections. To her, the bare tidal flats and strangely configured, towering rocks of Saint-Gildas, although beautiful, were desolate and lonely. One night, on the island, when she learned of her husband's intention to move to the area, she sat alone in the moonlight, trying to convince herself that if she learned to love the terrain, she would better understand "the landscape" of his mind. Unfortunately, on this particular night she was unable to gain a deeper insight into either the land or his psyche. Her spiritual musings were interrupted by Lindbergh's whistle, and she obediently jumped up and trotted to where he was sitting on some nearby rocks. As always, her need for his approval and love was so overpowering that she could not oppose his slightest wish, as a faithful dog will not disobey his master.

In 1938, during their Christmas visit to Mrs. Morrow, Charles had learned from Madame Carrel that Illiec, the island adjacent to Saint-Gildas, was for sale. On the island was a well-built stone house, with a small tower, which had been built by Ambroise Thomas, who had composed the opera *Mignon*. According to one of Lindbergh's scientific associates, Theodore Malinen, foreigners were not allowed to own property on the French coast, so the Carrels arranged for the island to be purchased by some of their friends, who formed a small company. The entire stock of the company was then turned over to Anne and was held for her by Madame Carrel.

But the thought of becoming an island owner filled Anne with dread. Already suffering from a high degree of nervous tension, in part triggered by the news that the Czechs and Germans were massing on the Czechoslovakian border in May 1938, she became overwrought at the prospect of leaving her beloved Long Barn. Fearing that war would break out at any minute, at night she was often sleepless. To make matters worse, her mother, always a source of inner conflict, had just arrived from the United States for a visit. An introspective woman who could not easily tolerate excitement, Anne had always needed time to analyze her feelings and write about them, but now her days had become crammed with activities and preparations for the move to Illiec, and there was no time for her to be contemplative. "I must learn to control my life and my nerves," she admonished herself. "I will not be a neurotic who cannot see people without going to pieces."

Not surprisingly, her writing was affected by these many pressures. Her diary entries, which formerly had been filled with charm and sensitive observations about life and nature, became a tedious vehicle for recording the development of her and her husband's political opinions.

Even she herself seemed to sense the change in her work. Months later, when she retrieved her old diaries from the Morgan, Grenfell vaults in London, where they were being kept for safekeeping and posterity, and reread them, Anne noted sadly, "It seems to me I *wrote* better in the old diaries, even in those depressed, nervous, unbalanced times. There is an intensity to it."

Although Anne hated the thought of leaving Long Barn, she had no regrets about leaving England, with its "ugly and mediocre" suburbs and "cheap" stores, or the English, with their "superior" ways. In fact, she had come to feel that most upper-crust Britons were literary snobs, and it continued to rankle her that they remained unimpressed with her writing, for her books did not sell nearly as well in Britain as they did in the United States. Her negative feelings, however, did not extend to the English countryside. It was the only aspect of the nation that never failed to inspire her. "The trees are so beautiful — the trees and the countryside are the only things in England that give you a feeling of ecstasy," she noted almost bitterly in her journal. "The dingy brick suburban houses, the iron fences, the Bovril signs, the buses — and those dreary, dreary-looking people in mackintoshes." Despite her supposed "spirituality," it was though she had no feeling for the ordinary people in life or their struggles to earn a living.

And so it was only Long Barn that she would miss intensely, with its ancient, crumbling house and beautiful, terraced gardens. Herself now interested in gardening as the result of Vita's influence, she sadly concluded that a similar garden would be out of the question at Illiec, with its inhospitable soil. Still, she hoped that it might be possible to grow flowers there, and before she and Lindbergh left for Illiec, they drove to Sissinghurst to say goodbye to Vita. "She looked quite lovely in her black corduroy knickers and coat and her black felt hat, with two police dogs straining at the leash," Anne reported. "We told her how we hated to leave Long Barn and I asked her what would grow in a garden by the sea. She said that if hydrangeas grew there, lots of other things might, and she gave me some names. I can see I am going to become one of those gardening women, after all! . . . I could not help thinking how much nicer it was than generally — some real contact."

Vita's impressions of the visit were similar to Anne's, although she was quick to pick up on her ex-tenant's unhappiness. "I think they really have been happy at Long Barn, and I think poor Anne dreads the idea of this desolate and rocky island," she wrote to Harold. "I wish you had seen the little notebook she produced for hints on seaside gardens! She has learnt to love flowers at Long Barn."

Shortly after the Lindberghs left Long Barn, however, Vita went down to check on the property. Its condition appalled her. "Now you know the Lindberghs are the last people on earth with whom one would ever wish to have an unpleasantness, but the state in which they have left the house is disgraceful," she raged to Harold.

> Not only is it filthy, but they have shifted practically every piece of furniture and made no attempt whatever to put it back in place. E.g. those large Dutch cupboards we bought from Luigi are now in different rooms, most of the beds have been moved, not to mention tables, chairs, and chests of drawers. And dust and cobwebs everywhere. Personally I should never expect anybody to take it in its present state, with every room looking ugly. (How they have managed to spoil it like this I don't know!)

Harold Nicolson too was rapidly becoming disenchanted with the "charming" Lindberghs. Violently against the Nazis, whom he thought had "exploited the worst in the German character . . . at the expense of all that is best," Nicolson felt that he would rather die than see Britain make an alliance with them. "Charles and Anne Lindbergh and Mrs. Morrow came over from Long Barn," he noted in his diary on May 22.

> Lindbergh is most pessimistic. He says that we cannot possibly fight since we should certainly be beaten. The German Air Force is ten times superior to that of Russia, France and Great Britain put together. Our defences are simply futile and the barrage-balloons a mere waste of money. He thinks we should just give way and then make an alliance with Germany. To a certain extent his views can be discounted, (a) because he naturally believes that aeroplanes will be the determinant factor in war; and (b) because he believes in the Nazi theology, all tied up with his hatred of degeneracy and his hatred of democracy as represented by the free Press and the American public. But even when one makes these discounts, the fact remains that he is probably right in saying that we are outmastered in the air.

Certainly not a pacifist, Lindbergh had begun urging Britain and France to build up their military and air power. At the same time he did everything he could to convince the two countries to reach an accommodation with Germany in order to prevent war. The French listened to what he had to say but failed to take effective action, while the

British, to his dismay, failed to heed his warnings. According to Wayne Cole, to whom Lindbergh granted unrestricted access to his personal letters and papers relating to his isolationist activities prior to World War II, "Though he [Lindbergh] did not use the term, both his emphasis on Germany's overwhelming air superiority and his appeals for accommodation with Hitler's Germany coincided with and may have encouraged appeasement policies at the time."

> In any event, Lindbergh became convinced that a war between Germany, on one side, and Britain and France, on the other, would be a tragedy whichever side won. It would, in his view, be a fratricidal conflict that could destroy the inherited genetic and cultural treasures slowly built by Western civilization over the course of countless centuries. The only beneficiaries, in his opinion, might be the Communists and the Soviet Union. If left to themselves, Lindbergh believed, the Germans under Hitler would turn east toward the Soviet Union, not west toward Britain and France. He did not view such a course with the same misgivings as he did a war in the west. Conceivably a Russo-German conflict would leave the ramparts of Western civilization secure against Communist Russia and the Asiatic hordes.

Before they departed for the stony isolation of Illiec, the Lindberghs spent some time with their good friend, the Virginia-born Lady Nancy Astor, who had often entertained them, since their arrival in England, at her opulent country estate, Cliveden, in Buckinghamshire. At the time many people suspected the "Cliveden Set," as they were called, of being pro-Nazi and pro-fascist, an accusation that was vehemently denied. Whether they ever participated in intrigues against the British government is open to question, but it is clear that the group was decidedly proappeasement. Their leader, Lady Astor, a celebrated society hostess, who was also the first woman member of Parliament, shared Lindbergh's conviction that Britain should abandon its French allies and adopt a policy of appeasement toward Germany. Or, as Lindbergh put it after meeting her and her circle, "[Lady Astor] wants better understanding with Germany. I was encouraged about the feeling of most of the people there in regard to Germany. They understand the situation better than most Englishmen do these days."

Witty, opinionated, and often outrageous, Nancy Astor was a powerful woman who boasted many important friends. She arranged for Lindbergh to express his views on Germany's strength to a number of decision-making British statesmen, as well as the American ambassador to London, Joseph P. Kennedy, who had independently come to the conclusion that the Nazis were invincible and that it was in the best interests of the British government to appease Hitler as quickly as possible.

Anne was entranced by Lady Astor and her circle, finding them even more charming and sympathetic than the king and Mrs. Simpson. She especially liked Lady Astor, an old friend of the Morrow family, who was as "gay and spontaneous and natural, as always." A woman whose painful seriousness about life often prevented her from seeing its humorous aspects, even Anne found it "screamingly funny" when Lady Astor put some false teeth in her mouth and, imitating a lower-class Englishwoman, began to twit Lindbergh about why he "didn't marry a Mae West sort of woman instead of that little shrimp?" As for Lady Astor's husband, Waldorf, Anne feared that he would discover that she "was *not* the intelligent daughter of a very intelligent father, or the intelligent wife of a very intelligent husband." Nevertheless, she pronounced him "*the* nicest man I've met in England, very quick, keen, perceptive and kind," entirely forgetting that not too many months before she had bestowed the informal honor on the former king, Edward VIII.

As for Ambassador Joseph Kennedy, another Nazi-appeaser, as well as an anti-Semite, he struck Anne as being "clean-cut, humorous, and intelligent." She liked him immediately, as did her husband, who, though usually uncommunicative at social gatherings, couldn't "tear himself away" from the ambassador when he met him at the Astors', finding him to be "someone he can really talk to." This proved to be something of an understatement; a few months later in September, when Hitler was threatening to seize the Sudetenland from Czechoslovakia, Lindbergh did more than talk to Joseph Kennedy about the strength of the Luftwaffe. At Kennedy's request, he wrote Kennedy a letter in which he stated that "German air strength is greater than that of all other European countries combined, and . . . she is constantly increasing her margin of leadership."

In the letter, he also stressed the importance of avoiding a general European war, which he felt might

> easily result in the loss of European civilization. I am by no means convinced that England and France could win a war against Germany at the present time, but, whether they win or lose, all of the participating countries would probably be prostrated by their efforts. A general European war would, I believe, result in something akin to Communism running over Europe, and, judging by Russia, anything seems preferable.

I am convinced that it is wiser to permit Germany's eastward expansion than to throw England and France, unprepared, into a war at this time.

We must recognize the fact that the Germans are a great and able people. Their military strength now makes them inseparable from the welfare of European civilization, for they have the power either to preserve or destroy it. For the first time in history, a nation has the power either to save or to ruin the great cities of Europe. Germany has such a preponderance of war planes that she can bomb any city in Europe with comparatively little resistance. England and France are too weak in the air to protect themselves.

Several of Lindbergh's critics believe that this letter, with its terrifying portrayal of Nazi air power, was partially responsible for the Munich Pact. One of those to whom Kennedy forwarded Lindbergh's gloom-and-doom missive was British prime minister Neville Chamberlain. It was rumored that he became so panicked after reading its contents that he, with French prime minister Édouard Daladier, decided at Munich on September 30, 1938, to sacrifice Czechoslovakia to Germany, a charge that Anne has spent her life denying. "His estimates of comparative European air strengths were rumored to have influenced Prime Minister Neville Chamberlain in his decision to go to Munich and to persuade the Czechs to yield to Hitler's demands," she wrote in her introduction to *War Within and Without,* the fifth volume of her diaries and letters, which was published six years after her husband's death. "The truth is that Lindbergh never spoke about German air power to Chamberlain or to the Secretary of State for Air, Sir Kingsley Wood. His reports to other air officials were no doubt repeated, but there is no evidence that these were influential in the decisions at Munich. The British, in fact, had long ignored other warnings from aviation experts and those of Winston Churchill."

How much influence Lindbergh's letter to Kennedy actually had on Chamberlain at Munich remains the subject of heated debate between Lindbergh's critics and Anne Lindbergh, but one thing is certain. For both Anne and Charles, the impending war in Europe had become an obsession. Political naifs, as she herself admitted many years later, they nevertheless felt that it had become their mission to prevent a conflict.

But there was also something in Lindbergh's temperament and background that made him an admirer of the Germans. Not only was he himself of Nordic descent, but as an aviator and scientist he was impressed by their military power and technical achievements. Naively, he believed that they had found a solution to the problems of crime and an uncontrolled press, which he had by now convinced himself was the cause of his family's tragedy.

Still professing to loathe his own legend, he nonetheless swiftly succumbed to German propaganda. This was not surprising, as the Nazis' bloated myth of the "master race" was similar to the mystique surrounding the elite nature of pilots in the twenties. For instance, an advertisement for an early New York flying school featured a banner headline proclaiming, THE AVIATOR — THE SUPERMAN OF NOW, and then went on to explain why a pilot was braver and tougher than other men: "The world has its eye on the flying man. Flying is the greatest sport of red-blooded, virile manhood."

The reason for Anne's tolerance of fascism was very different from that of her husband. It wasn't so much that she admired the Nazis, but rather that the prospect of a full-scale European war, similar to World War I, about which she had heard so much as a young girl, horrified her to the point that she felt she could not bear it. Unlike her husband, she had been converted to the cause of pacifism, by reading Erich Maria Remarque's *All Quiet on the Western Front* in college. Furthermore, according to a friend, "there was a strong Quaker influence on the family," even though the elder Morrows attended the Presbyterian church regularly. Millions of people would be slaughtered, as they had been in the earlier global conflict. In addition, the threat of another world war must have subconsciously conjured up all the old nightmarish feelings about her son's murder.

For this very sensitive woman, war, like her son's senseless death, was an unendurable prospect. As she saw people standing in line in London to buy gas masks in September 1938, she imagined that she saw death everywhere. "I feel as though I were watching the dead, seeing the doomed. Impossible to think it might all be interrupted with bomb holes and shattered buildings in another week. And yet so possible that I had the feeling I was looking on an old film, showing 'the good old days of prewar England,' before the destruction."

Like her husband, Anne believed that unless war could be averted, the treasures of Western civilization would be destroyed. "I do not agree at all with the 'We must stop the dictators now or never,' " she noted in her journal. "Unfortunately, it is most doubtful whether they can now be stopped. England and France are so piteously weak, and even with

America it would be a long struggle. And practically, I think the only way to stop them is to let them come up against Russia."

The remoteness of Illiec might have helped Anne escape temporarily her anxieties about the ominous world situation, but the primitive conditions only aggravated the tension for her. Shortly after moving to the isolated, rocky island off the Brittany coast in June 1938, she had discovered that "the 'simple' life that many men extol . . . is extremely complicated for women." The nineteenth-century turreted stone house lacked heating, plumbing, and electricity. Most of the furniture was in hideous taste and would have to be replaced. To make matters worse, the English nurse she had hired to take care of the children objected to the French servants' slovenliness and poor cooking, and then there was Dr. Carrel, who was always popping over from his neighboring island to offer some unwanted child-raising advice. Usually a paragon of patience and understanding, even Anne was becoming exasperated with the French surgeon's constant intrusions. When Evangeline Lindbergh came for a visit, he seized the opportunity to question her about the diet that her son had been fed as a baby. "There is never, I remark to Mrs. Lindbergh, such interest expended on what I was fed when I was a baby!" Anne wrote indignantly in her diary.

Even the seaside garden she had planned at Illiec was a dismal failure. As she had feared, the strong wind immediately killed all the fragile cuttings she had carefully transported from Long Barn. At night, exhausted by physical work and the servants' quarrels, she took refuge in pleasant dreams of the tranquil gardens of her former residence.

In fact, the only thing that was going well was her book, which she was able to finish by the end of June 1938 and send to Alfred Harcourt. Deeply impressed by its quality, the publisher immediately complimented her on a job well done. "He said it was one of the days that made publishing worth while — a grand job. But it makes me happy," she noted in her journal. "Besides C. will be *so* pleased."

Harcourt suggested a few changes, and rather than let his wife attempt them herself, Charles Lindbergh once more assumed the role of her editor. Why he felt qualified remains something of a mystery, as he had a poor grasp of the language and his own diaries, *The Wartime Journals of Charles A. Lindbergh*, are filled with grammatical errors, such as "the Ambassador invited Anne and I for tea at 4:30," which an editor, perhaps fearing his displeasure, let stand. Despite these lapses, he had a keen eye for repetitions and inaccuracies, and unlike his own editor, he did not hesitate to tell his wife bluntly what he thought about her work and how she could best improve it. In addition to correcting his wife's grammatical and factual errors, Lindbergh helped her decide on a title: *Listen! the Wind*. Not trusting the book cover to a professional artist, he also designed the jacket, which consisted of half-stars, a half-moon, and waves. Anne found it "striking and decorative."

It was on Illiec, with its wild, primordial landscape, that Charles Lindbergh began to grow disillusioned with science as a means of understanding the mysterious laws of life and started to search for answers elsewhere. Hoping that science would provide evidence of immortality, he had begun studying his own sperm under a microscope, becoming enthusiastic when he observed "thousands of living beings, each one of them myself, my life stream, capable of spreading my existence throughout the human race, of reincarnating me in all eternity." An hour later, however, when he returned to his microscope, he was disappointed to find that "the area within its lens field was as desolate and lifeless as a plain upon the moon . . ."

"But how far can scientific aids penetrate mystery?" he asked himself. "Will not we find in awareness itself the deepest penetration of all wonder? . . . Intuition and rationality converge in a supersensate penetration, and we learn how reality forms phantoms and phantoms form realities." His attempt to find a bridge between the mystical and scientific worlds was in part the influence of the Carrels, both of whom believed in the occult and experimented with a wide range of supersensory phenomena, including ghosts, mental telepathy, and clairvoyance.

For Lindbergh, watching Carrel operate in his all-black surgery at the Rockefeller Institute had been like having a supernatural experience. "I felt I had reached the frontier where the mystical and the scientific meet, where I would see across the indistinct border separating life from death . . . The moment I entered the black-walled room, I felt outside the world men ordinarily lived in. Black-gowned figures like my own stood erect, sat on stools, glided about spectrally."

Encouraged by Madame Carrel, Lindbergh began to search for ghosts, which were said to be lurking around a "haunted" well on Saint-Gildas. Although he never saw an apparition, he sometimes "had an eerie feeling" as he passed it, "as though its phantoms had receded to make way for my approach but would then close in behind me."

At the same time he also became fascinated by the supersensory phenomena associated with the yogic masters. While living at Long

Barn, he had received special permission to use the library of the Royal College of Physicians in London where he read medical reports on yogic and fakir practices. And in March 1937 he and Anne had flown to India for a conference of the World Fellowship of Religions, which was headed by Sir Francis Younghusband, the celebrated explorer and mystic. On his return to England, Lindbergh made a series of unsuccessful scientific experiments in which he tried to demonstrate that the yogi's slow, rhythmic breathing controlled his body's heat-regulating mechanism.

Although neither Lindbergh nor Anne ever made the connection between the violent death of their son and Lindbergh's sudden interest in the occult and mystical religions, it seems clear that like so many other people who have suffered a grievous loss he had turned to the supernatural for a possible explanation of his suffering.

Anne does not seem to have shared her husband's enthusiasm for occult phenomena and mystic religions. After attending the religious conference in India, she wrote to her mother,

> The effort of keeping a straight face at C., sitting up in the front row of a religious conference facing a large sugary picture of Ramakrishna decked with flowers. Banners all around the walls: "Religion is the highest expression of man" — "Blessed is he who is free from thoughts of I-Am," with crowds of barefoot Indian monks, holy men, students, and a few stray, wispy people from Pasadena, London, Boston, following an Indian swami in an orange turban, is simply too stifling to meet. I nearly died of the incongruity the first day. Also C.'s alarm watch went off in the middle of a prayer!

Never one to embrace any organized form of religion with fervor, Anne preferred to find solace, peace, and inspiration in nature. The sky, the sea, the wind, and the stars were the sources of her creativity, and her best writing would reflect this deep communication with the natural world.

In early August 1938 both Lindberghs were in the air again, this time on their way to visit Russia, where Lindbergh was going to meet with Russian aviation experts. As Anne later emphasized in one of her published diaries, his trip "was part of a larger project to make a comparative study of the air strength of the major European countries for U.S. Intelligence reports."

As she was about to leave on her trip, Anne was suddenly filled with a sense of foreboding that something would happen to Jon or to Land, who was beginning to resemble Charlie, while she was away. "I don't want much to go to Russia, but feel I must," she wrote unenthusiastically in her diary. "It is part of the European picture. C. must know it, and I must go so we can talk it over together . . ."

This was self-delusion on her part, considering that Lindbergh was in contact with many American and European aviation experts who possessed a far greater knowledge of Russian aviation than she. The real reason Anne had to accompany her husband to Russia was that she felt afraid and insecure whenever she was apart from him, even for short periods of time. Possibly she feared that if he went without her, he would find someone younger and more attractive. What would happen to her then? In a flash, her life of glamour, adventure, and fulfillment as a woman would vanish, and once more she would be that loveless, mousy girl who could not possibly compete with her brilliant, vivacious parents and sister. "I watch C. until he is a speck of white over the path across flats and islands and the bar of stones to the Carrels'," she wrote later that week in her diary.

> Why do I go? Why do I keep my eye on that white speck as far as I can see it? The two questions seem to be related.
>
> I must go. I must be part of C.'s life. I must go even though I am afraid to go. "Not to be afraid of this world, said Hari, one must belong to it."
>
> And for your children — perhaps sometimes you must do things that show them that you are not afraid of life, even if you die in doing them. Perhaps it might teach them more than staying at home and trying to protect them.

When they arrived in Russia, Lindbergh was shown a number of aircraft factories, which he privately thought were vastly inferior to the ones he had seen in Germany. Anne too was unimpressed by the Soviets. To be sure, the country had changed since their previous visit in 1933. There were new buildings and merchandise in the stores, but she could not help noting that the goods were of shoddy quality and the people looked undernourished. Not even the exploits of some women military pilots who had recently made a record flight across the Soviet Union could change her mind about the Soviet system. "I feel quite out of sympathy with this. They have taken women's work away from women in Russia and given it to the state," she noted. "I do not believe it can be done as well *en masse* by the state. A woman is just another tool, like a man, to be pressed into mechanization."

As for liking the Russians, I do, too — I really feel more sympathetic to them than to Germans, innately. Of course, you are "for them," but it doesn't mean you are for a system that believes in absolute leveling.

Besides, that system has disappeared, rightly or wrongly. There is definitely an upper class of officers, technical people, officials, etc.

And how does he (Stalin) explain, or include in his support, these terrific trials, murders, espionage system?

Although she liked them as people, the Russians, Anne concluded, were not nearly as smart and able as the Germans. In fact, they suffered from "a general mediocrity," the only exception being the ballet, which both she and Lindbergh attended one night and agreed was beautifully performed.

At the time of the Munich Pact, on September 30, 1938, in which Britain and France sacrificed their Czechoslovakian ally to the Nazis, Anne was at Cliveden with Lady Astor, while Charles was at the American embassy in London with Ambassador Joseph Kennedy. Although apart when they heard the news that the four powers — Hitler, Chamberlain, Mussolini, and Daladier — had agreed, both Lindberghs had a similar reaction — they were ecstatic. An unabashed admirer of Chamberlain, Anne had no doubt that after thirteen hours of bargaining, he had done the right thing in giving Germany Czechoslovakia's rich and strategically important Sudetenland and buying "peace in our time." "The account of Chamberlain in the House of Commons — that great humble and courageous man — completely justified in his efforts and faith, rewarded, sweeping the house with enthusiasm. I can hardly read it without crying," she wrote emotionally in her diary. "Also his words on getting into the plane to go back for the third meeting: 'I hope when I come back I shall be able to say with Hotspur in *Henry IV,* 'Out of this nettle, danger, we have plucked this flower, safety.' ' "

But not all the Lindberghs' friends regarded the events of Munich as "good news." Particularly outspoken in his criticism was Jean Monnet, the distinguished French economist who had been a close friend of Dwight Morrow. Correctly sensing that the Nazis were untrustworthy, he frankly told the Lindberghs that he believed France should arm in preparation for Germany's next action.

Monnet's opinions were, of course, the direct opposite of Lindbergh's, and although it pained Anne to hear her husband and dear friend argue, it was clear where her loyalties lay.

I keep longing to hear the old M. Monnet who used to talk with Daddy: "My dear Monnet . . ." It is worlds away. They are generations apart. A prewar split. It is so strange. The cockles of my heart warm to the conversation of one, and yet I have been converted to the practical, hard facts-of-life of the other. And yet that is not fair either, nor do I mean it exactly. C. is not only "practical hard-facts-of-life." He is idealism, too. But it is a new idealism, of another age. M. Monnet, in spite of his youth, belongs to another. My father's.

She often wondered how people would have classified her father's politics during this period and sadly concluded that he would have been considered a Communist. "How strangely the lines have fallen. Charles is a 'Fascist' and Daddy a 'Red'!"

By this time she was convinced that the Nazis were not to blame for their brutal aggressions. "Whereas I hated the unrestricted use of *force* with all my heart and disliked much that was being done, I felt that England, France and U.S.A. had *forced* the use of force on Germany (C.'s arguments) and that Germany had got nothing by a policy of non-force in her League days, her Stresemann days, and therefore had to do it this way."

It was her husband's disillusioned, bitter voice speaking through her lips, pure and simple.

The Lindberghs returned to Illiec on October 1, and then almost immediately left their island retreat for a two-week trip to Germany. Jon was upset when Anne told him that she was leaving on yet another trip, but she calmed him by promising to write him while she was away and to bring him some chocolate on her return. As for Lindbergh, she was ecstatic to note that he was as pleased as "a small boy" when he learned she would be going with him. On this particular trip, their third to Germany, he had been invited to Berlin by the Lilienthal Society, the German Air Ministry, and by Ambassador Hugh Wilson, who, as Anne later was careful to stress, "hoped the visit would help him develop personal contacts with Göring."

This proved to be the case, for Göring arranged for the aviator to visit any aeronautical factory that he wished and to fly various types of planes, including the new ME-110 twin-engine fighter and the JU-88 light bomber, which could fly at a top speed of 310 miles per hour. It was the first time any foreigner, aside from the Italians, had seen the JU-88. Later, Göring confided to Lindbergh that soon the Germans would have a plane that could fly at 500 miles per hour.

But Lindbergh failed to realize that to a large extent, this German air superiority was illusory and the Nazis had far fewer serviceable bombers than they claimed. "If any doubt had remained in my mind about Germany's current leadership in military aviation, that visit in October 1938 removed it," he wrote. "The slowness of France, Britain and other farther-west countries to face the implications of the Luftwaffe's strength was to me astounding and depressing."

While they were in Germany, word leaked out in England of Lindbergh's unfavorable impressions of the Soviet Air Force and that he was of the opinion that the Luftwaffe could beat the Soviet, French, and British air forces combined. Moscow immediately got wind of the story, and Lindbergh was soon denounced in the Soviet newspaper *Pravda*, which made it clear that he would be arrested if he ever returned to the Soviet Union. He also received a highly critical letter condemning his actions from some of the Soviet Union's most celebrated pilots, many of whom had entertained him and Anne during their recent visit. Although U.S. officials pleaded with him to retract his statements, saying they were damaging to U.S.-Soviet relations, Lindbergh refused to comply with their request. It was clear that he had no use for the Soviets, for during this period he wrote, "It always seems that the Fascist group is better than the Communist group . . . Communism seems to draw the worst of men."

Anne was outraged that the Soviet pilots had had the effrontery to write such a letter to her husband.

> I am startled at its crudeness, at the fact that all those jovial nice open fliers should rush to put their names to such abuse, except that of course any rumors coming back about C. having Fascist sympathies (and ten days ago he was supposed to be on a mission for "democracies" of the world!) would throw suspicion on them and that to save their necks they must deny him vigorously.
>
> But I mind C.'s being misquoted and labeled and I mind the blind stupid hate and fear and jealousy in it. It is the most dangerous thing on earth.

It was during that third trip to Germany, on October 18, at an all-male dinner at the American embassy given by Ambassador Hugh Wilson, that Hermann Göring presented Lindbergh with the Service Cross of the German Eagle, a high German decoration for civilians, which was in recognition of his achievements in aviation, particularly the 1927 flight. Anne was not present at the ceremony.

"I found that he had presented me with the German Eagle, one of the highest German decorations, 'by order of the Fuhrer,'" Lindbergh wrote that evening in his diary in his dry, prosaic style.

In her diary, Anne also briefly summed up the occasion without comment. "C. came back late from his dinner, with a German decoration presented him quite unexpectedly by General Göring. Henry Ford is the only other American to get it. The parchment is signed by Hitler."

Later, amid an avalanche of criticism, she rushed to her husband's defense, pointing out that not only had the medal been bestowed on him at a dinner given by the American ambassador, but that he had had no knowledge of it beforehand. Moreover, two other people, an Englishman and a Frenchman, had received a German decoration that same week without being violently attacked in the press.

Oddly, it was Major Truman Smith, the American military attaché in charge of army and air intelligence in Berlin, who was more illuminating than Anne about the ramifications of Lindbergh's medal. "When Colonel Lindbergh and the military attaché reached home later that evening, they found their wives had not yet retired," he recorded in his air intelligence report. "Colonel Lindbergh, without comment, drew the medal box from his pocket and handed it to Mrs. Lindbergh. She gave it but a fleeting glance and then — without the slightest trace of emotion — remarked 'The Albatross.'"

Although Anne quoted from Smith's report in *The Flower and the Nettle*, she herself has never commented on whether it was true that she regarded the medal as an albatross around both their necks.

While the couple was still in Germany, Anne's *Listen! the Wind* was published in the United States to almost uniformly excellent reviews. A critic for the *New York Times* described it as "the story of ten days of human experience, as set down by a writer whose responsiveness can catch the fullness of each rounded moment and whose artistry can make her readers feel place and people, hope and disappointment and question and triumph, the slow pulse of suspense." Equally impressed was Clifton Fadiman, who wrote in the *New Yorker*, "Mrs. Lindbergh writes well. There are scenes in *Listen! the Wind* which, for closeness to the quick of character and experience, are worthy of a first-rate novelist. Mrs. Lindbergh's books, quite apart from their value as aeronautical history, are small works of art."

Although thrilled by these comments, Anne fretted that the critics had overlooked her husband's contribution. "They do not see how much of the book *is* C., how much of it he made."

Ironically, in light of the future enmity that would exist between their husbands, one of Anne's most fervent fans was Eleanor Roosevelt, who thought *Listen! the Wind* "a gem" of a book. But not even the beauty of Anne's prose could temper Mrs. Roosevelt's serious reservations about Anne's husband. The pogrom against the German Jews that became known as Kristallnacht had appalled her, and she wrote from Cincinnati, where she was on a lecture tour, "The German-Jewish business makes me sick and when F.D.R. called tonight I was glad to know [Ambassador Hugh] Wilson was being recalled and we were protesting. How could Lindbergh take that Hitler decoration!"

Kristallnacht, which occurred three weeks after Lindbergh had accepted the German medal, had also deeply depressed Anne, who, realizing the depth of Charles's attachment to the Germans, had previously agreed to spend the winter with him and the children in Berlin. "You just get to feeling you can understand and work with these people when they do something stupid and brutal and undisciplined like that. I am shocked and very upset.

"How *can* we go there to live?"

Although the Lindberghs eventually decided to rent a small apartment across from the Bois de Boulogne in Paris for the winter, it did not dispel the persistent rumors that they were pro-Nazi. In the United States, it was widely reported that they were "going to live in Germany in a house of an evicted Jew." Lindbergh's name was hissed by movie audiences whenever it appeared in a newsreel, his name was removed from TWA, the "Lindbergh line," and Anne's new book, despite the excellent reviews, was boycotted by Jewish booksellers.

Unshaken in her loyalty, Anne continued to defend her husband vigorously.

> I hate to have such unfair labeling going on and have a body of hatred building up against C. for something that is not true. He is not and never has been anti-Semitic. C. is marvelously untouched by all this. Their scorn does not touch him any more than their praise once did.
>
> Only, I think, if he felt he had betrayed his own integrity would he mind.
>
> Femininely, I mind the injustice of it.

By now, she had convinced herself that she and her husband had done nothing to arouse the violent backlash against them. They had become innocent victims not only of the press, which invented wildly untrue stories about them, but of the "naturally oversensitive Jews" who "wrongly" accused them of being anti-Semitic.

In an attempt to remind herself of the time when the world had loved — and mourned — with her, Anne had her bust sculpted by Charles Despiau, a famous French sculptor who had been a disciple of Rodin. (Despiau later received permission from Lindbergh to make several copies of the head to be exhibited in national museums in London, Paris, and New York.) Simultaneously, Charles had his head sculpted by Jo Davidson, a well-known American sculptor living in Paris. Perhaps because Davidson heartily disagreed with Lindbergh about Munich, the bust lacked the vigor and intensity that was usually associated with his work. When she saw the bust of her husband, Anne was secretly disappointed, thinking it did not have "that extra thrill of surprise . . . the mystery that is in every human being, the divinity." Although skillfully executed, both busts, the Lindberghs felt, failed to capture their true essence, and so they approached the celebrated — and eccentric — English painter Augustus John about painting their portraits. Anne in particular felt that only an artist like John would be capable of catching Lindbergh's intensity on canvas. "He would be superb for C., I have always thought, after seeing his Lawrence. He is the only person who could get C.'s 'burning glass' quality," she wrote in her diary. She was thrilled when she learned, through a friend, that John would be delighted to paint either Charles or herself, or preferably both of them.

On their return to London, the Lindberghs dined with the Duke and Duchess of Windsor. Although struck by the vapidity of their lives since the king's abdication, Anne could not help noting the similarities between themselves and the Duke and Duchess. Both couples had chosen a life of self-imposed exile, and like her husband's, the duke's recent trip to Germany had been severely criticized in the press, which he and the Duchess loathed as much as the Lindberghs did. "The *lies* they print about you, the way they set you up on the wrong issues, praise you for the wrong things. Prying into one's personal life.

"How strange it was — a pair of unicorns meeting another pair of unicorns."

It was during this visit to London that Anne, who traveled almost exclusively in the highest diplomatic and financial circles, made the acquaintance of several well-known writers and artists. They included the

American writer Gertrude Stein, her companion, Alice B. Toklas, the Chinese author and philologist Lin Yutang, and the Mexican painter Frida Kahlo, whom Anne immediately liked when they met at a luncheon given by Jo Davidson. Anne's affinity for Frida, the wife of famed muralist Diego Rivera, was not surprising under the circumstances. Both women had allowed their considerable talents to become vehicles for exploring their obsessive relationships with their husbands. "Frida Rivera is there, enchanting in a Tehuantepec costume," Anne later remembered. "Her dark hair around her head with a band of yellow wool (braided into it) and some little yellow orchids caught in the braid in front, like a tiara of flowers.

"She looked enchanting, not artificial at all, but natural as a child — as she is."

On March 16, 1939, Germany annexed Bohemia and Moravia, and Anne was shocked into the realization that Jean Monnet, and not her husband, had been right after all — Germany was not to be trusted. Despite her personal liking for the Germans, she felt deeply betrayed.

> I feel fiercely and instinctively angry inside. This time you have gone too far. You are *wrong*... Of course all treaties are broken. All nations break their word eventually, but the Germans break their word the moment it leaves their lips. The ink not yet dry on the paper . . .
> And all the [Anthony] Edens and [Cordell] Hulls are right. I can't bear it. Poor Chamberlain. I still feel he was right to do what he did.

Lindbergh did not share his wife's dismay at the Nazis' making a sham of Chamberlain's policy of appeasement. On April 1, Hitler spoke at Wilhelmshaven, using the occasion of the launching of the battleship *Tirpitz* to justify his actions. When he read Hitler's speech in the newspapers the following day, Lindbergh was impressed. He did not understand why people failed to realize that "civilization depends upon his [Hitler's] wisdom far more than on the action of the democracies." Although he disapproved of many of the Nazis' actions, he still staunchly believed that the country "has pursued the only consistent policy in Europe in recent years. I cannot support her broken promises, but she has only moved a little faster than other nations have in breaking promises. The question of right and wrong is one thing by law and another thing by history."

Now deeply concerned that the United States might be drawn into the ensuing European conflict, which he felt was inevitable, and convinced that only a man of his stature and experience could persuade his fellow Americans as to the folly of taking on such a formidable foe, Lindbergh abruptly decided to return to the United States. This was not an easy decision on his part, for the prospect of having to live once more in what he felt was a degenerate democracy was an unappealing one. As he wrote in his journal,

> How can democracy hold its head high when there is no freedom for those who have attracted the interest of its public and its press? For twelve years I have found little freedom in the country which is supposed to exemplify freedom. What I have found I have had to seize, and I did not find real freedom until I came to Europe. The strange thing is that of all the European countries, I found the most personal freedom in Germany, with England next, and then France. But in comparison to America we move freely in any country over here.

Despite Lindbergh's grave misgivings about the quality of life in his homeland, the thought of the country's becoming involved in a futile war aroused all his old feelings of protectiveness, and he decided to return to the United States with the hope that one day there would be "less crime and more freedom than exist today."

On April 8, 1939, he sailed alone on the *Aquitania* for the United States. He instructed Anne and the children to stay behind in Paris and await his decision on whether he intended to remain in the United States. If he decided to do so, he would send for them. It all depended on whether anyone would listen to his warnings about the true nature of the European situation.

"If there was to be war, then my place was back in my own country," he wrote many years later.

> I felt I could exercise a constructive influence in America by warning people of the danger of the Soviet Union and by explaining that the destruction of Hitler, even if it could be accomplished through using American resources, would probably result in enhancing the still-greater menace of Stalin. I would argue for an American policy of strength and neutrality, one that would encourage European nations to take the responsibility for their own relationships and destinies. If they prostrated themselves once again in internecine war, then at least one strong Western nation would remain to protect Western civilization.
>
> I was greatly concerned about the strength of America. Although I feared the combination of military strength with our idealism — it was an uneasy mixture — I believed that military strength was essential to our security. I was convinced that aviation would play a major role in

future wars, and I knew we had lost our leadership in military aircraft. Germany's research and production facilities were much more extensive than ours. . . . Back in the United States I could do something about this situation. I could help stimulate American aviation activities.

On the ship, Lindbergh kept strictly to himself, as was his practice during all crossings. At dinner he avoided sitting with the other passengers for fear that they would later misquote his conversation to members of the press, who would surely swoop down on them like vultures once the ship docked in New York. Fortunately, for Lindbergh, the crossing was a rough one, and so he was able to stroll around the decks undisturbed.

When the *Aquitania* docked in New York on April 14, he was met by the Carrels and his friend Jim Newton. But as he himself had predicted, his reunion with these old friends was swiftly interrupted by the press, who barged their way into his stateroom, and made him "wonder where freedom ends and disorder begins — It was a barbaric entry to a civilized country."

Shortly after his arrival, Lindbergh met with President Franklin Roosevelt in Washington. He had never met the president before and was unsure how he felt about the man. On the one hand, Lindbergh liked him; on the other, he felt that Roosevelt was glib and untrustworthy, and "lacked a statesman's wisdom." Despite these grave reservations, Lindbergh agreed to be called back temporarily into the U.S. Army Air Corps. He thought it would be better for him and the president "to work together as long as we can." Now feeling "needed," he cabled Anne to join him, and she immediately booked passage for herself and the children on the SS *Paris*, which was to set sail on April 19. But, in a strange twist of fate, the ship burned at the dock, and so she and the two boys sailed for the United States one day later, on the *Champlain*.

As the ship left Le Havre, Anne suddenly felt depressed at the thought of leaving the country that she had grown to love so deeply. It was like discovering upon leaving someone the depth of one's love for him or her.

This was an extraordinary reaction, considering the reason she was leaving France: to rejoin her husband, who had gone home with the precise purpose of convincing his countrymen not to aid any of the people who had been so good to them in their exile and who were now in mortal danger.

CHAPTER 16

"Poor Anne"

Lindbergh had summoned Anne, and she had done his bidding, a dutiful wife who had once again uprooted herself to be with her husband. But when she and the children arrived in New York in the early morning hours, he was not there to greet their ship. Believing that his presence would attract even more publicity, he had entrusted his family's care to a guard of roughly one hundred policemen. He was still asleep at Next Day Hill when they arrived in the chauffeur-driven limousine that his mother-in-law had provided.

When her mother opened the door, Anne was struck by the change in her appearance. The usually indefatigable Mrs. Morrow looked pale and worn, and considerably older. Her weariness was not surprising, considering that all her children, though well into adulthood, were living with her. Recently her household had expanded to include Dwight, Jr., and Margot, who were now married, as well as Constance, her husband, Aubrey, and their new baby daughter, Saran. Now Anne, Charles, and their two children would also be residing at Next Day Hill until they found their own home. Mrs. Morrow had noted her son-in-law's lack of warmth and sensitivity to others; she once described him as being like "a very beautiful woman who lends grace just by *being* present. He doesn't have to say anything or do anything — just be there." The prospect of having him under her roof and listening to his views for an extended period must not have been an appealing one for her.

When Anne arrived at the mansion, she found her husband still in bed, "tousled and tired" from a long drive he had taken the night before from Washington, D.C. Although exhausted from her trip, Anne immediately perked up when she saw him. It thrilled her to see Charles looking so happy, obviously absorbed by his new job.

The new job that currently absorbed Lindbergh's attention involved increasing the efficiency of American aeronautical research organizations for General Henry H. Arnold, then the chief of the Air Corps, to whom he had reported on the status of German aviation shortly after his return to the United States. Many years later, when Anne was still devoting most of her time and energy to defending her husband's role in the prewar era, she would point with pride to Arnold's assessment of Lindbergh's report, which the general had called "the most accurate picture of the Luftwaffe, its equipment, leaders, apparent plans, training methods, and present defects received up to that time."

Although overjoyed to see Charles, Anne was not looking forward to staying with her mother. As she herself was well aware from previous extended visits to Next Day Hill, living as an adult woman in her mother's home was not an easy experience. This particular visit proved no exception and in fact was even more a test of her patience. After the primitive life on Illiec, the Morrow mansion, with its antiques and priceless objets d'art, struck her as obscenely grand and luxurious, so filled with possessions that she often yearned to burn her own belongings. Another conflict had to do with the way she liked to savor each individual experience, while her energetic mother and siblings rushed from one activity to another. Observing her mother's hectic schedule, Anne concluded that the older woman's philanthropic pursuits were an escape from her husband's and Elisabeth's deaths. She felt it might help her mother regain her emotional equilibrium if she too began to write, for some reason overlooking the fact that Mrs. Morrow had indeed started writing following Dwight Morrow's death, and was a well-established writer, with several published children's books and a volume of poetry, appropriately entitled *Quatrains for My Daughter,* to her credit.

Realizing that their present sojourn in the family mansion was also getting on her husband's nerves, Anne began hunting for a place of their own. To her relief, she soon found one — a large, white eighteenth-century clapboard house on Lloyd Neck, on Long Island Sound, which they rented for two thousand dollars a month under the name of their private secretary. Behind the house was a small beach for swimming, and there were three majestic oak trees at the back of the property which Lindbergh especially admired.

Another adjustment was getting used to living again in the United

States. In comparison with France, where she had led a slow-paced, "mature" life, the United States seemed incredibly fast-paced, immature, and gaudy. "I see only false high-pressuring newspapers and magazines, flashy and cheap; racy and material advertising; sex-appeal movies; blustering politicians," she wrote disapprovingly in her diary. Even having a permanent at the hairdresser's became something of an ordeal. She felt as if she were trapped inside a "cheap magazine advertisement world." Only by reading Lord David Cecil's *Lord Melbourne* under the hair dryer did she manage to make the experience bearable.

Once she had moved her family into the house at Lloyd Neck, Anne resumed her writing, but again the work was slow and frustrating. Although she had brought a young Swiss nursemaid, Soeur Lisi, with her from Paris to take care of the children, the young woman occasionally had a day off, and to Anne's dismay the children swarmed all over her whenever she tried to write in her diary on the porch. Desperate to distract them, she ordered a children's wading pool by phone, but then thought she had acted precipitously. Always careful about money, despite her wealth, she began to feel that such a purchase was an "extravagance," because "after all, they have the sea."

Still pondering the tragic brevity of Elisabeth's life, she began toying with the idea of writing a book of reminiscences of her sister. At night, when the children were finally asleep, she began rereading her correspondence with Elisabeth, as well as the adulatory letters about Lindbergh she had written to Constance shortly after she had met him in Mexico City. She stayed up half the night, "overcome with the romance of my own life, my own youth."

But her elation shifted characteristically to depression, which was alleviated only when she opened a letter from the French publisher of *Listen! the Wind* and found enclosed a preface for the French edition. Anne was thrilled when she realized that the person selected to write it was the famous French aviator and author Antoine de Saint-Exupéry. She was one of his most ardent admirers; indeed, she had recently read and admired his *Wind, Sand and Stars,* which had just been published to accolades in the United States. For Anne, reading her fellow flier's book had been an "incredibly beautiful and gripping" experience, and in some respects she wished that she had written it herself. "It is all I ever wanted to say and more of flying and time and human relationships."

Saint-Exupéry, as the publisher had explained to Anne in his note, had originally planned to write only a one-page preface, but after reading her work, he had been so impressed by it that he had expanded the preface to nine pages. As she read it, she was not only struck by the profundity of his analysis, but also a little unnerved by his uncanny perceptions of her personality: her fear of not being able to compete with others, as well as her constant need to prove her worth.

According to her French publisher, Saint-Exupéry was in New York and wanted to see her. When Anne thought of meeting the man she so deeply admired and who seemed to know all about her secret self, she was overcome with fear and shyness. Still, she yearned to meet him. Although Saint-Exupéry was a daring aviator like Lindbergh, he was, like herself, a writer, someone who, unlike her husband, shared her imaginative inner world.

As it turned out, Lindbergh, who was supposed to pick up the French flier in New York, had a previous engagement, and so it was Anne who was entrusted with the task. Arriving at Saint-Exupéry's hotel, she was dismayed to learn that he was in the bar. "Heavens, I think, he is one of those drunken aviators — *why* did we do this?" she asked herself, obviously having second thoughts. But she was delighted to discover on meeting him that not only was he completely sober but in person even more fascinating than she had imagined. "He appears, tall and stooped and a little bald, beginning to be not as young as he once was; an inscrutable sort of face, not at all good looking, almost Slavic in its solidity and inscrutability, and his eyes turn up at the corners a little," she noted later in her diary, writing with the same kind of rapturous prose that she had once reserved for Lindbergh.

As luck would have it, Anne's car broke down as she was driving Saint-Exupéry out of New York to Lloyd Neck. After leaving it in a garage for repairs, she and the French flier took a taxi to Penn Station. But before they boarded the train for Long Island, they stopped for an orangeade at a stand and, as they sipped their drinks, engaged in a passionate discussion in French about their lives and work. Their discourse had an intoxicating effect on Anne. "I felt gay, freed and happy," she later wrote. "I and this absolute stranger who understood so well everything I said and felt!" Forgetting that Harold Nicolson had similarly encouraged her creative talent, she also noted, "It was very exciting. Perhaps it was only because it was almost the first time anyone had talked to me purely on my *craft*. Not because I was a woman to be polite to, to charm with superficials, not because I was my father's daughter or C's wife; no, simply because of my book, my mind, my *craft!*

"My heavens, what a joy it was to talk, to compare, to throw things out, to be understood like that without an effort. Summer lightning."

When her husband came home later that evening, Anne introduced him to the French flier. Although fascinated by Saint-Exupéry, who had also started his career as a mail pilot, Lindbergh was a bit wary of him, for it was evident that Anne found him very attractive. Perhaps for the first time in their long relationship, Charles Lindbergh sensed that he might have a rival for his wife's affections. Although the Lindberghs usually retired early, they sat up talking with Saint-Exupéry until midnight, with Anne acting as translator, for neither Saint-Exupéry nor Lindbergh understood the other's language. Two days later, when the couple was driving Saint-Exupéry back to his hotel in New York, Lindbergh, who was usually meticulously observant about the running of machines, became so absorbed in their conversation that he ran out of gas. Or perhaps it was worry about his wife's obvious attachment to her new friend that made him neglect to keep an eye on the fuel gauge.

After Saint-Exupéry returned to France, Anne expressed her admiration for his work in a glowing review of *Wind, Sand and Stars* which was published in the October 14 issue of the *Saturday Review of Literature*. Although this piece was later used as a foreword to the eighth edition of *Wind, Sand and Stars*, it was removed from subsequent editions because of the outrage many of the French felt toward the Lindberghs for their isolationist views.

September 1, 1939, was the day the Germans attacked Poland, and when Anne heard the news, she was devastated. Not only was the reality of a European war monstrous to contemplate, but it also revived her sense of loss about Charlie and Elisabeth. For the first time in many years she referred to her son's murder in her diary. It was as if the coming war had forced her to relive that bleak, windy March night when he was found to be missing from his crib, and she was hoping against hope that she would find him unharmed.

> This long and terrible week is like the week before Elisabeth died, a week of piling up hopes and then fears . . . I look at the newspapers piled up on our table, fruitless words, fruitless telegrams, letters, meetings, negotiations, airplane trips of diplomatists, words of pleading, of hope, prayers. All useless. It makes me think of Hopewell — that tremendous machine set going: state troopers, handwriting experts, ticker tapes, telephone services, detectives, specialists, politicians, friends, reporters, letters . . . For what use, for what purpose?

The child is dead.
The child is dead in Europe.

On September 3, when Britain and France declared war on Germany, which continued to advance into Poland, Anne's despair deepened. She was disillusioned not only with Germany, a country she had found admirable in many respects, but also about the prospects for peace. Plagued by a splitting headache, she spent a good part of the day in bed, trying "to face this war — all of it at its worst — what it means."

Unlike some of her friends, she did not believe that it was going to be a short war or a "humane" one.

But one is led little by little into the full horror of it. By little shocks, by little horrors, by small doses, one is led at last into the final draught of poison. And I suppose it is the kindest way. And yet I want to face it all now — like seeing little Charles, his head bashed in, dead, laid out before me, in that first flash of realization that he was gone; or Elisabeth lifeless, at the first word of pneumonia.

... But not only in the "*big*," in the "*little*" I see war — women gassed, babies with legs blown off, men with their brains blown to bits. One cannot conceive of the horror, only I felt that I must. I have always felt it. If there is such horror in the world and other human beings have suffered it, then it might be mine, too, it must be mine.

Clearly, for Anne Lindbergh the war in Europe had come to represent a magnification of her own personal tragedy. She could not bear that millions of men and women would now suffer as deeply as she and her husband had. From bitter experience, she knew the futility of standing up to an aggressor. She and her husband had seemed invincible, a golden couple in a fairy-tale romance, and yet they had been helpless against the machinations of one man.

Now that the war in Europe had started, Anne thought desperately, there must be a quick way to bring it to an end and to keep Americans from entering it — and dying in it.

But who possessed the strength and vision to make the people of the United States realize that it would be sheer folly to enter this conflict? Only one man, she knew, possessed such courage, and she continued to have total faith in him, her husband.

That evening Anne and Charles listened to Roosevelt's speech on the radio. Although Lindbergh did not care for the president as a speaker, that night he had to concede that his address was far more persuasive than usual, undoubtedly because Roosevelt was assuring the American people that he would do everything in his power to keep the United States neutral in the uncertain months ahead.

Still, there was something about Roosevelt's speech that left Lindbergh apprehensive. In his estimation, the president still seemed too suave and glib, and the aviator again seriously doubted whether he could be trusted.

After Roosevelt's radio speech, Lindbergh holed up in his study for the next few days, writing two radio speeches as well as an article outlining his stand on the war in Europe. His words, which echoed his father's speeches opposing American entry into World War I, left no doubt as to his position: "I do not intend to stand by and see this country pushed into war if it is not absolutely essential to the future welfare of the nation," he wrote in his journal. "Much as I dislike taking part in politics and public life, I intend to do so if necessary to stop the trend which is now going on in this country."

When Anne read her husband's two speeches and his article, "Aviation, Geography and Race," she was deeply moved by their contents, even though the article and at least one of the speeches contained racist opinions, such as the importance of maintaining the strength of the "White race," and preventing "the infiltration of inferior blood." (When "Aviation, Geography and Race" was published in the November 1939 issue of the *Reader's Digest,* many readers, disturbed by the similarities between its racist theories and Nazi ideology, wrote to President Roosevelt and J. Edgar Hoover, director of the Federal Bureau of Investigation, demanding not only that the authorities keep a close eye on Lindbergh, but also that he be prevented from gaining access to secret aviation documents or attaining any position of authority in the U.S. government.)

Lindbergh's writings contained such statements as these: "It is time to turn from our quarrels and to build our White ramparts again"; "[Aviation] is a tool specially shaped for Western hands . . . another barrier between the teeming millions of Asia and the Grecian inheritance of Europe — one of those priceless possessions which permit the White race to live at all in a pressing sea of Yellow, Black, and Brown." If Anne was disturbed by these racist views, she does not seem to have voiced her objections. On the contrary, she seemed determined to help him get his views across to the American people. "The speech is good but not as good as the article, which is his deepest, best thinking," she noted in her diary. "I say the end (of the speech) needs to be on a broader and higher note. I write a page for an ending as I feel he means it and take it up to him. He says it is very good and he will use part of it, changing it slightly."

Although Charles Lindbergh always denied the rumors that Anne or Truman Smith, the American military attaché who had become his close friend, wrote his speeches, Anne's help was apparent when he gave his first speech on September 15, 1939, urging the American people to stay out of the European conflict. "These wars in Europe are not wars in which our civilization is defending itself against some Asiatic intruder," Lindbergh cautioned. "There is no Genghis Khan marching against our Western nations. This is not a question of banding together to defend our White race against foreign invaders. This is simply one more of those age old quarrels among our own family of nations. . . . We must not permit our sentiment, our pity, or our personal feelings of sympathy to obscure the issue to affect our children's lives. We must be as impersonal as a surgeon with his knife."

At a time when the Nazis were killing thousands of Poles, the phrase "We must be as impersonal as a surgeon with his knife" struck many people as cold-blooded and tasteless. Because of its quasi-poetic tone, some listeners speculated that Anne Lindbergh had written it for her husband. Although she has never admitted or denied its authorship, it is highly probable that she did in fact pen the phrase, as her own work contains similar metaphors, equating logic and reason with a cutting instrument. For example, two years later, when she referred to Charles Lindbergh's Des Moines speech in her diary, she described it as being "direct and honest as a clean knife." And her poem "The Stone," which was published in 1956 in a volume of poetry entitled *The Unicorn and Other Poems*, contains a similar metaphor in which she refers to "the surgeon's scalpel of analysis."

But as Anne was rapidly discovering, wifely loyalty had its price. Lindbergh's isolationism had already alienated many of their oldest and closest friends, who staunchly supported aid to Britain. These included Henry Breckenridge, Lindbergh's lawyer and trusted friend; Harry Guggenheim, the Jewish tycoon who had sponsored Lindbergh's three-month tour following his solo 1927 flight; and Thomas Lamont, a close friend of the family who had been Dwight Morrow's business partner.

More significantly, Anne's family was in total disagreement with Lindbergh's isolationist views. The Morrows had been solidly pro-Allies in World War I, and Betty Morrow, knowing full well which side

Dwight Morrow would have supported in the present conflict, was involved with many pro-British organizations. Adding to the tensions was the fact that Aubrey Morgan, Anne and Charles's brother-in-law, had recently been made the assistant chief of the British Information Services in New York, an organization that Lindbergh, who had no use for the British, was convinced was attempting to "trick" the United States into war.

Unmoved by his wife's family's opposition to his isolationist views, Lindbergh continued to crusade against American involvement in the war. Although deeply upset by the private acrimony that had developed between her husband and her family, and despite her greater sympathy for the British, Anne made it clear whose side she was on. Although exhausted by continuing family tensions, she remained her husband's best cheerleader. When Lindbergh was asked to make an address in Washington, D.C., she immediately put aside her work and duties toward her children to sit beside him on the platform. "I knew that I had done right to come to Washington to be with C., *one,* because I believed in him and his stand (no matter how hard it was emotionally to turn one's back on Europe), and *two,* because it might please him, help him a little — release him to talk — give him a better sleep," she wrote in her diary. "And that in spite of all the criticism it might call forth — it was right to give the speech."

Predictably, Lindbergh's sudden re-emergence as a public figure, after many years in self-imposed isolation, only strengthened his contempt for the way the United States treated its celebrities. He was now under constant attack in the liberal press for his political views, and, further, he and Anne again began to receive thousands of letters. For many years their mail from people other than their relatives and closest friends was sent to the police, and several anonymous messages, which the authorities immediately brought to their attention, were especially frightening. The letter writers threatened to kidnap — and kill — Jon and Land.

It soon became obvious to Anne and Charles that fame and notoriety were holding them captive once again. No longer could they go for a peaceful stroll in public, as they had been able to do in Europe. Once recognized, they would be followed for blocks or hounded for autographs. Oddly enough, both Lindberghs often waxed nostalgic for England and France, where, even if the people were "decadent" and "effete," they at least had had the decency to leave them alone.

Although the Lindberghs considered most contemporary films to be cheap and tasteless — a sign of the country's decay — they still occasionally enjoyed going to the movies. Because of the public's renewed avid interest in their lives, this soon proved practically impossible, especially if they went as a couple. So Lindbergh often went alone, wearing a peculiar disguise consisting of horn-rimmed glasses without lenses. Feeling "angry and bitter and trapped again," Anne voiced her discontent to her husband, who suggested that a solution might lie in their moving out West, renting a ranch, and discovering their "real roots." But for the moment nothing came of this plan.

Of course, a large part of Anne's rage and bitterness derived from her awareness that many influential people were appalled by her husband's views and were attacking him in the press. In her opinion, their assaults were deeply unfair. When columnist Dorothy Thompson described Lindbergh as a "pro-Nazi recipient of a German medal," Anne dismissed the attack as "petty, personal and bitter mudslinging." She felt that only her father's old friend Walter Lippmann had the decency to criticize her husband "fairly, intellectually on issues," unaware that ever since Lindbergh had been decorated by Hermann Göring, the columnist had been privately describing him to friends as "a Nazi lover." As for Harold Nicolson, she no longer considered him and Vita to be friends after reading Nicolson's biting comments about her husband in an article in the *Spectator*. "It was such a temptation to write that little article, that clever little article, that biting little article. He could do it so well," she fumed in her diary. " 'The boy from Minnesota,' all that. I try to remember that after all he is a disillusioned idealist and his two boys might be sent to the front."

In the article to which she was referring, Harold Nicolson had observed about his former friend Charles Lindbergh that "it was almost with ferocity that he struggled to remain himself, and in the process of that arduous struggle his simplicity became muscle-bound, his virility-ideal became not merely inflexible, but actually rigid; his self-control thickened into arrogance, and his convictions hardened into granite. He became impervious to anything outside his own legend — the legend of the young lad from Minnesota whose head could not be turned."

In Nicolson's opinion, the change in Lindbergh's personality was the result of the kidnapping and murder of his child. "The suffering which that dreadful crime entailed upon himself and those he loved pierced his armor. He identified the outrage to his private life first with the popular press and by inevitable association with freedom of speech, and then with freedom. He began to loathe democracy . . . Let us not allow this incident to blind us to the great qualities of Charles Lindbergh. He is and always will be not merely a schoolboy hero, but a schoolboy."

Harold's views were echoed by Vita, who, like her husband, had once been attracted by Lindbergh's "charm," his naturalness and simplicity, which, in Harold's words, were as "refreshing as a mountain stream." But now, whenever Vita mentioned Lindbergh in her letters to her husband, she referred to him as "a shit."

Anne continued to defend her husband against his attackers. "C. is criminally misunderstood, misquoted and misused. And I have fought this, too," she raged in her diary. "I believe in him and in his absolute integrity and in what he is trying to do. But it has been so misunderstood. And that I beat against in my heart . . ."

She could not understand why many people had labeled him "pro-Nazi" when he was simply voicing his staunch belief that a war would reduce the United States' power and destroy most of Western civilization. As she stressed many years later in *War Within and Without*, the fifth volume of her diaries and letters, which dealt with the prewar period,

> Lindbergh's isolationist stand . . . was backward-looking to a younger and pioneering America whose image was self-reliant and self-sufficient. The Lindbergh speeches are full of the character, the stories, and the cadence of the old West. Although their factual content rests firmly on "the capabilities, limitations and consequences" of the air power of his day, the emotional thrust and language are those of his father and grandfather. One recognizes the rhetorical tone of those hardy immigrants who had left Europe behind them for the "new world of the West"; the American with an "independent destiny" which would not be "forever entangled in these endless wars in Europe." Lindbergh had his ancestors' staunch belief in our representative government, an issue that he felt was "even more fundamental than war itself." He was quick to perceive that the powers of Congress were being abrogated and the people of America led into an undeclared war, without the opportunity to voice their decision.

If Anne's way of dealing with stress and unhappiness during this period was to pour out her feelings in her diary, Lindbergh's method was quite the opposite. Evidently influenced by his wife to keep a permanent record of his thoughts and actions during this important period, he too had begun keeping a journal. Unlike his wife's diary, which was filled with feelings and emotion on every page, his journal was for the most part a dry and factual account of his political and professional activities. In keeping with his aeronautical training, he meticulously recorded the times he woke up, shaved, or boarded a train from Long Island to Washington or New York City. Perhaps it was no coincidence that on the rare occasions when he expressed his feelings, he wrote about the family pets — by this time both his dogs, Thor and Skean, were old and ailing — or about a visit to the museums where his planes, the *Spirit of St. Louis* and the *Tingmissartoq,* were on display. After making sure that no one had recognized him, he stood for a long time gazing up at the machines that he regarded as extensions of himself and remembering the miraculous journeys they had taken together.

In the middle of June, Lindbergh drove down to his country estate in Hopewell, New Jersey, which was now known as High Fields. He had not been in the house where his son was kidnapped for four years, and he was now considering not turning it into a children's home, as he and Anne had planned, but using it as a small center for viral and other medical research.

Charles Lindbergh's diary entry of June 18, 1939, was indicative of how he coped with his emotional past — at least in prose.

> The place has changed considerably since I last was there. The bushes have jumped upward, and there is a feeling of much heavier foliage. The house needs a new coat of whitewash, and the shutters should be painted, but everything is in good condition. I went to the back door and was met by the watchman. We went through the house from basement to attic, through the pump house and out around the grounds. We walked down to the little brook to the north.

He might have been describing someone else's country house, which had no connection with violence, horror, or personal agony.

When the Lindberghs discovered that their rented house on Lloyd Neck could not be heated for the winter, they found another house to live in at nearby Lloyd Manor. But the house they wanted to rent was not yet ready for occupancy, and so they moved back temporarily to Next Day Hill. As anyone might have predicted, this was not a wise decision on their part, for no sooner did they arrive there than family tensions swiftly escalated. Mrs. Morrow had been appointed interim head of Smith College after President Neilson's retirement, and moreover, she was now actively involved in a number of local and national organizations providing aid to the Allies. She was permitting Next Day Hill to be used as a sort of informal headquarters for some of these groups, and so, as soon as Anne and Charles joined the household, they found themselves face to face on a daily basis with people who were working feverishly to help the British and French fight the Nazis.

Even though most of her friends politely avoided discussing their political differences, Anne could not help but feel ostracized and out of place. While they were downstairs, packing bundles for Britain, she was upstairs, in another wing of the house, writing an article at her husband's request. It was a plea to stop the war before it really got started.

Although from the beginning Anne had had grave misgivings about her qualifications to write such an article, she decided to go ahead anyway. Even if, as she feared, it was already too late for such an article to have an effect on the world situation, it would at least demonstrate her deep commitment to her husband and his views.

As Anne later recalled, writing the article itself was an easy task. Unlike her own literary efforts, which often seemed to progress at a snail's pace, this political diatribe seemed to flow out of her easily. Perhaps this was because she was able to vent all the rage and bitterness she felt toward the people who had "misunderstood" her husband, although later, when she realized that such emotionalism undermined the article's effectiveness, she toned down the anger in subsequent drafts.

When Lindbergh read his wife's article, which was entitled "Prayer for Peace," he was deeply touched by the depth of her love for him and her commitment to his cause. Not one to bestow compliments easily, he later noted in his journal, with gratitude, "And thank God Anne has the courage to do that if it is necessary. I don't believe a woman exists who is her equal — if one ever did."

After some discussion, the Lindberghs came to the conclusion that for maximum impact, Anne's article should be published at Christmastime in the *Reader's Digest,* which in their opinion was "by far the best magazine of large circulation in America."

Most of the January issue of the magazine (which was on the stands December 25) had already gone to press. But the *Digest* editors, realizing the drawing power of the Lindbergh name, told the couple that by eliminating two other articles scheduled for the same issue, they would find room for Anne's piece.

Although they liked Anne's article in general, the editors wanted her to make some revisions. Anne always made her final corrections in pen, and Lindbergh, realizing that she would not have the opportunity if she waited until morning for her secretary to finish typing the manuscript, stayed up all night, retyping it in the third-floor room he and Anne used as an office. Anne knew nothing of his scheme. As they were going to bed, he had told her that he felt "restless and would sleep in another room." Since Lindbergh was by his own definition a "two-finger typist," he did not finish typing the manuscript until six o'clock in the morning. But not getting any sleep did not bother him. On the contrary, he felt exhilarated. "I felt I was doing something essential and worth while, and hard work is a real satisfaction when you have that feeling," he wrote in his journal. "Fatigue never does catch up with you if the goal you have is great enough, and I felt that Anne's 'Prayer for Peace' was great enough."

"Prayer for Peace," like most of Anne's writing during this period, was sincere and full of good intentions, the work of a well-meaning woman who had allowed her blind devotion to her husband to cloud her better judgment. Still unconvinced about the intellectual qualifications and abilities of her own sex, she began her article by stressing her own lack of authority as a woman to write a piece about the war: "But here I am speaking as a woman, a weak woman, if you will — emotional, impulsive, illogical, conservative, dreaming, impractical, pacific, unadventurous, any of the feminine vices you care to pin on me."

Things hardly got better as the article progressed. For in large part, it was a dreamy-eyed reinterpretation of the political opinions of her husband, who believed that Britain and France could not possibly survive another major war, that Germany was in some way justified in its aggression because of the raw deal it had received from France, Great Britain, and the United States after World War I, and that the United States should stay out of the conflict, for which it was largely responsible by not only failing to support the League of Nations but also by agreeing that Germany should be punished harshly.

In Anne's opinion, the best way to end the present conflict was to start by establishing an armed truce, which, if handled correctly, with that powerful combination of "science and spirituality" advocated by Alexis Carrel in *Man, the Unknown,* would eventually lead to a resolution of the conflicts leading up to the war.

As for Hitler himself, Anne believed that it was futile to oppose him. According to her, he was not merely an evil individual, but "the spirit of an embittered Germany," and it was useless to attempt to destroy him and his regime for unless the root causes of Germany's discontent were corrected, "other Hitlers will arise from the seeds of hate in another twenty years."

Despite the cloudiness of her thinking, many Americans responded enthusiastically to Anne's message that peace could still be achieved. (At the time the article was published, the hostilities were only four months old.) To the Lindberghs' joy, *Digest* readers rated "Prayer for Peace" as the best article of the year. But as far as we know, Adolf Hitler was not a subscriber to the magazine, and even if he had been, he had no intention of participating in a truce, armed or otherwise. Five months later he invaded France.

CHAPTER 17

Working for Charles

Anne was pregnant again, this time after returning from a five-day trip in early April 1940 to explore the then unspoiled Everglades with her husband. Having a baby was always a momentous occasion in her life, and this time was no exception, except that as the pregnancy advanced she became sensitive about strangers' seeing her protruding stomach. Her fear of the public's knowing about her condition was not surprising under the circumstances. As the nation's criticism of her husband mounted, she felt increasingly exposed and vulnerable. Where once he had been hailed by millions of people all over the world, he was now being attacked and ridiculed by intellectuals and liberals. In fashionable New York literary circles, even the kidnap-murder of their son was being made light of, and there were tasteless jokes making the rounds about "that fellow Hauptmann having kidnapped the wrong baby."

It was Anne's fourth pregnancy, and she was now thirty-three years old. Even though she often felt spiritually "old," she still looked physically trim and youthful. Her small, delicate face, with the astounding violet-blue eyes that continued to entrance her husband, gave the impression that she was serene and untroubled, as if the dark experiences of life hadn't touched her.

Her demure, composed demeanor was, of course, a facade. Inside, she seethed with conflicts and tensions, which were exacerbated by the escalating private war between her mother and her husband. On May 19, 1940, shortly after the Nazis had conquered Denmark and were attacking Belgium and Holland, Lindbergh spoke for the third time in

Washington. The title of his address was "The Air Defense of America," and when she heard it on the radio, Mrs. Morrow was furious. In his speech, her son-in-law referred to "powerful elements in America" that he believed hoped to profit by U.S. involvement in the war. This time Lindbergh was not referring obliquely to his enemies, who included President Roosevelt, in his opinion a warmonger, or the Jews, who he felt were in control of the press, or the British Information Service, which he was convinced was pushing the American people into a disastrous war. The "powerful element" to which he was referring was none other than Dwight Morrow's former employer, the House of Morgan, whose illustrious members were all decidedly pro-British. Like his father, whose economic views he had once discounted as being extreme and oversimplified, Lindbergh appears suddenly to have become a foe of the money trust into which he had married. Now he was convinced, as his father had been prior to World War I, that its members were propelling the country into a war to further their interests abroad.

According to Ron Chernow, author of *The House of Morgan,* "Five days after the radio speech, she [Betty Morrow] had an emotional lunch with Anne at the Cosmopolitan Club. Betty felt ashamed that America hadn't rushed to join England and said in anguish to Anne, 'How they will *hate* us — oh, how they will *hate* us.' Yet despite her candor with her daughter, Morrow felt constrained in challenging her son-in-law. The day after the lunch, she secretly wrote to [Thomas] Lamont asking him to reason with Lindbergh: 'I am in a difficult position just now . . . but my chief worry is over Anne. She is torn in spirit and it is telling on her health.' "

Lamont, Dwight Morrow's former business partner and a personal friend of the couple, wrote Lindbergh an amicable and polite letter, in which he asked him to name openly the group to which he had been referring in his address. The reply he shortly received from Lindbergh both dismayed and angered him. Not only was it completely impersonal, as if he and Lindbergh had never been friends, but in the letter the aviator clearly stated that he had deliberately elected not to name publicly the group involved because in his opinion it would create "a class conflict." Judging from Lindbergh's cool and unemotional response, it was apparent to Lamont that he could be of no help to Mrs. Morrow in resolving her personal differences with her son-in-law. There was, however, a way for him to resolve his own political conflicts with Lindbergh and with Anne, whom he had known since childhood. He ended their relationship.

Realizing that her son-in-law was not to be persuaded by personal appeals, Betty Morrow, after some soul-searching, decided to make public her pro-British views. She made a speech for the William Allen White's Committee to Defend America by Aiding the Allies, a rebuttal to Lindbergh's isolationist statements. According to Anne, the Committee was made up "chiefly of high-minded idealists" such as President Neilson of Smith, a man she had formerly looked up to until he became an interventionist. Before Betty gave her speech, she called Anne to explain why she was making it. "Your father would have wanted me to do it," she told her daughter. Fortunately, for Anne, Lindbergh was not at home when her mother's speech was broadcast on the radio, and she was able to listen to it alone.

"I urge the sending of munitions and supplies, food, money, airplanes, ships, and everything that could help them in this struggle against Germany. There are some things worse than war. There are some things supreme and noble that are worth fighting for," Betty Morrow reminded her listeners.

Although Mrs. Morrow's speech convinced many people to become interventionists, she did not win over her own daughter. Many years later, however, in her preface to the last volume of her diaries, *War Within and Without,* Anne echoed her mother's sentiment in an explanation of her own political views when she had been a student at Smith College. "In these years Erich Remarque's *All Quiet on the Western Front* converted me early to a pacifist point of view," Anne noted. "The Nazi era was still in the future, and I had yet to learn that there were worse things than war."

But at the time Anne was as dismayed by her mother's interventionism as she was by her opulent lifestyle and confident manner. Obviously, her lifelong competition with her had escalated into a power struggle in the political arena. "It is a beautiful speech, a fighting speech, with much of her faith and spiritual force in it," she conceded, "but I cannot agree with its premises, and I feel only sad at not being able to and very much alone and separated from all those good people."

Privately Anne felt that the White Committee had asked her mother to speak as a means of gaining publicity for the interventionist movement. Later Betty Morrow reluctantly admitted that perhaps her daughter was right after White himself made it known that he thought it had been "a smart trick" to pit Elizabeth Morrow and Charles Lindbergh against each other.

Nevertheless Mrs. Morrow continued to crusade for immediate aid to the Allies. When the Lend-Lease bill, which her son-in-law publicly opposed, came up for adoption, she advocated its immediate passage in a nationwide radio address on March 8, 1941, "without weakening amendments or strangling clauses." In the speech, she bluntly rebutted Lindbergh and Anne's isolationist position, without directly referring to them. "As I have listened to the arguments against this bill," she said, "I have said to myself 'Is Hitler hypnotizing this country?' "

The political, as well as personal, conflicts between mother and daughter intensified when Betty Morrow was named chair of the women's division of Fight for Freedom, the most extreme and powerful of the interventionist groups, which advocated that the United States enter the war as a full military participant. In a broadcast speech given during a luncheon for the organization in November 1941, Mrs. Morrow again set forth her position, which was clearly the opposite of Lindbergh and Anne's isolationism. She stated that she was pleased that the Neutrality Act had been repealed, and grateful that "its hypocrisy had been removed from our statute book." She also said that Americans must frankly meet the risk of war and must face the "deepening danger to all that we believe in" for an all-out war might be necessary in order to prevent a Nazi victory.

Betty Morrow was not the only person close to Charles Lindbergh to be baffled by his strange personality, which resonated to the power of machines but not to the souls of human beings. A growing estrangement had developed between Lindbergh and his closest friend and mentor, Alexis Carrel. Although Carrel's theories concerning eugenics and euthanasia bore some uncanny similarities to those of the Nazis, and he was accused after the war of being a Nazi collaborator, Carrel was, in the opinion of several historians, no Nazi-lover. He was deeply grieved when the Germans occupied Paris and worried intensely about his wife, who insisted on remaining alone on Saint-Gildas. Hoping that Lindbergh might do something to ease the situation, Carrel called him before one of his radio addresses, urging him to include "some friendly reference to France." But as he had with Lamont, Lindbergh flatly refused, telling his friend that he "would like to do so, but did not see how I could appropriately include a reference to France in this particular address, since it was primarily an argument against our entry into war." Although Alexis Carrel was by no means Anne Lindbergh's favorite person, she was upset by the coolness that had developed between the two men. "I feel uneasy and unhappy about it though I respect C.'s integrity completely and understand him."

Selden Rodman, poet and coeditor of *Common Sense,* met the Lindberghs during this period. An antiwar activist, he was also an admirer of Anne's writing, and he asked her to write several book reviews and essays for his publication. As a visitor to the Lindbergh home and one of Anne's frequent correspondents, he was in a unique position to observe the Lindbergh marriage during this period, and he learned firsthand that once Lindbergh had made up his mind about something, it was impossible to change it.

Rodman, with some friends, visited the Lindberghs for the first time on July 22, 1941, at their home in Lloyd Neck. His first impression of Lindbergh was that "he still looks young, thirty-five at most, though he must be forty; a little heavy in the waist perhaps, but clear of skin and very agile. He speaks precisely, choosing words carefully, listens well, asks many questions for information, is tolerant of disagreement but unflinching in his position. I launched at once into the subject on which I thought I might influence him."

Columnist Westbrook Pegler had recently attacked the aviator for his failure to criticize the Nazis, and Rodman bluntly asked Lindbergh if he might not silence his attackers by separating his own philosophy from that of the Nazis.

"Perhaps it would — temporarily, at least — but I am not a politician and I can see no reason why I should take the defensive," Rodman quotes Lindbergh as saying.

> I have repeatedly said that I believe in our way of life and would defend these shores against any importation from abroad, but who am I to tell the German people what kind of politics they should have? That is their business, and as far as I can understand it, they made the only choice possible for them in 1933. It was Nazism or Communism, and certainly if I had to make the unwelcome choice between living in Germany or Russia today, I would be obliged to choose Germany. Coming from Russia into Germany I felt as great a sense of liberation as I did in returning to France from Germany . . .

Undaunted, Rodman then tackled the question of Lindbergh's alleged prejudice against the Jews. "What about anti-Semitism?" he asked. "Surely if you assailed that, half the ground would be cut from under your critics."

Rodman remembered that Lindbergh then "spoke with considerable feeling . . . almost bitterly." Rodman quotes him as saying:

> Anti-Semitism is growing in this country for almost the same reason it grew in Germany and I am afraid that nothing can stop it. The Jews will have themselves to blame. As in Germany, they control the press, the radio and the movies — at least out of all proportion to their numbers. I am not against their controlling them, but the use they make of such weapons is going to end with their undoing. Instead of acting in the interests of their country and of the majority of their audience, they are acting in the interest — or the presumed interest — of their race . . . No, I will not criticize the Jews. But I shall certainly not take it upon myself to defend them.

It was Rodman's impression after spending the afternoon and evening with the couple that Anne was in almost total agreement with her husband's political views. "In the main, Anne seems to agree with him, but she is not so sure," he observed in his journal.

> During dinner she and Archie [a friend of Rodman's] discussed Indian philosophy and poetry, but after dinner she entered the argument Charles and I were having and deplored the negativism of the isolationist position. "The dominant 'new idea' of this epoch," she said, "is the rediscovery of the will to sacrifice, to give up life itself for the spirit, or at least for a cause or an idea, and we are handicapped by being forced to point out that the interventionists are fighting for a cause, lost though it may be, and are making people ready to die again. They have on their side the fact that people *want* to sacrifice themselves." Later on, however, she said that the real tragedy of the times is in the fact that the little man is caught between the fanaticisms of the Left and Right, Isolationism and Intervention, and simply wants to be left alone to work out his own salvation or security in less apocalyptic terms. "He is caught in this cross-fire and the fanatics, shouting over his body at each other, make themselves think that it is 'the people' who are shouting . . ."

Like many men, Rodman was entranced by Anne's gentle personality and the deft way she handled her husband.

> My final impressions of them? Her charm and many-faceted mind, her combination of emotional maturity and little-girl enthusiasm, are captivating. With him she is very understanding and sweet and he obviously adores her. "But of course," she said to me roguishly, "when Charles finally becomes convinced of something it's impossible to shake him, and I've long ago given up trying. I'm afraid I'm not much help to him in his present work, though I do understand people better than he does

and can at least warn him about the ones who are out for themselves and want to use him."

About Lindbergh, Rodman was forced to reach a far different conclusion. "As for Lindbergh himself, he has charm too, and simplicity and shyness and boyishness that are attractive. One cannot help admiring his courage and integrity," he noted in his journal. "But the fact is we don't speak the same language politically; and though he has none of the brassy jingoism and sadistic power-worship that make the Nazis so unspeakable, he seems destined to end up in their camp."

Puzzled by what he felt was the aviator's flirtation with Nazism, Rodman then speculated about the factors that might have caused him to become attracted to fascism.

> Perhaps it is because he [Lindbergh] has been cut off for so long from common people, that he is incapable of being outraged by their degradation under fascism. Perhaps it is because his initial isolation, and the memory of his father's martyrdom (during World War I which he opposed almost alone to the end), that drives his son logically as well as emotionally into the enemy's camp. Perhaps it is the conservatism of his friends, and the aristocratic racism of Alexis Carrel that have made him incline toward Nazism. Perhaps it is the symbolism of his lonely flight and the terrible denouement of mass-worship and the kidnapping that have driven him into a cause that is so unpopular among intellectuals; that always makes the Byronic hero spurn fame and fortune for guilt and solitary persecution . . .

When Charles Lindbergh's wartime journals were published many years later, Selden Rodman immediately turned to the day of their frank discussion. All these years he had hoped that his probing questions had moved Lindbergh to do some soul-searching. But with sadness he noted that "there was no entry at all for July 21, the day of our long debate about war, the isolationists, and anti-Semitism."

Although Rodman had the distinct impression that the Lindberghs were still very much in love, some tensions had in fact developed in their relationship. Lindbergh was starting to chafe at his wife's constant adoration, while she was beginning privately to resent his domination.

"C. back. As usual he is not in the house ten minutes before he is telling me gently to 'quiet down.' I know I am high strung and apt to be nervous but it is such a cold shower to be told to 'quiet down' one's joy and excitement, which always spring up when he comes home, even from a short trip," Anne confided to her journal. But then, as if shocked by her own disloyalty, she immediately added, "But he does it only for my own good and health, so I should not mind. And he is also nervous himself when he comes back from a trip, but chiefly it is his concern for me."

Her husband's criticism of her slowness as a writer had also begun to rankle her secretly: "He goes over the record — nine years, and only two books and wonders why it is. Has he not given me the right kind of environment?" And when he tried to pressure her into finishing an anthology of her favorite poems that she was collecting before the birth of their fourth child, she became furious, though it is unclear whether she worked up the courage to express her anger to him directly.

> But you ask too much, I want to cry out. I cannot be having a baby and be a good housekeeper and keep thinking and writing on the present times (in my diary) and be always free to discuss anything with you and give to the children and keep an atmosphere of peace in the family (the bigger family which is so scattered and distraught now, all of us disagreeing) and keep my mind clear and open on the present-day things and write a book at the same time. I cannot be an efficient woman and house-manager *and* an artist at the same time.

As Anne herself admitted, all her strength and creativity was going into the making of her child. Perhaps as a justification for her decision to become pregnant again, she had come to feel that

> the richest writing comes not from the people who dedicate themselves to writing alone . . .
> . . . For instance, in spite of my admiration for their beautiful writing, I think there is a kind of fungus quality in the books of both Vita Sackville-West and V. Woolf. I know they are married. V.S.W. has children, but it is a question of attitude. They think of themselves as *writers,* not as mothers or wives *ever* (what a statement!), so their point of view, it seems clear, is always the same.

But she did not have much time to brood about which type of female writer was best equipped to tell the truth about her sex. Her husband was again being attacked in the newspapers. After a May 19, 1940, speech, in which he had exhorted his audience not to be alarmed by the German advance into France and not to "listen to this hysterical chatter of calamity and invasion which has been running rife these last few days," Lindbergh was roundly attacked in an editorial in the *New York Times,* a publication that he and Anne had once admired.

"The hysterical chatter" is the talk now heard on every side of the democracies if France and Britain stand in danger of defeat by Germany. Colonel Lindbergh is a peculiar young man if he can contemplate this possibility in any other light than as a calamity for the American people. He is an ignorant young man if he trusts his own premise that it makes no difference to us whether we are deprived of the historic defense of British seapower in the Atlantic Ocean. He is a blind young man if he really believes we can live on terms of equal peace and happiness "regardless of which side wins this war" in Europe. Colonel Lindbergh remains a great flier.

Although still caught in "the eternal struggle of what I must be for Charles, and what I must be for Mother, and what I must be for myself," Anne Lindbergh at this point in her life seems at least temporarily to have resolved the conflict. By adopting political views that were entirely opposed to Mrs. Morrow's, for the first time in her life she stopped trying to be her "mother's good little girl." More important, however, she also stopped developing that part of herself that yearned to be a creative and independent woman with her own identity apart from her marriage. Now she lived only to please and help her husband. Abandoning her own work, she decided to use her considerable literary talent to help promote his political views.

Laying aside her proposed anthology of favorite poems, which she had entitled *O to Whom,* she began work on a very different sort of book. She began to write it in August 1940, the fifth month of her pregnancy, and as much as the new child growing inside her it was an act of love for her husband.

As had been the case with "Prayer for Peace," the writing went swiftly. As Anne recalled, it seemed to "flow" out of her, "unmindful of how it is 'written.'"

A political essay, the book attempted to answer the question whether Nazism was a monstrous or an understandable form of government that had grown out of the deprivations of the German people after World War I. After completing her manuscript, Anne decided to call it *The Wave of the Future,* seemingly unmindful of the fact that Lawrence Dennis, the leading intellectual of the American fascist movement, had also used the "wave" metaphor to describe the appeal of fascism.

Although aware that the book might arouse bitter controversy, Anne was willing to take the risk. As she wrote to her mother in an impassioned letter, she "*had* to write it, all the arguments and counter arguments, all my own carving out of a conviction, building of a bridge between C.'s beliefs and my own, and not least, my deep sense of the injustice to him and to his side."

It is unclear what Anne meant by a "bridge" between her beliefs and her husband's, since whenever she wrote about her own opinions concerning the war, her writing became uncharacteristically unclear. Undoubtedly this ambiguity was partly the result of feeling torn between Lindbergh's and her family's opposing views, even though she basically agreed with her husband. Another reason for her imprecision was that she was not an expert in politics and history, and her writing reflected it.

Although Anne Lindbergh was a pacifist and Charles Lindbergh was in favor of military action if it became necessary, there appears to have been little divergence in their views. In fact, most of the reasons Anne gave for staying out of the war parroted her husband's opinions. However, while Lindbergh's arguments for keeping the United States out of the conflict were based on logic and abstraction, Anne's were more personal and humane. She was horrified by the impact of the war on the lives of millions of people. After Mrs. Morrow had given her impassioned radio speech urging intervention, Anne wrote to her,

> You know I cannot agree with the application of your text when I personally feel that they should have never begun this war, that they should, once that mistake was made, have stopped it last fall; and that they should stop it now as quickly as possible. I personally believe, rightly or wrongly, that every day they go on fighting, they, their children, their grandchildren and ours will be worse off . . . Everything I love in the way of people, places, beliefs, dreams, and the general way of life over there, is going down before things and people that I personally hate.

The Wave of the Future, a mere forty-one pages in length, was published in October 1940. A month later it was on the top of the best-seller list. But Anne's book was a very unusual best seller. Unlike other works with a vast appeal for the reading public, it did not enhance its author's popularity or her literary reputation. On the contrary, this slender volume destroyed the public's image of Anne Morrow Lindbergh, and it would take almost two decades of hard work and harsh self-examination before she would regain her place as one of America's most beloved women authors.

CHAPTER 18

The Wave of the Future

I N THE EARLY MORNING HOURS of October 2, 1940, Anne gave birth to her fourth child, at Doctors' Hospital in New York. After three sons, she and Lindbergh desperately wanted a daughter and were delighted when their new baby proved to be a girl. This time the couple did not deliberate for days about a suitable name for their child. There was no question about it — she would be called Anne Spencer, after her mother.

Shortly before the birth, *The Wave of the Future* was published. Few books in the recent history of literature have aroused as much controversy.

Like "Prayer for Peace," Anne wrote *The Wave of the Future* to persuade Americans not to enter the European conflict. In the author's opinion, a major revolution was coming which would transform the entire world. As Anne saw it, the nationalist movements in Germany, Italy, and Russia were parts of this "vast revolution" — and here her writing again becomes cloudy and imprecise: "This is not to claim that the things we dislike in Nazism *are* the forces of the future. But it is to say that somehow the leaders in Germany, Italy and Russia have discovered how to use new social and economic forces; very often they have used them badly, but nevertheless, they have recognized and used them . . . They have felt the wave of the future and they have leapt upon it. The evils we deplore in these systems are not in themselves the future; they are scum on the wave of the future."

The precise nature of this "wave," or "revolution," Anne did not make clear, although she cautioned her readers that it was so powerful that all the United States could do was to submit to its strength. "The wave of the future is coming and there is no use fighting it."

Although Anne's style was generally praised by the critics — Clare Boothe, for example, writing in *Current History and Forum*, called it "clear, chiseled, cadenced — almost classic" — many readers were appalled by the author's equating Germany's aggression and persecution of the Jews with the faults of the democracies. "They are *sins*, there is no doubt about it, and I stand against them," she had written. "But there are other sins, such as blindness, selfishness, irresponsibility, smugness, lethargy, and resistance to change — sins which we 'Democracies,' all of us, are guilty of . . ."

Some readers interpreted the book as German propaganda, among them Harold L. Ickes, the secretary of the interior, who was convinced that Charles Lindbergh was a Nazi. He publicly damned *The Wave of the Future* as "the Bible of every American Nazi, Fascist, Bundist and Appeaser." At his third inaugural address, on January 20, 1941, Roosevelt himself refuted the book's premise by assuring the American people, "There are men who believe that . . . tyranny and slavery have become the surging wave of the future — and that freedom is an ebbing tide. But we Americans know that this is not true."

Irving Berlin's wife, Ellin Mackay, was one of many readers who strenuously objected to the book's seemingly antidemocratic stance. In a radio debate on the question "Is propaganda endangering the United States?" Mackay, who represented the Committee to Defend America by Aiding the Allies, described Anne as a "sensitive and gentle woman who has been bewildered and frightened by skillful German propaganda . . . No one can be blamed for being frightened, but it is heartbreaking to find an American woman burying Democracy in quotation marks. She speaks of it tenderly, but she speaks of it as though it were dead . . . That is not true. Democracy is alive here — it is alive in England. The Nazis have disguised old-fashioned tyranny to look like something new. They have touched the heart of a poet like Mrs. Lindbergh."

In Mackay's opinion, Anne had allowed herself to become a dupe of the Nazis. "We must not romanticize the Nazis," she cautioned. "They are a group of unscrupulous militants who mean to conquer the world. That is not what I say. That is what they say — 'Today we rule Germany, tomorrow the World.'"

Although Mackay attempted to soften her criticism of Anne by portraying her as a "frightened" and easily intimidated woman, columnist Dorothy Thompson could find no such excuses for her beliefs. In her syndicated column *On the Record,* Thompson, who, like Roosevelt, already suspected Lindbergh of being a Nazi, made it clear that she was now convinced of the fact after reading *The Wave of the Future.* In a blistering attack on both Lindberghs, she wrote,

> If one adds to Col. Lindbergh's speeches and writings the book written by his wife, where, in words that parallel the writings of the avowed advocate of American Nazi-ism, Lawrence Dennis, she described Nazi-ism and Communism as "waves of the future," the picture becomes even clearer: The growing youth movement around Col. Lindbergh, being carefully cultivated in American colleges and the support for Colonel Lindbergh of all the rabble-rousing American Fascists, the prophecy of the Nazi "Scribner's Commentator" that "the man" is at hand, and you have a picture closely resembling the composition of forces typical of all Nazi movements.

By "growing youth movement around Col. Lindbergh" Thompson was referring to the small student organization at Yale that had invited Lindbergh to speak on foreign affairs on October 30, 1940. By that time, the noninterventionist student group, led by R. Douglas Stuart, Jr., a twenty-four-year-old law student and son of the first vice president of the Quaker Oats Company, had won the support of a number of influential Midwestern business and political leaders. Less than a week after Lindbergh's address, it became a national noninterventionist organization, the America First Committee, with headquarters in Chicago.

By "rabble-rousing American Fascists" Thompson meant William Dudley Pelley, an open admirer of Hitler, who organized "Silver Shirt" brigades in North Carolina, California, and other states. According to Alan Brinkley, author of *Voices of Protest: Huey Long, Father Coughlin, and the Great Depression,* Pelley was "a disturbed and vicious man" who

> enthusiastically emulated the Nazis in his militarism, supernationalism, and anti-Semitism. But he never became a genuinely important force in American politics . . . There were, however, other American fascists, men of a very different sort. . . . Lawrence Dennis, Georgia born, Harvard educated, bright and literary, was perhaps the most prominent of such fascist "intellectuals." In several articulate books, he argued that capitalism was doomed by the pressures of modern society, and he claimed that fascism offered the only hope of saving America from communism.

Although Dorothy Thompson was on the mark in many of her opinions, her accusation that Charles and Anne were supported by the American fascist movement appears to have no basis in fact. When Pelley was brought to trial for sedition a year later by the Justice Department in Indianapolis, Lindbergh was subpoenaed by the defense. In his wartime journals, Lindbergh maintained that he had "never seen or had any contact with Pelley or his organization," but felt that it was his duty to appear because he had "always been under the impression that a subpoena was something to be answered, both from a standpoint of honor and of law." Although on the stand for only twelve minutes, "the episode," according to Wayne Cole, "further identified him in the public mind with unsavory and seditious elements in America."

As for Lawrence Dennis, Lindbergh wrote in a memorandum dated August 21, 1969, "I met Lawrence Dennis on only a few occasions, and read only parts of his book. I was interested in his philosophy, but doubtful about its wisdom and practicality. His influence on my thought and action was negligable [*sic*]."

Mrs. Morrow, Constance, and Aubrey Morgan discreetly refused comment on the book, but Anne's cousin, Richard B. Scandrett, Jr., wrote her a denunciatory letter that later became public:

> Your book seems to me to be the effort of a troubled woman, aghast at current world horrors, eager to have their area restricted and to find a conception of duty towards the situation which, if accepted, might keep life running on much as usual in America. . . . I have read and reread your book several times and each rereading adds to my original impression that it is, to an appreciable extent, a lyrical and silver-coated exposition of the views expressed by Charles. Both you and Charles seem to me to have accepted the totalitarian definition of a democracy as a static or decayed material concept.

Of the reviews, which were largely unfavorable, one of the most widely read and quoted was that written by E. B. White, which appeared in the *New Yorker* in December 1940:

> It is called a "confession of faith," but I couldn't make out what it is she believes in and did not think it a clear book or a good one. . . . She herself states that the evils in the system are the "scum on the wave," but makes it clear that this *is* the wave. It is of course anybody's privilege to believe that a good conception of humanity may be coming to birth through the horrid forms of nazism; but it seems to me far more likely that a good conception of humanity is being promoted by the stubborn resistance to nazism on the part of millions of people whose belief in democratic notions has been strengthened . . . Mrs. Lindbergh says it is the duty of a writer to state the problem correctly, and I agree with her

but do not think she has done a good job, because many of her state-ments, although accurate in themselves, are followed by an inferential remark which a logician would find inadmissible. She tells me that the German people are not innately bad, which is correct and is not even news as far as I am concerned; but then she draws the inference that therefore the star the German people are following is good, which I think is illogical and a perversion of the facts. . . .

. . . And even after my conclusions I do not believe that Mrs. Lind-bergh is any more fascist-minded than I am, or that she wants a different sort of world, or that she is a defeatist; but I think instead she is a poeti-cal and liberal and talented person troubled in her mind (as anybody is today) and trying to write her way into the clear. . . .

Although Anne tried to shrug off the scathing reviews, it still both-ered her intensely that people had misinterpreted her message. "I never said Totalitarianism was the Wave of the Future; in fact, I said emphati-cally that it was *not* — and that I hoped *we* in America could be, in our way," she insisted.

In an attempt to clarify what she had meant to say in *The Wave of the Future,* she wrote an article entitled "Reaffirmation," which was sub-sequently published in the *Atlantic Monthly.* In the piece, she stressed that the "wave of the future" was not Nazism, Communism, or fascism, but "a movement of adjustment to a highly scientific, mechanized, and material era of civilization, with all its attendant complications, and as such it seems to me inevitable, I feel we must face this wave; that we must not be overwhelmed by it . . .

"I do not say we must meet it in the same way as the dictator-governed nations," she added. "I opposed that way from the depths of my conviction."

Nevertheless the fact that most readers of *The Wave of the Future* had failed to grasp the book's essential message undermined Anne's self-confidence as a writer. She had meant the book to be a "pacifist docu-ment" and blamed herself for what she considered her lack of literary skill in not making the idea clearly understood. Despite her good inten-tions, her intended "pacifism" had come across as a defeatist attitude that played into the hands of Hitler.

If she expressed herself so poorly, Anne thought bitterly, perhaps she should stop being a writer.

Even more painful for Anne than reading the bad reviews was her estrangement from the people she had once regarded as kindred spirits. "I find I am hurt, not by the reviews exactly, but by the growing rift I see between myself and those people I thought I belonged to," she rue-fully admitted. "The artists, the writers, the intellectuals, the sensitive, the idealistic — I feel exiled from them. I have become exiled for good, accidentally, really. My marriage has stretched me out of my world, changed me so it is no longer possible to change back."

One of those friends from whom she felt "exiled" was Antoine de Saint-Exupéry. In January 1941, when she learned that he was back in New York, she longed to contact him. "I keep looking for someone to be left like that from my world, my world of writing," she explained to Lindbergh, who was still suspicious of her relationship with the French aviator. But she could not bring herself to call him. Although she con-sidered Saint-Exupéry to be a very special person in her life, she knew that as a Frenchman risking his life to fight the Nazis, he had absolutely no sympathy with her and her husband's refusal to aid the Allies. She feared that if she dared call him, he might be cold to her or, worse yet, he might hang up in disgust, and she knew that she could not bear his rebuff.

On Christmas Eve, 1940, Anne spoke on the radio on behalf of the Quak-ers, urging that food be sent to the starving people living in the occu-pied European countries. Lindbergh was busy with a previous engage-ment.

But public opinion was still heavily against her. When footage of her address later appeared in a newsreel, a photograph of Roosevelt pre-ceded it and the caption read, ANNE LINDBERGH SUGGESTS WE FEED HITLER'S EUROPE. With the exception of this newsreel coverage, her speech was largely ignored in the press.

Of all the groups involved in the antiwar movement, Anne was most drawn to the Quakers, to whom she planned to donate the royalties of *The Wave of the Future.* "I felt I could breathe with them — such a re-lief not to be fighting up the stream, as one is most of the time. At least here are some 'good' people on our side. For it is this that has upset me the most this year, to find all the right people on the wrong side and — even more appalling — all the *wrong* people on the right side. The Quakers are both practical and 'good.' I can go almost 'all the way with them.' But C. cannot."

The organization that Lindbergh could "go all the way with" was the America First Committee, the most powerful noninterventionist pres-sure group in the United States. He joined the committee in April 1941, soon becoming its most influential and crowd-pleasing speaker.

The purpose of America First was to keep the United States out of the war and, by extension, to oppose the interventionist policies of Roosevelt, even though at this point the president was still declaring himself to be in favor of nonintervention. Its heterogeneous ranks included such powerful archconservatives and zealous Roosevelt haters as General Robert E. Wood, chairman of the board of the Sears, Roebuck Company, and Robert R. McCormick, publisher of the *Chicago Tribune.* Other members included J. Stanford Otis, vice president of Chicago's Central Republic Bank; Jay C. Hormel, president of the Hormel Meat Packing Company; Oswald Garrison Villard, former editor of the *Nation;* Avery Brundage, president of the Olympic Association; R. Douglas Stuart, Jr.; Kingman Brewster, a Yale student who later became president of the university; Chester Bowles, the advertising executive; and Edward Rickenbacker, the air ace and aviation expert.

Although many of the people in America First were pacifists or men and women who regretted the United States' participation in World War I, there were also some Nazis and Bundists in the organization.

"In some of the local America First Committee branches, there was an infiltration of Bundists and people that could be called Nazis," Senator William Benton, who was involved with the committee, later recalled.

I had a butler, not long before that, a German butler, working for me who pointed out about the *New York Times*— that the word "Times" is "Semite" spelled backwards, and he claimed that the *Times* was owned by Jews — which of course it was, by the Sulzberger family — but that it was primarily an organ to promote the Jewish people and the welfare of the Jews. Stuff of this kind was not uncommon in this country. Further, there was a substantial group, only some of whom were Bundists and Nazis, who thought Germany was going to win the war. Some of them got infiltrated into some of the America First local groups. But very few, and it was very much exaggerated.

Although Anne herself never joined America First, a number of other distinguished American women were members of the organization. They included Lillian Gish, the silent-film star, Kathleen Norris, the writer, Alice Roosevelt Longworth, Theodore Roosevelt's witty and irrepressible daughter, and Adelaide Hooker Marquand, the novelist John Marquand's off-beat wife who was a good friend of Anne's.

With the exception of the Marquands and Lillian Gish, whom she found "charming — fragile and intelligent," Anne didn't especially care for the people who were drawn to America First. "The young on our side are good stuff, but the older generation are pretty seedy and washed out," she noted in her diary. "All the good ones are on the other side."

This unfavorable assessment of her husband's colleagues included socialist Norman Thomas, who, although not a member of America First, occasionally spoke on its behalf. Thomas and his family lived in Cold Spring Harbor, not far from Lloyd Neck, and the two families occasionally saw each other socially. On one occasion, Lindbergh, according to Anne, talked to Thomas "about the Jewish problem and the need for tolerance." Although impressed by the socialist leader's intelligence, she quickly summed him up as a monstrous egotist who constantly interrupted his wife and whose overbearing maleness made her feel deeply appreciative of her own husband, whom she now regarded as "more of a feminist" than herself.

Anne's unflattering assessment of Thomas's personality is noteworthy in that it was one of the few times in her life she was ever highly critical of a man. Clearly, his chauvinism upset her more than the racist views of many of the prominent men she liked and admired, including the Duke of Windsor, Ambassador Joseph Kennedy, Alexis Carrel, Henry Ford, and, of course, her own husband.

Norman Thomas's impressions of Anne are unknown. However, according to his biographer W. A. Swanberg, he considered her husband to be "the kind of heroic and glamorous person the anti-war movement could use if he would only take a little tutoring. Though friendly, he was as independent as his late father, blunt and tactless. He had uttered and written undemocratic sentiments and made enemies." Like Thomas Lamont, Betty Morrow, Alexis Carrel, Selden Rodman, and, undoubtedly, Anne herself, Thomas attempted to modify Lindbergh's views of the Nazis. In a letter, he urged the aviator to speak out against Hitler, advice the stubborn Lindbergh refused to heed.

Although a strong force in both New York and Boston, America First attracted its mainly Republican followers mostly in the Midwest, which had long been the traditional seat of the nation's isolationist sentiments. However, thanks to Lindbergh's charisma and the persuasiveness of his speeches, many Americans across the country were now against becoming involved in the European conflict. In fact, Lindbergh was so successful in drumming up antiwar feeling that Roosevelt had become deeply suspicious of his motives. He now considered Lindbergh to be a major threat to his presidency.

At a news conference on April 25, 1941, a reporter asked the president why he did not call Lindbergh, an army officer, into uniform. The reason, Roosevelt replied, was that Lindbergh was a defeatist, and he then compared Lindbergh to Representative Clement L. Vallandigham, a Civil War congressman from Ohio, the chief spokesman of a group called the Copperheads, who said the North could never win.

Considering his honor impugned, Lindbergh immediately resigned his commission in the U.S. Army. "If I did not tender my resignation," he wrote in his *Wartime Journals*, "I would lose something in my own character that means even more to me than my commission in the Air Corps."

"No one else might know it, but I would," he continued proudly. "And if I take this insult from Roosevelt, more, and worse, will probably be forthcoming."

Deeply upset by Roosevelt's statement, Anne tried to convince her husband not to give up his commission, pointing out that it might hurt the cause of America First and the antiwar movement. But Lindbergh refused to change his mind, telling her that under the circumstances he had no choice but to resign.

That night Anne couldn't sleep. She had been working on her rebuttal to the criticism of *The Wave of the Future* for the *Atlantic Monthly*. The piece wasn't going well, and she knew that she was writing it out of desperation, but it wasn't her own problems that were making her feel restless and unhappy. It was the grief she felt about Charles having to give up his commission. She knew how much it had meant to him.

The next few days proved even more emotionally draining. Editorials in several of the nation's leading newspapers attacked Lindbergh personally, characterizing him as a "mechanical, hard and unfeeling" man. Some also pointed out that although he had no trouble resigning his commission in the U.S. Army, he had refused to return his German medal.

Anne was still in a state of emotional turmoil a few days later when Sue Vaillant, a close friend, accused her of never having had the courage to write truthfully about her husband. Stung by Sue's criticism, Anne defended herself in her diary, writing,

> If this is true, it is because I respected his very strong feelings about privacy — his passionate feeling of not wanting to be exposed, written about, journalized, interpreted. So strong is this feeling of his and so strong is my feeling that I must protect him from this kind of intrusion — that

his wife, at least, should not journalize him, betray him, that I have, rather than give a *false* picture, given an incomplete one. And one equally false. It is very bitter to think so. But I hoped, oh I hoped so, that the truth would shine through, that my love itself would illuminate it. For some people it has.

In June, the Lindberghs flew to Los Angeles, where Lindbergh was to speak at an America First meeting at the Hollywood Bowl and then travel through the West on a speaking tour. Feeling fed up with the quality of their life on the East Coast and determined to find their "roots" at last, the couple decided to use the opportunity of the Western trip to look for a house that might be suitable for them and their three young children, whom they had left behind in the care of servants. As usual, Anne had felt torn about being separated from her offspring, in particular Jon, with whom she hadn't spent much time recently, as she had been "occupied with C. or writing or war."

The Lindberghs departed for Los Angeles from La Guardia Airport in a sleek, modern TWA Douglas DC-3. It was the first time Lindbergh had flown over the air route as a passenger, not as a pilot, and Anne could not help noting the difference between this flight and the ones they had shared together during the early days of aviation. She observed,

> It is so strange to leave this airport where we went off in the *Sirius* for the trip to the Orient and to Greenland (it was North Beach then — a converted dump heap), now in a silvered limousine of a plane, soft seats, small curtained windows, muffled noise, air conditioning, sky hostesses . . .
>
> I cannot get used to it, and it does not seem like flying to me. I push back the curtains and peer out of the tiny window and look down at the earth below the great silver wing. But it is separated from me. It is unreal, like a movie.

It was during this trip to the West Coast that Lindbergh decided to make peace with his old enemy, newspaper publisher William Randolph Hearst. This was a peculiar decision on Lindbergh's part, as Hearst had paid for Bruno Hauptmann's defense in exchange for exclusive interviews with him and his wife, Anna. And it was Hearst reporters who had hounded the flier and his family to the point where their lives became unbearable and they had to seek refuge in England.

Although Anne always characterized her husband as a man of firm convictions and integrity, it seemed that he could change his mind about someone when it served his purpose. And in Hearst's case, Lindbergh's purpose was clear. The newspaper tycoon shared his belief that the United States should stay out of the European conflict, or, as Lindbergh himself put it, Hearst was "so good on the war issue." And Hearst's newspapers, with their enormous circulation, could be counted on to spread the flier's message of nonintervention to millions.

Ironically, the Lindberghs' visit to the Hearst ranch in Medford, Oregon, coincided with Anne's thirty-fifth birthday and what would have been the eleventh birthday of Charles Augustus, Jr., had he lived.

Considering the emotional trauma Hearst and his reporters had inflicted on her and her family, Anne reacted to the newspaper tycoon in an extraordinary way. "He [Hearst] is a great figure in a tan raincoat, his head bent forward with age, at about the same angle to his coat as a turtle's head to its shell," she observed. "His face is lined and rather flabby and it gives an impression of general kindliness, even benevolence. It is without emphasis except for the eye — a pale and even watery eye — but intensely aware, observant."

Although her diary contained a wryly amusing account of the aging newspaper publisher's relationship with movie star Marion Davies, whom she characterized as a perpetually "charming child" whom Hearst deliberately kept in a state of arrested development, Anne never once referred to the past, when Hearst had been such a powerful and destructive influence on their lives. Nor evidently did her host. Judging from Anne's account, he adroitly avoided mentioning Hauptmann. Nor did he apologize for the often outrageous tactics of his reporters. On the contrary, he appears to have said little to his famous guests, emerging from his zombielike state only when they were on their way out the door, at which point he suddenly pressed on Lindbergh an autographed photo of himself.

Oddly enough, it was the usually close-mouthed Charles Lindbergh who proved more forthcoming in print on the subject of the couple's new friendship with the newspaper tycoon. "Hearst has been assisting us, and I intend to assist him as far as this war issue is concerned," Lindbergh wrote. "I cannot forget the past, but I have put it in the background, at least for the time being."

On July 7, after returning from the Western speaking tour, Lindbergh learned that his phone, as well as the phones of other prominent people in America First, was being tapped by the FBI. Unperturbed by the surveillance, which had been going on for some time, Lindbergh told the man who informed him about the tapping to tell his friends at the bureau that "if there was anything they didn't understand in my own phone conversations, I would be glad to give them additional information. . . . It really makes very little difference as far as I am concerned. My main interest lies in knowing whether or not these tactics are being used by the Administration."

Although wiretapping had previously been outlawed by the Supreme Court, on May 21, 1941, Franklin Roosevelt wrote a letter to Attorney General Robert Jackson, giving him permission, on an individual basis, to authorize wiretaps of persons suspected of subversive activities against the government of the United States, including suspected spies. Although Jackson was instructed "to limit these investigations so conducted to a minimum, and to limit them insofar as possible to aliens," the attorney general realized the directive "opened the door pretty wide to wiretapping of anyone suspected of subversive activities." With his radio addresses proclaiming the Luftwaffe's invincibility and Britain's certain defeat, Charles Lindbergh was, of course, one of those persons "suspected of subversive activities," and his activities could now be legally investigated.

Charles Lindbergh's FBI file, released under the Freedom of Information Act, begins on September 16, 1939, the day after his first major public address against U.S. involvement in the war. Alarmed by the flier's political allegiances, many American citizens wrote to President Franklin Roosevelt or FBI director J. Edgar Hoover, warning them to keep an eye on Lindbergh because, in the opinion of the correspondents, he was a "Nazi agent" or a "fifth columnist."

Other letters to Roosevelt or Hoover contained theories to explain why Lindbergh had become enthralled by the Nazis. Most of these theories are so fantastic that they must be discounted, although it cannot be denied that they make for fascinating reading. For example, one man claimed he was certain that the Charles Lindbergh who was presently in the United States was an imposter and that the "real" Charles Lindbergh was imprisoned in Berlin, together with his wife, Anne Morrow Lindbergh. "The person now masquerading in this country as Lindbergh is a cleverly duplicated Charlie McCarthy brought into being under the legerdemain of Dr. Goebbels," the letter writer warned.

Another equally wild theory about Lindbergh's sudden political activism was advanced by Maurice Leon of Irvington-on-Hudson, New

York. A well-known columnist, Leon contacted the FBI and was interviewed on March 30, 1942. According to the FBI report,

He [Leon] advised that he had been told by a French diplomatic representative, prior to the fall of France, that the French Military Intelligence
had carefully investigated the captioned subject [Lindbergh], and remembered that while an obscure pilot in the United States, he had acted as an
informant for the German government on air conditions in this country. Mr. Leon further advised that he had been told that after the subject's well known flight to Paris, he attempted to break this tie with the
German government. He stated that Hauptman [*sic*] was an escaped German prisoner, subject to extradition by the German government, and
the German government apparently used the pressure of extradition, of
Hauptman, to compel him to act as their "strong-arm" man to keep Lindbergh in line.

Mr. Leon continued that it is a well-known fact that the pro-Nazi circles in the United States raised defense funds for Hauptman's trial for
the kidnapping and murder of the Lindbergh baby. Leon informed that
according to French Intelligence, Lindbergh then left the United States
and fled to England to protect himself from further prosecutive action
by the Germans. He stated he left England and went to a desert island in
France to further attempt to protect himself, and finally, to protect his
wife and child, Lindbergh went to Berlin, and made his peace with the
Nazis. Leon advised that was at the time Lindbergh received a medal from
the German government, and he has been acting under the influence of
the German government since, because of fear of further violence to his
wife and child.

Mr. Leon concluded that he cannot prove these things, but the story
was told to him by a reliable French diplomat.

From the files, it is obvious that Charles Lindbergh's sudden political
activism was as baffling to the FBI as it would be to his subsequent biographers. The bureau concluded:

The files and other reference material examined contain no indication
that Charles A. Lindbergh expressed any opinions or engaged in any activities which indicated that he took an interest in anything other than
flying until the latter part of 1935 or early 1936. Up to that time the only
factor which might explain his later isolationist views was his father's
career and isolationist position in the First World War; however, there
are no public statements of Lindbergh's to indicate that such was the
case.

It is to be noted that even during the time he was being questioned
concerning the circumstances surrounding the kidnapping of his first son,

Lindbergh allegedly would avoid the main issue and would tend to discuss aviation at every opportunity.

Perhaps the only incriminating evidence of Lindbergh's alleged anti-Semitism came from a man who himself was also the recipient of a German medal and was openly anti-Semitic. The FBI contacted maverick automobile manufacturer Henry Ford, with the hope that he might provide the name of whoever it was at the War Department who might be giving Lindbergh restricted and confidential information that Lindbergh, in turn, might be transmitting to Germany. The FBI report said, "It is also to be noted that during the course of an interview with Henry Ford, he stated on one occasion that he had been counseling Lindbergh concerning his anti-Semitism and had been cautioning him against openly expressing it."

The FBI interview with Ford took place on December 13, 1941, six days after Japan bombed Pearl Harbor.

> Henry Ford stated that he asked Colonel Charles A. Lindbergh to come out to Detroit and to visit him at the plant because he wanted to talk to Lindberg [*sic*] about Lindberg's attitude toward the Jews. Henry Ford told Bugas [an FBI agent] that he had heard a speech which Lindberg had made several nights before, and Ford did not like some of the things he said about the Jews. Accordingly, he asked Lindberg to come out and see him so that he could give some views on that score.
>
> Henry Ford stated that Lindberg had stayed overnight and that the conversations were principally about Jewish matters. Henry Ford does not recall any conversations on the part of Lindberg with regard to Lindberg's obtaining or securing any information from the War Department.

The contents of this particular report are open to serious question, however. Why would Henry Ford, an avowed anti-Semite, be so shocked by Lindbergh's alleged anti-Semitic remarks that he would invite Lindbergh out to Detroit to chastise him? And to which speech of Charles Lindbergh was Ford referring? The last time Lindbergh spoke publicly was not in December but on October 30, in Madison Square Garden, and his speech contained no mention of the Jews.

The FBI file on Charles Lindbergh essentially ends on December 16, 1942, when Hoover was advised by the head librarian of Yale University that Charles Lindbergh had recently deposited a voluminous collection of mail he had received during the time he was the most prominent member of America First. The director declined to read it. His reason is unknown, but perhaps it is fair to say that he knew that examining Lindbergh's mail would be a waste of his time.

Aside from some letters from private citizens concerned about Lindbergh as a possible risk to national security during the Second World War, no significant documents were added to the file until September 8, 1954. That was the day after Evangeline Lindbergh died at her Grosse Point Park home at the age of seventy-nine. J. Edgar Hoover used the occasion of her death to write Lindbergh, who was now a brigadier general, a sympathy note, which, considering their past association, was a masterpiece of hypocrisy.

> Dear General:
>   It was with the greatest regret that I learned of the passing of your mother.
>   Words alone, I know, can provide little comfort on such an occasion as this. I want to tell you, however, that your friends share your deep sorrow, and you have my heartfelt sympathy in your bereavement.
>   Sincerely yours,
>   J. Edgar Hoover

In a postscript that was clearly intended as an interdepartment memorandum, the director added, "There have been numerous derogatory allegations against the General in the past concerning America First and pro-Nazi leanings. Presently, however, the Bureau is completing an investigation of him requested by AEC in connection with his appointment as Consultant to the Secretary of the Air Force, and none of the derogatory allegations have been substantiated in any way. Our few contacts with him have been cordial . . ."

As for an FBI investigation of Anne's political activities, there appears to have been none. She was mentioned only in passing in Lindbergh's FBI file. The most substantive reference to her was in connection with her supposed professional relationship to the fascist intellectual Lawrence Dennis, who advocated a totalitarian form of government in the United States which would cooperate with the Nazi regime.

According to the FBI, "In December, 1940, Dennis stated that he was then working on something for his (Lindbergh's) *Scribner's Commentator* [a conservative noninterventionist magazine] and to be reprinted for the Marshall No Foreign War Committee which he is the prime mover of." On another occasion in December 1940, Dennis said that he had just seen J. B. Kelly, an alleged Fascist, who had just seen Lindbergh. A confidential source has also advised that Dennis was writing articles put out by Anne Lindbergh."

Once again, this rumor had no basis in fact. Although many interventionists claimed that Lawrence Dennis was Anne's ghost, the truth was that she wrote her own articles and her relationship with the fascist was a superficial one at best. In fact, like her husband, she had met him only once or twice. "Lawrence Dennis is by far the most interesting of this group we have met because of the war situation," she admitted without apology in her diary. ". . . From his *Letter* (*Weekly Foreign Service Letter*, a right wing publication), and the things people say about him, I had expected the devil incarnate ('Foremost Fascist of America,' etc.) . . . But though very brilliant he did not seem hard, and I would say that, far from being assertive, he was rather reserved and extremely sensitive . . . But I feel in what he says a profound bitterness — the ring of 'the people is a great beast.' This is where I leave him."

How accurate is the information in these FBI files? Was J. Edgar Hoover, at Roosevelt's request, "using tactics" to ruin Lindbergh politically? And was the director himself acting out of personal motives?

First of all, it is important to realize that Hoover owed his very career to Lindbergh. It was the Lindbergh kidnapping case that had thrust both him and his agency into national prominence. According to Ovid Demaris, author of *The Director: An Oral Biography of J. Edgar Hoover*,

> The Bureau slept through the violence of the Roaring Twenties . . . It was not until the Lindbergh baby was kidnapped in March 1932 that the nation became conscious of the large number of criminal gangs that were abducting citizens and fleeing to other jurisdictions to avoid capture . . . This alarmed Congress enough for it to pass the Lindbergh Law, which made it a federal crime to send a ransom demand or a kidnapping threat through the mails. For the first time the federal government was authorized to act against crimes of violence committed in jurisdictions other than on government reservations.
>
> This legislation literally marks the beginning of J. Edgar Hoover's rise from obscurity . . . Companion bills to the Lindbergh Law enacted between 1932 and 1934 put the Bureau foursquare into the crime business.

Although the Lindbergh kidnapping case helped make Hoover's career, the director himself had never forgiven Lindbergh for crediting the Treasury Department, rather than the FBI, with the capture of Bruno

Hauptmann. In preparing the ransom money, Elmer Irey, from the Treasury Department, had insisted, against Lindbergh's wishes, on including a large number of gold certificates, which had been previously withdrawn from circulation when Roosevelt took the country off the gold standard. The numbers of the ransom bills were recorded in a forty-six-page list and then circulated to banks throughout the country. Hauptmann's use of one of the gold certificates more than a year later led to his subsequent arrest.

According to Curt Gentry, author of *J. Edgar Hoover: The Man and the Secrets,* "At the time of the trial, Charles Lindbergh told Elmer Irey of the Treasury Department: 'If it had not been for you fellows being in the case, Hauptmann would not now be on trial and your organization deserves full credit for his apprehension.' Hoover would never forgive Lindbergh for that remark."

Five years later, in Gentry's view, he had an opportunity to get even with Lindbergh.

> On May 16, 1940, the president addressed a joint session of Congress on the subject of national defense. It was an explosive issue — many considered it a giant step toward U.S. intervention in the European conflict — and Roosevelt's critics were quick to respond.
>
> On May 18 Steve Early, the president's press secretary, wrote Hoover, "I am sending you, at the President's direction, a number of telegrams he has received since the delivery of his address . . . These telegrams are all more or less in opposition to national defense. It was the President's idea that you might like to go over these, noting the names and addresses of the senders."
>
> Hoover went one better. He checked the names against FBI files, then made "comments and reports" on what he had found — going beyond what FDR had requested, but probably giving him exactly what he wanted.
>
> . . . By the end of May, Hoover had conducted background checks on 131 critics of the president . . . including Colonel Charles A. Lindbergh . . .

According to Gentry, Roosevelt asked his presidential secretary, Major General Edwin M. ("Pa") Watson, to write a brief letter to Hoover under his signature, thanking him for his investigative reports. The president's comments were deliberately noncommittal, but Hoover was "moved" by them and sent back an "effusive reply."

"Roosevelt obviously knew just how to handle Hoover," Gentry added. "In addition to his letter, the FBI chief sent the president a new batch of reports on his political enemies. It was as if, amid all the rhetoric, a bargain had been struck."

Following Lindbergh's infamous speech on September 11, 1941, in Des Moines, Iowa, in which he blamed Roosevelt, the British, and the Jews for pushing the country into war, Steve Early forwarded Hoover thirty-six more telegrams from people who, like Lindbergh, were opposed to U.S. intervention.

"This time, however, Hoover went beyond making 'comments and reports,'" Gentry wrote. "He leaked some of the most interesting materials to [Walter] Winchell and [Drew] Pearson. According to Oliver Pilat, Pearson's son-in-law and biographer, the FBI director wasn't acting on his own but 'was harassing isolationists under orders from the White House.'"

Obviously, the bureau, at the request of the administration, was "harassing" Lindbergh, with the hope of turning up something on him that would cause his political downfall. Not surprisingly, both Hoover and Roosevelt lost interest in his activities after he "self-destructed" with his Des Moines speech, which will be discussed later, and no longer was considered a threat. This is significant in itself, because if Roosevelt and Hoover had actually believed that Lindbergh was a Nazi spy or a threat to national security, they would have continued to investigate his activities and contacts. But the investigation was essentially terminated after Des Moines, on September 11, apart from some perfunctory interviews with Henry Ford and Harry Bennett, Ford's vice president.

Still, no evidence exists that Hoover and Roosevelt were the organizers of a plot to topple Lindbergh. If that had been the case, it seems logical to assume, they would have concocted a more cohesive and believable story about his pro-Nazi activities and then leaked it to the press. Other than some scattershot, unverifiable rumors that were fed to Winchell and Pearson, this did not occur.

It was during these tumultuous years that the Lindberghs decided to transfer their old files and records from vaults and warehouses to the Sterling Library at Yale University, which would be the "safest possible location" in the event of an attack on the United States. The many documents they deposited at the library, which now number well over a million items, were not to be examined during their lifetimes without their permission. Obviously hoping that posterity would view him more favorably than did his contemporaries, Charles Lindbergh noted, "There are portions of everyone's life that could be improved if they could be lived again in the light of later experience; but Anne and I are not ashamed of the way we have lived our lives, and there is nothing in our records that we fear to have known. I wonder how many of our accusers would be willing to turn their complete files and records over for study in the future."

Also with an eye toward posterity, they had been working for the past year on editing Anne's old diaries, which Lindbergh had especially copied. Anne had mixed feelings about the project. "For six months this has gone on. It is, in a way, a strain, although I believe it should be done," she commented. "Each day that I read the lies about us in the newspaper I think there must be some honest personal record to show what it really was like. And that record must be assured of permanence as C. is doing now. But it bothers me — especially the early adolescent diaries. We have had dreadful arguments about it. I wish I had got hold of them before C., and had them all burned. It is so painful to read them and see all my faults in exaggeration and recognize that I still have them."

When Lindbergh started helping his wife edit her diary for 1935, he realized for the first time how close she had been to a nervous breakdown. "I did not realize the depth of her depression that year, although it was one of the main reasons that led me to take her and Jon to Europe," he admitted in his own journal. "I could see she was very unhappy and that Jon was feeling the abnormal environment under which we were living — Englewood, press, guards, police etc. I knew that pressure would increase during the appeal . . . But as I read Anne's diary for that year, I feel I should have taken her abroad before I did — although I do not know how we could have gotten away much earlier."

The time-consuming diary project made Anne's normally busy schedule even more hectic and regimented. Mornings were spent writing, although, as she confessed to Selden Rodman, she really did not have the heart to work on anything new for fear that it would be misunderstood. In the afternoon, she and Lindbergh attended to business matters. Between teatime and 7:00 P.M., she spent time with her children. Evenings were spent correcting her old diaries and writing in her current one. With this crammed schedule, it was practically impossible for her to have a moment to herself.

By midsummer of 1941 the Lindberghs had convinced themselves they could no longer live in Lloyd Neck. They felt that too many of their friends were intruding on their privacy, and that they were being trapped into "the deadly type of social life" that they considered typical of Long Island's upper classes. But the real reason they needed to leave their pres-

ent home was that their political views had made them personae non
gratae with their neighbors. Many residents of Lloyd Neck politely
avoided them and their children whenever they went to the beach.

Again they deliberately sought solitude and seclusion, this time finding it in mid-August 1941 in a small rented house on the loneliest part of
Martha's Vineyard. The house had been the property of the late Harvard dean Nathaniel S. Shaler, and there were only a few other houses
nearby on the rough landscape, which consisted of sand dunes, sheep
pastures, and straggly brush. As she was packing, Anne kept telling herself how happy she was to be moving from Long Island, although when
it actually came time to leave Lloyd Neck, she suddenly felt nostalgic,
for she "had loved that house and the garden."

With its view of the sea and of rocky islands in the distance, their new
home, which was named Seven Gates Farm, reminded Anne of Illiec,
which had been occupied by the Germans in 1940. From the Carrels,
they had gotten word that the Nazis had stripped the house of all its
possessions, with the exception of Anne's cherished wooden Madonna,
which fortunately the indomitable Madame Carrel had managed to rescue
and take with her to Saint-Gildas.

But Seven Gates Farm, with its serene views and lovely hills, on which
she could take long, solitary walks, brought Anne little tranquillity. She
was still being vigorously attacked in the press not only for her political
views, but also for her unswerving loyalty to her husband, who many
people were convinced was "a Nazi who dominated her."

In fact, many Americans, convinced that there was something sinister
in the Lindberghs' move to Martha's Vineyard, were sending the FBI letters warning of the potential dangers. "Lindbergh is living on an island
off U.S.A. shores — a perfect base for German invasion," read one
typical letter. "What is being done to guard this island? Who is watching
this man who so loves the Germans and the New Order?" Other correspondents suggested that it might be prudent for the bureau to relocate
Lindbergh and his family to a town in the Midwest. "Most of us would
appreciate knowing that 'enemy Americans' are being controlled as
well as German and Japanese suspects," urged one letter writer. "Martha's Vineyard, being not only a very remote spot but a place easily accessible from a boat off the coast, would of course be an ideal location
for a person whose sympathies lay with Germany, for instance."

Although Anne knew nothing about these letters, she wasn't spared
the persistent rumors that she and Lindbergh were separating over his
involvement in America First. Although there were many things Anne

disliked about the organization, she quickly pointed out to her relatives and friends that her commitment to her husband was stronger than ever. "There are lots of things (and people) I don't like in the work," she wrote to her mother.

> There are lots of things I don't like about my side and about America First. Especially in Cleveland. They had an exhibit in a park of a lot of coffins marked *Bundles from Britain.*
>
> But Charles stands for integrity. No matter who turns out to have been right in judgment of what is best for this country — war or peace — the issue of integrity in government remains the most important.
>
> And Charles stands for it — almost more than any person I ever met. And so I stand behind him.

There would be no greater test of Anne's loyalty to her husband than that of Charles Lindbergh's September 11, 1941, speech at Des Moines, Iowa. Like his father, who had brought about his own political defeat by attacking the Roman Catholic Church, Lindbergh made the serious blunder of injecting the issue of race into his antiwar campaign. In his speech, he bluntly stated:

> I can understand why the Jewish people wish to overthrow the Nazis. The persecution they have suffered in Germany would be sufficient to make bitter enemies of any race. No person with a sense of dignity of mankind condones the persecution of the Jewish race of Germany. Certainly I and my friends do not.
>
> But though I sympathize with the Jews, let me add a word of warning. No person of honesty and vision can look on their pro-war policy here today without seeing the dangers involved in such a policy, both for us — and for them.
>
> Instead of agitating for war, the Jewish groups in this country should be opposing it in every possible way, for they will be among the first to feel its consequences. Tolerance is a virtue that depends upon peace and strength. History shows that it cannot survive war and devastation. A few far-sighted Jewish people realize this, and stand opposed to intervention. Their greatest danger to this country lies in their large ownership and influence in our motion pictures, our press, our radio, and our Government . . . We cannot blame them for looking out for what they believe to be their own interests, but we also must look out for ours. We cannot allow the natural passions and prejudices of other people to lead our country to destruction.

As was her custom, Anne had read her husband's speech before he delivered it. Although she usually applauded his remarks, this time they filled her with "black gloom." She thought it sheer folly for him to "touch the Jews at all. For I dread the reaction on him.... And the price will be terrible. Headlines will flame 'Lindbergh attacks Jews.' He will be branded anti-Semitic, Nazi, Führer-seeking, etc. *I can hardly bear it. For he is a moderate.*"

The wife who usually deferred to her husband now violently argued with him to omit the references to the Jews, but Lindbergh stubbornly refused to heed her advice. In desperation, she then rewrote what she referred to as "the Jewish paragraph," "putting in some of the things he believes but never says — to avoid all traces of rancor or bitterness."

Perhaps because she had decided to dissociate herself from her husband's inflammatory remarks, Anne did not accompany him to Des Moines. Instead, she listened to his speech on the radio. Using one of her peculiar metaphors that equated truthfulness with a cutting instrument, she thought it "direct and honest like a clean knife," but was frightened by "the frenzied applause of the crowd." Possibly their response reminded her of the drunken, bloodthirsty mob at the Flemington courthouse which had not wanted to wait for the state to execute Hauptmann.

Within the next few days Anne's worst fears were confirmed. Her husband was no longer one of the nation's most respected heroes but a racist, spreading Nazi doctrine. According to Wayne Cole, who published an exhaustive study of Lindbergh's role in America First,

> Denunciations were most concentrated in New York, but they came from all across the United States. They came from Jews, but also from Protestants and Catholics. They came from interventionists, but also from noninterventionists.... They charged Lindbergh with anti-Semitism, Nazism, and sympathy for Hitler....
>
> Newspapers across the land joined in editorial attacks on Lindbergh and his speech. The *Des Moines Register* called it "the worst speech he has made so far." ... The *San Francisco Chronicle* concluded that "The voice is the voice of Lindbergh, but the words are the words of Hitler."

For the first time in their long marriage, Anne Lindbergh did not look forward to her husband's homecoming. Lying alone under the stars at Vineyard Haven, she contemplated their hypnotic pull toward "eternity and death" and dreaded "like a Lazarus — tomorrow's emotions with C.'s return." And then reminding herself of his paramount importance in her life, she wrote almost bitterly, "What *time* marriage takes — but it is life. It would be death without it."

When Lindbergh arrived at noon the following day, they discussed "the Jewish question and his speech," and Anne made clear to her husband her "profound feeling of grief." She told him frankly that by segregating the Jews as a group, he had established the ground for anti-Semitism.

"Because it is at best unconsciously a bid for anti-Semitism," she later admitted in her diary. "It is a match lit near a pile of excelsior. Of course he does not mean or does not want to light that pile of excelsior, but his match, lit only to show the ground, may light the excelsior."

In an argument that was almost as heated as the one they had had before his Des Moines speech, Anne told her husband that she "would prefer to see this country at war than shaken by violent anti-Semitism." But, to her dismay, he disagreed with her, countering that he could not let his country become involved in a "disastrous war" simply because he lacked the "courage" to name the groups that wanted to push the country toward it.

In his published journal, Lindbergh made no mention of Anne's desperate efforts to tone down his racist comments in his Des Moines speech and their subsequent argument. In fact, he saw nothing anti-Semitic in his remarks, noting in his diary, "I felt I had worded my Des Moines address carefully and moderately. It seems that almost anything can be discussed today in America except the Jewish problem. The very mention of the word 'Jew' is cause for a storm. Personally, I feel that the only hope for a moderate solution lies in an open and frank discussion."

Nor would he admit that he was following his father's example when he battled the United States' entry into World War II. In fact, for the rest of his life, he would stubbornly maintain that his father's views on foreign policy had nothing whatsoever to do with his own isolationism.

But millions of Americans, including many people associated with America First, saw nothing "moderate" in his remarks. Norman Thomas was so outraged by Lindbergh's speech that he dissociated himself and the Socialist party from the isolationist organization. "Didn't our friend Lindbergh do us a lot of harm? . . . I honestly don't think Lindbergh is an anti-Semite, but I think he is a great idiot," he lamented in perhaps the most astute analysis ever made of Lindbergh's actions. "Not all Jews are for war and Jews have a right to agitate for war if we have a right to agitate against it . . . It is an enormous pity that . . . the Colonel will not take the advice on public relations which he would expect an amateur in aviation to take from an expert." When asked by a reporter who wrote Lindbergh's speeches, Thomas snapped, "Most emphatically he writes his own speeches. That's why part of them have been so bad."

Deeply anguished that her husband had now become a symbol of anti-Semitism, Anne desperately tried to exert more control over the content of his speeches. It was an almost hopeless task, for Lindbergh was an extremely stubborn man, who, once he had made up his mind about something, refused to listen to anyone's advice, even his wife's. Nevertheless, she tried her hardest to make other people see him through her eyes and was happy when he incorporated the passages that she thought should be there, the ones she hoped would reveal to the world his essential "nobility and goodness."

As much as Anne dreaded the thought of the United States' entering the war, it must have come as something of a relief when Japan attacked Pearl Harbor on December 7, 1941, thus ending the great debate about intervention versus nonintervention.

At lunch that day Anne and Lindbergh listened to Roosevelt's declaration of war on the radio. Like her husband, Anne had little faith in the president's abilities, and his handling of this momentous event did not improve her estimation. "There is a lot of fanfare and excitement about the dramatic occasion and yet I feel chiefly a desperate lack of dignity, lack of seriousness, lack of humility about the whole scene," she lamented.

Lindbergh had been scheduled to speak again for America First, and Anne, who considered his address to be one of his "very best," was disappointed when the organization dissolved shortly after Pearl Harbor and he did not have a chance to deliver it. In lieu of the speech, Lindbergh, who was convinced that the United States had been "prodding" the Japanese "into war for weeks," issued a statement. In his wife's opinion, it was an excellent one. "Now it [war] has come and we must meet it as united Americans regardless of our attitude in the past toward the policy our government has followed . . . We must now turn every effort to building the greatest and most efficient Army, Navy and Air Force in the world . . ."

Soon after Pearl Harbor, Anne learned she was pregnant for the fifth time. It had been only fifteen months since she gave birth to her daughter, and this time she was not exactly thrilled by the thought of having another child. "I want another one, of course, but it seems just a little soon — physically and mentally. I feel as if I had just got over the last one," she admitted. "And I half dread going back under the lid pregnancy puts on me — three or four months ill, five months ugly and heavy and stupid and tired, and five months tied to the baby nursing it. The burden of the war, coming worries, conflicts, hates seem heavy enough. One should be in one's best health to carry them, to understand them and not be downed by them."

Nor was Lindbergh enthusiastic about becoming a father again. Now that war had come, he wanted to be a part of it, and as far as he was concerned, the best way for him to serve his country was in the military. "It is definite now. Anne is bearing her fifth child," he briefly noted in his diary.

CHAPTER 19

Outcast

As anne had feared, her pregnancy prevented her from doing any major writing — she felt so nauseated that she had to stay in bed for the first two months. Although her family and friends knew she was expecting a baby, with people she knew less well she passed off her condition as a severe case of "nervous indigestion."

Her deception may have been closer to the truth. Chronic tension and unhappiness, rather than morning sickness, were undoubtedly largely responsible for her symptoms. Although she pretended she didn't care what people thought about *The Wave of the Future,* the overwhelmingly negative response to the book had shattered her self-confidence. It unnerved her to think that people had not only misread her message, but now regarded her as a leading apologist for fascism. "Will I have to bear this lie through life?" she wrote despairingly in her diary.

With regret, she turned down the opportunity to review Saint-Exupéry's new book, *Flight to Arras,* for Selden Rodman's *Common Sense.* Although she had been deeply moved by the book, a moral and spiritual account of the aviator's feelings about the war during a long reconnaissance flight made over France during the German invasion, she feared that any review of his work bearing her name might "injure a writer still untouched by political controversy and smearing."

In contrast, her husband remained a highly controversial figure. After Pearl Harbor, he had wanted to rejoin the Army Air Corps, but his bid to serve his country was immediately rebuffed by the War Department. Obviously yielding to government pressure, the management of several major U.S. aircraft companies, including Pan American, Curtiss-Wright, and United Aircraft, also refused to hire him. Both Lindbergh and Anne blamed the Roosevelt administration for his ostracism. This was not paranoia on their part, for both Roosevelt and his secretary of the interior, Harold L. Ickes, continued to be skeptical of Lindbergh's allegiances, even though the FBI investigation of his activities was essentially terminated. In a letter to the president, written shortly after Lindbergh had offered his services to the Army Air Corps, Ickes made it clear that he still personally regarded the aviator as a threat to national security: "To accept Lindbergh's offer would be to grant this loyal friend of Hitler's a precious opportunity on a golden platter," he wrote to Roosevelt. "It would, in my opinion, be a tragic disservice to American democracy to give one of its bitterest and most ruthless enemies a chance to gain a military record. I ardently hope that this convinced fascist will not be given the opportunity to wear the uniform of the United States . . . He should be buried in merciful oblivion."

Anne's period of bed rest gave her plenty of opportunity to brood about their plight. Yet as much as she minded being "excluded from the world of books," she felt that it was far worse for her husband to be cast out from "the world of Aviation," in which he had been a pivotal figure for so long. She could not help but marvel at his equanimity in the face of these latest, most bitter rejections, finding a measure of courage herself in his resilience.

As it turned out, she didn't have to worry about her husband's prospects for very long. Lindbergh soon found work with a man who couldn't care less what Roosevelt thought about him, since he distrusted the president even more than Lindbergh did. His new employer's name was Henry Ford, and he was currently manufacturing B-24 bombers for the U.S. government.

In April 1942, when Charles Lindbergh went to work for Ford as a technical consultant at the colossal Willow Run plant in Dearborn, Michigan, the individualistic car manufacturer was in his dotage. Almost eighty, he had suffered two strokes. The second one had left his memory severely impaired, and the company was now mainly run by subordinates, but Ford still fancied himself indispensable to its operations and would not consider relinquishing control.

Although no longer in full command of his faculties, Ford was in many respects the perfect boss for Lindbergh, since the two men shared many traits. Not only did Ford share Lindbergh's hatred of Roosevelt, but he also admired the Germans. And if Lindbergh was opposed to what he perceived as the Jews' "large ownership and influence in our motion pictures, our press, our radio, and our Government," Ford was openly anti-Semitic. According to Robert Lacey, author of *Ford: The Men and the Machine,*

> Anti-Semitism has come to a particularly ugly and obscene climax in the twentieth century, and if any one American were to be singled out for his contribution to the evils of Nazism, it would have to be Henry Ford. His republished articles [from his anti-Semitic newspaper, the *Dearborn Independent*] and the currency which he gave to the *Protocols of the Learned Elders of Zion* [a purported czarist document that attempted to prove the Jews planned to kill Christians and take over the world] had considerable impact on Germany in the early 1920s — a vulnerable and, as it proved, crucially formative time. Hitler, still an obscure figure in those years, read Ford's books, hung Henry's picture on his wall, and cited him frequently as an inspiration.

Like Lindbergh, Ford had been the recipient of a Nazi medal. In 1938, the same year Lindbergh received his medal from Göring, the car manufacturer had received the Grand Cross of the German Eagle, the highest award Hitler could give to a foreigner.

According to Lacey, Henry Ford, like Lindbergh, had "professed surprise at the widespread outrage that greeted his acceptance of a Nazi honour. The medal came, he said, from the German people, who 'as a whole are not in sympathy with their rulers in their anti-Jewish policies. . . . Those who have known me for many years realize that anything that breeds hate is repulsive to me.' "

"But this was disingenuous," Lacey stressed.

> Though Henry Ford had maintained his support for pacifist causes throughout the 1920s and 1930s, it was remarkable how often these seemed to have a pro-German tincture. At Clara's [Ford's wife's] urging, he provided support for the "moral rearmament" campaign of Frank Buchman's Oxford Group [of which the Lindberghs' close friend James Newton was a member] . . . and he also endorsed the America First lobby of Charles A. Lindbergh, who had himself accepted the Order of the German Eagle in 1938, from the hands of Hermann Göring.

In her published diaries Anne never mentioned meeting Henry Ford, although, according to her friend Jim Newton, she and Charles dined at Ford's home in Detroit where the automobile manufacturer, a health enthusiast like her husband, served them carrot juice, his favorite beverage. It is possible that the reason she neglected to publish her impressions was that she was shocked by his senility and anti-Semitic views. Fearing that any candid description of Ford would further tarnish her husband's reputation, she tactfully omitted mention of him in her published diaries.

She did, however, acknowledge meeting Harry Bennett, Henry Ford's ruthless right-hand man, who employed gangsters and thugs to beat up union organizers. They met at a rodeo party held at Bennett's Ann Arbor estate, which that night was transformed into a fantasy Western setting. Still not a very astute judge of character and obviously unaware that Bennett was informing on her husband to the FBI, Anne described him as an engaging host, "a compact little man" in a Western riding outfit who gave her "the impression of youth and taut trigger health," and who sang to his guests with such gusto that she thought he might have "a hankering to be a troubadour."

When Lindbergh went to work for Henry Ford at the Dearborn plant, he left a pregnant Anne behind at their home in Martha's Vineyard. Although he tried to come home as often as he could on the weekends, the couple was mostly apart — it was the first time they had been separated in their thirteen-year marriage. At the beginning at least, Anne felt lost without him, her sense of loneliness increased by the fact that he seldom wrote to her. Herself a prolific correspondent, she soon discovered that her husband did not share her love of writing letters, and the few times he did write, his letters were perfunctory and disappointing. "I always forget how little of him gets across in a letter," she ruefully admitted to a friend. "All that warmth and charm and life that you feel when he walks into a room."

In July 1942, in the seventh month of her pregnancy, Anne, who had become fed up with their "divided" lifestyle, moved out of the house on Martha's Vineyard and joined Lindbergh in the new home he had found for the family in Bloomfield Hills, a Detroit suburb. Although she was overjoyed to be reunited with her husband and liked the location of their new home, which was near the famous Cranbrook Academy of Art, she didn't care for the house itself. It was entirely too ostentatious and filled with gadgets and appliances for her taste. "I feel rather depressed by all the ersatz elegance. I long for Illiec, bare as white driftwood or as those rocks on which the women of Brittany pound their wash," she lamented in her diary.

Her sense of dislocation was intensified by the deaths of two beloved family pets shortly after she moved to Bloomfield Hills. First, Kelpie, the Lindberghs' new dog, was struck and killed by a car in front of their home. And then Thor, the German shepherd who had guarded the family ever since the death of Charles Lindbergh, Jr., died of old age.

When Lindbergh realized that Thor was close to death, he dug the animal's grave in the woods close to the house. He had hoped to be able to bury the animal himself, but on the day Thor died he was in Indianapolis, having been subpoenaed to testify for the defense at the trial of William Dudley Pelley. Anne, who was expecting her baby at any minute, buried Thor herself with the help of her servants. In a poignant diary entry, she mourned the loss of her devoted friend:

> There is a stillness about the day on which even a dog dies. Life goes on around it but the stillness remains like these black holes in the Milky Way that drop one through to a further depth of the infinite . . .
> . . . Thor was a symbol of something — of devotion and love and family unity. A great unity of my life — the child-bearing years. His going ends a chapter.

Thor's death, painful as it was, nevertheless forced her to re-examine her feelings about suffering and the human condition. "I keep realizing all the time that suffering isn't enough for true learning, for true understanding, for true vision," she concluded philosophically. "I used to think it was. 'One learns by suffering.' One doesn't, though. One learns through suffering *and* beauty. One *alone* won't do it. You've got to have both . . . You must remain open — vulnerable."

Nine days after Thor's death, on August 13, 1942, Anne gave birth to her fifth child, at the Henry Ford Hospital in Detroit. Although her new doctor looked askance at the idea, Lindbergh attended the birth, as he had all of Anne's other deliveries. For Anne, his calm presence was immensely comforting — she always refused to be given any sedatives or an anesthetic until right before the baby's birth. To ease her labor pains, she chose to concentrate on some objects that held special significance for her and which she hoped might protect her from the complications of childbirth. For this, her fifth delivery, her choice of talismans was rather unusual: a postcard featuring a wooden deer with shell eyes which had been carved by Florida Indians many years before, an oval eyeglass case, and a favorite carved Madonna.

Her good luck pieces appear to have done their job. The baby was born without complications shortly after five o'clock in the morning. While pregnant, Anne had hoped for another girl like little Anne — who was growing up to look like an enchantingly beautiful blonde fairy-tale princess — but the new baby was a robust boy, weighing in at seven and a half pounds. She and Lindbergh named him Scott, after their good friend O. E. Scott, manager of Lambert Field in St. Louis, where Lindbergh had once been an airmail pilot.

That fall, after recovering from the baby's birth, Anne accompanied her husband to the iron foundry at the enormous seventy-acre River Rouge plant, just outside Detroit, which Lindbergh had once described as "a sort of Grand Canyon of the mechanized world." Afterward she wrote a powerful account in her diary of the foundry's depressing "inferno-like" atmosphere, but discreetly neglected to mention that by this time the operations of the enormous Ford plant, which the public had once considered a symbol of American victory, were themselves under fire. According to Robert Lacey, "Continuing manufacturing tie-ups meant that the grand total of B-24s produced at Willow Run by the end of 1942 amounted to fifty-six — less than three days' production at the vaunted plane-an-hour rate — and as the truth became public, the great Ford plant was transformed from a source of inspiration into a national disgrace."

The hellish atmosphere of the foundry reminded her of the war, which continued to dominate her thoughts. "Mass shootings, the planned extermination of all Jews in Europe by the Nazis," she wrote despairingly in her diary. "In moments like these I feel I cannot bear it."

Although by now she knew that she could "never trust the German race," she tried to excuse the Nazis' brutality by telling herself that "other races have been as cruel, as brutal. Other atrocities have been done — by English, by Americans, in war. Must one accept it as possible in the human race? How can one?"

The argument was a feeble one, and at the time she undoubtedly realized it. But it was hard for her to admit, even to herself, how naive she and her husband had been to admire a people who were now in the process of slaughtering millions.

By her own admission, the war years would be "a marking-time period" for Anne. In fact, her diary entries during this period contain surprisingly few references to major battles, military figures, or historical events. While others, including her own husband, were engrossed in the war effort, she remained apart from it. In March 1944, she wrote, "It is hard for me to participate in this war — because I stood against it believing it would only destroy the things we were fighting for. Even though we are or seem to be slowly winning. The destroying, the com-

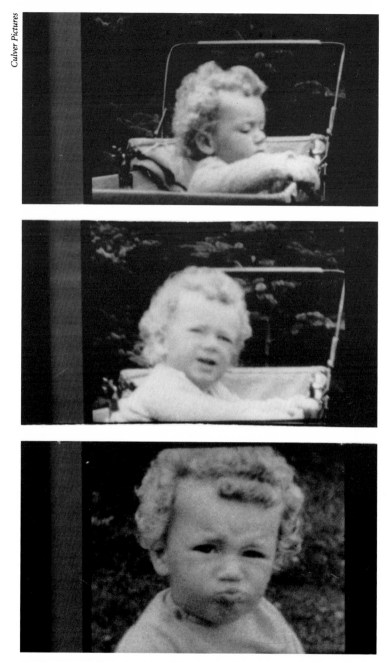

Lindbergh took these charming photographs of his fair-haired, blue-eyed
son, Charles Augustus Lindbergh, Jr., who was just beginning to talk when
he was kidnapped at age twenty months. Protective of his family's privacy,
Lindbergh usually shunned the press but released these pictures in the vain
hope that his son was alive and would be recognized.

The Lindberghs' brand-new, secluded country house near Hopewell, New Jersey, from which their son was kidnapped on March 1, 1932.

A photograph of the child's nursery, taken shortly after he was discovered to be missing. The kidnapper or kidnappers entered the room through the window; a ransom note was found on the windowsill.

Bronx carpenter Bruno Richard Hauptmann *(left)* and his wife, Anna, confer during his 1935 trial for the kidnap-murder of Charles A. Lindbergh, Jr. Two members of the New Jersey State Police are monitoring the conversation.

A rare photograph of Anne Morrow Lindbergh on the witness stand at Hauptmann's trial.

Charles and Anne leaving the courthouse with Mrs. Norman Schwarzkopf *(center)* after Anne's testimony. During the highly publicized trial, Mrs. Schwarzkopf, whose husband had directed the kidnapping investigation, helped shield the Lindberghs from the press.

Harold Nicolson and Vita
Sackville-West in 1933.

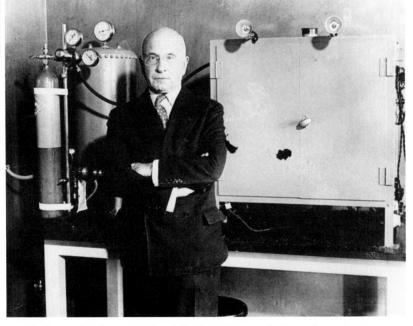

Dr. Alexis Carrel at the International Cytology Congress in Copenhagen in 1936.
Behind him is the perfusion pump, a precursor of the artificial heart that he and
Lindbergh developed together.

Antoine de Saint-Exupéry in 1939.

Left: The Lindberghs socialize with Field Marshal Hermann Göring *(center),* chief of the Luftwaffe, and his wife in Berlin in 1938.

Prominent members of America First, the isolationist organization, on the speakers' platform at a 1941 rally. *From left to right:* Charles and Anne Lindbergh, Senator D. Worth Clark of Idaho, novelist Kathleen Norris, and actress Lillian Gish.

Anne and Charles at the dedication
of Falaise, their friend Harry
Guggenheim's estate on Long
Island, as a museum in 1973. During
their long marriage, they had often
sought refuge there.

Seldom seen in public after 1941,
the Lindberghs attended a New
York dinner given by the National
Institute of Social Sciences in 1968.
Both Charles and Anne were given
medals for "distinguished service to
humanity."

Anne and two of her children, Land and Reeve, at a gala dinner at the Waldorf-Astoria commemorating the fiftieth anniversary of Charles Lindbergh's solo New York-to-Paris flight.

Seated in front of a portrait of her husband, Anna Hauptmann pleads in San Francisco's Court of Historical Review for the Lindbergh kidnapping case to be reopened. After considering new evidence produced by her attorney, the court, a forum with no legal authority, recommended in 1986 that there was "historical need to reopen the case."

Anne Morrow Lindbergh in 1985, with a statue of her husband by the Minnesota sculptor Paul Granlund. The artist depicted Lindbergh as both a young boy and a heroic aviator.

plete nullification of the values we went to war for, seems to be happening even faster than we feared, both here and abroad . . ."

The devastation of war continued to disturb her more than the right or wrong of either side, and thus, she was able to write a few days later, when more than half of Berlin, where she and her husband had been so feted in the late thirties, was destroyed by enemy bombs,

> Most of it is blind bombing from above clouds, no shadow of excuse as precision military-objective bombing. When the guilt of having done this catches up with us, what will it do to us? Or will it be better than this horrible callousness that covers all of us now: "They had it coming," we say placidly as we sit back in our comfortable chairs. And the fliers lost — bringing about this hell . . .
>
> People are "waking up" but Europe has been destroyed in the meantime. "The child is dead."

In the fall of 1943, Lindbergh, who by this time had his own reservations about the quality of operations at Willow Run, started working as a technical consultant for the United Aircraft Corporation in Hartford, Connecticut, which was manufacturing Corsair fighters for the U.S. Navy and the Marine Corps.

Once more the Lindberghs were separated. And again Anne, staying behind in Michigan, felt lost, missing intensely not only her husband's companionship but also their sexual relationship. In her diary she delicately alluded to their continuing passion for each other by quoting some favorite lines from a poem that read, "I went in tears up to my lonely bed, / Oh, would it be like this if you were dead?" Yet despite her neediness, the separation was good for her. For the first time in their relationship, she seemed not to be obsessed with her husband. Freed from the demands of the marriage, she began to take genuine pleasure in being alone with her children, discovering them as individuals with their own needs and desires.

During the time Lindbergh was working in Connecticut, Anne made the acquaintance of several artists associated with the Cranbrook Academy of Art. To her delight, she discovered they were people who talked the same language she did and also loved literature, music, and philosophy. Her new circle included Lily Swann Saarinen, wife of the Finnish architect Eero Saarinen, whose father, Eliel Saarinen, had built Cranbrook; Carl Milles, the famous Swedish sculptor; and Janet de Coux, a talented sculptor who taught at the academy.

Despite her views on the war, Anne still keenly missed France and identified emotionally and intellectually with Europeans (most Americans, she felt, were far "younger" than she). Considering her affinity for Europe, it was perhaps not surprising that all of her new friends were Europeans.

"It was for *Europe* that I wanted the war to cease, not for America First," she admitted in a remarkably candid statement. "And I found myself incredibly separated from both sides. Cut off from the America Firsters because I simply could not feel as they did about Europe. And cut off from the interventionists because they would have none of me . . ."

During Lindbergh's absence, Anne began work on a new writing project. While recuperating from Scott's birth, she discovered an outline she had written before the war about a dangerous flight they had made over the Alps in 1937. Convinced that it would make a compelling novel, she spent the mornings working on it in the mobile trailer Lindbergh had bought for her and set up on the property as a separate writing studio.

Yet even though she had ample time for working undisturbed on her novel, it did not go smoothly at first, undoubtedly because, after the fiasco of *The Wave of the Future*, she felt pressured to write something that was not only important and noble but clear in its message. "I am not content to write anything that has not in it *everything* that I know. Not quite that — but I can't bear to write down half a truth, when I know better," she admonished herself.

But soon it became obvious to her that without her husband around to absorb her attention, writing was once more consuming her. She was becoming as obsessed by it as she had been by him.

"Writing, of course, the sheer concentration, is exhausting. To write, I have decided, is to be possessed by the Demon Lover the ballads talk of," she observed. "In ordinary life, you look sane. You act sane. Just as sane as any mother of four children, any wife. But once you start to write — No. You are possessed. You think incredible things. You say incredible things. You are another person. You even love other people. You don't love your children and your husband at all."

The thought frightened her.

"I have had three big things to fight against in my life," Anne Lindbergh wrote during this period. "The first was just sorrow (the Case), the second was fear (the flights) and the third is bitterness (this whole war struggle). And the third is the hardest."

By "bitterness," Anne meant not merely her horror of the war itself, but also that although two years had passed since Pearl Harbor, she was still being ostracized by those in literary and intellectual circles. By this time she undoubtedly was painfully aware that maintaining a friendship with her was a liability for many people. Recently, she had been upset to learn that Adelaide Marquand, a close friend from America First, had gotten into a bitter argument about her. The disagreement had occurred when Adelaide and her husband, John, who was collaborating with George S. Kaufman on the dramatic version of his novel *The Late George Apley*, had gone to visit the playwright and his wife, Beatrice, at their Bucks County country home for the weekend.

During the Marquands' visit, Anne had tried to call Adelaide. Unable to reach her, she had left word with the Kaufmans' maid for her friend to return her call. When Beatrice, who was both Jewish and an ardent pro-Roosevelt Democrat, learned that Anne Lindbergh had called Adelaide at her home, she was outraged and told Adelaide frankly that if she wanted to return the call, she could not use the Kaufmans' phone. Words were exchanged. Adelaide burst into tears, then packed her bags and demanded that her husband drive her immediately to the railway station.

After Marquand had put his wife on the train, he returned to the Kaufmans'. According to Stephen Birmingham, one of Marquand's biographers,

> There had been no discussion of the scene that had occurred, and quite obviously both men were somewhat embarrassed by their respective wives' behavior, Kaufman for his wife's insulting a guest and John for Adelaide's poor taste in giving the Kaufmans' telephone number as the one where the Lindberghs could reach her. The two stood in silence for a while, and finally Kaufman said, "John, why do you associate with people like the Lindberghs?" Marquand thought for a moment and replied, "George, you've got to remember that all heroes are horses' asses."

One weekend when Lindbergh was home, Anne showed him the manuscript of *The Steep Ascent*, which she had recently finished. Although he told her that it was wonderfully written, Lindbergh advised her to postpone publishing it for several years since public opinion was still heavily against them. He said that he himself planned to put off publication of a book he was currently writing — a new version of his historic 1927 flight — until people put him and his war stand into proper perspective.

Although she rarely disagreed with her husband, Anne was dismayed by his request. "In two or three years I shall not want to publish it and I shall not be able to go on writing if it is not given," she told him heatedly. "You learn nothing from a book until it goes to the publisher. And then, the moment it reaches the press, you know everything and can start out again."

In August 1943, against Lindbergh's wishes, Anne sent the manuscript to Alfred Harcourt. By this time the Lindberghs could count on Harcourt, Brace to publish anything they wrote, as well as any book about them by an author who expressed an admiring view, and Alfred Harcourt's response was a predictable one. He wrote to Anne, "Anything so beautiful is without a date-line; it is about a flight of the spirit as well as about the flight of a plane. The plane is merely the vehicle for conveying the heightened sense of awareness. The last two or three chapters are, I'd guess, the best writing you have done so far."

Yet despite this encouragement, Anne once again began to question seriously whether she wanted to continue writing — it was an art, she was beginning to feel, that had serious limitations. "What a crippling art writing is, no body to it, no *craft*, really," she observed resentfully. "It's all in the mind and you never *see* it or *feel* it — only sometimes hear it. It uses only such a small part of man. I wish I were a sculptor."

Two months before, in June, she had taken a course in modeling and line drawing at the Cranbrook Academy of Art in an attempt to discover how she felt about channeling her creativity into another art form. The experience, she discovered, was a revelation. For the first time in her life she was an anonymous person, merely another student in a class of many others. More important, she was at last free of the tyranny of deadlines and the need to publish frequently.

Yet as much as she enjoyed her courses, she rapidly found that she had no talent for sculpture. She also realized that the people she met through her courses stimulated her imagination more than the classes themselves. She pictured them in different situations and wondered what they thought about when they were alone. Obviously, she was a born writer, despite her intense love-hate relationship with the profession.

Still, for a woman in her unique situation it wasn't simple to be a writer. Although her husband continued to urge her to have her own career, he remained sharply critical of her output, demanding to know why, when she complained that she had no real time to write, she couldn't run her life "like a business." And then there was her ever-present guilt about her large family. She felt she simply couldn't hand over the entire care of her four children to a nurse, even though, unlike most women, she could easily afford an entire staff of nannies. "Writing comes out of life; life *must* come first," she informed her husband in one of their several heated discussions on the subject.

And then there was the other side of the dilemma. Although writing took her away from life, she had to admit, "My life does not go well *without* writing. It is my flywheel, my cloister, my communication with myself and God. It is my eyes to the world, my window for awareness, without which I cannot see anything or walk straight."

This inner struggle between woman/wife/mother and artist was one that many creative women have had to contend with, but Anne's conflict appears to have been more intense than most. A great deal of this, of course, was caused by the continuing pressures of her extraordinary lifestyle, including her marriage to a famous and demanding man, whom she both respected and wanted to please, and her lingering doubts about her own literary abilities. It was a conflict with which she would struggle for the rest of her long life, and, unfortunately for her development as a writer, it was one that she would never quite resolve.

The publication of a book is never an easy time for any author, but Anne was frankly nervous about the reception of *The Steep Ascent.* She had ample reason to worry. Recently she had learned that the Book-of-the-Month Club had refused to consider the book — many readers had threatened to cancel their membership if it became a selection. Even her faithful editors at *Reader's Digest* had declined to run an excerpt, attempting to soften the blow by writing her that the book was too "beautifully written" to be cut. But perhaps the most stinging rejection came from her own publisher. Despite Alfred Harcourt's glowing comments, the sales staff of Harcourt, Brace was of the opinion that a large segment of the book-buying public was not going to buy any work with Anne Morrow Lindbergh's name on the cover. To her dismay, she learned that the first printing for *The Steep Ascent* was only twenty-five thousand copies, half that of the first edition of *Listen! the Wind.*

The Steep Ascent, Anne's first novella, was published in March 1944. On the surface, it bore a close resemblance to her two earlier books about flying in that it was an account of a perilous flight taken by a woman and her husband. However, this being fiction, it was not Anne Morrow Lindbergh and Charles Lindbergh who were on the flight, but Eve Alcott, an American who was five months pregnant, and her British airman husband, Gerald. At first, their flight appears a routine one. They are traveling from England to Italy and must cross the Alps en route. But once they reach the highest point of the mountain range, Eve and Gerald are surrounded by thick clouds, and they have no idea of their location. In desperation, Gerald finally decides to chance a careful descent, and as they make their perilous downward journey, a fearful Eve suddenly becomes accepting of death. Although they eventually manage to land safely in Italy, she realizes that her terror has evaporated, and she experiences "a strange ecstasy," which leads to a renewed appreciation of life. "This then was life: not to be hurried, not to be afraid, not to be imprisoned in oneself. To be open, aware, vulnerable — even to fear, even to pain, even to death. Then only did one feel ecstasy filling one up to the brim."

Like Saint-Exupéry's *Flight to Arras,* to which it was indebted, Anne's book was a philosophical account of a spiritual and moral passage. Although obviously thinly disguised fiction, she had conceived of it from the beginning as an allegorical tale for all women. "It is a flight over the Alps but it could be anything. Childbirth or getting married, or the mental and moral struggles one has," she had written to her friend Sue Vaillant. "There are those same peaks ('Is this all there is to the Alps?') and those same abysses ('I am abandoned — they have abandoned me!')."

In this, her first work of fiction, Anne largely succeeded in her mission to make her story a universal one. To be sure, at the beginning, the reader is aware that the tremulous Eve Alcott in the back cockpit is in actuality Anne Morrow Lindbergh, and that it is not some ruddy, cheerful Englishman piloting the plane but Charles Lindbergh himself. (Clearly, the author hoped to soften the effect of her husband's strong anti-British views by making his fictional counterpart an Englishman.) Yet Anne's writing is so delicate, introspective, and poetic, with a soaring lyrical quality not unlike the rhythm of flight, that the reader rapidly forgets who the fictional characters are based on and becomes absorbed and moved by the story itself.

Although Anne had feared that *The Steep Ascent* would be panned, the reverse happened. To her surprise, the book was almost universally well received, which encouraged the initially skeptical sales director at Harcourt, Brace to reprint it some time later. Amy Loveman wrote in the *Saturday Review,* "It would be a pity if those who were disturbed by Mrs. Lindbergh's last book were to ignore this one because of it. For they would lose in so doing one of the most beautifully written, sensitive, and lovely volumes which has appeared since those earlier ones which were akin to it, 'North to the Orient' and 'Listen! the Wind.' " This opinion was echoed by a critic for the *New Yorker,* who observed,

"One of the most arresting short novels of recent years. There is not a whiff of politics anywhere, either, which, in view of a certain wave that the author once saw engulfing the future, is probably all to the good." Another highly enthusiastic review came in the *New York Times Book Review* from Beatrice Sherman, who pointed out that "as an adventure story it is keen and exciting, but it is much more than that. Its charm and grace are rooted in the fabric of the author's mind and in the fruit of her philosophy."

There were, however, a few dissenters. Some critics felt that her metaphysical writing was pallid in comparison with Saint-Exupéry's, while others, obviously bitter about the Lindberghs' prewar views, found it no accident that Eve and Gerald somehow managed to make a safe landing in Mussolini's Italy. Another reviewer thought that the book demonstrated the author's secret egotism and snobbery toward her husband. Predictably, it was this last accusation that bothered Anne the most. After reading the critic's review, she lay awake all night, brooding about his comments.

But Anne's anxieties about the reviews — both good and bad — were soon cast aside. In early April, Lindbergh was sent to the South Pacific as a civilian technical representative for the Chance Vought Division of United Aircraft to observe in action the planes he had been testing. He was very excited about going into the combat zone, and Anne did her utmost not to convey to him her fears for his survival. Despite her growing independence from him, he was still "all of life," and merely the sight of him descending a flight of stairs flooded her with indescribable happiness. She was convinced that "to have given all one could give — to make a man happy — is so very much in life."

This spirit of self-sacrifice, she had always felt, was especially necessary for aviators' wives. "They are like war wives," she had once written to a friend. "Only the 'war' has been always."

But now her husband was in fact going off to a real war, and when and whether he would return, she was uncertain. Unlike their previous separations, he was going too far away for them to be in touch by telephone or to visit on the weekends. For the first time in their long marriage, she was entirely on her own.

"I am a woman approaching forty, with a young figure, the intensity of a girl, lines on the forehead, an occasional gray hair, and eyes that still glow suddenly and unexpectedly," Anne wrote in a candid self-description shortly after her husband left for the Pacific.

What she did not mention was that she was also a woman who was beginning to discover her own identity after so many years of willingly living in her husband's shadow. Without Lindbergh around to scrutinize her lifestyle, she continued to see a great deal of her Cranbrook friends, enjoying a constant round of social activities where everyone talked about the arts and only occasionally about politics. For the first time, she felt that she could go out socially without her husband and find a group to which she could "give my true self as I have never done to a group of people before . . . Certainly not in my marriage, because the groups we have entered have never been *my* people. In political groups, aviation groups, quite naturally everyone looked to C. But here I am perpetually my own self — and they like me!"

Away from the demands of marriage, domesticity, and his own self-imposed political zealotry, Lindbergh too was discovering his own niche. During the months he was away, he flew fifty combat missions with Marine and Air Corps squadrons, in which he tested the combat capabilities of the Marine F4U Corsair and the P-38 Lightning, increasing the effective range of the P-38 fighter plane by hundreds of miles. In July 1944, while flying a P-38, he narrowly missed a head-on collision with a Japanese plane before shooting it down.

Although he was so busy that he seldom had the chance to write to her, Anne astutely sensed that her husband's rough-and-ready lifestyle, with its omnipresent dangers, was thoroughly agreeing with him. Not since his barnstorming days "has he had such basic and satisfying companionship with his fellow men. He is not a hero — he is working with them, he is really contributing, he is anonymous (the glory goes to the war heroes), and he is completely and warmly accepted as one of them. They love him."

Surprisingly, it was in defeat and humiliation, and not in fame and triumph, that both Anne and Charles at last began to discover their real identities, she with her work, children, and circle of sophisticated European friends in Michigan, and he with American soldiers, fighting in the Pacific.

In July 1944, Anne traveled by train out West for a brief reunion with her husband at the home of her brother, Dwight, in California. Although she had learned before her departure from Bloomfield Hills that she would be unable to get an extension on the lease of the new, much simpler, and attractive house they were living in, her worries about the future rapidly evaporated as soon as the train left the station.

Not only was she struck by the awesome beauty of the country, but for the first time since her marriage, she felt liberated from the "unreal newspaper personage of Mrs. Lindbergh." Seeing the crowds of soldiers, sailors, and their wives at the various stations, she felt "a secret joy in being ordinary, in being let in a door I have never been allowed in before. 'Yes, my husband is in the South Pacific. Yes, I'm hoping to see him . . .' "

"So many things have separated me from life," she wrote candidly in her diary. "First, money. For money certainly does it . . . And fame has insulated me from life — the Midas touch. And then, finally, '*Par delicatesse, j'ai perdu ma vie.*' I realized on this trip how hungry I was for life, starved for it, fell on it ravenously, all the little scraps. People would laugh at such scraps; they are precious if one has starved."

Realizing how cut off she had been from average human relationships, Anne was more determined than ever to live simply, like an ordinary housewife and mother. On her return from the West Coast, she found a new house for the family in Westport, Connecticut. Although she hated the idea of giving up her artistic Cranbrook friends, she knew that Charles would be working in Connecticut once he returned home from the Pacific, and she wanted to be with him. She had come to the conclusion that Michigan was no longer the ideal place for either of them to live. Her restless, energetic husband was happiest when living out of a suitcase and did not belong "in the production-minded Ford plant," any more than she could continue to hide from life in "the Ivory Tower of Cranbrook, in spite of that wonderful circle of friends." They both clearly needed change, new horizons, and a more normal life for themselves and their children.

On August 25, Anne was elated to learn of the liberation of Paris — France was the part of Europe to which she was the most emotionally attuned. But her joy was short-lived. As she was packing to leave Bloomfield Hills, she read in the newspaper that Saint-Exupéry was reported missing on a lone reconnaissance flight over southern France.

Anne was devastated by the forty-four-year-old French aviator's death. Although she had met him only once, his loss was almost as shattering as Elisabeth's death, for she felt that she had lost the one person who had understood her work. "Of what use to write if he were not there to read it, perhaps, sometime, somewhere?" she mourned in her diary. "And my last book, which had gone out like a letter to him and never reached him, of what use was that? No one could really understand it, not as he could have . . . I felt like this at Elisabeth's death — completely alone to the end of my life — but that was personal. This is something more. This man's beliefs and his voicing of them made it possible, just possible, for me to live in the world as it is today, as it will be tomorrow . . ."

And then, perhaps aware that such sentiments reflected dissatisfaction with her marriage, she reminded herself that her love of life was "very strong" and that she had a husband whom she adored. "Charles is earth to me, the whole world, life. St.-Ex. was not earth but he was a sun or a moon or stars which light earth, which make the world and life more beautiful. Now the earth is unlit and it is no longer so beautiful. I go ahead in it stumbling and without joy."

Shortly after Anne had moved the family to Connecticut, Lindbergh returned home from the South Pacific. Anne was overcome with joy when she gazed out the window of the house and saw his tall, slightly stooped figure emerging from a taxi. Suddenly her days of independence receded into memory. "It is hard now to go back to the days without C. To remember what it was like — that strange unbalanced creature I was, never really at rest, suspended, never touching earth," she wrote in her journal.

With his return, she no longer had to endure the prospect of climbing into her "big lonely bed," the "sleepless nights," and the early morning awakenings caused by having to live her life without him.

He was home and hers again. And suddenly nothing else mattered.

CHAPTER 20

Comeback

WHEN THE WAR ENDED, Anne and Charles, after seventeen years of shuttling from one rented house to another, finally settled permanently, in Darien, Connecticut. In a sense the large house they purchased in 1946 at Scott's Cove was their first real home. By this time they could hardly be considered youngsters applying for their first mortgage, as Anne was almost forty years old, Charles, forty-four.

Of English Tudor style, their new house was roomy and comfortable, with a bedroom for each of their children. It was located on several secluded acres of land overlooking an isolated stretch of water that flowed into Long Island Sound. With its partially rocky terrain, small sandy beach, and three small offshore islands to which they could walk when the tide was out, the property reminded them of Illiec.

It was here in Scott's Cove that the Lindberghs retreated into semi-anonymity, quietly pursuing their own activities and raising their large family, which now included five children. In the fall of 1945, when she was thirty-nine years old, Anne gave birth to her sixth and last child, a daughter they named Reeve. To everyone's surprise, the baby was born on October 20, which was the birthday of five-year-old little Anne, whom everyone was now calling "Ansy" so as not to confuse her with her mother.

Both Anne and Charles were determined that their offspring not become spoiled by their celebrity and wealth. They insisted on sending them to public schools, where they made friends with the local children. They encouraged them from an early age to be self-reliant and to share their father's love of nature and rugged outdoor activities.

Although the Lindberghs were millionaires, their Scott's Cove home was far from luxuriously appointed. In fact, it bordered on the monastic, and a first-time visitor was dumbfounded to discover that although their living room contained a piano and some paintings by notable artists, it was meagerly furnished, lacking even a sofa. The children's rooms were similarly Spartan. With their identical iron bedsteads and austere décor, the rooms resembled a barracks.

It was obvious to the Lindbergh children that their parents feared that they might share the terrible fate of their brother. When the children were asleep, the doors to their bedrooms were deliberately left ajar. They were taught to mumble their surname when they were introduced to strangers and not to announce who they were when they answered the telephone. They were also instructed never, under any circumstances, to speak to anyone whom they suspected of being a reporter.

"The kidnapping was always sort of in the background, but it had a very strong impact on both my parents' lives," Jon recalled recently. "They tried to protect us as much as they could and as the years went by, it eased off. But they were always worried."

Whenever Lindbergh was home, discipline was rigid. The children had to make their own beds and they were not permitted a television set, so they had to sneak off to a neighbor's house whenever they wanted to watch a program. Since their father believed that white bread was not as nutritious as whole wheat, they were not allowed to eat it. Nor were sweets permitted — he believed the stuff would rot their teeth. White sugar was also verboten, although Anne had their cook sneak it into certain dishes. To everyone's relief, he never noticed.

The children did exactly as they were told when their father was home, but when he was away, they relaxed and did pretty much what they wanted.

"When I was little, he was sort of a stern, scary figure who was also very exciting," Reeve, Lindbergh's younger daughter, remembered many years later. "You'd love it when he came home and then, after a while, you'd kind of wish he'd leave again because he was very, very exacting in what he wanted us to do. But he was also very exciting; he was always taking us for trips in the plane."

His larger-than-life presence unsettled everyone whenever he came home. "[My father] seemed to demand more oxygen than there was air," Reeve also remembered. "He would fill up the house, and they would co-exist."

Of their two parents, the children were far more comfortable around Anne. "My mother was calm and calming, although she did not think of herself that way," Reeve recalled. "When my father was away, Mother was not so much a disciplinarian as she was an example." Friends noted that Anne expressed her affection for her children in an open, warm-hearted manner, while Lindbergh, although there was no doubt he loved them, was far more restrained in showing his affection.

In the summer of 1947, Anne returned to Europe. She wanted to experience for herself the impact of the war on the countries in which she had lived happily for several years and to re-establish contact with her old friends. As she had anticipated, it was a deeply depressing experience. Although people tried to be polite, it was obvious that many of her acquaintances were still appalled by her husband's noninterventionist views, in Europe as in much of the United States considered pro-Nazi. Others, to whom she and Charles had been particularly close, had either died in the interim or were living elsewhere. Alexis Carrel had died of a heart attack in France in November 1944, although some people said the actual cause of his death was a "broken heart" after he was branded a Nazi collaborator by the liberation government. After burying Carrel in a small, vine-covered chapel on Saint-Gildas, his embittered widow fled to Argentina.

When Anne returned from Europe, she wrote five articles about her impressions of postwar Europe which were subsequently published between 1948 and 1950 in the *Reader's Digest, Life,* and *Harper's* magazines.

In several of the essays, she deplored the turmoil and living conditions in Europe, where people were not only deprived of food, supplies, and hope, but forced to live in a Kafkaesque bureaucracy. In her opinion, Britain and France were almost as badly off as Germany. Like her husband, she continued to believe that the war itself wasn't entirely responsible for this poor standard of living and lack of values. The "decay" of the modern democracies was also responsible. "This house, with its roof on the ground, its interior despoiled, its foundations crumbling — this house is a symbol," she maintained in "The Flame of Europe," which was published in the *Reader's Digest* in 1948. "The basic values of our civilization are crumbling away like this rubble."

In terms of Anne's literary development, these five postwar essays were important in that, like her novella *The Steep Ascent,* they represented a maturation in her work from a sophisticated reporting of external events to a spiritual meditation about their inner meaning.

Although Anne had looked forward intensely to resuming her life with her husband at the end of the war, she soon discovered on his return that their relationship had undergone a change. In fact, the years immediately following the war were the most difficult ones in her marriage. It soon became obvious to her that after experiencing the adventure, drama, and ever present danger of battle, where he had been in his element, he was having trouble adjusting to both the ordinariness and the stress of civilian life. "I think he was very happy in the military," Reeve Lindbergh later commented about her father during this period in his life. "Everything was very well ordered, and there was a kind of camaraderie, and there wasn't the confusion and the tension of the rest of the world."

On May 17, 1945, ten days after Germany surrendered, Lindbergh had flown to Munich as a United Aircraft representative with a naval technical mission that was sent to examine advanced German warplanes. The city, which was reduced to "a mass of rubble," depressed him deeply. After returning briefly to Paris, he traveled through the areas occupied by the Americans in Germany and Austria. He was moved by the plight of the German people, especially the children, whom he felt were starving and maltreated by the American GIs who were looting and gorging themselves with food in front of them. "What right have we to stuff ourselves . . . what right have we to damn the Nazis and Japs while we carry on with such callousness and hatred in our hearts?" he wrote in his diary. Whenever possible, he would slip small gifts to the Germans, such as a cake of soap or a pack of cigarettes.

In June, while inspecting the underground factory at Nordhausen that had produced the V-1 and V-2 weapons, Charles Lindbergh was shown Camp Dora, a Nazi extermination camp. There, he was confronted with the horrors of the Nazi regime, which he had once admired. At Camp Dora, there were no "virile" and able people, no medal-bedecked German generals listening attentively to his opinions on aviation, but only dying men and women who were reduced to walking skeletons and the crematoriums that had consumed twenty-five thousand bodies of their fellow human beings in a year and a half. Camp Dora revolted him, and he wrote in his journal, "Here was a place where men and life and death had reached the lowest form of degradation. How could any reward in national progress even faintly justify the establishment and operation of such a place?" But then, as if he could not bear to admit that his admiration of the Nazis had been a gross mistake, he tried to justify their monstrous crimes by telling himself that in the South Pacific some Americans had been equally brutal to the Japanese, shooting prisoners and keeping their skulls as souvenirs. "We, who claimed that the German was defiling humanity in his treatment of the Jew, were doing the same thing in our treatment of the Jap," he noted in his journal, adding preachily that "what is barbaric on one side of the earth is still barbaric on the other. 'Judge not that ye be not judged.' It is not the Germans alone, or the Japs, but the men of all nations to whom this war has brought shame and degradation."

As far as Charles Lindbergh was concerned, a government-sponsored systematic extermination of 6 million people was as morally reprehensible as the despicable acts of savagery committed by a small number of soldiers against their enemies. As he flew back to the United States, he was convinced more than ever of the rectitude of his decision to oppose the war and the United States' entry into it.

After the war, as restless and disturbed by global events as ever, Lindbergh swiftly buried himself in a multitude of projects and activities. These included being a member of the secret Army Ordnance's CHORE project at the University of Chicago, which was involved in military weapons research, as well as serving as consultant to the secretaries of the Air Force, Stuart Symington and Harold Talbott. He also took part in the postwar reorganization of the Strategic Air Command, developing supersonic bombers and extending the range of the planes through air refueling, and he was a member of scientific ballistic missile committees of the Air Force and the Defense Department. A great deal of his work during those years was concerned with top secret projects focusing on rocketry and space flight programs.

The sophisticated strategic bombers that he flew were a far cry from a simple monoplane like the *Spirit of St. Louis*. Yet the feeling of separateness and remoteness that he got flying them was the same as in his youthful days, and if anything it was intensified by the fact that he was flying many thousands of feet above the ground. Alone, soaring far above the world of ordinary men, he had the uncanny feeling that he was no longer part of the earth, but omnipotent, divine. "I sensed a godlike power that comes of viewing the earth below," he wrote in his memoirs. "Continents and oceans were no longer barriers of distance or of substance. The Sierras, the Rockies, and the Appalachians became frozen ripples underneath my wings and the Atlantic and Pacific were glass-smooth tints. Were not Zeus's thunderbolts less awesome than the atom bombs we carried? But I also sensed a separation from earth and men that had not existed in the pioneering days of aviation."

In April 1954, Republican president Dwight D. Eisenhower, in a gesture obviously intended to compensate Lindbergh for the "wrongs" he had suffered at the hands of a Democratic president, restored his commission in the armed forces. On April 7, 1955, once more wearing his wings, Lindbergh was sworn in as a brigadier general in the U.S. Air Force Reserve.

At some time after the war, Lindbergh rejoined Pan American as a director and consultant. He advised its president, his old friend Juan Trippe, about new air routes and construction of airports, and later on the specifications for the design of the Boeing 747. In the course of his work for the airline, he traveled to almost every part of the world.

For the time being it was the perfect combination of jobs for a searching, dissatisfied man who had long despised most aspects of his celebrity and yearned to recapture his essential nature, which was one of an unencumbered adventurer and explorer, with no ties to anyone, including his adored wife. He relished living out of suitcases, flying from continent to continent with a birdlike freedom, but for Anne, his transient, incessantly on-the-go lifestyle was far from ideal. Unlike the early days of their marriage, when they had been inseparable, he seldom took her with him. More often than not, she was left at home alone to cope with their five children, whose ages now ranged from five to eighteen. Although she had plenty of help — a full-time servant and cook, as well as a cleaning woman — it was she who had to be both mother and father to their large family, helping her children with their homework, chauffeuring them to and from after-school activities, and listening to their problems.

As in the past, Anne at first had difficulty adjusting to life without her husband. Her stimulating Cranbrook friends might have helped ease her sense of loneliness, but they were thousands of miles away in Detroit, and as yet she hadn't found a similar circle in Connecticut. Nevertheless, she tried her best to learn to become "a person on my own."

Paradoxically, although she looked forward to her husband's return, she also felt that his comings and goings were a disruption. A shy and reserved woman who did not make friends easily, she managed eventually to establish some new, gratifying relationships, but these had to be put on hold whenever he came home. A man who did not require or enjoy the company of others for mental stimulation, Lindbergh insisted that their social obligations be kept to the barest minimum. So they rarely entertained and remained aloof from their neighbors.

"When he came back, he was always in wonderful spirits, and he had so much to tell me. It was a very alive pattern of marriage, but sometimes it was difficult for me to manage," she once admitted to an interviewer. "When he came back, Charles, not being a social person, never wanted to go out. I couldn't see people when he was there. So I had to balance, to adjust my life from being a social creature to being a recluse." Then, as if afraid of sounding disloyal, she quickly added, "But it worked out very happily for us."

Lindbergh's antisocial behavior appears to have been inherited in part from his mother, from whom he had become estranged during the prewar years. Staunchly pro-Allies, Evangeline had no sympathy with her son's isolationist views and did not understand his affinity for the Germans. They had a rapprochement, however, when Lindbergh joined the war effort in 1941.

Evangeline herself was becoming even more reclusive and eccentric with the passing years. To the amusement of her students and colleagues, she insisted on wearing her hat to the chemistry classes she still taught at the Cass Technical High School in Detroit. Refusing to participate in staff meetings, she sat aloofly on one side of the room, reading a book.

While Anne and Charles were living in Bloomfield Hills, Mrs. Lindbergh developed the unmistakable symptoms of Parkinson's disease, for which there was unfortunately no treatment at the time. She had retired from teaching in 1942 and stayed at home with her brother until her death in the fall of 1954. What little money she had by then — a meager five thousand dollars — was divided between her son and her brother. Originally she had wanted to leave all her money to Lindbergh to "recognize a devotion to me which has been full and constant and in many material and spiritual forms," but realizing how loyal her brother had been, Lindbergh persuaded her to divide her estate between them.

Shortly after Mrs. Lindbergh's death, Anne suffered the loss of her own mother. In late December 1954, the active, intelligent, and seemingly indomitable Elizabeth Morrow suffered a severe stroke. For eight weeks she lay in a coma. On the evening of January 23, 1955, she died at age eighty-one at Next Day Hill.

During other family crises, Anne had had Charles to lean on, but this time he wasn't there to comfort her. When her mother died, he was in

Europe on one of his frequent business trips. Upon hearing the news, however, he immediately flew home to be with her and the children.

At Mrs. Morrow's funeral, held two and a half days later, on January 26, at the First Presbyterian Church in Englewood, Anne heard Dr. Henry Pitney van Dusen, president of the Union Theological Seminary, eulogize her mother as "one of the great women in the history of our country," who was outstanding for her contributions to women's education, welfare, philanthropy, and poetry.

What Dr. van Dusen tactfully neglected to mention was that Betty Morrow was also one of the country's richest women. Her gross estate amounted to $9,399,935. Its principal assets were securities, among them 9,750 shares of the Kennecott Copper Corporation, appraised at over a million dollars. Anne and Constance, her surviving daughters, each received $50,000 and life interests in trusts of one-third of the residuary estate. Another $50,000 and the balance of residue (or other two-thirds) were left to her son, Dwight, Jr. Still plagued by mental instability, Dwight had recently suffered yet another severe nervous breakdown, this time shortly after his divorce from Margot Loines. For several years he had been institutionalized at an exclusive private psychiatric clinic in Bucks County, Pennsylvania. Eventually, however, he recovered, taught history at a small college in Pennsylvania, and later happily remarried and moved to California.

No matter what Betty Morrow's private feelings were about her son, she obviously wanted to ensure that if he did in fact suffer another breakdown and institutionalization after her death, he and his children would be more than amply provided for. This spirit of generosity extended not only to her son and his family, but also to her and her husband's alma maters, Smith and Amherst colleges — she left each institution $100,000. She also dutifully left the son-in-law who had caused her such pain and embarrassment in recent years a separate bequest of $10,000.

Despite her complicated feelings about her gregarious, strong-willed mother, Anne was deeply affected by her death. Shortly afterward, she wrote to Jim Newton, who had lost his own father, "No matter how much one is prepared for death of one's parents by age or illness, it does not lighten the blow of tangible separation . . . It is a great wrench and a great testing of all our powers and faith . . ."

With her inheritance from her mother, Anne Morrow Lindbergh was now a very rich woman. But even if her share of the estate had been less than substantial, most people would have considered her exceedingly well-off. In addition to her own money, which would continue to be managed by J. P. Morgan and Company, Anne had access to her husband's considerable wealth, which in recent years had increased substantially, since he had become a best-selling author.

In 1953, after fifteen years of work, Lindbergh finally completed *The Spirit of St. Louis,* his second autobiographical account of his 1927 flight. A best seller and winner of the Pulitzer Prize for biography in 1954, the book earned him royalties of nearly $1.5 million.

A classic in the genre of true adventure stories, *The Spirit of St. Louis* is very different from *We,* Lindbergh's awkwardly written first account of the historic flight, which was published in 1927. In tone and level of sophistication, the two books are vastly different, and it is hard to believe that the same person wrote them both. The second version is a compelling minute-by-minute account of the famous flight, but it also contains sections that are so luminous that they verge on poetry.

I climb higher as I approach Avalon Peninsula. Bleak mountain summits glow coldly against a deepening sky. A thin layer of cloud burns molten gold. The wind lifts me up and carries me with it over the mountains, blowing hard and nearly on my tail, rocking my wings as it swirls past ridges and stirs in valleys. Each crevice fills with shades of gray, as though twilight had sent its scouts ahead to keep contact with a beaten sun. The empire of night is expanding over earth and sea.

By contrast, a descriptive passage in *We* is written in a rather different style:

There was no moon and it was very dark. The tops of some of the storm clouds were several thousand feet above me and at one time, when I attempted to fly through one of the larger clouds, sleet started to collect on the plane and I was forced to turn around and get back into clear air immediately and then fly around any clouds which I could not get over.

A reader comparing these descriptions might well ask who was really the author of the passage from *The Spirit of St. Louis.* Was it written by Charles Lindbergh, a pedestrian writer at best, or by his wife, a consummate stylist and poet? Unfortunately, the various drafts of *The Spirit of St. Louis,* which Charles Lindbergh subsequently gave to the Library of Congress, cannot be examined without Anne Lindbergh's permission. However, since eleven years had elapsed between the publication of *The Steep Ascent* in 1944 and her next book, *Gift from the Sea,* published in 1955, it is possible to assume that a great deal of her time during those intervening years may have been devoted to rewriting and polishing her husband's manuscript. To be sure, he supplied the sequence of events, as well as a record of his own emotions as the flight progressed, but it was she who undoubtedly added the beautiful descriptions of the flight and his spiritual musings about aviation, life, and death which elevated the book into something more than a mere adventure tale.

It says something about the character of Charles Lindbergh that he did not claim sole authorship of the book, but gave his wife ample credit for her time and help. His book was dedicated to her, with the words: "To A.M.L., who will never realize how much of this book she has written."

With her mother's death, Anne's "eternal struggle" became focused on what she "must be for Charles . . . and what I must be for myself." In an effort to resolve the conflict that had bedeviled her entire married life, she began to explore its ramifications in prose. She resumed writing a month after her mother's death, clarifying in words what she felt about the relationships of men and women, becoming middle-aged, and the need for a woman to achieve not only a simple, uncluttered life in a restless world of technology and change, but also her own identity within the confines of marriage and motherhood. The result was a group of eight short essays, entitled *Gift from the Sea*, which deservedly was to become her most successful and enduring work. Significantly, it was written shortly after the death of her mother and after a vacation spent alone — Anne had spent a week without Charles at a simple beach-house on the island of Captiva, Florida, where she had gone alone in an attempt to get away from the distractions and responsibilities of both him and their five children.

Each essay in the book takes the form of an exquisitely written meditation on a seashell, symbols for the various aspects of modern life and relationships for which she was trying to find an answer, and, as Elizabeth Gray Vining later noted in the *New York Times Book Review*, the book "is like a shell itself, in its small and perfect form, the delicate spiraling of its thought, the poetry of its color, and its rhythm from the sea, which tells of light and life and love and the security that lies at the heart of intermittency."

Gift from the Sea, published by Pantheon Books, sold hundreds of thousands of copies and was on top of the best-seller list for more than six months. Thirty-seven years later, it still remains in print, a book especially cherished by women, old and young alike. Ironically, Anne's editors at Pantheon had feared that the book had no chance for commercial success. They tried to get her to change the title to "The Mass of Men Lead Lives of Quiet Desperation," a suggestion that she wisely vetoed.

The publication of *Gift from the Sea* immediately re-established Anne's reputation as one of the country's most popular and beloved women authors. Thousands of American women immediately identified with the problems and concerns voiced in her inspirational essays. Although the book did not offer any revolutionary solutions to the age-old stresses of being a wife and mother (after a week of blissful freedom and solitude at the beach, Anne dutifully trudged home with her shells to Charles and her family), it did advocate that a woman occasionally take time away from her responsibilities to nourish herself spiritually. This was rather startling advice at the time, for the midfifties were a complacent, chauvinistic era in which most well-educated women did not question their roles as housewives and mothers but were vaguely restless, unhappy, and searching for answers. (The book was published eight years before the liberationist *Feminine Mystique,* written by Betty Friedan, another Smith graduate, in 1963.) By stressing the value of the inner life, *Gift from the Sea* offered inspiring answers to their frustrations, and after reading it, many women wrote to Anne, thanking her for writing a book that so perceptively echoed their concerns with such passages as these:

> I want . . . to live "in grace" as much . . . as possible . . . an inner harmony, essentially spiritual, which can be translated into outward harmony.

> What a circus act we women perform every day of our lives . . . Look at us. We run a tight rope daily, balancing a pile of books on the head. Baby-carriage, parasol, kitchen chair, still under control. Steady now! This is not the life of simplicity but the life of multiplicity that the wise men warn us of. It leads not to unification but to fragmentation. It does not bring grace; it destroys the soul.

With the enormous success of both *The Spirit of St. Louis* and *Gift from the Sea,* Anne and Charles Lindbergh attained something far more important than critical success and commercial reward. They reclaimed their reputations. The controversy about their prewar activities and *The Wave of the Future* was largely forgotten. When Anne's name, at least, was mentioned by one of her numerous female fans, it was usually with reverence, as if she were a saint or a guru. For a woman who less than fifteen years before had been accused of being a Nazi propagandist, it was no mean feat to become almost deified, and even those people who could never forgive her and her husband for their isolationist views grudgingly had to concede that Anne Morrow Lindbergh had talent and endurance. By the power of her pen, she had managed to transform her and her husband's public images, so that they were no longer tarnished and ugly but shining and noble.

CHAPTER 21

"To Club a Butterfly"

Encouraged by the enormous success of *Gift from the Sea*, Anne published her next work the following year, in 1956. It was a slim volume of poetry entitled *The Unicorn and Other Poems*. Unfortunately, it did not meet with the same reception accorded her previous work. In fact, despite its refined, ladylike title, her collection of poems became almost as much of a cause célèbre as *The Wave of the Future*. Although some reviewers praised its "beautiful lyrics," the majority did not share this opinion, the most vocal being John Ciardi, the newly appointed poetry editor of the *Saturday Review of Literature*. As his long review made abundantly clear, he found reading Anne's poetry an excruciating experience.

"As a reviewer not of Mrs. Lindbergh but of her poems I have, in duty, nothing but contempt to offer," Ciardi furiously began his attack. "I am compelled to believe that Mrs. Lindbergh has written an offensively bad book — inept, jingling, slovenly, illiterate even, and puffed up with the foolish afflatus of a stereotyped high-seriousness, that species of esthetic and human failure that will accept any shriek as a true high-C. If there is judgment it must go by standards. I cannot apologize for this judgment. I believe that I can and must specify the particular badness of this sort of stuff . . ."

To prove his point, Ciardi went on to shred Anne's technique.

She is constantly in trouble with the simplest of rhymes (here "heart-apart") and that, lacking first a sound grammatical sense and second anything like a poet's sense of words and their shades of meaning, she is defenseless against her rhyme schemes and will commit any absurdity while entangled in her own harness.

Nor is "absurdity" too strong a word. I can certainly sense the human emotion that sends Mrs. Lindbergh to the writing, but I can only report that what emerges in the writing is low-grade poetry and low-grade humanity. As a person Mrs. Lindbergh must certainly have richer resources than these, but whatever those personal resources the fact remains that they simply do not make their way through bad writing.

To illustrate what he perceived as Anne's lack of ability as a poet, Ciardi then proceeded to pick apart a stanza from one of her poems:

> Down at my feet
> A weed has pressed
> Its scarlet knife
> Against my breast.

"The neatest trick of the literary season," he pointed out triumphantly.

"Compare the now classical examination answer that reads: 'Dante was a great transitional figure: with one foot he stood in the Middle Ages, while with the other he saluted the rising sun of the Renaissance,' " Ciardi continued, not content to have delivered the coup de grâce. "The student could perhaps be forgiven — he was racing the clock. But what will forgive Mrs. Lindbergh this sort of miserable stuff?"

As any author might feel about receiving such a review, Anne was deeply wounded by Ciardi's scathing comments. Her loyal and equally angry husband tried to lessen the blow by telling her that Ciardi's comments had nothing whatsoever to do with the quality of her work — the critic was simply attempting to get even with Lindbergh for his war stand by attacking her poetry. Although both Lindberghs yearned to make some sort of public statement refuting Ciardi's criticism, they wisely refrained from doing so.

As it turned out, a rebuttal was unnecessary. Hundreds of Anne's outraged fans deluged the *Saturday Review* with letters protesting Ciardi's "unnecessary cruelty" and threatening to cancel their subscriptions. "Why take a baseball bat to club a butterfly?" was one typical response from a female reader. "Why don't you find a new poetry editor?" suggested another not so subtly, while still another female subscriber advised that the magazine "let some other reviewer take over women poets, especially if they are successful."

Reporters got wind of the controversy, and soon many Americans

were debating at the dinner table whether John Ciardi had been justified in attacking Anne Morrow Lindbergh's work. Such was the intensity of the debate that *Saturday Review* editor Norman Cousins was
jolted awake in the middle of the night by a phone call from a librarian
who reported that only that afternoon a local reading group had considered the issue and voted three to one in favor of "Mrs. Lindbergh."
Finally, Cousins was forced to offer an explanation for his reviewer's
criticism.

"John Ciardi's review of Anne Morrow Lindbergh's 'The Unicorn
and Other Poems' has produced the biggest storm of reader protest in
the thirty-three year history of the *Saturday Review*," Cousins wrote in
an attempt to pacify his irate subscribers. "Hundreds of readers have
hastened to tell us of their pointed disapproval of Mr. Ciardi's review;
four have written in his support. Many of the letters have raised questions about our editorial policy and procedure. How is it, they have
asked, that the review was allowed to appear?" Although Cousins defended his reviewer's right to his opinions, he made it clear that he did
not entirely agree with them.

> Our main argument with Mr. Ciardi, however, involves the basis of his
> criticism. It seems to us that his critical yardstick for Mrs. Lindbergh's
> book was better adapted to the measurement of prose than poetry . . .
> Nor can we accept the adjective "illiterate" when applied to Mrs. Lind-
> bergh or her books. There are few living authors who are using the Eng-
> lish language more sensitively or with more genuine appeal. There is in
> her books a respect for human responses to beauty and for the great con-
> nections between humankind and nature that gives her work rare dis-
> tinction and that earns her the gratitude and loyalty of her readers, as
> the present episode makes clear.

In the same issue, John Ciardi defended his review of *The Unicorn* in
a long, semihumorous essay entitled "The Reviewer's Duty to Damn: A
Letter to an Avalanche." Featured above his article were photographs of
the two antagonists in semiprofile, which suggested to the already
fired-up reader that Anne wasn't going to take it anymore and that the
two were about to engage in a round of fisticuffs. Judging from appear-
ances, it wasn't going to be an even match. Gazing dreamily heaven-
ward, Anne resembled a woman about to be canonized, while Ciardi,
who looked more like a prizefighter than a literary critic, appeared
eager to knock her out.

"I am not yet persuaded, however, that the avalanches of indignation are an intellectual measure I can respect. If the excellence of poetry were determinable by a national election, I have no doubt that Edgar Guest would be elected the greatest poet in the English Language — by a landslide," an unregenerate Ciardi noted, and then went on to defend what he believed was the responsibility of the critic to provide the public with an honest, even brutal evaluation of an author's work, even at the cost of being crucified himself.

Today, when critics routinely savage the style and subject matter of popular, best-selling authors without getting any response from readers, the public uproar over Ciardi's review seems like a quaint anachronism, a throwback to a more literate, committed time when readers had a sense of personal loyalty to their favorite writers and didn't hesitate to defend them publicly.

Without question, Ciardi's review of Anne's slender volume was needlessly venomous. Once on the attack, he seems to have fallen in love with his own rhetoric and lost all sense of restraint. But even though his style often suffered from the same clumsy syntax that had marred his target's poetry, his critical evaluation of her work seems in the main correct. Although a careful stylist who was capable of creating many lovely and delicate images, Anne Morrow Lindbergh was not a very good poet. With the exception of one or two poems in the volume, including the moving "Second Sowing," which alludes to her feelings about her dead child, her work strikes the contemporary reader as old-fashioned, insipid, and sentimental. Her real talents lay in her seemingly effortless prose style, which conveyed her own subtle gradations of feelings about her inner life and the natural world from which she derived comfort and inspiration.

As for the "stereotyped high-seriousness" of her work that Ciardi found so offensive, his criticism appears to have some justification. For both Anne Lindbergh's prose and poetry, which are largely autobiographical in nature, tend to be cloying if read in large doses. In print, at least, she gives the distinct impression that her days were spent rushing from one high-minded activity to another — from contemplating the spiritual meaning of a withered tree branch, to listening to the "pure sounds" of Bach, to analyzing a quotation from a favorite philosopher. The reader never imagines that she ever enjoyed ordinary or mundane things, such as eating a hot dog, laughing at a tasteless joke, or reading a trashy novel for the sheer fun of it. In fact, her humorless intensity seems even to have gotten on *her* nerves. In her diary she once observed, "I try not to *waste* any of the day. By waste I don't mean exactly what other people do. Waste is being unaware. And yet sometimes I feel I wear myself out being 'aware.' Is this why I am so tired at the end of the day?"

Although the uproar about Ciardi's review eventually subsided, for years people talked about it as a kind of intellectual curiosity. In the bland, TV-dominated Eisenhower era, some Americans had actually turned down the volume of the set at dinner so they could debate an esoteric subject like the values in literary criticism. But for Anne, the knowledge that her "slovenly" and "illiterate" poetry had helped briefly raise the nation's literary IQ must have offered scant comfort. In her entire career she would publish only one more poem.

CHAPTER 22

"The Most Attractive Couple"

B Y THE 1960s, Anne and Charles's public reputation had come full circle. The past largely forgotten as the national memory became hazier, they had re-entered the ranks of such revered American couples as George and Martha Washington, James and Dolley Madison, Abraham and Mary Todd Lincoln, and their old nemeses Franklin and Eleanor Roosevelt. Charles's image as a national hero had been fully restored, in part due to Anne's literary plastic surgery. In fact, her writing on her husband's behalf amounted to one of the most skillful and successful campaigns ever mounted in the history of public relations. Thanks to the power of her graceful prose, the image of the Luftwaffe-saluting, Jew-hating Charles Lindbergh had been largely erased. It was replaced by an earlier, far more sympathetic and attractive portrait, that of the modest and courageous young aviator who had accomplished the impossible. It must have been with enormous pride that Anne noted that many Americans now regarded her husband as one of the most influential figures of the twentieth century. As they had in the past, even presidents stood in awe of him.

Remembering how close the celebrated couple had been to his father, Joseph Kennedy, when he had been ambassador to London, President John F. Kennedy invited the Lindberghs to a state dinner in 1962 for André Malraux, the French minister of cultural affairs. It was not the first time the Lindberghs had met the younger Kennedy. They had been introduced to him many years before, when he was a Harvard student, at a luncheon given by Ambassador William C. Bullitt in Paris in May 1939. "The most attractive couple I've ever seen," an entranced

Kennedy had written to a friend. "She takes a rotten picture and is really as pretty as hell and terribly nice."

That was the spring Jack had decided to take a leave from Harvard for the spring semester so he could go to London with his father. Before their return to England, father and son had visited Palm Beach, where, while lolling beside a pool, rubbing cocoa butter into his skin, the ambassador had given off-the-record briefings to Damon Runyon, Walter Winchell, and a host of other reporters in which he made it clear that he had no regrets about Munich. In fact, he boasted that his plan to bring Charles Lindbergh to London at the height of the crisis in Czechoslovakia was one of the reasons Chamberlain had decided not to defy the Nazis.

But now Jack Kennedy, his son, was going to renew his acquaintanceship with the Lindberghs, and he was as thrilled about seeing the famous flier as he had been as an impressionable young college student. As Jacqueline Kennedy Onassis remembered some years after her husband's assassination,

> The person that President Kennedy was most anxious to have attend the dinner was Charles Lindbergh, because of his life-long admiration for him and for Mrs. Lindbergh. We knew that Colonel and Mrs. Lindbergh did not like to attend public functions and for that reason we invited them to stay in the White House where they might be spared some press attention. I will never forget how sweet the Lindberghs were to the children. Mrs. Lindbergh gave an inscribed copy of *North to the Orient* to Caroline and Colonel Lindbergh gave *The Spirit of St. Louis* inscribed to John. They treasure these books now, and that occasion will always remain one of my happiest memories.

The Kennedys' admiration for the Lindberghs was carried on by their successors, Lyndon Johnson and his wife, Lady Bird. Mrs. Johnson not only invited the celebrated pair to a number of social occasions at the White House, but agreed to be interviewed by Anne for an article she wanted to write about the First Lady for *Look* magazine.

Lady Bird's initial impression of Anne was that she was "so attractive and quietly magnetic." Although their interview had been scheduled to last only an hour, it went on much longer. As the First Lady commented,

> Because I liked listening and talking to her, I myself prolonged it.
> I was interested in the diversity between her book, *Gift from the Sea*, which was so introspective and delicate, and her later book, *Dearly Be-*

loved, which had humor in it and some bitterness. The characters lived pretty painful lives in *Dearly Beloved.* That they should both come from the same mind intrigued me.

The book to which Lady Bird was referring, *Dearly Beloved: A Theme and Variations,* had been published by Harcourt, Brace the previous year, in 1962. Significantly, like *Gift from the Sea,* it was written during a time of dissatisfaction and turmoil in Anne's marriage, but unlike the former work it presented a far different portrait of its creator.

Of all Anne's works, *Dearly Beloved* was perhaps the most daring and honest, as if she had at last managed to break free of her well-bred, soulful image to write candidly about the subject that had shaped her entire life: love and marriage. Her philosophical reflections on this universal theme were framed in the form of a novel about nine guests attending the wedding ceremony of a young couple, Sally McNeil and Mark Gallatin, who were based on Anne's oldest daughter, Anne, and the young Frenchman, Julien Feydy, she had recently married. Within this fictional framework, the guests express their personal thoughts on marriage as they listen to the solemn words of the wedding ceremony, with its opening, "Dearly beloved, we are gathered together," and this allowed Anne the freedom she had not enjoyed previously in her nonfiction to explore her conflicts about her own marriage.

Like Virginia Woolf's *To the Lighthouse,* Anne's book explored the subtle variations in the moods and thoughts of her characters as they tried to evaluate the experience of marriage.

The novel begins with Deborah McNeil, the mother of the bride, who is obviously based on the author herself. As she anticipates her daughter's marriage, she reflects on her own relationship with her husband, John, a man who, not surprisingly, is very much like Charles Lindbergh: "One of those lean silent boys at college; quite a hero on the track team ... They said he was a hermit, mysterious. Some kind of locked-up treasure in him, they imagined, had never been discovered. Each of them thought she alone had the key to the treasure. Except for her, actually."

But John proves something of a disappointment on their first date. He sits miles away from her in the car, and his idea of conversation is a discussion of "the effect of carbon monoxide in city streets." Still, he is so good-looking that she can't take her eyes off him. With so many pretty and popular girls to choose from, she can't believe that he has actually asked her for a date. To her surprise, however, she discovers that not only is he breathtakingly handsome, but he's also very intelligent and logical (though after their marriage this trait exasperates her to the point where she notes despairingly, "He would nail her down, with the good strong nails of his logic . . . Nailed to her faults forever").

Yet as Deborah listens to the words of the wedding service, she realizes that she "didn't know" her husband at all. Swiftly she reminds herself, "Oh, of course, she *did*; it was only that she couldn't talk to him. She had another language: feelings, poetry, music; and she couldn't talk about carbon monoxide. He lectured; she listened."

During the wedding ceremony, Deborah begins to fantasize about being married to a foreigner, in particular a Frenchman. Although John thought Frenchmen "silly," especially when they kissed her hand, as one had when they had been abroad recently, she had always felt attracted to them. "You could talk to them. They understood things; a bride like a newborn baby — closed gentians."

Suddenly aware that such thoughts are tantamount to betrayal, she quickly reminds herself that "marriage was different: solid, real, lasting. This didn't last, wasn't solid. Just daydreaming, imaginary conversations." And then aware of what her marriage is lacking, she laments, "But conversation itself . . . wasn't that real? Communication with another person — wasn't it the realest thing in life?"

Don's is the next soliloquy. A psychologist who deals daily with the misery and unhappiness of many married couples, he is married to Deborah's sister, Henrietta. Cynical and thoroughly modern in his viewpoint, he views marriage as a trap that forces people to relinquish their individuality and sexual freedom. In his opinion, a good sex life is the only thing that manages to make it palatable. Spiritual love isn't enough. And if one of the partners finds the other sexually lacking, Don believes in adultery. Obviously bored with Henrietta, he starts to imagine an affair with her sister, Deborah, and then rapidly dismisses the idea.

How about Deborah? . . . She was a faithful wife, all right.

So what? No man would think of touching her . . . too delicate and cool, virginal — almost more virginal than the bride. . . .

That was the trouble with Debby. Not a bad figure, either, but she hid it in those sad-sack clothes. . . . Every attractive-to-man line — breast, hip, leg — covered up by a careful fold. Each wrinkle of cloth cried: Keep off the grass!

In total, nine guests — four men and five women — voice their observations on love and marriage, ranging from eager expectancy (one of the bridesmaids) to the resigned (the bridegroom's mother, who has decided for her son's sake to remain in an unhappy marriage) to the intensely spiritual (Deborah's father, Theodore, who believes that life should be "a stream of compassion which fed the world"). Theodore — a character obviously based on Dwight Morrow — is still grieving for his dead wife, Suzannah (Betty Morrow), with whom he had an intensely close relationship. In a revealing passage he muses about why neither of his daughters has been as happy with her husband as he and his wife had been with each other during their long, incredibly happy marriage. "What happened to them? . . . Did he and Suzannah not give them the proper example of marriage? Their own great all-absorbing happiness — did it shut out the children? Where had they failed?"

It is obvious from *Dearly Beloved* that by this stage in her life Anne had come to believe that most marriages were basically unhappy. Still, after describing in often excruciating detail the guests' mainly depressing marital experiences, she comes out firmly in favor of marriage as an institution. During the wedding banquet, Deborah glances at John at the other end of the table and suddenly realizes what he means to her: "She felt the firm bond between them, and the relatives on either side held by this bond . . . *Community* was what they had together. And perhaps this was the meaning of marriage, not the communication she was forever looking for."

In style and content, *Dearly Beloved* was clearly a departure for its author, and predictably, reviews were mixed. Some critics had trouble coping with the fact that the sensitive and ladylike Mrs. Lindbergh had written about sex and other bodily functions. They were offended by the book's frank passages, such as the one in which Don describes his refined Boston wife in a Mexican outhouse: "God, she looked funny, sitting on air . . . so she wouldn't pick up any horrible germs, she said."

Pamela Marsh commented in the *Christian Science Monitor,* "Mrs. Lindbergh is honestly attempting to deal with problems as urgent as infidelity, sexual morality and the need for love. But in presenting some attitudes the writing becomes as tasteless as the situation described." Other critics felt that the book, although dealing with an intriguing and universal theme, contained few exceptional insights. Noted *Time* magazine, "Mrs. Lindbergh frequently manages a small memorable insight. But for the most part, her symposium on matrimony . . . rediscovers too much that is old or borrowed, too little that is new."

What these reviews neglected to point out was that, for its author, *Dearly Beloved* was a step forward. For the first time Anne was able not only to talk about sexual relations and bodily functions, but, more important, to write about life from a point of view other than her own. For years, she had hungered for "real life" and to observe and write about people with different backgrounds. Granted, it was the upper middle class she was portraying in her "fictional meditation," and several of the characters were based on herself and members of her family, but apart from its roman à clef fascination, *Dearly Beloved* revealed growth, both personal and artistic, on the part of its author. She was developing as a fiction writer, and furthermore, her work was becoming less self-centered. She was no longer Anne Morrow Lindbergh writing just about her relationship with Charles Lindbergh but about other men and women and their equally complex marriages.

Unfortunately, *Earth Shine,* published seven years later, was a reversion to her earlier fervidly soulful style. Too old by now to be adventurers themselves, the Lindberghs were now witnessing the explorations of others, and they had been invited to Cape Kennedy on December 21, 1968, to watch the launching of Apollo 8 for its first moon-orbiting mission.

They arrived a day early, and Anne was shocked by the transformation of the cape, which she had remembered as Cape Canaveral, a quiet desolate place where they and their children used to camp but which was now spoiled with motels, gigantic supermarkets, and neon-lit restaurants. But she was impressed by the enormous NASA complex, and when she visited the open-air museum, with its display of early rockets, she was reminded of their old friend, Robert Goddard, the American rocketry pioneer who had always believed that it was theoretically possible to design a multistage rocket that could reach the moon. Before the takeoff, they were invited to have lunch with the astronauts, and as they were eating, Lindbergh told the amused spacemen that Goddard had given up the idea because it would cost too much — perhaps a million dollars.

Anne recorded her feelings about the awesome launch in an essay, "The Heron and the Astronaut," which was published in *Life* magazine. A revised and expanded version was later included in *Earth Shine,* which was published in 1969. The book also contained the essay "Immersion in Life." Previously published in *Life* in 1966, it recalled a safari the Lindberghs had made to the teeming wild animal preserves of East

Africa. Written in Anne's poetic prose, the two essays celebrated the beauty and fragility of the planet and grew out of her deep reverence for life.

Although eloquently written, *Earth Shine* was not an honest, self-exploratory work like *Dearly Beloved*. Despite its appealing philosophy, it was essentially a record of experiences that Anne had shared with her husband and, in the case of the first moonshot, was unlikely to have had if she had not been Mrs. Charles Lindbergh. It was as if after a period of artistic and personal experimentation, she had suddenly become timid and scrambled to reclaim her old literary image, namely, that of the soulful, poetic wife of the world-famous aviator. In short, she became "Anne Morrow Lindbergh" again, and one wonders if her marriage had suddenly taken a turn for the better.

Earth Shine was Anne's last book dealing with her observations about the modern era, with its confused personal relationships, awesome technical achievements, and capacity for destruction. Although she later wrote occasionally about environmental issues, she would spend the next decade preparing for publication the monumental collection of diaries she had been keeping for many years about her marriage.

CHAPTER 23

"Argonauta"

As ANNE HAD WRITTEN in *Gift from the Sea*, a simple, unencumbered lifestyle might be one of life's answers. Now, with their children grown and off on their own, she and her husband began divesting themselves of their possessions, something that Charles Lindbergh had longed to do ever since his 1927 flight, when he had been inundated with so many gifts from admirers that he began to regard possessions "as debts rather than assets."

In 1963, the year their youngest child, Reeve, entered college, the Lindberghs sold the roomy Tudor-style house at Scott's Cove and built a small, five-room white cottage for themselves on the property, where at dusk they could gaze out the large picture window in the living room and see the geese and other waterfowl gathering on the quiet waters. The preservation of nature had long been of great concern to the Lindberghs, and it was around this time that Charles Lindbergh decided to break his public silence and become active in the fight to save the environment. As an active — and prestigious — member of at least half a dozen conservation organizations, including the World Wildlife Fund, he jetted around the globe helping to save the blue whale in Peru, the one-horned Jacan rhinoceros in Indonesia, the water buffalo and the monkey-eating eagle in the Philippines, as well as other endangered species. In 1968 he made his first public speech in twenty-seven years to the Alaska legislature on the protection of wildlife, and the following year he granted his first newspaper interview in thirty-five years, to Alden Whitman of the *New York Times,* about his conservation activities in the Philippines, which included his efforts to protect an endangered primitive tribe called the Tasadays. Lindbergh subsequently told Whitman that "he had unveiled himself because he thought the cause of conservation so urgent. 'I have had enough publicity for fifteen lives,' he noted, 'and I seek no more of it, but where I can accomplish a purpose I will do things I otherwise abhor.' "

By then, Lindbergh had become as disillusioned with civilization as he had with science and aviation as solutions to humanity's problems. To his dismay, he realized that in addition to the airplane's destructive capabilities, the "fast communication" made possible by commercial aviation was responsible for "a deadly standardization" throughout the world. "When I began surveying air routes of the world, every place I landed had its character and beauty," he recalled. ". . . A few decades later, the communication I helped to bring with my airplane is rapidly standardizing all cities, towns, villages, and even remote tribes — so much so that there is no longer a city in the world I have a desire to visit."

Questioning whether "civilization was progress," Lindbergh began to believe that "there is wisdom in the primitive lying at greater depths than the intellect has plumbed, a wisdom from which civilized man can learn and without whose application his survival time is limited. It is wisdom born of instinct, intuition, and genetic memory, held by the subconscious rather than the conscious mind, too subtle and elusive to be more than partially comprised within limits of rationality."

Of all the primitive places he visited, Africa was perhaps the most fascinating, because in its jungles he could observe for himself the evolutionary struggle that for him was the determining force behind all animal and human life. "Prolificacy. Competition. Selection. In the topi, the principles of nature were clearly manifest," he wrote in his memoirs. "Strength, skill, endurance had won for the buck who would return, victorious, to breed the herd and pass on to future generations those genetic characteristics that tend to support survival. The result was seen in the animals themselves. Among hundreds we passed, no blemish was visible." Still a firm believer in social Darwinism, he was disappointed to find that when African tribesmen killed their foes, a "similar selection of qualities" did not result, in his view. "Most of the human bodies I saw showed obvious defects — defects of form, of energy, of alertness, of muscle, tooth and eye. Even in tribal organization — considered extremely primitive by civilized man today — competition has become separated from selection on biological standards of life."

Although by no means a confirmed social Darwinist like her husband, Anne did share his deep concern about ecology and conservation. When he visited the Masai tribe in Kenya in 1964, she went along and was fascinated by the wildlife and the Masais' customs. Her real satisfaction, however, seems to have come from the knowledge that her husband had at last latched onto a cause that absorbed his prodigious energies and satisfied his chronic wanderlust.

At a two-day meeting at Smith College on environmental pollution in February 1970, Anne made a rare public speech in which she argued that "human values spring from earth values and must be supported by them." (Entitled "Harmony with the Life Around Us," it was published in the July 1970 issue of *Good Housekeeping* magazine.) During her visit, she was awarded an honorary doctorate by her alma mater.

Although Anne and Charles were growing old, physically they both seemed to defy the passage of time, as if the 1920s had happened only yesterday. Charles Lindbergh's hairline had receded to some extent and his face was lined, but he was still lean, long-limbed, and athletic, giving the impression that, if circumstances were to permit it, he still possessed the stamina to duplicate his celebrated feat. Though Anne was approaching her midsixties, her face was still virtually unlined, and her brown hair was abundant and curly. Her figure, of which she had always been vain, was still slender and youthful, kept in trim by her daily morning exercises and long, brisk walks alone through the countryside.

Although growing older, she had lost none of that quiet magnetism that many people, especially men, found so entrancing. Robert McKinstry, a close friend of Dwight, Jr., met Anne on several occasions when she was visiting her brother at his home in Bucks County. "She was interesting from any point of view," McKinstry remembered. "She was the most gracious and certainly the most feminine woman I ever met in my life . . . For all her keenness of intellect, she was modest. She was nice-looking, but spiritually she was beautiful." Charles Lindbergh was not present on those occasions, and it was McKinstry's impression after talking with Dwight that "she wasn't anywhere nearly as attractive when Colonel Lindbergh was around. When he was around she was diffident, and absolutely nonassertive . . . apparently, he overwhelmed her."

In the 1970s, she and Charles built a small, simple house on the edge of a cliff on four acres of land on Maui, in the Hawaiian Islands. They called their new home Argonauta, after the rare paper nautilus Anne had described so eloquently in *Gift from the Sea*. The part of the island on which they chose to build their house was characteristically very isolated (they were twelve miles away from the nearest store), but it was very beautiful, with waterfalls, natural swimming pools, and a spectacular view of the Pacific Ocean. Although the Lindberghs made Argonauta their legal residence, they did not live there permanently, spending only six to eight weeks there every year. They spent the summers in a chalet they rented every year in the mountains above Vevey, Switzerland.

Of course, enormous wealth as well as freedom from responsibility enabled them to have a lifestyle in which they could jet from one "simple" home to another. Their five children were all adults and living their own lives. Despite certain drawbacks to Lindbergh's severe style of parenting, they had all turned out well and were people in whom Anne and Charles could take a great deal of pride.

Jon, who was dark and shorter than his father (according to his mother, "more of a Morrow than a Lindbergh"), had graduated with a degree in biology from Stanford University in 1954. He had married a college classmate named Barbara and was the father of six children. Like his own father, he was an ardent conservationist and explorer. Fascinated by deep-sea diving, he made a record-making dive of forty-nine hours at 432 feet off the Bahamas in 1964 and was a frogman officer in the U.S. Navy. Later, he made a distinguished career for himself in deep-sea diving and oceanography. He is a director of Oceanographic Fund, an investment company, at Puget Sound, Washington, and develops salmon farms in the Pacific Northwest. "He is as much of a pioneer in the field of marine biology as his father was in aviation," one of his friends said. "He's tall, better looking than his father, and he has his mother's modesty and his grandfather Morrow's completeness."

In the early 1970s, Jon and his wife and their two daughters, Krissy and Wendy, were seriously injured when their car was struck by a drunk driver. With the exception of Krissy, all were knocked unconscious, and Jon, who suffered a brain injury, was pinned between the seat and the wheel until the local fire department extricated him. For Anne and Charles, the accident must have brought back all the suffering they had endured when Charles, Jr., was found dead, and they were greatly relieved when Jon and the other members of his family recovered without any permanent damage.

Land, who resembled his father and shared his love of the soil, had married a college classmate. As a young boy, he spent every summer on a Western ranch. He loved being outdoors and was now running a large cattle ranch the family owned in Montana.

Anne's older daughter, Anne Spencer, became the author of several well-known children's books, including *Osprey Island, The People in Pineapple Place,* and *Nobody's Orphan.* People who knew the elder and the younger Annes were often quick to point out the similarity between them. Both were sensitive, perceptive women who could be socially charming with people they liked. An observer once noted that "Anne also shares her mother's characteristic composure, an air of reserve that suggests a shy nature, a notion that dissolves when either woman speaks about subjects that involve their interests."

Neither Anne nor her younger sister, Reeve, went to Smith, their mother and grandmother's alma mater. Anne attended Radcliffe and the Sorbonne. After completing her studies, she married a Frenchman, Julien Feydy, and went to live in France.

The marriage did not last, and following her divorce, Anne married composer-conductor Jerzy Sapieyevski in January 1978. She had three children, two by her first marriage, Charles and Constance, and one, Marek, by her second.

Like her mother, Anne had always wanted to be a writer. "I've been a writer since I can remember," she once told an interviewer. "We were a writing family. My brothers, my sister and I started right in while we were little, inventing things, taking characters from books and adding more stories about them — having them interact . . . My father was extremely encouraging. He'd listen to everything and type up each story for us. So it was natural . . . our parents convinced us that it was just as possible to write as to read."

In Anne's opinion, it was her father who was of more practical help to her than her mother in her writing career. As he had with his wife, Lindbergh encouraged his daughter to develop her talent.

> I would willingly hand anything over to my mother, and she would willingly read it. But you know, she's too much of a mother. She would offer support rather than suggestions: "It's very nice, dear," no direct literary criticism . . .
>
> My father was much more helpful, although my mother was right when she warned, "Watch out. Don't let him at it or you'll find yourself with a skeleton." He visited me in Paris, the year before he died, and spent days going over my first manuscript and saying things like, "This

is repetitive; this is too long." I was just dizzy from the comments! He was absolutely able to take a book apart and find all the weak spots.

After graduating from Radcliffe, Anne's youngest child, Reeve, married photographer Richard Brown. She lived near St. Johnsbury, Vermont, where she taught school and raised two daughters. Like her mother, grandmother, and sister, she was an accomplished writer who has written both adult fiction and children's books. Like her parents and her siblings, she preferred to live in an unostentatious and inconspicuous manner.

As the years passed, it was Reeve, who was not born until after World War II, who became the most forthcoming and candid of all the Lindbergh children on the subject of their famous controversial parents.

"When I was in Radcliffe, some of my collegemates were curious about my father's non-interventionist role just before World War II, and some asked me if he were anti-Semitic. I answered no to the second question and said, quite truthfully, that I really didn't know much about the prelude to the war," she told Alden Whitman in 1977. "In college generally I was not singled out as the daughter of a famous man. A number of my friends, in fact, were more impressed with my mother — I think, because she is a writer."

But the truth was that the lingering controversy about Lindbergh's prewar role did have a profound effect on his children. "We are all still reeling from it, though in general the public has forgotten the whole business," Reeve admitted at about the same time to Julie Nixon Eisenhower. "When I learned that because of my father's war speeches some people saw him as a bigot, I was dumbfounded. Reading things that were said about him during the war; parents of certain of my friends acting a little oddly toward me . . . all the time, nothing corresponded to *my* view of my father, so that each experience of this kind was a crazy kind of nightmare."

If Reeve was the most accessible of the Lindbergh children, Scott, their third living son, was the most reticent, fleeing reporters every time he spotted them. Scott was the rebel and free spirit in the family. As a young man, he liked to speed in his flashy sports car, much to his father's annoyance.

Reportedly, when Scott was a child, he knew nothing of his brother's kidnapping. He later recalled that it seemed to be a taboo subject to his parents, adding that he was more than ten years old when he "learned" about it "through a newspaper story."

Now in his late forties, Scott is an expert on primate behavior, an interest that began when he and his wife, Alika, a Belgian former movie actress and novelist, started observing the habits of some rare monkeys they had collected from friends who had tired of them as pets. In 1973 the couple bought a ramshackle seventeenth-century manor house at Verlhiac, one hundred miles northeast of Bordeaux, and turned it into a simian paradise.

Their particular field of study was South American primates. By this time they had collected thirty-seven monkeys, which appeared to live in better style than Scott and Alika, who kept only two of the manor's ten drafty rooms heated.

"I couldn't help becoming absorbed in the things that my father and mother were interested in. But when I began studying monkeys seriously, he was not at all sure I was doing the right thing," Scott once admitted in a rare interview. "He was a great one for not wasting time. You had to have a definite goal. The goal here can sometimes seem indistinct."

Father and son did not see eye to eye on other issues besides Scott's interest in monkeys. Much to Anne's sorrow, they were estranged for many years and only reconciled when Lindbergh became terminally ill. Although Anne agreed with her husband that it was a waste for young people to fritter away their time and talents, she was obviously sympathetic to Scott's unorthodox lifestyle and choice of profession. Often, when she was driving around Maui, she would stop and pick up a young hippie hitchhiker.

In 1973, Lindbergh, who had been robustly healthy all his life, suddenly fell ill with a rash and fever. He consulted a doctor, who diagnosed his condition as shingles. However, he still continued to feel unwell and began to lose an alarming amount of weight. Friends who hadn't seen him for a while were shocked by how thin and gaunt he looked. In 1974 he became very ill with what his doctors thought might be pneumonia. But when he was admitted to the Columbia Presbyterian Medical Center in New York City, his condition was diagnosed as an advanced case of lymphatic cancer.

When Anne learned that her husband was terminally ill, she didn't ask his doctors how long he had. She wanted to live in the moment. But Lindbergh, always the realist, knew that he could not go on much longer, and he wanted to spend the time he had left at his home on

Maui. His doctors were appalled. The journey was a long one and they were convinced that he would die en route. But Lindbergh had always been stubborn ("a stubborn Swede," Anne sometimes called him), and he told the doctors, "I'd rather live one day on Maui than thirty in the hospital."

As usual, he got his way. On August 17, 1974, with Anne, Jon, and Scott accompanying him, he was placed on a stretcher in a United Airlines plane that would fly him directly to Honolulu. Airline attendants placed his stretcher high up on the backs of three window seats. In Honolulu, he was met by his son Land and then flown by a smaller hospital plane to Maui. The nature of his illness was kept secret at his request, as was the flight. Landing at Maui, he was taken to a small cottage near the medical center at Hana.

As she had during the other great crises of their lives, Anne acted with stoic calm during her husband's final days. "The last ten days were very peaceful and quite timeless, really rather timeless," she later remembered. While Jon, Scott, and Land took over the practical matters involved with his illness, she sat by his bed, holding his hand, as he drifted in and out of consciousness, and, when he was lucid, helped him plan every detail of his funeral, which included having a physician make out and sign his death certificate, with only the date left blank, and a swift burial after death in a nearby Hana churchyard. Lindbergh requested that his grave and style of coffin be handled by the local people in the traditional Hawaiian fashion. He insisted on being buried in the simple khaki work clothing he habitually wore. With Anne's help, he even planned his tombstone. It would be a simple marker made of granite. Its inscription, taken from the 139th Psalm, would read: "If I take the wings of the morning, and dwell in the uttermost parts of the sea . . ."

They had been married for forty-five years, and Anne knew she was losing him. For forty-five years, he had been her connection to a "real life" that, as she had long ago convinced herself, she might not have had the emotional stamina to endure alone.

Whenever he was conscious, they both tried not to discuss his impending death, but for Anne, her husband had always been her most important and exacting teacher, and she could not resist asking him what dying was like.

"Charles, tell me what it is like. I know I'll be next."

"It isn't something to be afraid of. It's a very natural thing," he said, trying to reassure her, as if they had suddenly encountered a dense fog on one of their early flights. "I felt that I could have died any time in the last few days and it would have been easy for me. It's harder on you watching me die than it is for me."

This time there was no doubt about the correctness of Charles Lindbergh's words. His death, when it occurred early in the morning of August 26, 1974, was much harder for his wife than it was for him, for it seemed to those present that he simply drifted away. Yet even though he was gone, Anne did not succumb to sadness and despair. The calm and even adventuresome manner in which he had approached his death gave her courage, not only about living without him but about her own inevitable end. Even in his dying, he remained the sustaining power in her life, her shining hero.

CHAPTER 24

"The Hardest Lesson"

Hᴇ ᴡᴀs ᴅᴇᴀᴅ, and for the first time in her life, Anne was completely independent, freed from his overwhelming presence, and released from "the eternal struggle of what I must be for Charles and what I must be for myself." At last, she could find her own identity and spend weeks combing the beach for rare and beautiful shells, returning home only when the spirit moved her. But even in death he seemed omnipresent. Although she was the grandmother of thirteen grandchildren, to whom she was known as "Granny Mouse," and was now on the board of directors of Harcourt Brace Jovanovich, most of her time was taken up with settling her husband's complicated estate and helping to ensure his heroic niche in American history.

She continued to live in their small cottage at Scott's Cove, with only her Cairn terrier, Berwick, for company. The sun-filled living room where she liked to sit and watch the finches, chickadees, and sparrows at the several feeders outside her two big windows was plainly furnished, with a window seat and couches in a worn and faded blue-patterned material. The two Vlaminck paintings she and Lindbergh had bought in Paris in the late thirties adorned the walls. At the far end of the room was a massive desk that had belonged to her father. On the desk was the sensitively sculpted bust that Charles Lindbergh had commissioned Charles Despiau to do of her during their self-imposed exile in Europe.

Unlike many widows devoted to the memory of a beloved husband, she did not turn the house into a shrine. There were no photographs of Charles Lindbergh, no memorabilia celebrating his famous flight and aeronautical achievements. Only a blue china mug with CHARLES inscribed on it served as a reminder of his monumental place in her life.

But their fabulous life together was still very much in her mind, and she continued the monumental task of editing and publishing her letters and diaries. She had begun the process in 1972, with the publication of the first volume, *Bring Me a Unicorn,* and in the next five years, from 1973 to 1980, she would publish four more volumes: *Hour of Gold, Hour of Lead,* 1973; *Locked Rooms and Open Doors,* 1974; *The Flower and the Nettle,* 1976; and *War Within and Without,* 1980. Three of the volumes were published while Lindbergh was still alive, and his sharp eye had scrutinized every word for misrepresentations and factual errors. But the next two volumes, *The Flower and the Nettle* and *War Within and Without,* she edited on her own, with the help of Helen Wolff, her meticulous editor at Harcourt. In her mind, these last two volumes were especially important for they dealt with the Lindberghs' political views during the prewar era. Anne hoped that their contents and the new introductions she wrote for each volume, in which she admitted being "appalled at my innocence of politics and the violence of my indignation" when she reread the diaries forty years later, would convince the present generation of readers to regard her husband with a new perspective.

In total, Anne's published diaries and letters come to more than two thousand pages. Most, though not all, of their contents are devoted to her personal relationship with Lindbergh and the extraordinary events of their lives. The first two volumes, *Bring Me a Unicorn* and *Hour of Gold, Hour of Lead,* which cover their meeting, marriage, and the kidnapping of their baby, are especially compelling documents, so vividly written that readers may feel that they are no longer living in their own time but in a bygone era, with one of the most famous couples of the age.

Many readers were eager to learn the details of what it was like to have been loved by the world's most worshipped hero, as well as the couple's reaction to the kidnapping of their son, which was movingly described in *Hour of Gold, Hour of Lead,* and the first two volumes enjoyed good sales and some excellent reviews. Observed Glendy Culligan in the *Saturday Review,* "The letters and diaries achieve both spontaneity and art, thanks in part to her style, in part to a built-in plot and a soul-searching heroine worthy of a Brontë novel." And Helen Bevington, writing in the *New York Times Book Review* about *Bring Me a Unicorn,* was of the opinion that "the decision not to shape this extraordinary material into an autobiography took courage, and I think, perfect wisdom of choice. . . . The picture that emerges is neither girlish nor partial. In a charming self-portrait that might be labeled 'before and after meeting Colonel Lindbergh,' she reveals herself as the complex person she was — strong-willed yet meek, firm yet apologetic, timid yet independent, terribly vulnerable, a poet fond of unicorns, a girl falling in love."

Unfortunately, the other three volumes, with their self-serving politicizing and intense narcissism, cloaked in the guise of discreet modesty, are far less impressive. Repetitious and far too long, they lack the charm and the intensity of the earlier volumes. Their major purpose seems to be to make Charles Lindbergh's views palatable to succeeding generations. One reads these last three volumes with a sense of sadness because by then it is all too obvious that instead of developing her own extraordinary talent, which might have classed her with the outstanding writers of our time, Anne Morrow Lindbergh had chosen to squander her unusual gifts on the enshrinement of a husband whose views were highly moot. Ultimately, she sacrificed her talent to become not the perfect wife and mother but the perfect public relations woman.

Predictably, the last volume of her diaries, *War Within and Without*, was the most controversial. Reviewing the book for the *National Review*, Selden Rodman noted with regret that, although Charles Lindbergh had omitted mentioning the frank discussion they had had about the Nazis and Jews in his *Wartime Journals*, he had hoped "Anne, who prizes the whole truth, will deal with it when her own diary of that fateful year appears." But even though they had seen each other and corresponded throughout the war, "not a word about any of this appears in the published version of Anne Lindbergh's day-by-day journal either. Is it unfair to suppose that there were other loving friends whose testimony proved equally embarrassing and was similarly suppressed?"

Rodman then went on to state his conviction "that there have always been two Anne Lindberghs. One is the poor little rich girl who, if she had 'married within her class,' would have spent the war years making 'Bundles for Britain' or typing Mom's interventionist speeches . . . The naiveté of this Anne is astonishing. She is susceptible to anyone and anything that will justify her husband's insensitivity." He then went on to quote from her journal: " 'Petain asks for peace terms. It is very moving, that old man taking hold at such an hour. They can trust him . . . I feel relieved that they had such a man at such a terrible hour.' "

"The other Anne, happily, is in the ascendant most of the time, and *all* of the time when removed from the ugly political orbit along which her stubborn husband bulls ahead," Rodman continued. "Her love for him is not just loyalty — though loyal she is. She responds to what is truly heroic in him. 'C. coming out of the sky with a kind of directness, a kind of magnificence that is only his . . . It catches my breath. I have always taken it for granted. But to see it in the sky . . . it is an act of creative beauty, a work of art.' "

Other reviewers were also troubled by Anne's tendency not merely to gloss over the negative side of her relationship with her husband, but to write about him in such an unreal way that he remained an idealized, romantic figure, a "heroic mask." Observed Kathleen Leverich in the *Christian Science Monitor,*

> In Mrs. Lindbergh's case, the difficulties of total honesty were compounded by the knowledge that her entries, by her own wish, were regularly perused by their chief subject. Charles Lindbergh emerges as the central figure of these diaries, while the author appears as the Devotee, the True Believer, the Keeper of the Flame. Here lies the value and fascination of the book. It is an unwitting, ingenuous self-portrait of a highly sensitive, intelligent woman who . . . dedicated her life to the service of one she could look up to. While disapproving the practice in others, Mrs. Lindbergh had herself elevated her husband to the status of a god.

Finally, Anne's commitment to her husband had profound ramifications for her writing. Unable to develop her own views independently, she remained so caught up in the conflict between her desire to be a perfect wife and her need to find her own identity that her work became highly fragmented. As David Kirk Vaughan has pointed out in his analysis of Anne's literary output,

> Critical evaluation of Anne Morrow Lindbergh's written work is almost nonexistent. Practically the only commentary about her thirteen books of memoirs, poetry, essays, and fiction is in the form of book reviews issued at the time of publication. Only the French writer Antoine de Saint-Exupéry, of all her readers, was able to appreciate Lindbergh's style and subject and to see it as part of an integral, unified artistic expression.

One important reason for this literary neglect is that the critics, like Anne herself, found it impossible to separate her literary achievements from her marriage. They could not respond to her work independently, as they could to that of a Dorothy Parker, Anita Loos, or Martha Graham, all of whom were Anne's contemporaries. But then, none of these exceptionally talented women was married for forty-five years to a man of Lindbergh's fame and with his dominating personality.

Another reason for this lack of critical analysis is that Anne did not produce a consistent body of work. Her first two books of travel writing, in which she celebrated the aeronautical achievements of her husband, were followed by a highly controversial political book on his behalf, then by a novella, followed by an inspirational book about the need for feminine solitude and privacy which was in essence a philosophical essay. Then came a slim volume of poetry, followed by a quasi novel about marriage which in actuality was a literary symposium, and then finally, five massive volumes of her diaries and letters which chronicled in minute detail her life with Charles Lindbergh. Vaughan points out correctly that literary critics had a hard time assessing her work on publication because she almost never wrote the same type of book twice and her writings did not easily fit into the usual literary classifications.

Nevertheless, although she skipped from genre to genre, and in some cases invented her own, all of Anne's work is unified by one theme, or rather one dilemma, namely, that "eternal struggle" of what "I must be for Charles and what I must be for myself." Sadly, most of her considerable talent was used up on Charles's behalf, and only *Gift from the Sea,* the ill-fated *Unicorn and Other Poems,* and *Dearly Beloved,* all of which were written during a low point in their marriage in the mid-fifties and early sixties, give testimony to her artistic independence. Yet even with *Gift from the Sea* and *Dearly Beloved,* she did not entirely break free from her husband's hold on her, for both works were in part confessionals for exploring her conflicted feelings about her marriage.

Besides editing these final volumes, Anne also prepared her husband's *Autobiography of Values* for publication. Obviously she hoped that this posthumous volume would help rescue his reputation, for his *Wartime Journals of Charles Lindbergh* had been published in 1970 to overwhelmingly negative reviews, since many critics, as well as his contemporaries, strongly reacted to his continuing unshakable conviction that it had been wrong for the United States to enter World War II. Others were appalled by his failure to say anything derogatory about the Nazis, even though by then the unspeakable evils of the concentration camps and gas chambers had been known for decades.

Autobiography of Values, which was published in 1978, was received with mixed reviews. Although some critics found Lindbergh's obsession with social Darwinism, which, among other things, had influenced his decision to marry Anne, "pretty spooky," others were moved by "the beauty and power of the reflections, so deeply troubled, of one of the major developers of technological civilization as he contemplated his handiwork." As was the case with *The Spirit of St. Louis*, it is debatable whether Charles or Anne was responsible for the "beauty and power" of the prose. Twelve days before his death, Charles Lindbergh had summoned his friend, William Jovanovich, head of Harcourt Brace Jovanovich, to the hospital and presented him with a three-thousand-page manuscript which he had been working on for the past thirty years. Realizing that the manuscript needed an enormous amount of work (it consisted of rough drafts of chapters, different versions of the same chapter, and, in many cases, sketchy outlines of chapters), he asked his friend to edit and publish it after his death. Jovanovich carried out his wishes, editing the massive, shapeless document with the help of Judith A. Schiff, a Yale archivist who was in charge of the collection of the Lindberghs' personal papers.

Although uncredited as coeditor, Anne Lindbergh clearly had a hand in preparing the manuscript for publication. Her gift for poetic imagery was evident in such passages as the following, in which Lindbergh describes an operation by Alexis Carrel: "Life sometimes merged with death so closely I could not tell them apart — click of scissors, cleave of scalpel, the surgeon's nimble fingers tying knots in silk." And some chapter titles also sounded as if she had written them. One such chapter was entitled "A Match Lighting a Bonfire," which was, of course, a variation on her phrase "a match lit near a pile of excelsior," which she had written to express her dismay over her husband's Des Moines speech, with its "unconscious bid for anti-Semitism."

On May 20, 1977, the fiftieth anniversary of Lindbergh's flight was celebrated in both the United States and France. Emerging from her reclusive life, Anne, along with Jon, Land, and Reeve, appeared and spoke at several of the "Spirit of St. Louis" banquets that were held in seven cities, raising hundreds of thousands of dollars for the Charles A. Lindbergh Memorial Fund, which supported scientific exploration, research, and conservation. To mark the occasion, the U.S. Postal Service issued a special stamp showing the *Spirit of St. Louis* in flight, and the Smithsonian Institution National Air and Space Museum, where the plane is permanently on display, exhibited a special collection of Lindbergh memorabilia, including his flying outfit and the twenty-five-thousand-dollar check for the Orteig Prize.

Ruth Dobrescu, a pilot who with her husband, Captain Charles Dobrescu, a former TWA pilot, was instrumental in persuading the Postal Service to issue the fiftieth anniversary stamp honoring Lindbergh's historic flight, met Anne at this time. "She's very gentle, unassuming, quiet, humble, unaffected," Mrs. Dobrescu remembered. "She's a very gracious, lovely lady."

During the course of their friendship, Anne asked Mrs. Dobrescu what she thought about Anne's public demeanor at the Paris Air Show, which both she and the Dobrescus had attended as part of the Lindbergh celebration. "When we were back in New York, having tea at the Cosmos Club, she asked me how I thought she had looked in the eyes of the public. Her daughter's little boy had been with her, and she asked me frankly if it appeared as if she were ignoring him. 'I didn't want anyone to know he was with me,' she confessed to me, 'because there are very strange people in this world.' "

To Mrs. Dobrescu, the implication was obvious.

Although Anne was initially dubious about the media hype surrounding the anniversary celebration, she did talk to Alden Whitman, a *New York Times* reporter who had been a friend of her husband. In a rare interview, she tried to set the record straight, explaining that Lindbergh had "resisted fame" and that "his disillusionment with material rewards propelled him in other directions. His search deepened and broadened into inner directions of exploration, study and thought. At the end of his life, he was thinking in terms of simplicity of living, of the basic qualities of life on earth, of the essential character of man himself, of the individual and his environment — not of man's machines, inventions, accomplishments, and exploits."

"I also think," she added lovingly, "that the continuing interest in Charles is not due to his 'hero image,' but due more to the fact that he continually broke out of the various images the public had of him. He continually surprised people by assuming a new role . . . He was, in a sense, a protean figure, impossible to simplify into a stereotyped picture, or to place into a limited framework."

As far as any writing of her own was concerned, Anne told Whitman that she was toying with the idea of writing another book, perhaps one on "the period in a woman's life when the children leave the nest." To another reporter, she said that she was thinking deeply about doing a book on widowhood and about "our unwillingness to face death, to meet it." But this was wishful thinking on her part. The truth was that she was too caught up in trying to restore her husband's image to write anything of her own.

When Julie Nixon Eisenhower interviewed her in 1976, Anne showed her the old gray toolshed at the back of the property where she had done her writing for many years. "She seemed quiet, a bit wistful when she showed me her little house," Eisenhower reported.

There was a hot plate with a kettle on it and a curtained-off corner with a wash basin and toilet so that she could spend the entire day in her studio if she desired, but from the cobwebs and the film of dust over everything, including the top of the desk, it was clear that she had not been working there lately. When I asked her why, she replied that there had been just too many requests, too many details of her husband's estate to attend to, and plans for his posthumous "Book of Values" that demanded her attention.

Anne also confessed to Eisenhower that "the final lesson of learning to be independent — widowhood" was "the hardest lesson of all."

"It is . . . so very difficult to be alone," she said. And then she confided that she still felt "married." "I don't say this in some Ouija-board sense, but in the way you approach things . . . always aware of how your husband would approach them . . ."

But in one area Anne refused to act in the high-handed manner that her husband had. After Charles's death, she made her peace with the press and consented to give interviews. Granted, the only reporters she was willing to see were in the top echelon, such as Alden Whitman and Julie Nixon Eisenhower, with whom Anne closely identified because she too had experienced a family member's fall from power and public disgrace.

In 1977 Anne was interviewed on television for the first time by respected correspondent Eric Sevareid. Had he been alive, Lindbergh would never have permitted such a public appearance. In his lifetime he had refused to appear on television, once declining an invitation by telling a reporter, "The publicity involved would be much too great, with resulting on-the-street recognition, and . . . I already had enough personal publicity to last me for a lifetime and several reincarnations."

Three years later, to promote the publication of *War Within and Without,* Anne appeared on CBS's "60 Minutes." On this occasion, she was interviewed by Morley Safer. Now seventy-three years old and still amazingly fit and in command of herself, she was surprisingly candid about her relationship with her husband. "He was not a demi-god," she informed Safer, adding that she "thought we made too much of him." She also said that as time went on she had found his fear of newsmen to be "irrational," but defended his paranoia by reminding viewers that after her child's skeletal remains were discovered, some unscrupulous reporters had broken into the Trenton morgue and taken a photograph. Her husband, she said, had never forgiven them for it.

She also used the opportunity to emphasize her dismay about his Des Moines speech, with its inflammatory remarks against the Jews, and how she had tried to prevent him from delivering it and had failed. "It's like lighting a match next to a pile of excelsior and saying you're just doing it in order to show your path . . . In fact, he did light the pile of excelsior," she said, quoting from her own diary. "It was terribly stupid. Well, I was horrified, *horrified*. I accused him of using this as a threat, and he said, 'No, I'm not doing that, I'm just saying the facts.'

"We had a terrible row about it. I felt terrible and he just didn't believe me about it, *terrible*. I said I think that to rouse anti-Semitism in the country is much worse than war. I'd rather have war, but he said, 'That's not what I'm doing.' He simply couldn't see it."

And then she pointed out a characteristic of her husband that she had not revealed in her diary. "One thing I think you have to realize is that he was not a great reader. Had he read Goebbels and Hitler and all of them, he would have known that people who really are anti-Semitic start with these statements."

When Safer bluntly asked her why she hadn't divorced her husband for his racist views, she did not evade his question but answered him frankly.

"Well, I think that was a terrible thing, I think that's a much worse thing to say. You know, when someone you've been with for years and that you love and you know does something that seems to you a total aberration, you don't walk out the door. You say, why did he do it, why did he do it? And I think he did it because of a kind of blindness."

"Did you love him less for that?" Safer pressed her.

"No, I can't say I did, but I pitied him. I *pitied* him. I mean, it was so awful to see this happen to him. I had a great belief in him, a *great belief*, and that was some of the pain. I couldn't bear it that people saw someone that I didn't see, that I didn't think was there."

There was one subject, however, that Anne refused to discuss publicly, and that was the murder of her son and whether she was convinced it was Bruno Hauptmann who had kidnapped and killed him. Reportedly, she has never read any of the recent books that have raised doubts about the fairness of the trial.

But it is clear from her words and actions that even after the passage of so many years, her feelings about her son remain painfully intense. "Charles had to escape. He went flying and went on with his work. But I couldn't take it in one draught at all, and I still can't," she said in a recent interview. She also has never been able to bring herself to return to the Hopewell house from which he was kidnapped. And perhaps her decision is a wise one. Although the interior of her former home has been completely transformed, a visit to Hopewell today would undoubtedly bring back a flood of painful memories. Called the Highfields Residential Group Center, it is now an institution for male juvenile offenders in danger of being sentenced to New Jersey detention facilities. During the last half century, nearly 1,600 troubled youths have received rehabilitation in the place where Anne and her little boy once played so happily, unaware of the hideous fate that awaited them. The small nursery of Charles Lindbergh, Jr., with its charming fireplace of blue and white delft tiles, is now a computer training center, and Anne and Charles's bookcase-lined bedroom is a classroom where the adolescent boys receive lessons in sex education. It is an odd use of both rooms, computer training and sex education, but, considering the intense enthusiasms and passionate relationship of their former inhabitants, perhaps a fitting one.

Although Anne and Charles made it clear that the scene of their tragedy was never to be turned into a tourist attraction, the current directors of the school now conduct tours of Highfields twice weekly. Today the curious visitor is permitted to wander at leisure through the house that thousands of people in the twenties clamored to visit, to walk the endlessly long, forbidding, tree-lined driveway, imagining what it must have been like to be the kidnapper, carrying his poorly made ladder in the darkness, and asking the still haunting question, could one man really have committed this crime without the help of someone who had an intimate knowledge of the Lindberghs' plans? One is also permitted to take photographs of the nursery and the rest of the house, with its surprisingly small and cramped rooms, though not of the children themselves. Like the memory of Charles Lindbergh, Jr., himself, to whom the house is a living memorial, they are inviolable.

Although the directors keep Anne informed about the center's activities, she never replies to their letters. Nor, it is reported, has she ever personally been in touch with members of the New Jersey State Police. There, outside Trenton, at police division headquarters, is a small log cabin–like museum that houses not only thousands of documents relating to the celebrated case, but also physical evidence from the trial, including the peculiar fold-up ladder and the ransom notes, with the strange double circles, that Hauptmann is said to have written. Safe and secure in illuminated glass cases are the deteriorated sleeping garments that Charles Augustus Lindbergh, Jr., wore on the last night of his brief life, along with small vials containing strands of his golden hair, tiny fragments of his bones, and an intact toenail.

Yet although sixty years have passed, that windy early spring night still continues to hold special significance for Anne. Recently, on March 1, 1990, at her home in Connecticut, she met with biographer Scott Berg and granted him unrestricted access to Lindbergh's papers for a comprehensive profile of her husband, to be completed on May 21, 1997, the seventieth anniversary of the day Lindbergh landed in Paris. Denied to other biographers over the years, the collection is rumored to contain more than 1 million items. Berg has stressed that he would not "do the book if there were any taboos, any controls on the manuscript." He has stated, further, that Mrs. Lindbergh "thought the book should tell the whole story and the truth. It was very clear that she didn't want a hagiography." Evidently, Anne Morrow Lindbergh, who is now well into her eighties and, according to her daughter Reeve, in frail health, hopes to be able to live long enough to see her husband vindicated. For after a return to glory in the midfifties and sixties, Charles Lindbergh is again in need of some restorative work, and she is too old and feeble to undertake it herself. For the most part, modern historians have dealt with him unkindly, saying that, intentionally or not, many of his beliefs echoed Nazi dogma.

On June 13, 1990, another elderly woman spoke out against the terrible injustices suffered by her husband. At a news conference in Trenton, New Jersey, the town where he was executed fifty-four years before for the murder of the Lindbergh baby, Anna Hauptmann, the elderly but still feisty ninety-one-year-old widow of Bruno Richard Hauptmann, demanded to meet with New Jersey governor Jim Florio. The reason Anna said she wanted to meet with him was to clear her husband's name.

"I want to talk to Florio and tell him the truth," Anna Hauptmann insisted, in a thick German accent. "My husband did not kidnap the Lindbergh baby."

As she has for the past fifty years, Anna Hauptmann was trying to get from the New Jersey governor a formal declaration that her husband's 1935 trial had been filled with manufactured evidence, false witnesses, and false testimony, and that he should never have been found guilty. The state had executed an innocent man.

"I am ninety-one years old and haven't much time left on this earth," she wrote to Florio. "If you believe in truth and justice you will see me. I want to have my husband's name cleared before the world. God knows he did not commit this terrible crime."

Anna, who still wears her wedding ring, insisted to reporters that her husband could not possibly have committed the crime. On the night of the kidnapping in Hopewell, New Jersey, he had called for her at the Bronx bakery where she had worked since 1929, and they had driven to their home in the Bronx.

"God saw us drive home together. We didn't even know there was a kidnapping until someone told us the following day," she insisted.

But Florio declined to meet with Anna Hauptmann. Through a spokesman, he said he did not intend to open an inquiry into the case.

In that hushed, packed courtroom of 1935, as she testified about the events leading up to the kidnapping, Anne had barely glanced at Anna, but now, because of an infamous crime and a stubborn loyalty to their husbands, they had become spiritual sisters, their lives dedicated to defending the men whom each had loved.

Aside from the new introductions to her diaries and letters, an address she gave at Smith College in 1978, and a brief foreword to her old friend Jim Newton's 1987 book of heavily retouched portraits of Charles Lindbergh, Henry Ford, and Alexis Carrel, Anne Morrow Lindbergh has not published any new original material since her husband's death in 1974. Perhaps her abiding adoration of him was at the heart of her inspiration. For in a sense he and their extraordinary life together were her only subject, and she gladly used up her exceptional talent to create what she hoped would be his enduring image. When he died, she was suddenly bereft of something to write about. The epic novel of her life was finished, and, as far as she was concerned, there could never be a sequel.

Acknowledgments

Works by Anne Morrow Lindbergh

Notes

Selected Bibliography

Acknowledgments

Believing like Anne Morrow Lindbergh that "the realest part" of a writer exists in his or her creative work, I have tried to interpret my subject's extraordinary life by analyzing her autobiographical writings. However, there are many aspects of Mrs. Lindbergh's life and literary career that she chose not to explore, and I am especially indebted to the following people for helping me shed light on them.

My deepest gratitude goes to Nigel Nicolson for his reminiscences of Anne and Charles Lindbergh and for his help in encouraging me to read the correspondence of his parents, Harold Nicolson and Vita Sackville-West, at the Lilly Library, Indiana University, in Bloomington, Indiana. I am indebted both to him and to Saundra Taylor, Curator of Manuscripts, for permission to publish excerpts from his parents' letters concerning the Lindberghs in the Vita Sackville-West manuscript collection.

For her generous assistance in helping me research the tragic period in Mrs. Lindbergh's life when her son was kidnapped, I am grateful to Dolores Raisch, the Lindbergh Archivist at the New Jersey State Police office in Trenton, New Jersey.

To Alex Handy, a photographer who covered the Lindbergh kidnapping case and was a personal friend of the aviator, my deepest appreciation for sharing his reminiscences and for allowing me to include some of his photographs of the Lindberghs and Amelia Earhart in the biography.

My special thanks also to Selden Rodman, writer and critic, for allowing me to read his personal journals concerning his relationship with the Lindberghs during the prewar period, as well as his correspondence with Anne Morrow Lindbergh during the late thirties and early forties.

The Ninety-Nines, Inc., an organization of international women pilots, also offered valuable assistance. I would like to express my appreciation to Gene

Nora Jessen, the president; to Ruth S. Dobrescu, a personal friend of Mrs. Lindbergh, who provided me with valuable information on the careers of the Mollisons and the Haizlips, two other famous flying couples of the thirties; and to Mrs. Courtney Bargerhuff, for her exhaustive research on my behalf.

Many other people have contributed to this biography, sharing their recollections in interviews or offering leads and encouragement. To all of them, I am immensely grateful: Jill Alexander, Jerry Bauer, Noel Behn, Sir Isaiah Berlin, Max and Renee Bierman, Richard M. Bissell, Jr., Mary Bode, Dr. Porter Brashier, Nikki Brierton, Toni Brown, Kent Chandler, Jr., Robert and Eve Chuse, Ella Merkel DiCarlo, Douglas Fairbanks, Jr., Marjorie Felice, Barbara Fisher, Alan R. Freestone, Constance Fulenwider, Maida Goodwin, Frances Greene, Dr. Ronald Grele, Peggy Guido, Alex and Stephanie Handy, Jon and Wendy Harlow, Janet Holbrook, Lesa M. Holstine, Ann Hook, Lady Shevan Hornby, Elizabeth Hunnewell, Sylvia Hutchinson, Dr. Abe Jankowitz, David Jenness, Joyce Jurnovoy, Dr. Carmela A. Karnoutsos, Ludovic Kennedy, Les Kippel, Carol Klein, Corliss Lamont, Dr. John K. Lattimer, Professor A. W. Lawrence, Reeve Lindbergh, Mrs. Henry Luce III, Florence Lundquist, John Marquand, Jr., Robert McKinstry, Joan Mellen, Horace Perry, Maggie Root, Bill Rowe, Judith Schiff, Gerri Schofield, Janice Selinger, Andrew Silverman, Bette Silverman, Jay Silverman, Peter B. Spivak, Betty Tilson, Lester Trauch, O. G. Villard, Jr., G. A. Vondermuhll, Jr., John and Sylvia Walsh, Cate Woods, and Dr. and Mrs. Ralph Wyckoff. I am also indebted to other persons who for reasons of their own do not wish to be identified.

To the libraries and librarians who assisted me in documenting Anne Morrow Lindbergh's life, I am most grateful: Captiva Memorial Library, Columbia University (Rare Book and Manuscript Library and Oral History Project), the Doylestown and New Hope public libraries, the Museum of Broadcasting, the New Jersey State Library, the New York Public Library, and the Roscoe L. West Library, Trenton State College, Trenton, New Jersey.

Under a Freedom of Information Act request, the Federal Bureau of Investigation released to me their voluminous files on Charles A. Lindbergh. These documents shed considerable light on Lindbergh's political activities prior to World War II.

No biographer could attempt a study of Anne Morrow Lindbergh without knowing a great deal about her husband, and I am grateful to the following biographers of Charles A. Lindbergh for their insights into his enigmatic personality and career: Kenneth S. Davis, *The Hero: Charles A. Lindbergh and the American Dream* (Doubleday, 1959); Walter S. Ross, *The Last Hero: Charles A. Lindbergh* (Harper & Row, 1968); and Leonard Mosley, *Lindbergh: A Biography* (Doubleday, 1976).

David Kirk Vaughan's *Anne Morrow Lindbergh* (Twayne, 1988) is also useful to biographers because it provides a thoughtful analysis of Mrs. Lindbergh's literary works, including the prose and poetry that she wrote while she was a student at Smith College as well as her shorter published pieces.

Cynthia Bayley generously shared with me her experiences in piloting a small aircraft. My thanks to her for answering my endless questions so patiently and for her friendship. I am also indebted to Stacy Schiff, author of a forthcoming biography of Antoine de Saint-Exupéry, who was kind enough to share information and offer leads and practical advice.

It would have been extremely difficult to complete this work without the help of Judith and Philip Toy, who are both gifted poets. I have been fortunate to benefit from their knowledge of poetry, as well as their friendship.

My father-in-law, Robert Silverman, generously donated his services as a photographer. My thanks for his work on behalf of the book and for his unfailing kindness and good humor.

I am also enormously grateful to Margo Shearman for her meticulous copyediting, and to Cindy Spiegel and Amy Hunerwadel of Ticknor & Fields and Becky Saikia-Wilson, Sigrid Wile, and Kathryn Blatt for their editorial assistance.

Three people have helped sustain me during what seemed at times to be an arduous and never-ending task. To my husband, Lance Silverman, my mother, Lucille Fletcher Wallop, and my friend and colleague Marion Meade, I owe gratitude for their encouragement and advice, and, most important, for their love and forbearance.

Finally, I would like to thank my agent at William Morris, Owen Laster, for his sage advice and loyal support during the years, and my editor at Ticknor & Fields, John Herman, a truly traditional editor who cares about his books and inspires his writers to do their best.

Dorothy Herrmann
NEW HOPE, PENNSYLVANIA
1992

Works by Anne Morrow Lindbergh

North to the Orient. New York: Harcourt, Brace, 1935.

Listen! the Wind. New York: Harcourt, Brace, 1938.

The Wave of the Future. New York: Harcourt, Brace, 1940.

The Steep Ascent. New York: Harcourt, Brace, 1944.

Gift from the Sea. New York: Pantheon Books, 1955.

The Unicorn and Other Poems, 1935–1955. New York: Pantheon Books, 1956.

Dearly Beloved. New York: Harcourt, Brace, 1962.

Earth Shine. New York: Harcourt, Brace, 1969.

Bring Me a Unicorn: Diaries and Letters, 1922–1928. New York: Harcourt Brace Jovanovich, 1972.

Hour of Gold, Hour of Lead: Diaries and Letters, 1929–1932. New York: Harcourt Brace Jovanovich, 1973.

Locked Rooms and Open Doors: Diaries and Letters, 1933–1935. New York: Harcourt Brace Jovanovich, 1974.

The Flower and the Nettle: Diaries and Letters, 1936–1939. New York: Harcourt Brace Jovanovich, 1976.

War Within and Without: Diaries and Letters, 1939–1944. New York: Harcourt Brace Jovanovich, 1980.

In addition, Anne Morrow Lindbergh has written numerous poems, articles, essays, prefaces, and reviews. For a complete list of these shorter published works, see David Kirk Vaughan's critical study, *Anne Morrow Lindbergh* (Boston: Twayne, 1988).

Notes

Preface

Page

xv "She has the quiet courage": *Christian Century*, August 14, 1935, p. 1039.

1. "The Sleeping Princess"

1 his estate taxes: George Waller, *Kidnap: The Story of the Lindbergh Case* (New York: Dial Press, 1961), p. 14.

1 kiss him again: Harold Nicolson, *Dwight Morrow* (New York: Harcourt, Brace, 1935), pp. 160–61.

2 aware of her existence: Ibid., pp. 162–63.

3 "physically rather revolting": James Lees-Milne, *Harold Nicolson: A Biography, 1930–1968* (London: Chatto & Windus, 1981), p. 50.

3 wearing his pajamas: Ron Chernow, *The House of Morgan: An American Banking Dynasty and the Rise of Modern Finance* (New York: Atlantic Monthly Press, 1990), p. 288.

3 coal dust: Nicolson, *Dwight Morrow*, p. 9.

5 "Another happy evening": Ibid., p. 83.

6 "It arose from an endeavor": Ibid., p. 126.

6 "*enormously* rich": Ibid., p. 124

6 real values: Ibid., p. 127.

7 "fantastic curlicues of paper": Ibid., pp. 158–59.

7 "frozen landscape of panic": Anne Morrow Lindbergh, *Bring Me a Unicorn: Diaries and Letters of Anne Morrow Lindbergh, 1922–1928* (New York: Harcourt Brace Jovanovich, 1972), p. xx.

8　severe mental illness: Author's interviews with Richard Bissell, Robert McKinstry, and Lester Trauch.

8　found him to be intelligent: Lees-Milne, *Harold Nicolson,* p. 50.

8　"the most wonderful person in the world": Author's interview with Robert McKinstry.

9　"Anne made a solemn compact": Quoted in Nicolson, *Dwight Morrow,* p. 158.

9　let her out: Lindbergh, *Bring Me a Unicorn,* p. xxiii.

9　her awe-inspiring father: Julie Nixon Eisenhower, *Special People* (New York: Simon & Schuster, 1977), p. 127. According to Eisenhower, the headmistress of the Chapin School in New York had asked Anne's class of 1924 to write about the kind of man they wanted to marry, and Anne, who at that time had not met Charles Lindbergh, responded, "I want to marry a hero."

2.　"A Modern Galahad"

10　"I want to go to Vassar!": Lindbergh, *Bring Me a Unicorn,* p. 5.

11　the nineteenth-century feminists: Dorothy M. Brown, *Setting a Course: American Women in the 1920s* (Boston: Twayne, 1987), p. 248.

11　"I want to write": Lindbergh, *Bring Me a Unicorn,* p. 82.

12　after her engagement: David Kirk Vaughan, *Anne Morrow Lindbergh* (Boston: Twayne, 1988), p. 5.

13　"a distinction between diaries and letters": Lindbergh, *Bring Me a Unicorn,* p. xvi.

13　"this marrying business": Ibid., p. 69.

14　an offer which Lindbergh graciously declined: Author's interview with John Marquand, Jr.

15　"a daring man alone": Alden Whitman, "Lindbergh Dies of Cancer in Hawaii at the Age of 72," *New York Times,* August 27, 1974, p. 18.

15　"A disillusioned nation": Frederick Lewis Allen, *Only Yesterday: An Informal History of the 1920's* (New York: Harper & Row, 1931), p. 220.

15　"So avid was the interest": Kenneth S. Davis, *The Hero: Charles A. Lindbergh and the American Dream* (Garden City, N.Y.: Doubleday, 1959), p. 212.

16　two antique celestial and terrestrial globes: Charles A. Lindbergh, *Autobiography of Values* (New York: Harcourt Brace Jovanovich, 1978), p. 318.

16　"aviation has changed into an established business enterprise": *Aviation Week,* August 12, 1991, p. 88.

16　"No living American": Allen, *Only Yesterday,* p. 221.

17　"I'm not sure that he ever knew himself": "Lindbergh," in "The American Experience," produced by Stephen Ives and Ken Burns, written by Geoffrey C. Ward, Public Broadcasting System documentary, 1990.

17 "the sort of man": Bruce L. Larson, *Lindbergh of Minnesota: A Political Biography* (New York: Harcourt Brace Jovanovich, 1971), p. 31.

18 "not good background": Ibid., p. 32.

19 financial interests abroad: Leonard Mosley, *Lindbergh: A Biography* (Garden City, N.Y.: Doubleday, 1976), p. 15.

20 "Lindbergh's character": Larson, *Lindbergh of Minnesota*, p. 207.

20 "see me in prison": Ibid., p. 241.

20 personality was so distant and eccentric: Davis, *The Hero*, p. 54.

20 "stay by the car": Ibid.

21 "The incident left me skeptic": Lindbergh, *Autobiography of Values*, p. 308.

21 His classmates: Davis, *The Hero*, p. 60.

21 "His mother is his only 'girl' ": Ibid., pp. 60–61.

21 "probably more because of its nearby lakes": Brendan Gill, *Lindbergh Alone* (New York: Harcourt Brace Jovanovich, 1977), p. 86.

21 "How wonderful": Charles A. Lindbergh, *The Spirit of St. Louis* (New York: Charles Scribner's Sons, 1953), p. 230.

22 "I ran to the window": Ibid., p. 231.

22 he wanted to fly himself: Lindbergh, *Autobiography of Values*, p. 55.

22 "My early flying": Ibid., p. 9.

22 "The life of an aviator": Ibid., pp. 63–64.

22 "The only modern counterparts": Walter J. Boyne, *The Smithsonian Book of Flight* (Washington, D.C.: Smithsonian Books, 1987), p. 116.

22 A pilot's life: Lindbergh, *Autobiography of Values*, p. 310.

23 "to rationalize away": Ibid., p. 297.

23 wheels sometimes touched: Davis, *The Hero*, p. 128.

24 He squirted mounds: Ibid., p. 117.

24 "his fellow cadets": Gill, *Lindbergh Alone*, p. 97.

25 "When reporters": Ibid., p. 82.

25 "frivolous explanation": "Lindbergh," in "The American Experience."

26 airmail pilots were killed: Ibid.

28 might well have ended in disaster: Boyne, *The Smithsonian Book of Flight*, p. 126.

28 The only clothing: Lindbergh, *Autobiography of Values*, p. 328.

29 "I wanted publicity": Ibid., p. 74.

30 "The national mind": Allen, *Only Yesterday*, p. 190.

30 the tabloids were crowded: Vicki Goldberg, "Voyeurism: The Mass Media and Photography," *New York Times*, March 8, 1992.

30 "Newspapering was entirely different": Author's interview with Alex Handy. Eric Mills, "Chronicler of an Eventful Era," *The Sunday Star* (Easton, Md.), March 15, 1991. Alex Handy, a *New York Daily News* photographer in 1926 and 1927, covered Lindbergh's takeoff from Roosevelt Field. In the next few years he became friendly with the aviator, who

avoided most newspapermen and -women, and was slated to take some formal portraits of Charles, Anne, and Charles, Jr. The child was kidnapped a few weeks later, and the pictures were never made. One of the first members of the press at the Hopewell house after news of the kidnapping was made public, Handy recalls that Colonel Norman Schwarzkopf, superintendent of the New Jersey State Police, wanted him to leave immediately, but Lindbergh told the colonel, "No, let him stay." Handy remembers Schwarzkopf as being "a self-important man who tried to run things and keep people at a distance," while Lindbergh was a man "who'd measure you before he'd say anything." However, at the time of the kidnapping, Lindbergh's determined attitude of aloofness toward the press seemed to falter. According to Handy, he seemed "confused. He didn't know what to say half of the time."

31 "I thought it cheaply sentimental": Lindbergh, *Autobiography of Values,* p. 75.

31 saw translucent figures: Ibid., p. 12.

32 "Life meant more to me than fame": Ibid., p. 320.

33 he was probably "the baseball-player type": Lindbergh, *Bring Me a Unicorn,* p. 89.

33 "Through Morrow, they got Coolidge": Chernow, *The House of Morgan,* p. 291.

34 Morrow himself became Lindbergh's personal financial adviser: Ibid., p. 292.

35 "the capabilities of modern aircraft": Lindbergh, *Autobiography of Values,* p. 83.

35 "to leave the flying problems": Ibid., p. 84.

35 "best maps of Mexico": Ibid., pp. 86–87.

36 "It was perfectly thrilling": Quoted in Nicolson, *Dwight Morrow,* p. 313.

36 "Suddenly, through the canyon": Lindbergh, *Bring Me a Unicorn,* p. 87.

37 "standing against the great stone pillar": Ibid., p. 89.

3. *"The Romance of the Century"*

38 sat tongue-tied with embarrassment: Lindbergh, *Bring Me a Unicorn,* p. 90.

38 "What kind of boy": Ibid.

39 "In her eyes": Davis, *The Hero,* pp. 273–74.

39 "He avoids us": Lindbergh, *Bring Me a Unicorn,* p. 96.

40 "not be happy": Ibid., p. 107.

40 that such a man existed: Ibid., p. 109.

40 "The idea of this clear, direct, straight boy": Ibid., pp. 109–10.

41 The only way: Ibid., pp. 116–17.

41 "The frightful sense of tragedy": Ibid., p. 117.

42   "He will turn quite naturally to E.": Ibid., p. 127.

42   two coveted literary prizes: Anne won the Elizabeth Montagu Prize, an annual award for the best essay on eighteenth-century women or women depicted in the literature of the period, for her paper on Mme d'Houdetot, and the Mary Augusta Jordan Prize for one of her sonnets.

42   "I sat sick with amazement": Ibid., pp. 130–31.

43   "Why do I meet people better": Ibid., p. 137.

43   "that sudden falling down": Ibid., p. 183.

43   "I want to be married": Ibid., p. 187.

44   "the coolest man": Ibid., p. 201.

44   "boots would have helped": Ibid., p. 204.

44   "Oh, it was priceless": Ibid., p. 211.

45   "be *perfectly* natural": Ibid.

45   "tremendous forces in the air": Ibid., p. 212.

46   "He never opens a book": Ibid., p. 226.

46   "Sometimes he will say something": Ibid., p. 239.

46   "He is amazingly understanding": Ibid.

46   "I don't think my parents": "Lindbergh," in "The American Experience."

46   "A barnstormer's relationships with women": Lindbergh, *Autobiography of Values,* p. 121.

47   "A girl should come from a healthy family": Ibid., pp. 118–19.

47   "There is the saying": Ibid., p. 122.

48   "The second daughter, Anne": Ibid., p. 123.

48   "Dating a girl": Ibid., p. 123.

49   "it's quite natural you should be weak": Lindbergh, *Bring Me a Unicorn,* p. 238.

50   "Apparently I am going to marry": Ibid., pp. 248–49.

50   "his lack of sense of humor": Ibid., p. 245.

50   brought her a spoon: P. J. O'Brien, *The Lindberghs: The Story of a Distinguished Family* (International Press, 1935), p. 46.

50   "My mother was surprised": Interview with Anne Morrow Lindbergh, "Crossing the Distance," "American Album," Discovery Channel, 1990.

51   "Although the Morrows were themselves": Quoted in Lees-Milne, *Harold Nicolson,* p. 50.

51   "He's going to marry Anne?": Television interview between Eric Sevareid and Anne Morrow Lindbergh, 1977 (Museum of Broadcasting).

52   "relationships with the press difficult": Lindbergh, *Autobiography of Values,* p. 125.

52   "creative darkness of anonymity": Anne Morrow Lindbergh, *Hour of Gold, Hour of Lead: Diaries and Letters, 1929–1932* (New York: Harcourt Brace Jovanovich, 1973), p. 3.

53   "Now here is the test": Ibid., pp. 17–18.

53 "I am sure *sure sure*": Ibid., p. 21.

4. Soaring

56 "The lid of caution": Lindbergh, *Hour of Gold, Hour of Lead,* p. 4.

56 "a knight in shining armor": Ibid., p. 2.

57 "the most terrible accident": Ibid., p. 72.

57 "Flying with my husband": Lindbergh, *Hour of Gold, Hour of Lead,* p. 6.

58 A daredevil as well as a dreamer: Robert Daley, *An American Saga: Juan Trippe and His Pan Am Empire* (New York: Random House, 1980), pp. 8–9.

59 "difficult from the S-38": Ibid., pp. 74–75.

59 "He was the hero": Ibid., p. 481.

59 "We rose above the harbor": Lindbergh, *Hour of Gold, Hour of Lead,* p. 81.

60 "a matter of course": Ibid., p. 107.

60 The *Sirius . . .* was a two-seater: "Crossing the Distance," in "American Album."

61 "most amazing person": Lindbergh, *Hour of Gold, Hour of Lead,* p. 119.

61 "a charming dignity": Quoted in "Anne Morrow Lindbergh," *Current Biography,* 1940.

61 "Amelia had unlimited admiration": Doris L. Rich, *Amelia Earhart: A Biography* (Washington, D.C.: Smithsonian Institution Press, 1989), pp. 100–101.

61 "Anne, the Colonel and AE": Quoted in Mosley, *Lindbergh: A Biography,* p. 150.

62 "The core of the Lindbergh make-up": George Palmer Putnam, *Wide Margins: A Publisher's Autobiography* (New York: Harcourt, Brace, 1942), pp. 238–40.

63 "greatest adventure": Lindbergh, *Autobiography of Values,* p. 7.

63 his search for ancient cave-dweller ruins: Davis, *The Hero,* p. 279.

63 The only woman: Ibid., p. 282.

64 "could not admit fear to my knight": Lindbergh, *Hour of Gold, Hour of Lead,* p. 8.

64 altitudes above the weather: Davis, *The Hero,* p. 284.

64 "about to have a baby": "Crossing the Distance."

65 "experiment in high-level flying": Quoted in Davis, *The Hero,* p. 284.

65 Many . . . had left the field: Mosley, *Lindbergh: A Biography,* p. 151.

65 "flying around in open cockpits": Lindbergh, *Hour of Gold, Hour of Lead,* pp. 7–8.

66 one of Mrs. Morrow's recently hired servants: Davis, *The Hero,* p. 283.

67 no longer be cooperating with . . . tabloids: Ibid., pp. 283–84.

5. "But She's Crew"

69 "I jumped from bed into a plane, almost": Lindbergh, *Hour of Gold, Hour of Lead,* p. 140.

70 "don't want to 'fondle' ": Ibid., p. 139.

70 "Never hug and kiss them": Quoted in Brown, *Setting a Course,* p. 120.

71 "where we finally built our house": Lindbergh, *Autobiography of Values,* p. 130.

72 "nice to see her": Lindbergh, *Hour of Gold, Hour of Lead,* p. 159.

72 She had always adored flying: Rich, *Amelia Earhart,* p. 100.

72 "it could land in a tree": "Crossing the Distance."

73 "to my husband's expectations": Ibid.

73 "like a queen": Ibid.

74 "boil with anger": Lindbergh, *Hour of Gold, Hour of Lead,* p. 151.

74 public drunkenness: Allen, *Only Yesterday,* p. 25.

74 "drank rather": Harold Nicolson to Vita Sackville-West, September 26, 1934. Sackville-West, V., mss., Lilly Library, Indiana University.

74 "selfish little *arriviste*": Harold Nicolson, *Diaries and Letters, 1930–1939,* ed. Nigel Nicolson (New York: Atheneum, 1966), p. 189.

74 "Dwight is so tired": Nicolson, *Dwight Morrow,* p. 379.

75 "That's nonsense": Quoted in Davis, *The Hero,* p. 295.

75 "Charles, never let yourself worry": Nicolson, *Dwight Morrow,* p. 395.

76 "The island falling away": Anne Morrow Lindbergh, *North to the Orient* (New York: Harcourt, Brace, 1935), pp. 52–53.

77 "Pan Am Radio gear": Daley, *An American Saga,* p. 111.

77 "*She* is *crew*": Lindbergh, *North to the Orient,* p. 61.

77 "equal footing with men": Ibid.

78 "How terrible to be left here": Ibid., p. 78.

78 "some timeless eternity": Ibid., p. 82.

79 "When I left": Ibid., p. 140.

6. "A Very Great Man"

80 "in a place of quiet": Lindbergh, *North to the Orient,* p. 188.

80 "back with the baby": Lindbergh, *Hour of Gold, Hour of Lead,* p. 191.

81 "Little Anne Pan": Ibid., p. 199.

81 "I felt quite exhilarated": Ibid., p. 200.

82 "How long . . . to repair": Ibid.

82 "what a hell of a mess": Nicolson, *Dwight Morrow,* p. 399.

83 "more composure than I can muster": Ronald Steel, *Walter Lippmann and the American Century* (Boston: Little, Brown, 1980), p. 243.

83 "a touch of madness": Nicolson, *Diaries and Letters,* p. 186.

83   "easier for me": Lindbergh, *Hour of Gold, Hour of Lead*, p. 201.
85   "a strong independent boy": Ibid., p. 202.
85   "look like himself ": Ibid., p. 160.
85   "anyone should hurt him": Ibid., p. 203.

7. *"Anne, They Have Stolen Our Baby"*

This chapter, which reconstructs the kidnapping of Charles Augustus Lindbergh, Jr., on March 1, 1932, is based on the files of the New Jersey State Police.

86   "Then my mind": Lindbergh, *Autobiography of Values*, pp. 129–30.
87   "my understanding of mechanical design": Ibid., p. 133.
89   "a highly sensitive girl": quoted in Ludovic Kennedy, *The Airman and the Carpenter: The Lindbergh Kidnapping and the Framing of Richard Hauptmann* (New York: Viking Penguin, 1985), p. 88.

8. *"He Was Such a Gay, Lordly, Assured Little Boy"*

97   "lack of sanity": *New York Times*, March 4, 1932.
97   "armed guards": Chernow, *The House of Morgan*, p. 301.
99   "symbolically perfect for the Depression": Barbara Goldsmith, *Little Gloria: Happy At Last* (New York: Knopf, 1980), p. 195.
99   Marion Parker kidnapping case: Hank Messick and Burt Goldblatt, *Kidnapping: The Illustrated History* (New York: Dial, 1974), pp. 52–56.
99   "Many children of the time": Goldsmith, *Little Gloria*, p. xii.
100 "distracted ghost": Quoted in Kennedy, *The Airman and the Carpenter*, p. 12.
101 "MOTHER MEETS ORDEAL": *New York Times*, March 3, 1932.
101 "MOTHER KEPT BUSY": *New York Times*, March 4, 1932.
102 "so terrifically unreal": Lindbergh, *Hour of Gold, Hour of Lead*, p. 235.
103 "an ultimate fortress": Ibid., p. 274.
103 "C. is *marvelous*": Ibid., p. 226.
103 "In a survey": Ibid.
104 "Their knowledge": Ibid., pp. 225–26.
105 "the two underworld kings": Ibid., p. 230.
106 Condon's account of his role as intermediary: Quoted in Kennedy, *The Airman and the Carpenter*, p. 98.
106 "scenario etched by Condon": Ibid.
107 "through letters": Lindbergh, *Hour of Gold, Hour of Lead*, p. 239.
107 "old and kindly professor": Lindbergh, *Autobiography of Values*, p. 140.
107 "sincere appreciation": Quoted in Walter S. Ross, *The Last Hero: Charles A. Lindbergh* (New York: Harper & Row, 1964), p. 208.
107 "a screwball": Quoted in Kennedy, *The Airman and the Carpenter*, p. 125.

109 "a sense of peace": *Hour of Gold, Hour of Lead,* p. 247. In 1932 a Mercer County coroner found that Charles Augustus, Jr., died of "a fractured skull due to external violence" (that is, caused by a fall when a ladder rung broke and the kidnapper accidentally dropped the burlap bag into which he had been placed). Some modern forensic experts, however, are not altogether convinced that the child's death was caused by a fractured skull, or, in fact, that it was accidental. In 1983 Dr. Michael M. Baden, deputy chief medical examiner of Suffolk County, Hauppauge, New York, wrote that "skull fractures in themselves do not cause death, but rather significant injuries to the brain" and that the child's brain was not described at all in the autopsy. He also points out that there were many people in the house on the evening of March 1, 1932, including Charles Lindbergh, who was in the room below, and that "a kidnapper could not rely upon the baby not crying out." In addition, the "perforated fractures" on both sides of the skull which the coroner noted postmortem could have been caused after the baby's death, perhaps when the body was thrown into a hasty grave in the woods or by wild animals or by the natural process of decomposition, which affects the bodies of children differently from the way it affects those of adults, so that "natural suture lines may separate and give the appearance of fracture lines." It was Dr. Baden's opinion that although the "circumstances of death and the autopsy description are consistent with the baby having died from cranio-cerebral trauma, perhaps in a fall, . . . the possibilities that the child was intentionally murdered by suffocation or strangulation while still in his crib cannot be excluded." (See M. M. Baden, "The Lindbergh Kidnapping: Review of the Autopsy Evidence," *Journal of Forensic Sciences* [JFSCA] 28:4 [October 1983]: 1071–75.)

110 Excerpts from Anne Morrow Lindbergh's diary entries, May 13–20, 1932: *Hour of Gold, Hour of Lead,* pp. 248–55.

112 "only I am old": Ibid., p. 256.

112 "He is gone": Ibid., p. 291.

9. Victims

113 "lost your faith": Lindbergh, *Hour of Gold, Hour of Lead,* p. 271.

114 "Life is captive": Ibid., p. 259.

115 "women take and conquer sorrow": Ibid., p. 268.

115 "old ladies": Ibid., p. 267.

116 "the publicity": Ibid., p. 297.

116 "do anything constructive": Ibid., p. 271.

117 Charles Lindbergh's reaction to Curtis's hoax: Mosley, *Lindbergh,* p. 164.

118 Anne's return to Hopewell: Lindbergh, *Hour of Gold, Hour of Lead*, p. 280.

118 "And I went towards him": Ibid., pp. 308–9.

118 "another house": Ibid., p. 284.

119 "this dog": Ibid., p. 287.

119 Anne's second delivery: Ibid., pp. 298–99.

120 "a door to life": Ibid., pp. 300–301.

120 Anne's reaction to new baby: Ibid., pp. 310–11.

123 "This was the old Elisabeth": Ibid., p. 322.

124 "*It did not happen*": Anne Morrow Lindbergh, *Locked Rooms and Open Doors: Diaries and Letters, 1933–1935* (New York: Harcourt Brace Jovanovich, 1974), pp. 12–13.

124 "The punctuation of anniversaries": Ibid., p. 17.

124 Psychological symptoms of crime victims: Sherrye Henry, "Can a Marriage Survive Tragedy?" *Parade*, July 15, 1990; J. L. Barkas, *Victims* (New York: Charles Scribner's Sons, 1978).

125 "that's exactly what he would do": "Lindbergh," in "American Experience."

10. *"Where Is My World?"*

127 "a clear calm light": Lindbergh, *Locked Rooms and Open Doors*, p. 24.

128 Dangers of survey flights: "Crossing the Distance," in "American Album."

128 "joined together the continents": Ibid.

128 world record: Lindbergh, *Locked Rooms and Open Doors*, p. 158.

128 The Mollisons: John P. V. Heinmuller, *Man's Fight to Fly* (New York: Funk & Wagnalls, 1944), pp. 183–92; Mary S. Lovell, *Straight on Till Morning: The Biography of Beryl Markham* (New York: St. Martin's, 1987), p. 199.

129 James and Mary Haizlip: Newspaper clippings, unidentified source.

130 "Very bad for you": Lindbergh, *Locked Rooms and Open Doors*, p. 110.

131 " 'handmaid to the Lord' ": Ibid., p. 107.

131 "in C.'s world": Ibid., p. 69.

131 "in a panic": Ibid., p. 148.

131 Florence Klingensmith's crash: Newspaper clippings, unidentified source.

132 William Hopson's death: Boyne, *Smithsonian Book of Flight*, p. 115.

132 "have faith in him": Lindbergh, *Locked Rooms and Open Doors*, p. 140.

132 "All this visit": Ibid., p. 127.

133 "Jon seems so wonderful": Ibid., p. 192.

134 Details of Bruno Hauptmann's arrest: George Waller, *Kidnap: The Story of the Lindbergh Case* (New York: Dial, 1961), pp. 212–16.

135   "a note at midnight": *Locked Rooms and Open Doors,* p. 202.
136   "eternal struggle": Ibid., p. 221.

11. *"The Geisha"*

137   "It was a brave gamble": Nicolson, *Diaries and Letters,* p. 175.
138   Anne's impressions of Harold Nicolson: *Locked Rooms and Open Doors,* p. 208.
138   Nicolson's impressions of the Lindberghs: *Diaries and Letters,* pp. 131–32.
138   "Anne like a Geisha": Ibid., p. 180.
139   a treatise: Lees-Milne, *Harold Nicolson,* p. 51.
139   "He is a very decent man": Harold Nicolson to Vita Sackville-West, October 13, 1934, Sackville-West, V., mss., Lilly Library, Indiana University, Bloomington, Indiana.
139   "He amuses and puzzles me": Nicolson, *Diaries and Letters,* pp. 182–83.
140   "this dramatic event": Ibid., p. 184.
140   "take another trip": Lindbergh, *Locked Rooms and Open Doors,* p. 209.
141   "a sudden recognition": Ibid., p. 210.
141   "Anne is so modest": Harold Nicolson to Vita Sackville-West, October 14, 1934, Sackville-West, V., mss., Lilly Library, Indiana University.
142   Vita's opinion of Anne's writing: Vita Sackville-West to Harold Nicolson, October 28, 1934, ibid.
142   "Some terrible fate": Harold Nicolson to Vita Sackville-West, November 23–24, 1934, Sackville-West, V., mss., Lilly Library, Indiana University.
143   "feel terrified": Lindbergh, *Locked Rooms and Open Doors,* p. 218.
144   "An observant person": Nicolson, *Diaries and Letters,* p. 191.
144   "All life ahead of me": Lindbergh, *Locked Rooms and Open Doors,* pp. 223–24.
145   writing had become even more important: Ibid., p. 229.
145   "write it out": Ibid.
145   "not to disappoint C.": Ibid., p. 232.

12. *Witness*

146   "frosted picture postcard": Quoted in Julie Goldsmith Gilbert, *Ferber: A Biography* (Garden City, N.Y.: Doubleday, 1978), p. 324.
147   Anne Morrow Lindbergh's direct examination by David Wilentz is taken from the transcript of the trial proceedings, *State of New Jersey v. Bruno Richard Hauptmann.*
147   Prostitutes working the streets: Mosley, *Lindbergh,* p. 188.

150   his young daughter, Dorothy: Lee Israel, *Kilgallen* (New York: Dela-corte, 1979), pp. 40–41.

150   "take careful handling": Adela Rogers St. Johns, *The Honeycomb* (Garden City, N.Y.: Doubleday, 1969), p. 288.

151   Excerpts from Adela Rogers St. Johns's columns: Quoted in Israel, *Kilgallen*, p. 43.

151   "I carried Anne Lindbergh": St. Johns, *The Honeycomb*, p. 344.

151   "I only saw them": Ibid., pp. 291–92.

152   "Great Moment": Ibid., p. 320.

152   "We who sit": Ibid., p. 319.

152   "Hauptmann's trial" : Alexander Woollcott, *The Portable Woollcott*, selected by Joseph Hennessey (New York: Viking, 1946), p. 575.

153   "I read the papers": Lindbergh, *Locked Rooms and Open Doors*, p. 249.

153   "On top of his sorrow": St. Johns, *The Honeycomb*, pp. 308–9.

154   "That pale profile": Lindbergh, *Locked Rooms and Open Doors*, p. 247.

154   Wood experts' testimony: Samuel G. Blackman, "The Trial of the Century," Associated Press, *Doylestown Intelligencer*, January 26, 1992; Waller, *Kidnap;* and Kennedy, *The Airman and the Carpenter*.

157   "Mr. Hearst took a poll": St. Johns, *The Honeycomb*, p. 340.

157   "reads more impartial": Harold Nicolson to Vita Sackville-West, February 14, 1935, Sackville-West, V., mss., Lilly Library, Indiana University.

158   Two radios were on: Ibid.

159   "That howling mob": Lindbergh, *Locked Rooms and Open Doors*, p. 249.

160   Kennedy's impression: Letter to author, June 12, 1990.

13. Interim

162   "good story": Lindbergh, *Locked Rooms and Open Doors*, p. 270.

162   "there is a place": Ibid., p. 271.

163   "a sense of drama": *Books*, August 18, 1935, p. 1.

163   "the seeing eye": *Saturday Review*, August 17, 1935, p. 6.

163   "delicate intimacy": Lewis Gannett, *New York Herald Tribune*, August 15, 1935, p. 16.

163   a copy to Virginia Woolf: *The Diary of Virginia Woolf*, vol. 4, 1931–1935, ed. Anne Olivier Bell (New York: Harcourt Brace Jovanovich, 1982), p. 335. Woolf's reaction to *North to the Orient* is unknown, but her husband, Leonard, liked Anne's work, defending it in a letter written in 1957 to a friend who had criticized him for his choice of authors as "not . . . in the very least degree bogus — sentimental, yes, but not bogus." *Letters of Leonard Woolf*, ed. Frederic Spotts (San Diego: Harcourt Brace Jovanovich, 1989), p. 360.

164   "give degrees": Lindbergh, *Locked Rooms and Open Doors*, pp. 253–54.

165 killed his nephew: New Jersey State Police files, letter dated May 13, 1932, from Michael H. Crowley, Superintendent of Police, Boston, Massachusetts, to Colonel H. Norman Schwarzkopf.

165 Dwight Morrow's will: Last will and testament of Dwight W. Morrow, dated January 24, 1927, filed and proved October 23, 1931, Bergen County, New Jersey, B11957.

165 "feel my heritage": Lindbergh, *Locked Rooms and Open Doors*, p. 288.

166 "wasn't worth talking to": Ibid., p. 275.

166 "baffles me": Ibid., p. 264.

169 a sizable bonus: Ferdinand Lundberg, *Imperial Hearst: A Social Biography* (New York: Arno & New York Times, 1970), p. 307.

170 "All my life": Lindbergh, *Locked Rooms and Open Doors*, p. 331.

14. Days of Heaven

172 Description of Long Barn: Nigel Nicolson, *Portrait of a Marriage* (New York: Atheneum, 1973), pp. 193–94.

173 some primroses: Victoria Glendinning, *Vita: The Life of Vita Sackville-West* (New York: Knopf, 1983), p. 77.

174 "A puissant blend of both sexes": Ibid., p. 286.

174 "metal meeting metal": Anne Morrow Lindbergh, *The Flower and the Nettle: Diaries and Letters, 1936–1939* (New York: Harcourt Brace Jovanovich, 1976), p. 28.

174 "suffered much more": Ibid., pp. 28–29.

175 "their marriage": Nicolson, *Portrait of a Marriage*, p. ix.

175 "Harold, I am sad": Ibid., pp. 98–99.

175 "could not relate easily": Glendinning, *Vita*, p. 131.

175 "The Lindberghs": Vita Sackville-West to Harold Nicolson, March 4, 1936, Sackville-West, V., mss., Lilly Library, Indiana University.

176 "they might be arriving": Ibid., September 2, 1936.

176 "No sir": Nicolson, *Diaries and Letters*, p. 247.

176 "inviting the lightning": Waller, *Kidnap*, p. 591.

177 "strange feeling": Lindbergh, *The Flower and the Nettle*, p. 29.

177 "It isn't really time": Ibid., pp. 20–21.

178 "something undefined": Ibid., p. 114.

178 "I had foreseen it": Ibid., p. 11.

179 "Who am I": Ibid., p. 44.

179 "That marriage": Ibid., p. 73.

180 "so much piecing": Ibid., p. 167.

180 "But I think": Ibid., p. 124.

181 "Those who have murdered": Alexis Carrel, *Man, the Unknown* (New York: Harper & Brothers, 1935), pp. 318–19.

181   "bore an uncanny resemblance": Mosley, *Lindbergh*, p. 220.

182   "Is the emphasis correct?": Lindbergh, *The Flower and the Nettle*, p. 90.

182   "women should develop": Carrel, *Man, the Unknown*, pp. 89–90.

182   "women should receive a higher education": Ibid., p. 302.

182   "females, at any rate": Ibid., p. 92.

182   "compact, alert": Lindbergh, *The Flower and the Nettle*, p. 66.

182   "an incredibly strong": Ibid., p. 44.

183   "Seeing their strength": Ibid., p. 108.

184   "appearance of youth": Ibid., p. 50.

184   "beautifully dressed": Ibid., p. 51.

184   "I have had so much": Michael Bloch, ed., *Wallis & Edward: Letters 1931–1937, The Intimate Correspondence of the Duke and Duchess of Windsor* (New York: Summit Books, Simon & Schuster, 1986), p. 212.

185   "a real person": Lindbergh, *The Flower and the Nettle*, p. 53.

185   "with my well-known charm": Quoted in Nicolson, *Diaries and Letters*, p. 263.

185   "in the name of General Göring": Quoted in Mosley, *Lindbergh*, p. 210.

186   Lindbergh's reply to Truman Smith: Ibid., pp. 211–12.

15. *"A Pair of Unicorns"*

187   "Aviation has brought": Quoted in Mosley, *Lindbergh*, pp. 216–17.

188   "blurred uncomfortable patches": Lindbergh, *The Flower and the Nettle*, p. 101.

188   "To me, Nazi Germany": Lindbergh, *Autobiography of Values*, p. 156.

189   "The Olympic games": William L. Shirer, *The Rise and Fall of the Third Reich: A History of Nazi Germany* (New York: Simon & Schuster, 1960), pp. 232–33.

189   "I was surprised": William L. Shirer, *The Nightmare Years, 1930–1940* (Boston: Little, Brown, 1984), pp. 236–38.

191   "Do you see": Vita Sackville-West to Harold Nicolson, June 23, 1937, Sackville-West, V., mss., Lilly Library, Indiana University.

191   *"My brother"*: Lindbergh, *The Flower and the Nettle*, p. 164.

191   "my two little boys": Ibid., p. 169.

191   "his investigation": Ibid., p. 176.

192   "Germans were so obviously friendly": Mosley, *Lindbergh*, p. 224.

192   manuscript about new apparatus: After five years of work, Lindbergh succeeded in developing a perfusion pump that could be used in experimental work. In April 1935, he and Carrel cultivated an entire organ (a cat's thyroid gland) successfully in vitro for the first time. In the following months, using Lindbergh's pump, Carrel and his colleagues were able to perfuse animal spleens, kidneys, and pituitaries. Three years later, in 1938, Carrel and Lindbergh published a book, *The Culture of Organs*, in

which they envisioned the day when "organs removed from the human body, in the course of an operation or soon after death, could be revived in the Lindbergh pump, and made to function again when perfused with an artificial pump."

Lindbergh's biomedical interests became secondary when he got involved with opposing the U.S. entry into World War II. However, in the mid-1960s, scientists at the Naval Medical Research Institute duplicated the Lindbergh-Carrel perfusion pump, and attempted to repeat their experiments with varying degrees of success until Lindbergh himself came to the laboratory and made the pumps operate properly. He subsequently designed a new perfusion pump, but it was never widely used as it had to be operated manually.

192 "Obtain technical parity with the U.S.A.": Quoted in Wayne S. Cole, *Charles A. Lindbergh and the Battle Against Intervention in World War II* (New York: Harcourt Brace Jovanovich, 1974), p. 37.

193 "Your father must go": Lindbergh, *The Flower and the Nettle*, p. 190.

193 "the excitement": Ibid., p. 203.

193 "Lindberghs . . . were not there": Vita Sackville-West to Harold Nicolson, December 7, 1937, Sackville-West, V., mss., Lilly Library, Indiana University.

194 "tough with his little boy": Author's interview with Nigel Nicolson.

194 "rather live on Saint Gildas": Quoted in Theodore I. Malinen, *Surgery and Life: The Extraordinary Career of Alexis Carrel* (New York: Harcourt Brace Jovanovich, 1979), p. 145.

195 foreigners were not allowed: Ibid.

195 "control my life": Lindbergh, *The Flower and the Nettle*, p. 273.

196 "I *wrote* better": Ibid., p. 519.

196 "The trees": Ibid., p. 494.

196 "She looked quite lovely": Ibid., pp. 253–54.

196 "happy at Long Barn": Vita Sackville-West to Harold Nicolson, May 24, 1938, Sackville-West, V., mss., Lilly Library, Indiana University.

197 "the Lindberghs are the last people": Ibid., June 14, 1938.

197 Violently against the Nazis: Nicolson had his own brief brush with fascism. During the Depression he joined Sir Oswald Mosley, later a professed fascist, in his New Party, becoming editor of *Action*, its weekly paper. However, Nicolson rapidly became disenchanted with the New Party's growing identification with Hitlerism. Although he was still fond of Mosley, he broke their association.

After finishing his biography of Dwight Morrow, Nicolson, a former diplomat, became active in politics again. In 1935, he was elected to the House of Commons as a right-wing Labourite, and he became popular in the late thirties for his firm stand against Hitler and Mussolini.

197 "Lindbergh is most pessimistic": Nicolson, *Diaries and Letters*, p. 343.

198 "Germany's overwhelming air superiority": Cole, *Charles A. Lindbergh*, pp. 48–49.

198 "[Lady Astor] wants better understanding": Charles A. Lindbergh, *The Wartime Journals of Charles A. Lindbergh* (New York: Harcourt Brace Jovanovich, 1970), p. 26.

199 "gay and spontaneous": Lindbergh, *The Flower and the Nettle*, p. 128.

199 "a Mae West sort": Ibid., p. 262.

199 "*not* the intelligent": Ibid., p. 256.

199 "*the* nicest man": Ibid., p. 255.

199 "loss of European civilization": Quoted in Mosley, *Lindbergh*, pp. 229–30.

200 "His estimates": Anne Morrow Lindbergh, *War Within and Without: Diaries and Letters, 1939–1944* (New York: Harcourt Brace Jovanovich, 1980), p. xvi.

201 "strong Quaker influence": Author's interview with Robert McKinstry.

201 "watching the dead": Lindbergh, *The Flower and the Nettle*, pp. 409–10.

201 "I do not agree": Ibid., p. 412.

202 "the 'simple' life": Ibid., p. xv.

202 "There is never": Ibid., p. 325.

202 "one of the days": Ibid., p. 380.

202 "the Ambassador invited Anne and I": Lindbergh, *Wartime Journals*, p. 47.

203 "thousands of living beings": Lindbergh, *Autobiography of Values*, pp. 392–94.

203 "reached the frontier": Ibid., p. 134.

203 "an eerie feeling": Ibid., p. 370.

204 "a straight face": Lindbergh, *The Flower and the Nettle*, p. 150.

204 "larger project": Ibid., p. 336.

204 "I don't want much": Ibid.

205 "I watch C.": Ibid., p. 337.

205 "out of sympathy": Ibid., p. 348.

206 "liking the Russians": Ibid., p. 361.

206 "The account of Chamberlain": Ibid., p. 419.

207 "I keep longing": Ibid., p. 421.

207 "How strangely": Ibid., p. 505.

207 "Whereas I hated": Ibid., p. 507.

207 "hoped the visit": Ibid., p. 425.

208 "If any doubt": Lindbergh, *Autobiography of Values*, p. 180.

208 "the Fascist group": Lindbergh, *Wartime Journals*, p. 75.

208 "I am startled": Lindbergh, *The Flower and the Nettle*, pp. 429–30.

209 "with the German Eagle": Lindbergh, *Wartime Journals*, p. 102.

209 "C. came back late": Lindbergh, *The Flower and the Nettle*, p. 437.

209 "When Colonel Lindbergh": Quoted in Mosley, *Lindbergh*, p. 235.

209 "the story of ten days": *New York Times Book Review,* October 16, 1938, p. 1.

209 "Mrs. Lindbergh writes well": *New Yorker,* October 15, 1938, p. 92.

210 "They do not see": Lindbergh, *The Flower and the Nettle,* p. 438.

210 "The German-Jewish business": Joseph P. Lash, *A World of Love: Eleanor Roosevelt and Her Friends* (Garden City, N.Y.: Doubleday, 1982), p. 264.

210 "get to feeling": Lindbergh, *The Flower and the Nettle,* p. 450.

210 "such unfair labeling": Ibid., p. 470.

211 "naturally oversensitive Jews": Ibid., p. 471.

211 "that extra thrill": Ibid., p. 550.

211 "superb for C.": Ibid., p. 538.

211 "The *lies*": Ibid., p. 510.

212 "Frida Rivera is there": Ibid., p. 559.

212 "instinctively angry": Ibid., p. 554.

212 "upon his [Hitler's] wisdom": Lindbergh, *Wartime Journals,* p. 173.

213 "How can democracy": Ibid., p. 166.

213 "less crime": Ibid.

213 "If there was to be war": Lindbergh, *Autobiography of Values,* p. 187.

214 "where freedom ends": Lindbergh, *Wartime Journals,* pp. 182–83.

214 "lacked a statesman's wisdom": Lindbergh, *Autobiography of Values,* p. 192.

16. *"Poor Anne"*

215 "very beautiful woman": Lindbergh, *Locked Rooms and Open Doors,* p. 273.

216 "accurate picture": Quoted in Lindbergh, *War Within and Without,* p. xvii.

217 "false high-pressuring newspapers": Lindbergh, *War Within and Without,* pp. 4–5.

217 "extravagance": Ibid., p. 17.

217 "romance of my own life": Ibid., p. 18.

217 "all I ever wanted to say": Ibid., p. 21.

218 "drunken aviators": Ibid., pp. 21–22.

218 "gay, freed and happy": Ibid., p. 23.

219 "long and terrible week": Ibid., p. 44.

220 "full horror": Ibid., pp. 47–48.

221 "this country pushed": Lindbergh, *Wartime Journals,* p. 252.

221 "turn from our quarrels": Charles A. Lindbergh, "Aviation, Geography and Race," *Reader's Digest,* November 1939.

221 "The speech is good": Lindbergh, *War Within and Without,* pp. 52–53.

222 "These wars in Europe": Quoted in Mosley, *Lindbergh,* pp. 259–60.

222   "direct and honest": Lindbergh, *War Within and Without*, p. 221.

222   "the surgeon's scalpel": Anne Morrow Lindbergh, *The Unicorn and Other Poems* (New York: Pantheon, 1956), p. 42.

223   "to come to Washington": Lindbergh, *War Within and Without*, p. 55.

224   "petty . . . mudslinging": Ibid., p. 59.

224   "a Nazi lover": Steel, *Walter Lippmann*, p. 375.

224   "such a temptation": Lindbergh, *War Within and Without*, p. 66.

224   "almost with ferocity": *Spectator*, reprinted in the *New York Times*, October 22, 1939.

225   "C. is criminally misunderstood": Lindbergh, *War Within and Without*, p. 65.

225   "Lindbergh's isolationist stand": Ibid., p. xxv.

226   "The place has changed": Lindbergh, *Wartime Journals*, p. 213.

227   "Anne has the courage": Ibid., p. 291.

227   "the best magazine": Ibid.

228   "doing something essential": Ibid., p. 292.

228   "speaking as a woman": "Prayer for Peace," *Reader's Digest*, January 1940, pp. 1–8.

228   "other Hitlers": Ibid.

17. *Working for Charles*

230   "that fellow Hauptmann": Alexander Woollcott, *The Letters of Alexander Woollcott*, ed. Beatrice Kaufman and Joseph Hennessey (New York: Viking, 1944), p. 243.

231   "after the radio speech": Chernow, *The House of Morgan*, p. 446.

232   "I urge the sending": Quoted in "Elizabeth Cutter Morrow," *Current Biography, Who's News and Why*, (New York: H. W. Wilson, 1943), p. 539.

232   "converted me": Lindbergh, *War Within and Without*, p. xiv.

232   "a beautiful speech": Ibid., p. 99.

232   "a smart trick": Quoted in Chernow, *The House of Morgan*, p. 447.

233   "without weakening amendments": "Elizabeth Cutter Morrow," *Current Biography*, p. 539.

233   "its hypocrisy": Ibid.

233   "deepening danger": Ibid.

233   "reference to France": Lindbergh, *Wartime Journals*, p. 358.

234   "I feel uneasy": Lindbergh, *War Within and Without*, p. 108.

234   "he still looks young": Journals of Selden Rodman, unpublished.

236   "C. back": Lindbergh, *War Within and Without*, pp. 120–21.

237   "goes over the record": Ibid., p. 129.

237   "you ask too much": Ibid., p. 130.

237   "richest writing": Ibid., p. 91.

237 "fungus quality": Ibid., p. 92.

238 " 'The hysterical chatter' ": *New York Times,* May 20, 1940.

238 "unmindful": Lindbergh, *War Within and Without,* p. 137.

238 used the "wave" metaphor: Davis, *The Hero,* p. 401.

238 "*had* to write it": Lindbergh, *War Within and Without,* p. 142.

239 "cannot agree": Ibid., pp. 99–100.

18. *The Wave of the Future*

240 "This is not to claim": Anne Morrow Lindbergh, *The Wave of the Future: A Confession of Faith* (New York: Harcourt, Brace, 1940), pp. 18–19.

240 "the wave of the future": Ibid., p. 37.

241 "They are *sins*": Ibid., p. 11.

241 "the Bible of every American Nazi": Quoted in Mosley, *Lindbergh,* p. 275.

241 "There are men who believe": Quoted in Frank Freidel, *Franklin D. Roosevelt: A Rendezvous with Destiny* (New York: Little, Brown, 1990), p. 364.

241 "Is propaganda": Quoted in Laurence Bergreen, *As Thousands Cheer: The Life of Irving Berlin* (New York: Viking, 1990), pp. 383–84.

242 "If one adds": *Washington Star,* April 25, 1941. Dorothy Thompson's dislike of Lindbergh appears to have started when she was the victim of one of his practical jokes. In 1930, when both she and Lindbergh were guests at a dinner party, Lindbergh poured mouthwash in a rare Burgundy wine that had been decanted on a sideboard. According to Vincent Sheean, author of *Dorothy and Red,* Dorothy, who was pregnant at the time, had "a real respect for good wine" and thought Lindbergh's joke "was an atrocious one." "She never forgot it; it formed, or helped to form, her impression of him; and ten years later, when he spoke for the isolationists . . . and she was one of the leading interventionists in the early stages of World War II, she made two tremendous attacks on him," Sheean wrote. "I do not believe that Dorothy could have been so thunderous on this subject if she had not retained a vivid personal distaste based upon the experience of that practical joke. To a pregnant woman at a dinner party with total strangers a glass of Burgundy with Listerine in it must have been a horrid infliction." (See Vincent Sheean, *Dorothy and Red* [Boston: Houghton Mifflin, 1963], pp. 172–73.)

242 "a disturbed and vicious man": Alan Brinkley, *Voices of Protest: Huey Long, Father Coughlin, and the Great Depression* (New York: Knopf, 1982), p. 275.

243 "never . . . had any contact": Lindbergh, *Wartime Journals,* p. 684.

243 "a subpoena was something": Ibid., p. 688.

243 "the episode": Cole, *Charles A. Lindbergh,* p. 230.

243 "I met Lawrence Dennis": Ibid., p. 255.

243 "Your book": Quoted in Mosley, *Lindbergh*, pp. 275–76.

243 "It is called 'a confession of faith' ": E. B. White, *One Man's Meat*, new and enlarged ed. (New York: Harper & Brothers, 1944), pp. 203–10.

244 "never said Totalitarianism": Lindbergh, *War Within and Without*, p. 170.

244 "a movement of adjustment": Ibid., p. 174.

244 stop being a writer: Eisenhower, *Special People*, p. 140.

244 "I am hurt": Lindbergh, *War Within and Without*, p. 148.

245 "could breathe with them": Ibid., p. 150.

246 "local America First Committee branches": Senator William Benton, Columbia University Oral History Research Office, Butler Library, Columbia University, New York.

246 "The young on our side": Lindbergh, *War Within and Without*, p. 179.

247 "about the Jewish problem": Ibid., p. 185.

247 "more of a feminist": Ibid., p. 209.

247 "the kind of heroic": Quoted in W. A. Swanberg, *Norman Thomas: The Last Idealist* (New York: Scribner's, 1976), p. 245.

248 "If I did not tender": Lindbergh, *Wartime Journals*, p. 480.

248 "respected his . . . feelings": Lindbergh, *War Within and Without*, pp. 181–82.

249 "occupied with C.": Ibid., p. 196.

249 "It is so strange": Ibid., pp. 196–97.

250 "a great figure in a tan raincoat": Ibid., p. 200.

250 "Hearst has been assisting": Lindbergh, *Wartime Journals*, p. 526.

251 "didn't understand in my own phone conversations": Ibid., p. 515.

252 "He [Leon] advised": Charles A. Lindbergh, Federal Bureau of Investigation files, File No. 65-11449, report dated April 10, 1942.

252 "The files": Ibid., report dated August 21, 1942, p. 5.

253 "interview with Henry Ford": Ibid., report dated December 13, 1941.

253 "Henry Ford stated": Ibid.

254 "Dear General": Ibid., letter dated September 8, 1954.

254 "Dennis stated": Ibid., report dated August 21, 1942, p. 11.

255 "Lawrence Dennis is by far": Lindbergh, *War Within and Without*, pp. 151–52.

255 "The Bureau slept": Ovid Demaris, *The Director: An Oral Biography of J. Edgar Hoover* (New York: Harper's Magazine Press, 1975), pp. 55–56.

256 "time of the trial": Curt Gentry, *J. Edgar Hoover: The Man and the Secrets* (New York: Norton, 1991), p. 163.

256 "On May 16, 1940": Ibid., pp. 225–27.

257 "portions of everyone's life": Lindbergh, *Wartime Journals*, p. 519.

258 "For six months": Lindbergh, *War Within and Without*, p. 166.

258 "the depth of her depression": Lindbergh, *Wartime Journals*, pp. 502–3.

259 "Lindbergh is living": Charles Lindbergh, Federal Bureau of Investigation files, report dated December 11, 1941.

259 " 'enemy Americans' ": Ibid., report dated December 24, 1941.

260 "lots of things . . . I don't like": Lindbergh, *War Within and Without*, p. 213.

260 "understand why the Jewish people": Quoted in *Des Moines Register*, September 12, 1941.

261 "touch the Jews at all": Lindbergh, *War Within and Without*, pp. 220–21.

261 "the Jewish paragraph": Ibid., p. 221.

261 "Denunciations were most concentrated": Cole, *Charles A. Lindbergh*, pp. 173–74.

261 "like a Lazarus": Lindbergh, *War Within and Without*, p. 223.

261 "What *time* marriage takes": Ibid.

262 "a bid for anti-Semitism": Ibid., pp. 223–24.

262 "this country at war": Ibid., p. 224.

262 "worded my Des Moines address": Lindbergh, *Wartime Journals*, p. 539.

262 following his father's example: Cole, *Charles A. Lindbergh*, p. 19.

262 "Didn't our friend Lindbergh": Swanberg, *Norman Thomas*, p. 254.

263 "a lot of fanfare": Lindbergh, *War Within and Without*, p. 241.

263 "[war] has come": quoted in Cole, *Charles A. Lindbergh*, p. 209.

263 "I want another one": Lindbergh, *War Within and Without*, p. 243.

264 "Anne is bearing": Lindbergh, *Wartime Journals*, p. 572.

19. Outcast

265 "bear this lie": Lindbergh, *War Within and Without*, p. 359.

265 "injure a writer": Ibid., pp. 250–51.

266 "To accept Lindbergh's offer": Letter from Harold L. Ickes to Franklin Delano Roosevelt, December 30, 1941, quoted in Mosley, *Lindbergh*, p. 308.

267 "Anti-Semitism": Robert Lacey, *Ford: The Men and the Machine* (Boston: Little, Brown, 1986), p. 229.

267 "professed surprise": Ibid., p. 405.

267 dined at Ford's home: James D. Newton, *Uncommon Friends: Life with Thomas Edison, Henry Ford, Harvey Firestone, Alexis Carrel, and Charles Lindbergh* (New York: Harcourt Brace Jovanovich, 1987), p. 218.

268 "a compact little man": Lindbergh, *War Within and Without*, p. 285.

268 "how little of him": Ibid., p. 251.

268 "ersatz elegance": Ibid., p. 274.

269 "There is a stillness": Ibid., pp. 284–85.

269 "suffering isn't enough": Ibid., p. 258.

270 named him Scott: Mosley, *Lindbergh*, p. 318.

270 "Continuing manufacturing tie-ups": Lacey, *Ford*, pp. 412–13.

270 "Mass shootings": Lindbergh, *War Within and Without*, p. 306.

270 "other races": Ibid., p. 277.

270   "It is hard . . . to participate": Ibid., p. 416.

271   "blind bombing": Ibid., p. 421.

271   "my lonely bed": Ibid., p. 373.

272   "It was for *Europe*": Ibid., pp. 370–71.

272   "not content to write anything": Ibid., p. 324.

272   "Writing . . . is exhausting": Ibid., pp. 325–26.

272   "three big things": Ibid., p. 328.

273   "no discussion of the scene": Stephen Birmingham, *The Late John Marquand* (Philadelphia: Lippincott, 1972), pp. 157–60.

274   "You learn nothing": Lindbergh, *War Within and Without*, p. 339.

274   "Anything so beautiful": Ibid., p. 382.

274   "What a crippling art": Ibid., p. 353.

275   "Writing comes out of life": Ibid., p. 360.

275   "It is my flywheel": Ibid.

276   "This then was life": Anne Morrow Lindbergh, *The Steep Ascent* (New York: Harcourt, Brace, 1944), p. 111.

276   "flight over the Alps": Lindbergh, *War Within and Without*, p. 331.

276   "It would be a pity": Amy Loveman, *Saturday Review*, March 18, 1944, p. 12.

277   "most arresting short novels": *New Yorker*, April 1, 1944, p. 82.

277   "an adventure story": Beatrice Sherman, *New York Times Book Review*, March 19, 1944, p. 3.

277   "make a man happy": Lindbergh, *War Within and Without*, p. 364.

277   "like war wives": Ibid., p. 364.

277   "woman approaching forty": Ibid., p. 417.

278   "give my true self ": Ibid., p. 427.

278   "He is not a hero": Ibid., p. 428.

279   "unreal newspaper personage": Ibid., p. 441.

279   " 'Yes, my husband' ": Ibid., pp. 441–42.

279   "production-minded Ford plant": Ibid., p. 444.

279   "Of what use to write": Ibid., p. 447.

280   "days without C.": Ibid., p. 450.

20. Comeback

282   never to speak to a reporter: Ross, *The Last Hero*, p. 351.

282   "The kidnapping": "Lindbergh," in "The American Experience."

282   "stern, scary figure": Alden Whitman, "Anne Morrow Lindbergh Reminisces About Life with Lindy," *New York Times Magazine*, p. 28.

282   "demand more oxygen": Eisenhower, *Special People*, p. 131.

283   "My mother was calm": Ibid.

283   his embittered widow: The following year, in June 1945, Madame Carrel returned to the United States for a visit and stayed with the Lindberghs.

Although Carrel appeared "worn and thinner," Anne was impressed that she was "still *amazingly* the same. She still gives the impression of enormous strength and even vitality."

283 five articles: "The Flame of Europe," *Reader's Digest*, January 1948, pp. 141–46; "One Starts at Zero," *Reader's Digest*, February 1948, pp. 73–75; "Anywhere in Europe," *Harper's*, April 1948, pp. 300–302; "Airliner to Europe," *Harper's*, September 1948, pp. 43–47; and "Our Lady of Risk," *Life*, July 29, 1950, pp. 80–91.

283 "This house": Lindbergh, "The Flame of Europe," *Reader's Digest*, January 1948, p. 143.

284 "happy in the military": "Lindbergh," in "The American Experience."

284 "What right have we to stuff ourselves?": Lindbergh, *Wartime Journals.*

284 "Here was a place": Ibid., p. 995.

285 "the German was defiling humanity": Ibid., p. 996.

285 a government-sponsored . . . extermination: Mosley, *Lindbergh*, p. 335.

285 "I sensed a godlike power": Lindbergh, *Autobiography of Values*, p. 224.

287 "When he came back": Alden Whitman, "A Conversation with Anne Morrow Lindbergh," *Ladies Home Journal*, May 1976, p. 186.

288 plagued by mental instability: Author's interviews with Robert McKinstry, Richard Bissell, and Lester Trauch.

288 Betty Morrow's will: *New York Times*, October 12, 1956, p. 32.

288 "death of one's parents": Anne Morrow Lindbergh to James Newton, April 7, 1955, quoted in Newton, *Uncommon Friends*, p. 307.

289 "I climb higher": Lindbergh, *The Spirit of St. Louis*, p. 272.

289 "There was no moon": Charles A. Lindbergh, *We* (New York: Putnam, 1927), p. 218.

290 most enduring work: In 1991, readers surveyed by the Library of Congress and Book-of-the-Month Club cited *Gift from the Sea* as one of the books that had most influenced their lives (*Parade*, December 29, 1991).

290 Captiva house: The two-bedroom cottage at the north end of Captiva Road which Anne rented for her week's vacation at the beach may not have been so simple and unpretentious after all. When its present owners recently put it up for sale, the asking price was $950,000 (*Captiva Current*, September 14, 1990).

290 "like a shell itself": *New York Times Book Review*, March 20, 1955, p. 1.

291 Pantheon Books: Pantheon, which later merged with Random House, had been started in 1942 by Kurt Wolff, a distinguished publisher in Berlin who had fled from the Nazis. In the 1950s, he and his wife, Helen, built Pantheon into a highly successful publishing house, with such best sellers as *Gift from the Sea*, *Doctor Zhivago*, by Boris Pasternak, *Born Free*, by Joy Adamson, *The Leopard*, by Giuseppe di Lampedusa, and *The King Must Die*, by Mary Renault. Unfortunately, with commercial success came infighting and internal struggles, and Wolff and his busi-

ness partner, Kyrill Schabert, soon had a falling out, with Wolff eventually selling his interest in Pantheon and making a deal with Harcourt, Brace. When the Wolffs started their own imprint, Kurt and Helen Wolff Books, a number of important Pantheon authors went with them, including Anne Lindbergh, whose previous books, with the exception of *Gift from the Sea,* had been published by Harcourt, Brace. When Wolff died in 1963, Helen, who was regarded as the grande dame of international letters and a brilliant editor, carried on his work.

In her diaries and letters, Anne does not mention why she decided to change publishers or how she came to meet the Wolffs. In his *Autobiography of Values,* Charles Lindbergh provides a clue, however. He recounts a meeting with the Wolffs in Switzerland, at the home of Carl Jung, whom he and Anne visited a few years before, in 1961. "An old wizard of a man, surrounded by books, mandalas, and collected charms, he sat and talked to us and to his friends Kurt and Helen Wolff, who had published his works in conjunction with the Bollingen Foundation," Lindbergh wrote. It is unclear whether this was the first time the Lindberghs had ever met the celebrated publishing couple.

291   "to live 'in grace' ": Anne Morrow Lindbergh, *Gift from the Sea* (New York: Pantheon, 1955), p. 23.

291   "What a circus act": Ibid., p. 26.

21. *"To Club a Butterfly"*

293   John Ciardi's review: "A Close Look at Unicorn," *Saturday Review,* January 12, 1957, pp. 54–55.

294   "Why take a baseball bat": Ibid., February 16, 1957, pp. 24–25.

295   phone call from a librarian: Norman Cousins, *Present Tense: An American Editor's Odyssey* (New York: McGraw-Hill, 1967), p. 55.

295   "John Ciardi's review": Norman Cousins, "John Ciardi and the Readers," *Saturday Review,* February 16, 1957, pp. 22–23.

295   "The Reviewer's Duty to Damn": February 16, 1957, pp. 24–25, 54–55.

296   "try not to *waste*": Lindbergh, *War Within and Without,* p. 325.

297   only one more poem: According to David Kirk Vaughan, author of a critical study of Anne Morrow Lindbergh's work, the poem, entitled "Mid-Summer," appeared nine months after the Ciardi review in the December 1957 issue of the *Atlantic Monthly.*

22. *"The Most Attractive Couple"*

298   "The most attractive couple": Peter Collier and David Horowitz, *The Kennedys: An American Drama* (New York: Warner, 1984), p. 112.

299   the ambassador had given: Ibid., p. 110.

299 "The person that President Kennedy": "America's First Ladies Honor Charles Lindbergh," *Good Housekeeping,* June 1977, p. 72.

299 "so attractive": Claudia Alta Johnson, *A White House Diary,* by Lady Bird Johnson (New York: Holt, Rinehart and Winston, 1970) p. 63. Anne's profile of Lady Bird Johnson, "As I see the First Lady," was published in *Look,* May 1964.

300 "One of those lean silent boys": Anne Morrow Lindbergh, *Dearly Beloved* (New York: Harcourt, Brace & World, 1962), p. 31.

301 "He would nail her down": Ibid., p. 35.

301 "couldn't talk to him": Ibid., p. 33.

301 "a bride like a newborn baby": Ibid., p. 34.

301 "marriage was different": Ibid.

301 "How about Deborah?": Ibid., p. 51.

302 "What happened to them?": Ibid., p. 170.

302 "God, she looked funny": Ibid., p. 48.

302 "Mrs. Lindbergh is . . . attempting": *Christian Science Monitor,* June 21, 1962, p. 7.

302 "a small memorable insight": *Time,* June 8, 1962, p. 92.

23. "Argonauta"

305 "as debts": Lindbergh, *Autobiography of Values,* p. 329.

306 "began surveying air routes": Lindbergh, *Autobiography of Values,* p. 421.

306 "wisdom in the primitive": Ibid., p. 286.

306 "Prolificacy": Ibid., p. 281.

307 "interesting from any point of view": Author's interview with Robert McKinstry.

308 "a pioneer in . . . marine biology": Ibid.

309 "Anne also shares": Jean F. Mercier, "PW Interviews Anne Lindbergh," *Publishers Weekly,* July 27, 1984, pp. 147–48.

309 "I've been a writer": Ibid.

309 "I would willingly hand": Ibid.

310 "When I was in Radcliffe": Alden Whitman, "Anne Morrow Lindbergh Reminisces," *New York Times Magazine,* May 8, 1977, p. 28.

310 "still reeling from it": Eisenhower, *Special People,* p. 134.

310 Scott Lindbergh: "Fond Monkey Business in France," *Time,* May 23, 1977; Rudolph Chelminski, "The Lindberghs Liberate Monkeys from Constraints," *Smithsonian,* March 1977, pp. 58–65; and Ross, *The Last Hero.*

310 taboo subject: Quoted in *Parade,* July 5, 1992, p. 2.

311 "began studying monkeys": *Time,* May 23, 1977.

311 Charles Lindbergh's last days: Newton, *Uncommon Friends;* Mosley, *Lindbergh;* "Lindbergh," in "American Experience"; and other sources.

24. *"The Hardest Lesson"*

314   Details of Anne Morrow Lindbergh's later years come from Alden Whitman's "Anne Morrow Lindbergh Reminisces About Life with Lindy," *New York Times Magazine*, May 8, 1977; Julie Nixon Eisenhower, *Special People*; James Newton, *Uncommon Friends*; and interviews with their friends.

315   "appalled at my innocence": Lindbergh, *War Within and Without*, p. xxi.

315   "The letters and diaries": Glendy Culligan, *Saturday Review*, March 4, 1972, p. 72.

315   "the decision not to shape": Helen Bevington, *New York Times Book Review*, February 27, 1972, p. 3.

316   "Anne, who prizes . . . the truth": Selden Rodman, *National Review*, October 17, 1980, p. 1274.

317   "In Mrs. Lindbergh's case": Kathleen Leverich, *Christian Science Monitor*, May 12, 1980, p. B1.

317   "Critical evaluation": Vaughan, *Anne Morrow Lindbergh*, p. ix.

319   "pretty spooky": Walter Clemons, *Newsweek*, February 13, 1978, pp. 92–93.

319   "the beauty and power": Eric F. Goldman, *New York Times Book Review*, February 5, 1978, p. 10.

319   "Life sometimes merged with death": Lindbergh, *Autobiography of Values*, p. 134.

319   Information about the fiftieth anniversary of Lindbergh's 1927 flight: Lance Morrow, "Lindbergh: The Heroic Curiosity," *Time*, May 23, 1977; Becky Bylen, "The People's Choice," *Air Line Pilot*, July 1978; and author's interview with Ruth Dobrescu.

320   "She's very gentle": Author's interview with Ruth Dobrescu.

320   "resisted fame": Whitman, "Anne Morrow Lindbergh Reminisces," *New York Times Magazine*, May 8, 1977.

320   "our unwillingness to face death": Eisenhower, *Special People*, p. 144

321   "She seemed quiet": Ibid., p. 145.

321   "The publicity involved": Quoted in Newton, *Uncommon Friends*, p. 323.

322   "He was not a demi-god": Anne Morrow Lindbergh's interview with Morley Safer, "Sixty Minutes," April 20, 1980.

323   the recent books: Whitman, "Anne Morrow Lindbergh Reminisces," *New York Times Magazine*, May 8, 1977.

323   "Charles had to escape": "Lindbergh," in "The American Experience."

324   remains of Charles, Jr.: There are some who believe it was not the almost totally decomposed body of Charles Augustus Lindbergh, Jr., that the truck driver discovered in the dense woods a mile away from the

Hopewell house. According to these theories, and there are a number of nonsensical ones, another child's body was substituted, and Charles Lindbergh, Jr., raised by other persons, is still alive today. Over the years, according to a member of the New Jersey State Police, at least twenty-seven people, including several women, have stepped forward claiming to be the real Charles Augustus Lindbergh, Jr. After Charles Lindbergh's death, at least two men, claiming to be his heir, tried to assert rights to a part of his estate. Anne Lindbergh, through her attorneys, has made it clear that she believes her child died on the night of March 1, 1932, and all these claimants are imposters.

324 Scott Berg as Charles Lindbergh's biographer: *Publishers Weekly,* April 27, 1990, pp. 33–34.

324 frail health: Author's interview with Reeve Lindbergh.

324 Anna Hauptmann: Mark Perkiss, "Hauptmann Widow's Plea," *Trenton Times,* June 13, 1990; Samuel G. Blackman, "The Trial of the Century," *Doylestown Intelligencer,* January 26, 1992; and Kennedy, *The Airman and the Carpenter.*

Selected Bibliography

Allen, Frederick Lewis. *Only Yesterday: An Informal History of the 1920's,* New
    York: Harper & Row, 1931.
————. *Since Yesterday: The Nineteen Thirties in America.* New York: Harper
    & Row, 1940.
Barkas, J. L. Victims. New York: Scribner's, 1978.
Bell, Millicent. *Marquand: An American Life.* Boston: Little, Brown, 1979.
Bergreen, Laurence. *As Thousands Cheer: The Life of Irving Berlin.* New York:
    Viking, 1990.
Birmingham, Stephen. *The Late John Marquand.* Philadelphia: Lippincott, 1972.
Bloch, Michael, ed. *Wallis & Edward: Letters 1931–1937; The Intimate Corre-*
    spondence of the Duke and Duchess of Windsor. New York: Summit Books,
    Simon & Schuster, 1986.
Boyne, Walter J. *The Smithsonian Book of Flight.* Washington, D.C.: Smith-
    sonian Books, 1987.
Brinkley, Alan. *Voices of Protest: Huey Long, Father Coughlin, and the Great De-*
    pression. New York: Knopf, 1982.
Brooks, John. *Once in Golconda: A True Drama of Wall Street, 1920–1938.* New
    York: Dutton, 1969.
Brown, Dorothy M. *Setting a Course: American Women in the 1920s.* Boston:
    Twayne, 1987.
Carrel, Alexis. *Man, the Unknown.* New York: Harper & Brothers, 1935.
Cate, Curtis. *Antoine de Saint-Exupéry.* New York: Putnam, 1970.
Chernow, Ron. *The House of Morgan: An American Banking Dynasty and the*
    Rise of Modern Finance. New York: Atlantic Monthly Press, 1990.
Cole, Wayne S. *Charles A. Lindbergh and the Battle Against American Interven-*
    tion in World War II. New York: Harcourt Brace Jovanovich, 1974.

Collier, Peter, and David Horowitz. *The Kennedys: An American Drama.* New York: Warner, 1984.

Cousins, Norman. *Present Tense: An American Editor's Odyssey.* New York: McGraw-Hill, 1967.

Daley, Robert. *An American Saga: Juan Trippe and His Pan Am Empire.* New York: Random House, 1980.

Davis, Kenneth S. *The Hero: Charles A. Lindbergh and the American Dream.* Garden City, N.Y.: Doubleday, 1959.

Demaris, Ovid. *The Director: An Oral Biography of J. Edgar Hoover.* New York: Harper's Magazine Press, 1975.

Eisenhower, Julie Nixon. *Special People.* New York: Simon & Schuster, 1977.

Elledge, Scott. *E. B. White: A Biography.* New York: Norton, 1984.

Felsenthal, Carol. *Alice Roosevelt Longworth.* New York: Putnam, 1988.

Freidel, Frank. *Franklin D. Roosevelt: A Rendezvous with Destiny.* New York: Little, Brown, 1990.

Friedan, Betty. *The Feminine Mystique.* New York: Norton, 1963.

Gilbert, Julie Goldsmith. *Ferber: A Biography.* Garden City, N.Y.: Doubleday, 1978.

Gill, Brendan. *Lindbergh Alone.* New York: Harcourt Brace Jovanovich, 1977.

Glendinning, Victoria. *Vita: The Life of Vita Sackville-West.* New York: Knopf, 1983.

Goldsmith, Barbara. *Little Gloria: Happy at Last.* New York: Knopf, 1980.

Heinmuller, John P. V. *Man's Fight to Fly.* New York: Funk & Wagnalls, 1944.

Higham, Charles. *The Duchess of Windsor: The Secret Life.* New York: McGraw-Hill, 1988.

Hobson, Laura Z. *Laura Z: A Life.* New York: Arbor House, 1983.

Hoyt, Edwin P. *Alexander Woollcott: The Man Who Came to Dinner.* New York: Abelard-Schuman, 1968.

Ickes, Harold L. *The Secret Diary of Harold L. Ickes.* Vols. 2 and 3. New York: Simon & Schuster, 1954.

Israel, Lee. *Kilgallen.* New York: Delacorte, 1979.

Johnson, Claudia Alta (Taylor). *A White House Diary,* by Lady Bird Johnson. New York: Holt, Rinehart and Winston, 1970.

Kennedy, Ludovic. *The Airman and the Carpenter: The Lindbergh Kidnapping and the Framing of Richard Hauptmann.* New York: Viking Penguin, 1985.

Ketchum, Richard M. *Will Rogers: His Life and Times.* New York: American Heritage, 1973.

Lacey, Robert. *Ford: The Men and the Machine.* Boston: Little, Brown, 1986.

Lamont, Corliss. *Yes to Life: Memoirs of Corliss Lamont.* New York: Horizon Press, 1981.

Larrabee, Eric. *Commander in Chief: Franklin Delano Roosevelt, His Lieutenants, and Their War.* New York: Harper & Row, 1987.

Larson, Bruce L. *Lindbergh of Minnesota: A Political Biography.* New York: Harcourt Brace Jovanovich, 1971.

Lash, Joseph. *A World of Love: Eleanor Roosevelt and Her Friends, 1943–1962.* Garden City, N.Y.: Doubleday, 1984.

Lees-Milne, James. *Harold Nicolson: A Biography, 1930–1968.* London: Chatto & Windus, 1981.

Lindbergh, Charles A. *Autobiography of Values.* New York: Harcourt Brace Jovanovich, 1978.

———. *The Spirit of St. Louis.* New York: Scribner, 1953.

———. *The Wartime Journals of Charles A. Lindbergh.* New York: Harcourt Brace Jovanovich, 1970.

———. *We.* New York: Putnam, 1927.

Lomax, Judy. *Women of the Air.* London: John Murray, 1986.

Lovell, Mary S. *The Sound of Wings: The Biography of Amelia Earhart.* New York: St. Martin's, 1989.

———. *Straight on Till Morning: The Biography of Beryl Markham.* New York: St. Martin's, 1987.

Lundberg, Ferdinand. *Imperial Hearst: A Social Biography.* New York: Arno & New York Times, 1970.

Malinin, Theodore I. *Surgery and Life: The Extraordinary Career of Alexis Carrel.* New York: Harcourt Brace Jovanovich, 1979.

Masters, Anthony. *Nancy Astor: A Biography.* London: Weidenfeld & Nicholson, 1981.

McCarthy, Mary. *The Group.* New York: Harcourt, Brace and World, 1964.

McCullough, David. "Aviator Authors: Saint-Exupéry's 'Wartime Writings' Recalls a Remarkable Body of Work." *New York Times Magazine,* October 12, 1986.

Mencken, H. L. *The Diary of H. L. Mencken.* Edited by Charles A. Fecher. New York: Knopf, 1989.

Millett, Kate. *Sexual Politics.* Garden City, N.Y.: Doubleday, 1970.

Morgan, Ted. *FDR: A Biography.* New York: Simon & Schuster, 1985.

Morrow, Elizabeth. *Quatrains for My Daughter.* New York: Knopf, 1931.

Mosley, Leonard. *Lindbergh: A Biography.* Garden City, N.Y.: Doubleday, 1976.

Newton, James D. *Uncommon Friends: Life with Thomas Edison, Henry Ford, Harvey Firestone, Alexis Carrel, and Charles Lindbergh.* New York: Harcourt Brace Jovanovich, 1987.

Nicolson, Harold. *Diaries and Letters, 1930–1939.* Edited by Nigel Nicolson. New York: Atheneum, 1966.

———. *Dwight Morrow.* New York: Harcourt, Brace, 1935.

Nicolson, Nigel. *Portrait of a Marriage.* New York: Atheneum, 1973.

O'Brien, P. J. *The Lindberghs: The Story of a Distinguished Family.* International Press, 1935.

Putnam, George Palmer. *Wide Margins: A Publisher's Autobiography.* New York: Harcourt, Brace, 1942.

Rainer, Tristine. *The New Diary*. Los Angeles: J. P. Tarcher, 1978.

Rich, Doris L. *Amelia Earhart: A Biography*. Washington, D.C.: Smithsonian Institution Press, 1989.

Ross, Walter S. *The Last Hero: Charles A. Lindbergh*. New York: Harper & Row, 1964.

Rothman, Sheila M. *Woman's Proper Place: A History of Changing Ideals and Practices, 1870 to the Present*. New York: Basic Books, 1978.

Saint-Exupéry, Antoine de. *A Sense of Life*. New York: Funk & Wagnalls, 1965.

St. Johns, Adela Rogers. *The Honeycomb*. Garden City, N.Y.: Doubleday, 1969.

————. *Some Are Born Great*. Garden City, N.Y.: Doubleday, 1974.

Scaduto, Anthony. *Scapegoat: The Lonesome Death of Bruno Richard Hauptmann*. New York: Putnam, 1976.

Sheean, Vincent. *Dorothy and Red*. Boston: Houghton Mifflin, 1963.

Shirer, William L. *Berlin Diary: The Journal of a Foreign Correspondent, 1934–1941*. New York: Knopf, 1941.

————. *The Nightmare Years, 1930–1940*. Boston: Little, Brown, 1984.

————. *The Rise and Fall of the Third Reich: A History of Nazi Germany*. New York: Simon & Schuster, 1960.

Sperber, A. M. *Murrow: His Life and Times*. New York: Bantam, 1986.

Steel, Ronald. *Walter Lippmann and the American Century*. Boston: Little, Brown, 1980.

Swanberg, W. A. *Citizen Hearst*. New York: Scribner's, 1961.

————. *Norman Thomas: The Last Idealist*. New York: Scribner's, 1976.

Vaughan, David Kirk. *Anne Morrow Lindbergh*. Boston: Twayne, 1988.

Waller, George. *Kidnap: The Story of the Lindbergh Case*. New York: Dial, 1961.

Weeks, Edward. *Writers and Friends*. Boston: Little, Brown, 1981.

White, E. B. *One Man's Meat: A New and Enlarged Edition*. New York: Harper & Brothers, 1944.

Wolfe, Tom. *The Right Stuff*. New York: Farrar, Straus & Giroux, 1979.

Woolf, Virginia. *The Diary of Virginia Woolf*. Vol. 4, 1931–1935. Edited by Anne Olivier Bell. New York: Harcourt Brace Jovanovich, 1982.

————. *The Letters of Virginia Woolf*. Vols. 5 and 6. Edited by Nigel Nicolson and Joanna Trautmann. New York: Harcourt Brace Jovanovich, 1979, 1980.

————. *A Room of One's Own*. Orlando, Fla.: Harcourt Brace Jovanovich, 1929.

Woollcott, Alexander. *The Letters of Alexander Woollcott*. Edited by Beatrice Kaufman and Joseph Hennessey. New York: Viking, 1944.

————. *The Portable Woollcott*. Selected by Joseph Hennessey. New York: Viking, 1946.

Television Interviews with Anne Morrow Lindbergh

Television interview between Eric Sevareid and Anne Morrow Lindbergh, 1977 (Museum of Broadcasting, New York, New York).

Television interview between Morley Safer and Anne Morrow Lindbergh, "60 Minutes," April 20, 1980 (Museum of Broadcasting, New York, New York).

"Crossing the Distance," in "American Album," David McCullough, host. Discovery Channel, 1990.

"Lindbergh," in "The American Experience," produced by Stephen Ives and Ken Burns, written by Geoffrey C. Ward. PBS, October 1, 1990.

Index